EQUALITY AND PU

The aim of this series is to fill a current gap in knowledge. As a number of historians, sociologists and literary critics have for some time been pointing out, there is a dearth of published research on the character-istics and effects of gender difference in Wales, both as it affected lives in the past and as it continues to shape present-day experience. Socially constructed concepts of masculine and feminine difference influence every aspect of individuals' lives; experiences in employment, in education, in culture and politics, as well as in personal relationships, are all shaped by them. Ethnic identities are also gendered; a country's history affects its concepts of gender difference so that what is seen as appropriately 'masculine' or 'feminine' varies within different cultures. What is needed in the Welsh context is more detailed research on the ways in which gender difference has operated and continues to operate within Welsh societies. Accordingly, this interdisciplinary and bilingual series of volumes on Gender Studies in Wales, authored by academics who are leaders in their particular fields of study, is designed to explore the diverse aspects of male and female identities in Wales, past and present. The series is bilingual, in the sense that some of its intended volumes will be in Welsh and some in English.

EQUALITY AND PUBLIC POLICY

EXPLORING THE IMPACT OF DEVOLUTION
IN THE UK

Paul Chaney

CARDIFF
UNIVERSITY OF WALES PRESS
2011

www.uwp.co.uk

British Library Cataloguing-in-Publication Data
A catalogue record for this book is available from the British Library.

ISBN 978-0-7083-2326-7
e-ISBN 978-0-7083-2327-4

Printed in Wales by Dinefwr Press, Llandybïe

Er cof am K. B. Sherwood

Acknowledgements

This volume draws upon the findings of three Economic and Social Research Council funded projects,[1] as well as a study funded by the University of Wales.[2] The work is also based on research conducted in relation to projects sponsored by the (former) Equal Opportunities Commission, the Disability Rights Commission and the Commission for Racial Equality, and the National Assembly for Wales,[3] as well as

[1] Economic and Social Research Council (ESRC) funded project: 'Social Capital and the Participation of Marginalized Groups in Government', award number: R000239410, 09/2001 to 01/2004. Co-investigator. Project led by Professor Ralph Fevre. ESRC funded project: 'Gender and Constitutional Change' (L219252023), part of the ESRC Devolution and Constitutional Change Programme. 1999–2004. Co-investigator. Project led by Dr Fiona Mackay and Professor Alice Brown. ESRC funded project: 'The Devolution Monitoring Programme', in conjunction with the UK Government Department of Constitutional Affairs. 2005–8. Co-investigator (with professors Richard Wyn Jones and Roger Scully in respect of the Welsh devolution reports). Grant holders, Professor Robert Hazell and Akash Paun at the Constitution Unit, University College London. Initial funding No. L219252016; subsequent funding by the Economic and Social Research Council; the Department for Constitutional Affairs; the Scottish Executive; the Scotland Office; and the Wales Office.
[2] University of Wales, Board of Celtic Studies funded project: 'Inclusive Governance: The First Years of the National Assembly for Wales'. 1999–2001. Project led by Professor Ralph Fevre (award holder).
[3] 'The Equality Policies of the Government of the National Assembly for Wales and their Implementation: July 1999 to January 2002'. A study commissioned by the Equal Opportunities Commission, Disability Rights Commission, Commission for Racial Equality and Institute of Welsh Affairs. Principal applicant and award holder.

the Welsh Assembly Government[4] and the UK government Department for Local Government and Communities,[5] the Equality and Human Rights Commission, the Wales Office, Scotland Office, Scottish Executive/Government, the Department for Constitutional Affairs and the Northern Ireland Office.[6]

Thanks go to colleagues, in particular those that I have been fortunate enough to collaborate with on research projects used in this volume – Professor Teresa Rees, Professor Ralph Fevre, Dr Fiona Mackay, Professor Laura McAllister, Ms Sandra Betts, Professor Charlotte Williams – as well as to professors Richard Wyn Jones and Roger Scully for the opportunity to participate in the Devolution Monitoring Programme. In addition, I wish to register my gratitude to students on the MSc in Equality and Diversity degree scheme at Cardiff University for their enthusiastic engagement and feedback on earlier work that has led to this book.

[4] 'Action against Discrimination in Pay Systems: A Preliminary Evaluation of the Welsh Assembly Government's Close the Pay Gap Campaign in Wales', commissioned by the Welsh Assembly Government, the Equal Opportunities Commission Wales and the Wales TUC. Principal applicant and award holder.
[5] 'Advice and Guidance to Public Service Providers: Promoting Multi-Strand Equality in the Welsh legislative Context and Beyond, Welsh Assembly Government/UK Government Department for Communities and Local Government (2007)'. Principal applicant and award holder.
[6] The Northern Ireland Section 75 Equality Duty: An International Perspective analysis commissioned by the Northern Ireland Office for the Section 75 Equality Duty Operational Review. Co-investigator with Professor Teresa Rees.

Contents

Tables

Figures

1

Introduction: Equalities and Public Policy

1.0 Equalities and Public Policy

Equality of opportunity is an often misunderstood and contested concept; deeply political in nature it evokes strong reactions from proponents and opponents alike (Temkin, 1993; Freeden, 1994). It is an example of what Newman, (2001: 59) terms 'wicked issues'. These are characterised by: differing interpretations of the social problem to be addressed; the fact that the relationship between different factors is sometimes hard to assess; they span traditional policy frames; and, require collaboration between agencies in both formulating and implementing policy responses. In the face of such challenges, the Equality Act (2006, Section 3) sets out a vision of an equal society as one in which:

(a) People's ability to achieve their potential is not limited by prejudice or discrimination.
(b) There is respect for and protection of each individual's human rights.

(c) There is respect for the dignity and worth of each individual.

(d) Each individual has an equal opportunity to participate in society.

(e) There is mutual respect between groups based on understanding and valuing of diversity and on shared respect for equality and human rights.

The different dimensions to the concept of equality (see chapter 2) underpin the growing use of the term 'equalities' (Carabine, 2004; Bowes, 2006; Department for Local Government and Communities, 2007; Håkan, 2008; Carr, 2008).[1] It is the general practice adopted in this volume for it recognises the contrasting needs and experiences of discrimination within and between diverse social groups. The following analysis therefore aims to move away from traditional approaches that have tended to treat 'gender' as a discrete policy issue. Instead, this volume aims to offer an holistic analysis; simultaneously examining gender (in)equality whilst also exploring 'equalities' 'in the round' by mapping policy developments in relation to a range of 'strands' including disability, age, faith, ethnicity, language and sexual orientation.

A vast and burgeoning literature centres on 'public policy' (e.g. Parsons, 1996; Hill, 2004; Dorey, 2005; Sabatier, 2006; Moran, Rein and Goodin, 2008; Hill and Hupe, 2008). It too is the subject of many contrasting definitions. At its simplest 'policy' can be seen as 'a course of action adopted and pursued by a government, party, ruler, states[wo]man etc; any course of action adopted as advantageous or expedient' (Hill, 1997: 6). In reality, it is often highly complex: involving a 'web of decisions'; it is something that continues to evolve after the initial decision-making; it involves implementation, adjustment and feedback; and is dynamic rather than static (Hill, 1997, op. cit.). The prefix 'public' simply refers to the fact that the state and/or state institutions are the 'owners' of a given policy and that, in consequence, it is backed by the resources and legal processes of the state. John (1998: 2) offers a more sophisticated definition that emphasises its political provenance:

> Public policy seeks to explain the operation of the political system as a whole . . . The policy-orientated approach looks at public decision-making from the viewpoint of what comes out of the political process

. . . one of the purposes of the policy-orientated approach is to sharpen up analysis of politics by examining the links between decision-makers as they negotiate and seek influence in the government system.

Analysis of public policy can therefore be seen as a way of interrogating organised activity; an approach sometimes referred to as the 'social construction perspective':

> This sees policy as something that has been constructed and sustained by participants in circumstances where they are likely to have choices about which interpretive map to use, which cues to follow. It draws upon work in a wide range of social sciences . . . all of which ask, 'what makes for collective action'? ... the concept of policy both explains and validates . . . action: it explains what people are doing, and it makes it appropriate for them to do it. (Colebatch, 2002: 20)

In addition to social constructionism, the comparative analysis in this book also draws upon a range of analytical frameworks to explore equality policy developments (see for example, Yanow, 1999; Fischer, 2003a; Weimer and Vining, 2004; Prokhovnik, 2005; Dunn, 2007; Bardach, 2008). These focus on:

- Setting the policy agenda.
- Understanding the nature of the problem(s) to be addressed.
- Policy venues, institutions and governance (inter alia: where policy is formulated and decided upon; as well as the role of networks and institutions).
- Policy content/policy discourse (a post-empiricist, interpretive approach that examines the language of policy documents and how dominant ideas are negotiated and framed).
- Implementation (how policy ideas are operationalised through public administration with reference to instrumental analysis, i.e. how policy outcomes can be monitored, measured and assessed).

Before presenting an overview of the analysis in each chapter, attention is first placed on contemporary legal and institutional developments, and the case for promoting equalities.

1.1 Contemporary Developments

The past decade in the UK has been marked by unprecedented and wide-ranging measures to promote equality. A number of factors have led to this unparalleled focus on equalities. They include:

- Legal directives from the European Commission (e.g. age, sexual orientation and faith directives on discrimination in employment).
- The racist murder of Stephen Lawrence, the official recognition of the concept of institutional racism and the subsequent legal requirement for wholesale change in 'race' equality practices in Britain.
- The signing on 10 April 1998 of the Belfast, or 'Good Friday' Agreement, putting in place measures to end the civil conflict in Northern Ireland.
- Continued pressure on government from new social movements and others concerned with identity politics.
- The rise of Islamaphobia and communal tensions along lines of faith.
- Increasing longevity and greater awareness of ageism and disability.
- Debates on community cohesion (particularly in relation to Northern Ireland and in the wake of urban riots in Bradford, Burnley and Oldham in 2001).

1.1.1 Equalities Law

Reference to the substantial number of equalities laws passed over recent years underlines extent of the political (re-)prioritisation of tackling discrimination and promoting equality. Thus, for example, the Race Relations Amendment Act (2000) signalled a general move to 'fourth generation' equality duties, requiring anticipatory and proactive measures to promote equality, in contrast to earlier anti-discrimination statutes that, retrospectively, set out redress for *individual* wrongs (see chapter 6). As noted, in accordance with European Commission Directives, in 2003, the Westminster government passed UK-wide Employment Equality Regulations on Religion or Belief and Sexual Orientation, followed in 2006 by the Employment Equality (Age) Regulations. In addition, the Civil Partnership Act (2004) gave legal recognition to same-sex partnerships for the first time. In 2005, the original Disability Discrimination Act (1995) was extended and updated, and set out new rights for disabled people. In order to achieve greater consistency in the legal protection afforded to different equality 'strands', the Equality Act (Sexual Orientation) Regulations (2007) made sexual orientation discrimination unlawful in the provision of goods and services. In addition, the Act (2006, s83) introduced a long-promised general 'gender' duty on public authorities in carrying out their functions to promote equality of opportunity between men and women, and to eliminate unlawful discrimination and harassment. Further significant legal changes are underway. The proposed Welsh Language Measure (2010) aims to give equal status to the Welsh language as well as create the office of language commissioner. Moreover, a more integrated legal framework around equalities for Britain is promised under the provisions of the Equality Bill (2009) currently before the UK parliament, and work is continuing on a Single Equality Bill for Northern Ireland.

1.1.2 Institutions

In addition to the foregoing legal developments, a significant number of new institutions have been created over the past decade with the aim of promoting equalities. For example, under the provisions of the Northern Ireland Act (1998), the Equality Commission for Northern Ireland and the Northern Ireland Human Rights Commission were established. In 2001, the Children's Commissioner for Wales was appointed, the first office of its kind in the UK. In order to enforce the law on additional learning needs the Special Educational Needs Tribunal for Wales was established in 2003. Subsequently, the Gaelic Language (Scotland) Act (2005) led to the creation of Bòrd na Gàidhlig (the Gaelic Language Board) in 2006. In relation to Britain as whole, 2007 saw the former Disability Rights Commission, Equal Opportunities Commission and Commission for Racial Equality replaced by the Equality and Human Rights Commission. More recently, in 2008, the Scottish Commission for Human Rights was established. In the same year, a new department was created in UK government, the Equalities Office, with its self-stated mission 'to put equality at the heart of Government'. Also, in 2008, the Older People's Commissioner for Wales was appointed under the terms of the Commissioner for Older People (Wales) Act (2006).[2] In addition to these developments, the 1998–9 devolution programme saw the creation of legislatures for Wales, Scotland and Northern Ireland. As this volume outlines, each has also impacted on the promotion of equality in public policy.

1.2 Why Bother About It?

Against the background of these recent legal and institutional changes, it is pertinent to question why the promotion of equalities is deserving of such attention? Not all see contemporary developments in this area as welcome or necessary. Various arguments have been used against promoting equalities. For example, those advancing the notion of meritocracy argue for a laissez-faire approach, asserting that individuals with the necessary skills and abilities will secure jobs and other posts that match their capabilities regardless of any barriers or prevailing structures and processes of discrimination (Cavanagh, 2002). 'Political correctness' is a further common attack made on equalities, whereby it is claimed designated activities are overly shaped not by considerations of effectiveness but by 'whether those activities offend (or are uncomfortable for) the sensibilities of others' (Furedy, 2002: 333). The 'political correctness critique' is also often founded on the trivialisation of the actual issues under consideration, the villainisation of those involved, conferring a sense of legitimacy on those opposed to the promotion of equalities (Ayim, 1998: 451), as well as the notion of 'oppressive petty bureaucracy . . . advancing some groups above others' (DLGC, 2007a: 93).

1.2.1 Making the Case for Equalities

In response those opposed to, or critical of, the promotion of equalities, a number of key arguments have been advanced (see Figure 1.1). The latter include economic arguments, issues of social cohesion, moral/ethical arguments, concerns for social justice, and democratic cases for policy interventions to end discrimination and inequality.

The economic case is partly based upon the idea of social diversity as a resource (Dickens, 1994; Business in the Community, 1993; CBI, 1996; Humphries and Rubery, 1995). This emphasises that different social groups possess varying rich forms of human capital and bring a wider range of skills and viewpoints to economic life than is the case when traditional reliance is placed on a comparatively homogeneous and unrepresentative pool of workers. In addition, the economic case

The Economic Case
According to the UK government's Equality Review (DLGC, 2007a: 20), 'Equality brings greater efficiency and growth. The efficiency of an economic system is impeded when the productive potential of individuals is wasted. For instance, a more equal society is one in which the average levels of education and human capital are higher than those present in unequal societies. It is also one in which there is more stability and less social conflict. All these factors are essential to sustained growth and prosperity.'

- The Women and Work Commission concluded that removing barriers to women working in occupations traditionally done by men, and increasing women's participation in the labour market, would be worth between £15 billion and £23 billion: equivalent to 1.3 to 2.0 per cent of Gross Domestic Product (GDP).[3]
- Disabled people are 30 per cent more likely to be out of work than non-disabled people with the same qualifications, age, place of residence and so forth. This costs the government almost £9 billion annually (including unemployment-related benefits) in lost revenue.[4]
- A study cited by the Leitch Review suggests that if half the women without qualifications gained NVQ Level 1 there would be benefits of between £300 million and £1.9 billion per annum in terms of reduced obesity and depression.[5]
- Young people excluded from school are much less likely to gain five good GCSEs and are more than twice as likely to report having committed a crime as other young people. The risk of exclusion is much higher among Black and some mixed race pupils, and for boys relative to girls. The social cost of failing to tackle the root causes of this inequality early on in life means that the taxpayer ends up paying between £15,000 and £50,000 per year for each prison place if these young people end up in prison – as many of them do.[6]

The Social Cohesion Case
The links between equality and social cohesion are well documented. Violence, conflict, insecurity and political instability are all more likely to occur in less equal societies.[7]

In the poorest areas of unequal societies, the quality of social relations and the social fabric are stretched to breaking point.[8] The report of the Community Cohesion Review into the disturbances in Bradford, Burnley and Oldham in 2001 argued that equality and social cohesion were closely intertwined.[9] The State of the English Cities report, published in 2006, also made a link between cities that were successful and cities that were inclusive,[10] highlighting the need to tackle inequalities in education, skills and housing if our cities are to become thriving, competitive and socially cohesive.

Figure 1.1. The economic and social cohesion cases for promoting equalities

asserts that ending the marginalisation of some groups in relation to the labour market (such as disabled people, for example) and increasing their consumer (and tax-paying) power through raised income boosts economic growth and reduces social welfare costs.

In contrast, the social cohesion argument is based upon studies of urban conflict and unrest. It draws upon a research literature that suggests that 'overt conflict is especially likely if economic instability continues . . . [such that] relative deprivation may lead to social conflict' (Freidrichs, 1998: 173; see also ECNI, 2005). Haylett (2003: 58) uses such empirical work to argue for policy responses based upon a 'politics of recognition', that is one sensitive to the interconnections between traditional equality 'strands' (e.g. ethnicity, faith, gender and so on) and economic inequality. He argues that 'recognition that economic differences are often inequalities, linked to cultural differences but not equivalent to them, allows for political priorities and discriminations between kinds of difference'.

The moral case for equalities stems from Enlightenment thinking that challenged earlier classical ideas of a natural human hierarchy; under the latter conception some groups and individuals were held as superior to others. Thinkers such as Locke (1690) and Rousseau (1762) advocated that all citizens posses equal natural rights to (self-) ownership and freedom. In a similar vein, Kantian moral philosophy claimed that the same freedoms should apply on an equal basis to all rational beings and be the sole principle of human rights (Kant,

1785). In this way, moral equality is concerned with treating individuals with equal respect, worth and dignity (Vlastos, 1962; Dworkin, 1977). A recent 'turn' in such egalitarian thought reflects a renewed focus on Aristotelian concerns over whether individual citizens are leading sufficiently 'good lives'. In other words, proponents assert that the policy focus should be on ensuring that people have enough to flourish (Brown, 1988; Cohen, 1989; Scheffler, 2003). Wolff (2007: 129) explains this moral dimension to equality in a way that links to Sen's 'capabilities approach' (Sen, 1997; see chapter 2). He states that 'evaluation of how well an individual's life is going . . . should measure neither the resources someone has, nor the welfare they are able to derive, but their 'capability to function'. Here a 'function' is held to equate to what a person can do or be (e.g. achieving nourishment, health, a decent lifespan, self-respect and so on) and a 'capability' is the freedom to achieve a function. As Sen (1997: 482) asserts, 'basic capability equality is a guide to the part of moral goodness that is associated with the idea of equality'.

According to Wolff (2007: 17), 'commonly it is assumed that social justice is in some way connected with ideas of equality, but how an idea of equality is to be formulated, and the relationship between social justice and equality, remain disputed'. Miller (2001:32) addresses this issue by asserting that the social justice case for equalities is based on claims for the equitable distribution of the benefits and burdens of society. This view stems in part stems from Rawls (1971) who argued that there are two main tenets of justice: all should have equal rights to extensive liberty, and social and economic equalities should be distributed in order that they are of the greatest benefit to the most disadvantaged. Thus, Miller (1997: 237) summarises the relationship between the two concepts: 'equality can shape the practice of social justice . . . [because] equal citizenship – and the concrete rights that attach to it [–] provide an essential starting point from which moves towards a wider social equality can be made'. In this way, as Young (1990: 174) asserts:

> Social justice entails democracy. Persons should be involved in collective discussion and decision-making in all settings that depend on their commitment, action and obedience to rules . . . Not only do just procedures require group representation in order to ensure that oppressed or disadvantaged groups have a voice, but such representation is also the best means to promote just outcomes of the deliberative

process . . . justice in a group-differentiated society demands social equality of groups, and mutual recognition and affirmation of group differences.

Lastly, Phillips (1999: 2) underlines the interrelationship between democracy and equality by observing:

Democracy erodes assumptions of natural superiority, and the experience of living in even the most enfeebled of democracies encourages citizens to look askance at privileges of history or birth. What was once taken for granted comes under closer scrutiny: in recent years this has included scrutiny not only of the rich and powerful, but of the relationship between the sexes, the unequal treatment of black and white citizens, and the one-sided assimilationism that threatens the integrity of minority cultural groups.

It should, of course, be noted that the foregoing cases for promoting equality are not discrete. Some, such as the business case and moral arguments can be held to be interrelated (e.g. Liff and Dickens, 1999). However, whether considered separately or in concert, these arguments constitute a powerful rebuttal to liberal opponents of equalities-oriented policy interventions.

1.2.2 A 'Minority' Issue?

In addition to criticisms about undermining meritocracy and 'political correctness', equalities are often characterised as a 'minority issue' (with the implied corollary that, if they only affect the few, they do not deserve consideration of the many). Reference to socio-demographic data reveal that to cast equality as a 'minority' issue is to mislead:

- Women constitute a majority of the population (52 per cent).
- The fastest growing age group in the population are those aged 80 years and over (currently constituting 4.5 per cent or 2,749,507 of the total UK population. This age group increased by over 1.1 million between 1981 and 2007).[11]
- There are over 10 million disabled people in Britain, including people with limiting longstanding illnesses, of which 4.6 million are over State Pension Age and 700,000 are children.[12]

- The number of lesbian, gay and bisexual people in the UK is estimated at between 3.05 and 4.27 million people.[13]
- One in ten people in the UK provide unpaid care to a friend or family member.[14]
- At the last Census the 'minority ethnic' population of the UK was 4.6 million people (7.9 per cent).[15]
- Whilst Christianity is the majority religious identity given in the last Census (42 million, 71 per cent), a significant number of people follow other faiths: Buddhist (152,000, 0.3 per cent); Hindu (559,000, 1.0 per cent); Jewish (267,000, 0.5 per cent); Muslim (1.59 million, 2.7 per cent); and Sikh (336,000, 0.6 per cent). In addition, 9.1 million people (15.5 per cent) said that they had no religion.

Recent UK government data also reveal the way in which major inequalities exist in many areas of life, including the labour market and education (see Figure 1.2).

'Snapshot' Measures
- Compared with men, women working part-time are paid around 40 per cent less per hour.
- The rate of employment of disabled people has risen from 38 per cent ten years ago to 48 per cent today, but if you are disabled you are still two and a half times more likely to be out of work than a non-disabled person.
- If you are from an ethnic minority, in 1997 you were 17.9 per cent less likely to find work than if you are white. The difference is still 15.5 per cent.
- 62 per cent of over-fifties feel that they are turned down for a job because they are considered too old, compared with 5 per cent of people in their thirties.
- 6 out of 10 lesbian and gay schoolchildren experience homophobic bullying and half of those contemplate killing themselves as a result.
- Women comprise the following percentages of all holding these elected posts: House of Lords (19.7 per cent); Scottish Parliament (34.1 per cent); National Assembly for Wales (47 per cent); local authority council leaders (14.3 per cent); UK Members of the European Parliament (25.6 per cent).

- People from an 'ethnic minority' background comprise the following percentages of all holding these positions: MPs, 15 (2.3 per cent); Peers, 28 (3.8 per cent); AMs, 1 (1.7 per cent); MSPs, 1 (0.8 per cent); directorships in FTSE 100 companies, 46; and high court judges, 3 (0.2 per cent).
- Women comprise the following percentages of all holding these senior positions: directors in FTSE 100 companies, 11 per cent; editors of national newspapers, 13.6 per cent; public appointments, 34.4 per cent; senior ranks in the armed forces, 0.4 per cent; senior judiciary (high court judge and above, 9.6 per cent; university vice chancellors, 14.4 per cent.

Momentum Measures:
At the current rate of progress:

- A representative House of Commons will be elected in 2080.
- The gender pay gap between men and women will not close until 2085.
- The ethnic employment gap will be closed in 2105.
- The 50+ year employment penalty will not be eliminated in this generation's lifetime.
- The ethnic educational attainment will 'never' be closed.
- The disability employment gap will 'probably never' be closed.
- It will take 55 years for women to achieve equal status at senior levels in the judiciary.
- It will take 73 years to achieve equal status for women directors in FTSE 100 companies.
- It will take another 27 years to achieve gender equality in civil service top management.

Figure 1.2. Contemporary indicators of inequality in Britain/the UK[16]

Overall, in response to the question 'why bother about equalities?', it is evident that, far from being a 'minority' issue, they affect a broad range of social groups; when aggregated, they comprise the *majority* of the population. In addition, instead of being a narrow and politically correct undertaking, the promotion of equalities relates to core debates about the nature of society, politics, the economy, morality, justice and democracy.

1.3 Equalities in a (Quasi-) Federal UK

Writing in the mid-1990s, Pierson (1995: 450) noted that 'comparative work on federalism is rare, and comparative research on the impact of federalism on social policy is non-existent'. Ten years later, Obinger et al. (2005: 2) detected little progress, stating:

> Recent comparative welfare research has acknowledged the importance of state structures in explaining cross-national variation in both the level and the dynamics of social policy formation. And yet the precise nature of this co-evolution of federalism and the welfare state, and the particular national combinations of state structures and social policy to which it gave rise have not been subject to systematic comparative investigation.

The latter conclusion also applies to the way in which equalities issues are addressed in public policy analysis, for existing texts tend to concentrate on developments at the unitary state level (e.g. Thompson, 2003; Daniels and Macdonald, 2005; White, 2006; Hill and Kenyon, 2007; Bagihole, 2009) or in relation to the European Union (Verloo, 2007; Kay, 2007; Elman, 2008; Schiek and Chege, 2008). In contrast, this volume aims to address existing lacunae by exploring the promotion of equalities at the 'sub-state' or 'regional' level by reference to devolution in Wales, with comparative reference to developments in Scotland and Northern Ireland. This is an appropriate focus for examining contemporary developments because, in a UK context, it represents an opportunity to analyse the impact that (re-) creating national legislatures at the sub-unitary state level has had on the promotion of equalities. This is important because, in the 1980s and 90s, some advocates of constitutional reform argued the case for the institutional design of the devolved legislatures to be configured with 'inclusive governance mechanisms' to promote equalities in the conduct of public business. Thus, the present approach allows for an assessment of progress made, for example, against the assertion in the 1997 devolution White Paper that the National Assembly for Wales would be 'a modern democratic institution that reflects the diversity of Wales . . . [and one that] promotes equal opportunities for all' (Welsh Office, 1997: 10). Yet, the present volume should not be seen as a 'before and after' exercise. Rather it engages with the developing process of constitutional reform in the UK, what Hazell (2007: 3) describes as 'a powerful political, legal and institutional dynamic, with further big changes still to come'. Hazell continues:

> Devolution still shows a great deal of dynamism, with the biggest piece of unfinished business being in Wales. There is a persistent and powerful myth that the people of Wales were ambivalent about devolution. Polling data suggest the reverse. When the Welsh have been asked about the options, the largest group is those in favour of the Assembly having law-making powers. (Hazell, 2007: 4)

Overall, the recent shift to quasi-federalism and the asymmetrical nature of devolution in the UK raises a series of significant issues and intriguing questions for the promotion of equalities. For example, how are the various governments and legislatures using their differing powers to promote equality in policy? What contrasts and commonalities exist in devolved policymaking in the UK? To what extent does devolution enable policy making to address specific equalities issues in each territory? Are the devolved polities characterised by inclusive modes of policymaking? Is there a legislative dimension to the promotion of equalities in the wake of devolution? How have the structures and processes of governance in each territory developed in relation to the 'equalities agenda'? Is there any evidence of innovative practice in devolved policymaking? What conceptual approaches to equalities are influencing practice in each country? What impact does the increased proportion of women parliamentarians have on equalities policies? To what extent does the promotion of equalities feature in electoral politics? And what have been the areas of progress, as well as issues, challenges and shortcomings evident in the promotion of equalities over the past decade?

It is these issues that the following chapters will address for, as the Equalities Review (DLGC, 2007a: 26) observes, the present marks a propitious time:

> Many of the necessary institutional conditions are now in place to support progress towards a more equal society . . . [for example] the establishment of the Equality and Human Rights Commission, [and] clearer government leadership on equalities . . . [and in addition] new opportunities are offered by devolution: the fresh legal responsibilities and powers for the Scottish Parliament and the Welsh Assembly . . . provide ways of innovating and making progress . . . The constellation of these favourable conditions may not arise again for some years.

1.4 The structure of this volume

As noted above, equalities are a contested concept – with ongoing debate about the way that they are theorised. In turn, this has major implications for the manner in which the promotion of equalities is operationalised in policy and law. Thus, chapter 2 explores the development of different conceptual approaches to equalities over the past two hundred or so years. Initial attention is placed on the historical development of the concepts of equal treatment, positive action and mainstreaming. In addition to these influential 'over-arching' equalities theories, discussion centres on 'strand-based' conceptualisations such as feminism, multiculturalism, queer theory and the social model of disability, as well as contemporary concerns with intersectionality, deliberative democracy, citizenship and capabilities.

In chapter 3 the focus shifts from theory to empirical data as the evidence base around inequalities and discrimination is explored in relation to gender and other social identities. The discussion is concerned with a core question: what is the nature and extent of present inequalities in Wales? Accordingly, the analysis draws upon official statistics and research evidence to assess inequalities between (and within) different social groups in relation to devolved policy areas such as education, the economy, health and housing. The chapter reveals their sometimes pronounced and enduring nature. A comparative perspective is provided by reference to data relating to Scotland and Northern Ireland. The chapter concludes with a summary of key equality issues in relation to gender. It shows that over the past four decades there have been major changes in the way that women participate in the labour market and higher education. And yet, despite modest progress in some areas based on a range of indicators, enduring and deep-rooted inequalities characterise today's society.

Chapter 4 begins with a concise theoretical outline of 'new governance'. As Newman (2001: 11) observes, this is 'an analytical concept, giving rise to questions about what forms of power and authority . . . typify a particular approach to governing'. As earlier work has outlined (Chaney and Rees, 2004: 36), this mode of analysis offers a systemic or 'constitutional approach', one that 'interrogates the way that the overall system of governance is supposed to operate in relation to the promotion of equalities'. This is important because, as Squires observes (2005: 380), 'enabling excluded groups to unsettle institutionally accepted conceptions of equality will require a parity of participation, which makes democratic inclusion central to both the meaning and realisation of equality'. Accordingly, a 'governance perspective' is applied to equalities developments in all three devolved UK polities and attention is focused on institutional developments such as cross-sectoral partnerships and constitutional equalities clauses.

In chapter 5, attention is focused on the 'state equalities infrastructure' in Wales and how it compares to developments in the UK's other devolved territories. The former term is used principally to denote public bodies that, wholly or in part, have an official remit to advise on, monitor, regulate and enforce equality policies and law across a broad range of public functions. The discussion explores the official remit of such organisations. It reveals that one consequence of the creation of the National Assembly is the rapid increase in regulatory capacity in relation to the devolved public sector. This gives the Welsh government significant powers to oversee, regulate and monitor equalities matters. The analysis also examines the adequacy of advice provision on equalities in and by the public sector. A comparative perspective is provided by reference to infrastructure developments in Scotland and Northern Ireland. Here too devolution has introduced significant change with the advent of bodies such as the Office of the Commissioner for Public Appointments in Scotland and the Equality Commission for Northern Ireland.

Examining the legal framework around gender and other modes of equality is central to understanding the effectiveness of state actions to tackle discrimination. However, as observed, contemporary analysis is principally focused at the level of the unitary state, with few studies offering combined examination of the legal framework emanating from the supra-, unitary and sub-state levels. Chapter 6 addresses such lacunae by examining the body of law on equalities in Wales. Initial attention is placed on the influence of the United Nations, European Union and Westminster. Subsequent analysis centres on the equality of opportunity clauses in the Welsh devolution statutes, as well as devolved lawmaking in relation to the promotion of equality. Attention is then focused on comparative developments in other devolved polities, such as Scotland, Northern Ireland, the Basque Country and Catalonia. This reveals that embedding equalities into constitutional law is an increasingly common aspect of 'regional' government in Europe. The chapter concludes with a critical evaluation of recent legal developments related to the promotion of equality at the sub-state level.

In chapter 7, attention is focused on developments in equalities policy since the creation of the National Assembly for Wales. Such a focus is appropriate for, as Mooney et al. (2008: 483) observe, 'through critical social policy analysis we can both evaluate and explain the complex interrelations between devolved governance and the continuing reproduction of inequalities and social divisions throughout the UK'. Analysis in this chapter discusses the way in which equality issues have been addressed in relation to gender and other 'strands'. The discussion draws principally upon policy discourse analysis (DeLeon, 1998; Edelmann, 1977, 1988) as part of a post-empiricist, interpretative approach that places an emphasis on the language of policy documents. It allows an appreciation of how policymakers formulate and construct problems, enabling us to focus on their claims and rhetoric, and acknowledging that policies are complex exercises in agenda-setting power, while policy issues such as equalities may be framed in particular forms of language reflecting the political viewpoints of those in power (Fischer and Forester, 1993: 5–7). A range of policy evaluations is also discussed, thereby providing instrumental analysis of the developing equalities agenda. The chapter concludes with a comparative analysis of policy developments in the UK's other devolved polities.

Both the mainstreaming literature on equalities (Rees, 1998) and research and theory in respect of new governance (Rhodes, 1997) emphasise a participatory, democratic dimension to public policy. Lobbying is a key component of this. It refers quite simply to 'the practice of attempting to influence the decisions of government' (Rosenthal, 2001: 11). Thus, the analysis in chapter 8 explores the evidence for a developing equalities policy lobby in Wales. Prefaced by a summary of theories of interest group mediation, policy networks and lobby formation, subsequent analysis delineates the membership and structures of the lobby and examines the connections and nature of interactions between agencies and groups in the Welsh policy domain, including the views of NGOs and other participants. The chapter also incorporates an analysis of a new dimension to the lobby; electoral competition around equalities as political parties and civil society organisations advance equalities policies in the context of elections to the National Assembly. A comparative perspective is provided by an outline of equality policy proposals in the election manifestos issued by political parties in devolved national elections in Scotland and Northern Ireland.

Chapter 9 summarises the book's core findings on devolution, equalities and public policy with reference to a political and social theory. In so doing, it details the principal contrasts and commonalities between the UK's three devolved polities, evaluates the nature and extent of progress and highlights ongoing issues and challenges.

2

Theoretical Perspectives on Promoting Equality

2.0 Introduction

Equality is a complex and contested concept based upon notions of social justice, rights, freedom and democracy. As Thompson, (2003: 45) observes, it often involves contestation: 'promoting equality inevitability involves entering into conflict with the 'powers that be', the dominant social arrangements that help to maintain existing power relations'. Burchardt (2006) identifies three core components of equality: equality of process, equality of outcome and, equality of opportunity. The first is principally about making sure that people are treated in the same manner. For Burchardt, this is 'the quality of relations between people, the interactions between them, and the interactions between people and institutions which are the focus of analysis, not the distribution of any particular outcomes' (Burchardt,

2006: 4). In contrast, equality of outcome relates to even shares as measured in relation to material resources and services (such as education and health). Whereas equality of opportunity refers to 'whether or not an individual has the opportunity to do something, for example, enter higher education . . . [this] depends on the resources available to her, her skills and talents, the effort she makes, the institutional setting in which she is operating and possibly a certain amount of luck' (Burchardt, 2006: 41). Against this background, the UK government's Equality Review defined an equal society as one that:

> Protects and promotes equal, real freedom and substantive opportunity to live in the ways people value and would choose, so that everyone can flourish. An equal society recognises people's different needs, situations and goals, and removes the barriers that limit what people can do and can be. (DLGC, 2007a: 7)

Accordingly, this chapter explores different conceptual approaches to achieving equality. Initial attention is placed on the historical development of the concepts of equal treatment, positive action and mainstreaming. 'Strand-based' theories such as feminism, multiculturalism, queer theory and the social model of disability are then summarised, before contemporary concerns with intersectionality are introduced. Two allied areas of social and political theory, deliberative democracy and citizenship, are then explored before a summary of contemporary theoretical developments, including the development of the 'capabilities approach' to equalities.

2.1 Equal Treatment, Positive Action and Mainstreaming

Equal treatment is a liberal approach to equalities that has its roots in the eighteenth century enlightenment. A prominent historical example of this approach is the preamble of the United States Declaration of Independence (1786): 'We hold these truths to be self-evident: that all men [*sic*] are created equal, that they are endowed, by their creator, with certain unalienable rights, that among these are life, liberty, and the pursuit of happiness'; in like fashion, Thomas Paine's 'The Rights of Man' (1792) and the writings of Rousseau advocated the extension of citizens' rights based on this notion of equality. Publications such as Wollstonecraft's 'Vindication of the Rights of Women' (1792) challenged the gendered bias of such claims, yet held to the basic premise of equal treatment.[1] Such approaches have endured into the twentieth-first century (e.g. the European Council Directive establishing a General Framework for Equal Treatment in Employment and Occupation, 2000).[2] Notwithstanding their enduring nature, they are fundamentally flawed in a number of key respects. As Rees (1998: 34) observes, 'the equal treatment approach suggests that people should be treated simply as individuals without recognising the impact of group membership in the allocations of positions and the implications of this for cultural reproduction'. Moreover, Howard (2008: 170) states: 'the concept does not look at any imbalances that have been created by past discrimination . . . because of its focus on equal treatment and on sameness; this notion ignores and negates the value of difference. This notion, therefore, leaves no room for any recognition of the positive aspects of difference or for a requirement that people should be treated appropriately according to their differences'. The need for an alternative to equal treatment was asserted in R. H. Tawney's classic text 'Equality':[3]

> Equality . . . is to be achieved, not by treating different needs in the same way, but by devoting equal care to ensuring that they are met in different ways most appropriate to them . . . the more anxiously, indeed, a society endeavours to secure equality of consideration for all its members, the greater will be the differentiation of treatment which, when once their common needs have been met, it accords to the special needs of different groups and individuals amongst them. (Tawney, 1931: 11)

Indeed, Tawney viewed difference as a positive resource, memorably stating that 'individual differences, which are a source of social energy, are more likely to ripen and find expression if social inequalities are, as far as practicable, eliminated' (Tawney, 1931; reproduced in Diamond, 2004: 143). Lister (1997: 96) underlines this point: 'the very notion of equality implies differences to be discounted or taken into account so that, despite them, people are treated as equals . . . equality and difference . . . are complementary rather than antagonistic'.

In turn, positive action emerged as an approach designed to address the shortcomings of equal treatment. It aims to create 'a level playing field' and conditions more likely to result in equality of outcome by equalising starting positions. It acknowledges that membership of a social group (for example, defined by age, sex, ethnicity, disability, language and so on) makes a difference to outcomes and can be a source of inequality and discrimination. Positive action therefore seeks to provide mechanisms that will allow certain social groups entry into particular activities by compensating for 'unequal starting positions'. Thus, it is principally concerned with 'perfecting or skewing the rules of the contest' (Rees, 1998: 40). There are numerous illustrations of the effective use of positive action in relation to gender equality. For example, as Lovecy (2002) underlines, one of the main policy frames of the Council of Europe (CoE) has been the construction of initiatives on women's rights around descriptive representation (in other words, securing equal numbers of women parliamentarians). Stemming from a CoE inter-ministerial conference report on promoting the participation of women in the political process, this agenda subsequently led to the adoption of various positive action measures including gender-quotas in elections. In the UK, it ultimately resulted in the Sex Discrimination Election Candidates Act (2002). The latter statute neatly embodies the conceptual shift in equalities theory, for it is concerned with enshrining in law a targeted suspension of earlier equal treatment statutes (specifically, the Sex Discrimination Act, 1975), so as to allow positive action in the case of political candidature. Recent legislative proposals in Britain indicate a renewed interest in application of positive action strategies. The documentation associated with the Equality Bill (2009) states the UK government's intention to 'extend positive action so that employers can take into account, when selecting between two equally-qualified candidates, under-representation of disadvantaged groups, for example women and people from ethnic minority communities . . . widening the scope of positive action will make a difference because it will increase opportunities for people from underrepresented groups' (Government Equalities Office, 2008a: 28).

However, as with equal treatment, positive action is also conceptually flawed. As Rees (1998: 37) observes of its application to promoting gender equality, it 'can be seen as providing window dressing; it facilitates some women in some areas, in particular, well qualified middle class women seeking to enter the professions, without affecting the status quo for the vast majority'. In addition, Howard (2008: 171) concludes that 'the main problem with positive action measures is that they are going against the principle of equal treatment, that they themselves constitute discrimination: preferential treatment of some is worse treatment of others and this is seen by some as 'unfair', although others see it as justified because of the inequalities suffered through historical discrimination'.

In response to the shortcomings of the equal treatment and positive action approaches, the theory of gender mainstreaming emerged from feminists' work on international economic aid programmes in the 1970s. As a new social and political priority, it came to wider prominence at the 1985 United Nations (UN) Third World Conference on Women in Nairobi, Kenya – a time when it was also developing in the domestic policies of several European countries, such as the Netherlands, Sweden and Norway (Hafner-Burton and Pollack, 2002). Continued focus was placed upon mainstreaming at the 1995 UN World Conference on Women held in Beijing and it has subsequently developed into an internationally recognised approach to delivering gender equality outcomes in a broad range of organisational contexts. Whilst the initial focus was on gender, in some circumstances a generic version of the mainstreaming concept has developed. One that has been applied to the breadth of equality 'strands' such as disability, language and ethnicity. There are competing definitions of mainstreaming. The UN defines it as a:

> Strategy for making women's as well as men's concerns and experiences an integral dimension of the design, implementation, monitoring and evaluation of policies and programmes in all political, economic and societal spheres so that women and men benefit equally and inequality is not perpetuated. The ultimate goal is to achieve gender equality. (UN, 1995: 2)

In contrast, the Council of Europe offers a more policy-oriented definition:

> Gender mainstreaming is the (re)organisation, improvement, development and evaluation of policy processes, so that a gender equality perspective is incorporated in all policies at all levels and at all stages, by the actors normally involved in policy-making. Gender mainstreaming cannot replace specific policies, which aim to redress situations resulting from gender inequality. Specific gender equality policies and gender mainstreaming are dual and complementary strategies and must go hand in hand to reach the goal of gender equality. (CoE, 2004: 23)

Mainstreaming has been characterised as 'a new approach to equality policy-making and practice' (EOC, 2003: 2). As the foregoing definitions suggest, it aims to build equality considerations into policy-making from the outset and is based upon a series of policy tools that includes gender disaggregated statistics; gender impact assessments; equality indicators; monitoring, evaluating, auditing techniques; gender balance in decision-making; and gender budgeting. In the burgeoning literature, Barnett Donaghy (2002: 327) distinguishes between the expert-bureaucratic and participative-democratic models of mainstreaming. The former

> Relies heavily on 'gender' expert(s) being located within the [government] bureaucracy, such as a women's unit ... [and in contrast] the participative-democratic model is the more recently developed (and tends to be the model which is most likely to incorporate multiple equality areas). It relies primarily on the participation of civic and community groups through a consultation process.

It is the participative-democratic model that relates to the first of three principles underpinning mainstreaming identified by Rees (1998), namely democracy; treating the individual as a whole person (by 'visioning' a person's different needs); and equity and justice. Overall, mainstreaming can be seen as a transformative approach to policy:

> Transforming involves designing programmes and projects informed by the knowledge of the diversity of needs of potential participants. It includes the development of mission statements, aims and objectives, performance indicators and output measures . . . particular attention should be paid to the development of a culture of equal opportunities awareness. Equal opportunities audits where appropriate are necessary to support the transformation process and invoke sanctions. (Rees, 1998: 48)

Against the backdrop of these major conceptual shifts in equalities theory, attention is now placed on conceptualisations that have emerged in relation to promoting equality for specific social groups and identities.

2.2 'Strand-based' Theories

In addition to the foregoing overarching conceptualisations of equality, there is a number of what might nominally be termed 'strand-based' theories (i.e. theories centred on a principal social characteristic, e.g. gender, age, disability etc.). Each is the subject of a burgeoning literature. The following summary delineates key features of selected examples with reference to core texts.

2.2.1 Feminism

Feminism is a theoretical approach founded on different historical phases and competing traditions. Each differs in its interpretation of the underpinnings of sex discrimination and the most appropriate solution. In contrast to nineteenth century/early twentieth century 'first wave' feminists' concentration on women's suffrage, during the period 1960–80 'second wave' feminists, notably liberal feminists, pushed for legal and policy reforms. Thus, liberal feminism emphasises women's autonomy, gender equality, individual rights and equal access to activities in the public sphere (see Friedan, 2001; Kaplan, 1992; Wolf, 1994). In contrast, radical, socialist and Marxist feminists emphasise the need to overthrow the oppression resulting from the capitalist and patriarchal ordering of society (see Rich, 1977; Daly, 1977; Dworkin, 2006; Rowbotham, 1992). In a manner that has acted as a spur to the development of intersectional approaches to equality (see section 2.3 below) and in reaction to the perceived essentialist position of second wave and liberal approaches, 'third wave' feminism has focused on issues of oppression faced by different groups of women (Gillis et al., 2007). Axiomatically, Black feminism has explored the intersection between class, sex and ethnicity (Hooks, 1981; Moraga and Anzaldúa, 1981). As Soper (1994: 14) warns, there are political implications stemming from the third wave:

> One is bound to feel that feminism as theory has pulled the rug from under feminism as politics. For politics is essentially a group affair, based on ideas of making 'common cause', and feminism, like any other politics, has always implied a banding together, a movement based on the solidarity sisterhood of women, who are linked by perhaps very little else than their sameness and 'common cause' as women.

2.2.2 Multiculturalism

According to Floya and Yuval-Davis (1993: 79) 'racism is a set of postulates, images . . . and practices which serve to differentiate and dominate . . . serving to deny full participation in economic, social, political and cultural life'. As Mac an Ghaill (1999: 28) observes, it is a phenomenon that is produced both ideologically and discursively. In conceptual terms, Miles and Brown (2003: 9) assert that 'racism is best conceived primarily as an ideology, for . . . racism was created historically and became interdependent with the ideology of nationalism'. In recent decades multiculturalism has been a common conceptual approach to addressing racism (Parekh, 2000). According to Modood (2000: 2) it is concerned with 'the recognition of group difference within the public sphere of laws, policies, democratic discourses and the terms of a shared citizenship and national identity' (see also Modood, 2007). Abbas (2005: 155) argues that multiculturalism has three central tenets:

> Humans are 'culturally embedded'; that is, they exist in a culturally-structured world and organise their social relations in a culturally-derived system of meaning and significance; second, 'different cultures represent different systems of meaning and visions of the good life'. Here, it is argued that one's way of life is likely to be enriched if there is access to others, and, more crucially, a culturally self-contained life is virtually impossible for most humans in the modern world. Third, every culture is internally plural and reflects a continuing conversation between different traditions and strands of thought.

2.2.3 The Social Model of Disability

The social model of disability makes a fundamental distinction between impairment and disability. Accordingly, the former refers to the loss or limitation of physical, mental or sensory function on a long-term or permanent basis; disability, on the other hand, is the loss or limitation of opportunities to take part in the normal life of the community on an equal level with others due to physical and social barriers (see for e.g. Barnes, and Mercer, 2004; Shakespeare and Watson, 1997; Oliver, 1996). The social model is a response to the pre-existing medical model of disability that stemmed from the 1940s work of Talcott Parsons and others. This emphasised that the 'normal' state of health was 'good health'; as a result sickness and impairments are seen as deviations from 'normality'. Thus, the academic focus was on the experience of 'illness' and the social consequences that come from it. In contrast, the social model posits that disability is a form of social oppression that needs to be addressed by civil rights. Despite its influence it has not been without its critics. For example, Shakespeare and Watson (2001: 13) question whether 'the "strong" social model itself has become a problem . . . [and query whether] a modernist theory of disability – seeking to provide an overarching meta-analysis covering all dimensions of every disabled person's experience – is a useful or attainable concept'. In response, Gabel and Peters (2004: 234) advocate a resistance theory of disability, for, they claim, it is 'inherently political . . . [and] accommodates diverse stakeholders in fluid coalitions and assumes that they can co-resist oppression, its processes can inclusively unite across paradigmatic boundaries . . . [and it] acknowledges the social forces opposing disabled people (also resistant processes) and illuminates responses to these forces'.

2.2.4 Queer Theory

Queer theory draws upon post-structuralism to expose and challenge heteronormativity and promote equality for gay, lesbian and bisexual people (see, e.g., Kosofsky Sedgwick, 1991; Spargo, 1999). It posits that 'sexuality is not natural, but rather, is discursively constructed . . . moreover, sexuality is constructed, experienced, and understood, in culturally and historically specific ways' (Sullivan, 2003: 12). However, critics of queer theory question the extent to which a focus on discourse and language can be extended to understand wider social processes. For example, Green (2004: 541) asserts that it:

> glosses over the ways in which sexual classifications are embodied in institutions and social roles, and thus under-theorizes their role as a principal axis of social organization. Similarly, the second strain of queer theory, radical subversion, neglects the shared social contexts in which sexual actors are socialized, and thus obscures the complexity of sexual marginality and its attachment to other institutionalized identities and social roles.

2.2.5 Anti-Ageism

As Bernard and Phillips (2004: 143) note, 'in social policy . . . old age has had a consistently high profile, but mainly as a social problem'. Contemporary proponents of age equality assert that 'biological determinism' and associated medicalised approaches to ageing have led to older people's subordination and marginalisation in many western countries. As Bytheway and Johnson (1990: 30) observe:

> It is on the basis of biological differences and, in particular, their visible manifestations, that people can be perceived to be of 'different kinds'. Just as it is biological variations which is employed to 'legitimate' distinctions on grounds of gender, disability and race, so it is biology of the ageing process which is popularly perceived to justify beliefs about age.

In response to these traditional perspectives, Phillipson and Walker (1986: 2) summarise the political economy approach to ageing as one whereby, 'the process of ageing and the experience of old age cannot be understood without reference to the elderly person's location in the social structure and their relationship to the economy' (see also Phillipson, 1998). Thus, over recent years, social conceptualisations of ageing have begun to emerge in order to underpin notions of equality for older people. Thus, Fredman and Spencer (2003: 38) assert, 'the aims of equality [for older people] should be seen as the facilitation of choice or autonomy, the protection of dignity and the enhancement of participative democracy or social inclusion'.

2.3 Intersectionality

The concept of intersectionality emerged in the work of Kimberlé Crenshaw (Crenshaw, 2000; Crenshaw et al., 1995). It also has its antecedence in the writing of Black feminists such as Hooks (1990) and Collins (1990). Hankivsky and Christoffersen (2008: 275) summarise this theoretical approach to equalities:

> Intersectionality is a theory of knowledge that strives to elucidate and interpret multiple and intersecting systems of oppression and privilege. It seeks to disrupt linear thinking that prioritizes any one category of social identity. Instead, it strives to understand what is created and experienced at the intersection of two or more axes of oppression (e.g. race/ethnicity, class, and gender) on the basis that it is precisely at the intersection that a completely new status, that is more than simply the sum of its individual parts, is formed.

There are various methodologies associated with intersectionality. McCall (2005: 1775) explains two main techniques: intracategorical and intercategorical approaches. The former 'acknowledges the stable and even durable relationships that social categories represent at any given point in time, though it also maintains a critical stance toward [such] categories'. This approach is called *intra*categorical complexity because authors working in this vein tend to focus on particular social groups at neglected points of intersection, 'people whose identity crosses the boundaries of traditionally constructed groups' (2005: 1782). In contrast, the *inter*categorical approach strategically uses the 'relationships of inequality among *already constituted social groups*, as imperfect and ever changing as they are, and takes those relationships as the centre of analysis' (2005: 1782; emphasis added).

Whilst these comparatively sophisticated conceptualisations may offer the potential to address some of the shortcomings of earlier approaches to equalities, the main challenge lies in their operationalisation in manageable and effective ways. As Squires (2008: 60) warns, 'if the complex interplay of multiple crosscutting structures of inequality is recognised, the demands of intersectionality require a policy response that may be too complex to be viable'.

2.4 Deliberative Democracy

Another body of social theory relevant to the promotion of equalities emphasises the role of discourse in democracy. For example, Habermas's Communicative Action Theory suggests that 'all interests need to be engaged in the discourse if a group is to . . . move beyond the assumptions and acceptance of a *status quo* which preserves the [pre-existing] power relations of society' (Habermas, 1981: 128). Applied to the promotion of equalities, this conceptualisation emphasises the need for deliberation to overcome subjective prejudice or bias 'in favour of a rationally motivated agreement' (Habermas, 1987: 315). Crucially for Habermas, the pursuit of consensus is the *raison d'être* of communicative encounters (Habermas, 1984: 247). Moreover, equal rights for citizens to participate in formal decision-making is central to the theory: 'access to political debates must be open for any person affected by the issue at stake, and within the debate it must be possible to raise all kinds of arguments freely' (Habermas, 1996: 72). Such assertions resonate with theoretical work around deliberative democracy (Bohman and Rehg, 1997; Gutmann and Thompson, 1996; Elster, 1998). This body of theory has two principal elements: 'collective decision-making with the participation of all who will be affected by the decision – or their representatives'; and 'decision making by means of arguments offered by and to participants who are committed to the values of rationality and impartiality' (Elster, 1998: 8). Dryzek restates the need for equality of participation: 'the essence of democratic legitimacy should be sought . . . in the ability of all individuals subject to a collective decision to engage in authentic deliberation about that decision' (Dryzek, 2000: v). The equality dimension to this conceptualisation lies not only with the emphasis on parity of access to deliberation but also in the idea of self-determination. This is defined by Young (1983: 180) as 'a principle that social decisions ought to be made by those most affected by the outcome of the decision, whether in terms of the actions they will have to take or in terms of the effects of the actions on them'. Thus, Elster (1998: 16) questions political systems where elected representatives do not fully reflect social diversity. He asks: 'will deliberation produce all of its good effects if it takes place mainly within an elite that is self-selected because it knows more about public issues and is concerned about them?' According to Cohen (1997), deliberative democracy is distinguished from more familiar adversarial politics by the commitment of the participants to pursuing consensus through deliberation. He states: 'not simply a form of politics, democracy, on the deliberative view, is a framework of social and institutional conditions that facilitates free discussion among equal citizens – by providing favourable conditions for participation, association, and expression' (1997: 412–13). It is a point that Gargarella (1998: 274) echoes when he observes that 'institutional system[s] could be examined in the light of at least two important observations. First, the diverse groups that comprise society find it difficult to express and defend their particular claims. Second, the system does not provide sufficient guarantees for the protection of the interests of minorities'. The foregoing has clear links to mainstreaming, for as Squires (2005: 381) asserts:

> We find in the deliberative democracy literature very similar concerns to those within the mainstreaming literature, though the language is different: both focus on the rule formation process and aim at impartiality through inclusivity. It is for this reason that it makes sense to think about mainstreaming with relation to deliberative democracy.

2.5 Citizenship

Theory on citizenship is also relevant to conceptualising equalities. According to Turner (1993: 2), it refers to 'practices (judicial, political, economic and cultural), which define a person as a competent member of society'. Thus, he continues, it is concerned with the 'debate about inequality, power differences and social class' (Turner, 1993: 3). Two broad theoretical strands are identifiable: liberal and civic-republican/ communitarian (Oldfield, 1994; Miller, 2000). Mistrustful of the state and collectivist practices, the former places emphasis on 'sovereign and autonomous beings' (Oldfield, 1994: 188) whereby the citizen is a 'unique subject and agent' (Byrne, 2005:3). In contrast, civic-republican/communitarian models emphasise civic duty (Arnot, 2003) and hold that the citizen 'plays an active role in shaping the future direction of her or his society through political debate and decision-making' (Miller, 2000: 53). According to this view, citizenship is concerned with participatory democracy (Lister, 2003) and 'sharing in rule as well as being ruled' (Lockyer, 2003: 2). The modern citizen is thus seen as an individual who 'is aware of their rights, but also of their obligations to other people and the wider society' and who is involved in voluntary activity and politics generally (Pattie et al., 2004: 129).

From an equalities perspective, the central issue is *who* is included in notions of citizenship (Marshall, 1950; Kofman, 1995). The exclusive nature of earlier models of citizenship has been the subject of a series of attacks from various equality 'strands'. For example, feminist critiques highlight the andocentric and patriarchal nature of traditional theories (Lister, 2003). In a similar vein, the civic pluralist model of multicultural citizenship emphasises the failure of pre-existing conceptualisations of citizenship to embrace ethnic diversity (Soutphommasane, 2005; Flores and Benmayor, 1997). Moreover, Field's (2007) analysis of theory and practice around citizenship in relation to lesbians, gays, bisexuals and transgendered (LGBT) individuals led her to propose a model of 'counter-hegemonic citizenship' which, she asserts, 'brings us to consider citizenship as a process, rather than a status or a set of rights, and to focus on meaningful struggles that can lead to the redrawing of the boundaries of the citizenship regime for all oppressed groups' (Field, 2007: 259). In a similar vein, critiques from age equality and disability perspectives refer respectively to the marginalisation of children and young people

(Gaskell, 2008) and due to the fact that 'disabled people are currently denied recognition or respect in ablist culture . . . [they] are denied not just full cultural citizenship, but also the formal rights and responsibilities which form the socio-political context for cultural association' (Marks, 2001: 168). Overall, Torres (2006: 538) concludes that 'traditional approaches are often founded on notions of a homogeneous citizenship through a process of systematic exclusion rather than inclusion in the polity'. Responding to the equalities critique, recent political discourse from across the political spectrum has emphasised citizenship as a means of strengthening democracy, and promoting equality and social cohesion (e.g. Faulks, 2000; Blunkett, 2001).

2.6 Contemporary Developments in Equality Theory

Recent developments in the way that equalities are conceptualised draw upon human rights law. As Phillips (2007a: 138) observes:

> Human rights can enrich our account of equality by taking us beyond narrow comparators and discrimination grounds to decide whether somebody has been treated unfairly and prevented from fulfilling their desires or potential. They help us by providing a way to talk sensibly about the differences that divide us. That surely must be a prize that anyone who seeks greater equality or assurance of human rights must value.

The move to integrate equalities and human rights stems in part from the findings of the UK government's Equalities Review (DLGC, 2007a); in response to this publication, the Equality and Human Rights Commission (EHRC) is currently developing a new way of measuring equality, the Equality Measurement Framework (EMF).[4] The latter will be based upon the 'capability approach' developed by Amartya Sen and is based on human freedoms in the form of 'human capabilities'. These are defined as 'the central and basic things in life that people can actually do and be' (Sen, 1984, 1992, 1993, 2005). These include such individual substantive freedoms as the ability to avoid premature mortality, to have access to adequate education and to participate in and influence public life. The new Measurement Framework is based upon the premise that there are three distinct aspects of inequality that can arise between individuals and groups:

inequality of outcome, that is inequality in the central and valuable things in life that individuals and groups actually achieve; *inequality of autonomy*, that is inequality in the degree of independence people have to make decisions affecting their lives, how much choice and control they really have given their circumstances; and *inequality of process*, reflecting inequalities in treatment through discrimination or disadvantage by other individuals and groups, or by institutions and systems.

The proposed new Measurement Framework will relate the foregoing three aspects of inequality to 'a list of the critical areas of life in terms of which the position of individuals and groups will be evaluated' (Burchardt, 2008: 12).[5] The list is principally based on a human rights framework of 'central and valuable freedoms'. Thus, the critical areas or 'capability domains' are: life; physical security; health; education; standard of living; productive and valued activities; individual, family and social life; participation and voice; identity, expression and self-respect; and legal security (Vizard and Burchardt, 2007). Such developments around the capabilities approach reflect the complexity of operationalising intersectional approaches to equalities within an integrated human rights-based framework. As such it has attracted a number of criticisms; for example, that subjective moral perspectives attach to the concept of capability (Cohen, 1993). Moreover, in a broadly similar vein, Nussbaum (2000) highlights shortcomings in theoretical neutrality, for there are diverse and culturally distinct conceptions of what constitutes a good life in which individuals possess the required capabilities to flourish.

2.7 Summary

Over recent decades there have been major developments in equalities theory. Notwithstanding the endurance of equal treatment approaches for over two centuries, positive action and more recently mainstreaming have had a significant impact upon the way in which (in)equalities are conceptualised. The present marks a pivotal phase characterised by the questioning of: (i) single theorisations relating to entire social categories (as, for example, witnessed in third wave 'attacks' on second-wave feminist approaches; or contemporary critiques of the social model of disability); and (ii) 'strand-based' discrete approaches to equality (for example, relating solely to gender or 'race' equality, as witnesses by the move to single equality commissions in Britain, Northern Ireland and elsewhere, as well as generic approaches to mainstreaming). In response, intersectionality has often been promulgated as the appropriate conceptual 'answer'. Whether hybridised with human rights (as in the 'capabilities approach') or seen as a standalone concept (variously operationalised by intracategorical and intercategorical techniques; see McCall, 2005, op. cit.), it offers the potential explanatory power to address earlier conceptual shortcomings. Yet, it is also marked by complexity, which may require further theoretical refinement before it is as widely adopted as its conceptual predecessors. Whatever the future for intersectional theory, a common thread running through recent theoretical developments in relation to equalities (and allied theory on citizenship and deliberative democracy) is the need to locate the theorising of equalities for different groups and identities within wider, complex social and political processes. Chapter 4 develops this theme as it examines the relationship between the promotion of equalities and new governance theory in the context of devolution in the UK. However, before this, the next chapter focuses on the evidence base related to (in)equality in Wales and the UK's other devolved polities.

3

Exploring Inequality and Discrimination in Wales, Scotland and Northern Ireland

3.0 Introduction

This chapter is concerned with exploring the evidence base around inequality and discrimination in relation to gender and other social characteristics in Wales. It draws upon official data and research evidence compiled over the past decade to analyse the extent of inequalities between different social groups in relation to devolved policy areas. Subsequently a summary of key gender equality issues is provided, following which attention is focused on social attitudes and the prevalence of discriminatory views in today's society. The chapter concludes with analysis of data relating to Scotland and Northern Ireland.

3.1 Demographic Context

The 2001 Census recorded that the population of Wales was 2,910,200.[1] A recent official estimate puts the figure at 2,993,000.[2] According to the Census, 52 per cent of the population is female and 48 per cent male. Just 2.1 per cent (61,580 people) comes from 'non-white' ethnic backgrounds (an increase of 0.6 per cent since 1991); this is principally due to increases in the number of people of Indian, Bangladeshi and Pakistani origin. The ethnic population is clustered in urban centres in the south of the country, with almost a half of the Black and Asian population living in Cardiff. In addition, recent estimates[3] suggest that there are approximately 2,000 Gypsy Travellers in the country.[4] Three quarters of the overall population was born in Wales. Recent Welsh government estimates indicate that there are 129,500 people born outside the UK resident in Wales,[5] and the proportion of those who were born in England constitute a fifth of the population (circa 2001, an increase from fewer than one in seven residents in 1951). It should also be noted that Wales, in common with the other UK countries, has seen significant in-migration of citizens from countries that joined the European Union in 2004, the 'Accession 8' or 'A8' countries. Between 2004–8, 23,800 people came to Wales from these countries.[6]

Christianity was the religious affiliation given by 97.9 per cent of Census respondents in Wales that said they had a faith;[7] one per cent said that they were Muslim. Almost one in five (18.5 per cent) said that they had no religion. As in the other UK countries, Wales has an ageing population; nearly one in four people are over the age of 60 years, a higher proportion than in England, Scotland or Northern Ireland.

Whereas the Welsh population as a whole grew by over 2 percentage points in the two decades prior to the last Census, the proportion of people of retirement age[8] grew by 9.1 percentage points (a total of 59,000 people); and, there was a decrease of 5.8 percentage points in the number of children and young people (for those under 16 years this represented a total decrease of 38,800 individuals). As Dunkerley (2007: 119) observes:

> Not only does Wales have a higher proportion of people of pensionable age than the rest of the UK (20.2 per cent compared to 18.4 per cent), but also, at 17.4 per cent, the country has a higher proportion of the

population aged 65 and over than all of what were then the 15 EU member states with the exception of Italy with 18.2 per cent.

In addition, the proportion of people aged 80+ years is slightly higher than the UK or EU average, and is at least one percentage point higher than over half of all EU countries.[9] It is not possible to set out detailed information on sexual orientation in the population for, as recent analysis concluded, 'very little creditable data have been collected on sexual orientation . . . no data have been analysed at a Wales level'.[10] However, Davies et al. (undated) estimate the number of gay, lesbian and bisexual people at approximately 175,000 (6 per cent of the total population). Moreover, in 2008, there were 137 male and 145 female civil partnerships in Wales.[11]

In terms of living arrangements, the 2001 Census revealed that there are 1.2 million households in Wales; 29 per cent are single person households (almost half of which are constituted by people of pensionable age). Just over a quarter (28 per cent) of households were families with dependent children. Married couple households constitute 17 per cent of all households, a decrease from 23 per cent recorded in the 1991 Census. Lone parent households (including dependent and non-dependent children) total 10.6 per cent of all households. Lone mothers head 89 per cent of lone parent households.[12]

The 1891 Census recorded that 54 per cent of the overall population could speak Welsh. This figure had declined to 19 per cent in 1981 and 1991, but increased to 21 per cent in 2001. A subsequent study in 2004 concluded that 21.7 per cent (611,000) of all those aged 3+ years could speak Welsh.[13] However, there are wide variations in Welsh language ability by age. For example, according to the last Census, 39 per cent of those aged 10 to 15 years could speak, read and write Welsh. Furthermore, the number of 'non-white' Welsh speakers was as follows: Mixed 2,910; Asian or Asian British 1,648; Black or Black British 443; and Chinese or Other Ethnic Group 535. In addition to those living in Wales, official estimates put the number of Welsh speakers resident in England at between 86,000 and 117,000, with a further 1,000 resident in Scotland and Northern Ireland (unknown numbers reside outside the UK).[14]

Measures of the number of disabled people in Wales vary owing to different official survey definitions and sampling procedures. Thus, estimates range from one in six of the overall population (from the

Welsh House Condition Survey), to one in three (from the Welsh Health Survey).[15] Of the 1.6 million people of working age in the country,[16] 380,000 stated they had a disability, of which 53 per cent were male and 47 per cent were female.[17] Amongst older people, one in fourteen people aged 70 to 80 have eyesight problems; for those over 80 years it is one in seven. In addition, there are 7,000 people over the age of 65 who are blind or partially sighted; a third of people aged 70 to 80 and half of the over 80s have hearing problems; and there are 9,000 people over the age of 65 who are deaf, or have a hearing impairment.[18] Overall, in relation to pupils with special educational needs (SEN), the official figures show that the total number with a statement is 3.2 per cent of pupils on the school roll, or 15,579; a further 82,100 had SEN but have not been 'statemented' by the local authority.[19] With regard to social disadvantage, combined data from the 2001 Census and the 2005 Welsh Index of Multiple Deprivation revealed that 10 per cent of the population of Wales live in one of the country's 10 per cent most deprived areas.[20] Lastly, Census data reveal that 11.3 per cent, or 344,000 individuals, provide some form of care for friends and relatives.[21] Against the background of a socially diverse and changing Welsh population we now consider the evidence relating to inequalities by policy area.

3.2 Education

Education remains an arena where inequalities are apparent; for example, gender differences in attainment are evident at Key Stage 4 (14–16-year-olds) with girls generally outperforming boys in GCSE results (see Table 3.1). Thus, 46 per cent of boys in Wales gain 5 or more GCSEs grade A*–C (or vocational equivalent) compared with 58 per cent of girls, and 64 per cent of boys gain 2 or more A/AS levels at A–C grades compared with 70 per cent of girls.[22] Furthermore, more boys than girls leave school with no formal qualifications (3.3 per cent compared with 2.1 per cent).[23] The gender gap in educational attainment is particularly marked amongst Pakistani-heritage pupils; boys attain an average score just 68 per cent of the average score for girls.[24]

Reflecting longstanding patterns of marginalisation in the education system, an attainment gap is also present for disabled people of all ages. For example, 62 per cent of disabled people in Wales attain up to four A*–C GCSEs compared with 87.2 per cent of non-disabled people; and 44.2 per cent of disabled people gain five A*–C GCSEs compared with 69.5 per cent of non-disabled people. In post-compulsory education, 25.4 per cent of disabled people attain up to two A levels compared with 47.4 per cent of non-disabled people; and 12.2 per cent of disabled people gain a degree compared to 26.7 per cent of non-disabled people. Furthermore, disabled people are more likely to have no formal qualifications (38 per cent compared to 12.8 per cent of non-disabled people).[25]

	2001		2005	
	Boys	**Girls**	**Boys**	**Girls**
Entered 5 or more GCSEs	84	89	84	90
5 or more GCSEs at A*–C	45	55	46	58
No GCSEs	10	6	9	5
A*–C in Science	47	48	47	50
A*–C in Maths	44	45	46	50
A*–C in English	46	64	46	64
A*–C in Welsh	26	43	28	46
A*–C in each core subject	34	39	35	42

Table 3.1. Gender and educational attainment: school pupils' qualifications (GCSE results (or vocational equivalent), percentage of 15-year-olds)[32]

In terms of attainment and ethnicity, pupils from the Black African ethnic group achieve the lowest results and pupils from the Mixed White/Black Caribbean group are in the lowest three performing ethnic groups. Thus, the Black African ethnic group have the lowest proportion of pupils attaining 5 or more GCSEs at grades A*–C (30 per cent, compared with 66 per cent for white and Asian pupils) and the lowest proportion of pupils achieving at least one GCSE at grade A*–G (77 per cent, compared with 95 per cent for white and Asian pupils). The three ethnic groups that attain the highest average scores in respect of compulsory-phase educational attainment also achieve the best results in terms of the proportion of their pupils attaining 5+A*–C GCSEs: 73 per cent of Chinese-origin, 67 per cent of White/Asian and 60 per cent of Indian-origin pupils attained this level.[26] In relation to socio-economic status and attainment, pupils eligible for free school meals (a proxy measure for low income households) at Key Stage 4 achieve an average point score of just over half of that attained by pupils from wealthier households.[27] When free school meal entitlement is analysed by ethnic background the figures reveal that 16.4 per cent of white pupils received such provision compared with 47 per cent of Black pupils and 61.4 per cent of Gypsy/Roma pupils.[28]

Inequalities are also evident in educational experience. With regard to ethnicity, a recent case study highlighted issues in relation to racist bullying in schools in Wales. It found that:

> Schools were generally felt to be poor at even acknowledging there is a problem with racism and racist bullying. Staff in schools are believed to be anxious about registering racist incidents, as they are required to do in law, in case they give the school a bad name.[29]

In a further study of bullying, seven per cent of gay and lesbian respondents reported being bullied while at school or college. However, few respondents in the study felt they had not been given the same educational opportunities as heterosexual people (2 per cent) or that they had been unfairly treated by teachers or lecturers (3 per cent), although a significant minority (7 per cent) stated that they felt excluded by the education system.[30]

In the face of increasing demand for Welsh medium education, there are mixed trends in state provision of Welsh medium schools.[31] Over recent years there has been a modest increase (2.4 percentage points) in the number of mainly Welsh medium primary schools from 455 (or 27.1 per cent of all primary schools) in 1991 to 458 (or 29.5 per cent) in 2006. The number of Welsh medium secondary schools has also increased from 47 in 1996 to 54 in 2006. In addition, the number of children learning Welsh as a second language grew over the same period from 111,647 to 155,978 (or 83.9 per cent of all children), an increase of 20.7 percentage points.

In relation to participation in post-compulsory education, over recent times there has been a marked change in the gender profile in higher education in Wales. In earlier decades the gender gap was pronounced. Prior to 1995/6, more males entered higher education. For example, in 1960 70.5 per cent of students were men; only 29.5 per cent were women. Throughout the 1960s the number of male university students was double that of women.[33] The difference in the sexes' respective participation rates declined steadily until 1996, when the ratio of males and females entering higher education was approximately fifty–fifty. Since then, females have outnumbered males and the gap is steadily increasing each year. In 2004/5, 57 per cent of students were female, compared with 43 per cent male. In addition to shifting participation rates, gender segregation in subject choice is an enduring equalities issue. When first degree subject choices in Welsh higher education institutions (HEIs) (see Table 3.2) are analysed, women predominate in subjects such as education, social sciences and law (73, 66 and 65 per cent respectively); men constitute the majority of students taking computer science and engineering technology (81 and 90 per cent respectively). Such gendered patterns also apply to vocational courses. For example, women constitute 74 per cent of first year students on initial teacher training courses at Welsh HEIs. Moreover, in terms of access to university-level studies, disabled people are under-represented compared with their proportion in the population as a whole. Thus, they constitute 7.5 per cent of undergraduate enrolments and 5.4 per cent of postgraduate enrolments.[34] Furthermore, only 7.6 per cent of disabled people have a degree or equivalent compared with 16.6 per cent of the non-disabled population.[35] In terms of ethnicity, the proportion of higher education enrolments from 'ethnic minorities' as a whole was greater than their proportion within the overall population. It was comparatively high amongst the Asian group (1.8 per cent of undergraduate students and 2.7 per cent of postgraduates). Moreover, recent figures show that 4.2 per cent of enrolments for undergraduate courses and 5.6 per cent of enrolments for postgraduate courses were from minority ethnic students (exceeding the 3.3 per cent of the general population recorded as being from the minority ethnic groups aged 16–24). Gender differences are also apparent in Black and Minority Ethnic (BME) enrolments to higher education; statistics reveal a higher proportion of males (5.2 per cent) compared with females (3.8 per cent). The disparity was particularly evident amongst Asian people, for 2.4 per cent of overall male enrolments at university were from Asian males compared with the 1.6 per cent of female enrolments constituted by Asian women.[36]

A gender participation gap is also evident in further education (FE) with males accounting for 53 per cent of enrolments compared with 47 per cent by women.[39] The gender gap was particularly evident amongst part-time learners. For both full-time and part-time FE students, the proportion of females increases with age. As with higher education, significant gender differences emerge when subject choices are analysed. Women predominate in courses on health (78 per cent)

41

Subject	Women		Men	
	No. students	%	No. students	%
Education	5960	73	2205	27
Social Sciences	6340	66	3235	34
Law	2345	65	1275	35
Medicine and dentistry	1130	64	640	36
Biological sciences		59	3460	41
Business and administration	4890	52	5020	48
Computer science	5395	19	3340	81
Engineering technology	800	10	6110	90
All subjects[37]	59,095	57	43,895	43

Table 3.2. Gender segregation in first degree subject: Welsh higher education institutions (2004/5)[38]

and sales and marketing (70 per cent) and are greatly under-represented in areas such as engineering and construction (both 2 per cent) (see Table 3.3).

Subject area	Women		Men	
	No. students	%	No. students	%
Health	14040	78	4070	22
Sales and Marketing	5480	70	2370	30
Business and Management	11185	60	7430	40
Science and mathematics	14310	50	14050	50
Media	14745	50	14770	50
Information Technology	10770	44	13660	56
Manufacturing	910	18	4255	82
Engineering	160	2	7500	98
Built Environment	140	2	6780	98
All subjects[40]	100,400	47	114,935	53

Table 3.3. Gender segregation and subject choice: Welsh further education institutions (2004)[41]

Disabled people are also under-represented in FE; only 6.9 per cent of learners report some form of disability.[42] In terms of age equality and learning, recent analysis concluded that 'Wales possesses one of the highest rates of adult participation in lifelong learning. Furthermore, the rate of growth between 2003 and 2005 was higher than those displayed by most other EU countries.'[43] An official report summarises the situation in the following terms:

> Just over half the people in adult education in Wales are over the age of 50. Nearly 1 in 4 people in further education are over the age of 50 and nearly 1 in 10 in higher education. 3 in 10 working age people over the age of 50 with no qualifications had taken part in some form of learning (not necessarily related to their work) over the past year; for those with GCSE qualifications (but nothing higher) it was 6 out of 10; and for those with a degree it was nearly 9 out of 10. For the under 50s the proportions are a shade higher (4 in 10 with no qualifications, 7 out of 10 with GCSEs and 9 out of 10 with degrees).[44]

In post-compulsory education there has been less progress in Welsh medium provision when compared with that in state schools. In FE the number of Welsh medium places *de*creased from 3,125 in 2003/4 to 2,535 in 2005/6. In HE, the number of enrolments with 'any element of teaching through Welsh', full-time equivalents declined from 1,691 in 2000/1 to 1,499 in 2005/6 and the number of students with any element of teaching through Welsh as a percentage of all enrolments, full or part-time, decreased by 0.4 percentage points over the same period.[45]

3.3 The Labour Market and the Economy

Prior to the onset of the latest economic recession (circa December 2007), analysis of gender and participation in the labour market revealed that 'over the past fifteen years in Wales unemployment for men has halved [from 11.5 to 6.0 percent]. For women it has fluctuated but has gone down slightly [from 5.4 per cent, peaking at 8.1, and declining to 5.1 per cent]. Since 2000, the unemployment rate for women has been about 1.5 percentage points lower than those for men'.[46] A recent study provided further insights into these gender-based differences:

> 4 in 10 working women work part-time compared with fewer than 1 in 10 men. Women working part-time are nearly twice as likely as men to say that they did not want full-time work. Women are five times more likely than men to give family reasons for working part-time. For women

the ratio of full-time to part-time workers is the same for all age groups. For men it is much higher for the 35 to 50 age group and lower for workers under 35 (but not as low as the ratio for women). Women are more than four times as likely as men to work under 35 hours: men are more than three times as likely as women to work over 42 hours.[47]

In addition, men are much more likely to be self-employed than women (in 2007 17.8 per cent of males aged 16+ years were self-employed compared with 7.1 per cent of females).[48]

Inequalities are also evident in disabled peoples' participation in the labour market.[49] They have lower employment rates than non-disabled people; 43 per cent of disabled women and the same proportion of disabled men work, compared with 82 per cent of non-disabled men and 76 per cent of non-disabled women.[50] Moreover, when economic inactivity rates of all those of working age in Wales are compared with those covering the UK as a whole, the gap between the respective rates was relatively small for the non-disabled population (15.8 per cent in the UK compared with 16.5 per cent in Wales). However, it was more pronounced for the disabled population (48 per cent in the UK as a whole, compared with 56.8 per cent in Wales).[51]

In terms of ethnicity and faith, economic activity rates are considerably lower in the Muslim community than in the general population, with the lowest rates amongst the Bangladeshi and Pakistani groups. This is principally the result of the low activity rates amongst Bangladeshi and Pakistani women (22 and 32 per cent respectively). As a result, the overall economic activity rate for Bangladeshi-origin people (53 per cent) was much lower than for the population as a whole (75 per cent).[52] In addition, self-employment was more prevalent amongst the Muslim population; notably, the proportion of female Muslims (aged 25–74) that were self-employed was 20 per cent compared with 9 per cent for women as a whole. For men, the respective figures were 33 and 20 per cent.[53] Partly based on such patterns of engagement with the labour market and resultant earnings levels, compared to the population as a whole, Muslims are more likely to live in the 10 per cent most deprived areas of Wales and less likely to live in the 50 per cent least deprived areas.[54]

In terms of age and labour market participation, two out of three people over the age of fifty are economically active (either in work or seeking employment) compared with more than three out of four for those below the age of 50. The proportion of the over 50s in Wales who are economically inactive is seven percentage points higher than in the UK as a whole. The employment rate in Wales for people over the age of 50 has increased by ten percentage points over the past 15 years (higher than in the UK overall and double the rise for the under-50s); almost one in three people over the age of 50 works part-time (a much higher proportion than the under 50s).[55] For disabled people, data reveal that they are more than twice as likely to be economically inactive (that is, neither in work nor looking for it) than other people (26.9 compared with 68.8 per cent), a difference that has increased slightly in recent years.[56] There is also a modest difference (4.4 percentage points) in the economic activity rates of Welsh speakers (61.9 per cent) compared with non-Welsh speakers (57.5 per cent) (in relation to language skills and income, one study estimates that Welsh/English bilingualism may increase earnings by between 8 and 10 per cent).[57]

Notwithstanding the provisions of the Equal Pay Act (1970), comparison based on median hourly earnings for all employees shows that in 2009 women earned 22 per cent less than men (a decrease from 22.5 per cent in 2008). Furthermore, women's median hourly earnings (excluding overtime) were 12.6 per cent less than men's (compared to 8.5 per cent in Scotland and 3.5 per cent in Northern Ireland).[58] In Wales, as in the rest of the UK, there is marked gender segregation in the labour market (see Table 3.4) with women over-represented in some routine and lower status occupations (such as administrative and secretarial posts, at 78 per cent) and under-represented in skilled trades and management (10 per cent and 35 per cent respectively).

Occupation Category	Women %	Men %
Skilled trades	10	90
Process, plant and machine operatives	18	82
Managers and senior officials	35	65
Elementary	49	51
Professional	49	51
Associate professional and technical	54	46
Sales and customer service	67	33
Administrative and secretarial	78	22
Personal service	82	18

Table 3.4. Gender and occupational distribution in Wales (2005)[59]

Whilst notable gains have been made in women's political representation in the National Assembly, reference to a range of posts such as local government councillors, head teachers and hospital consultants shows that the vertical gender segregation is particularly evident in the Welsh labour market (see Table 3.5).

Position	Female %		Male %	
	2005	2009	2005	2009
Welsh Assembly Government Cabinet	44	40	56	60
Assembly Members	52	47	48	53
Members of Parliament	20	20	80	80
Members of European Parliament	75	75	25	25
Local Government – Council leaders	18	18	72	72
Local Government – Councillors	22	25	78	75
NHS Wales Trust Chief Executives	38	23	62	77
Hospital consultants	20	-	80	-
GPs	31	-	69	-
All NHS Wales staff	79	79	21	21
Secondary school head teachers	19	16	81	84
Secondary school governors	41	-	59	-
All teachers	69	74	31	26
University vice-chancellors	0	0	100	100
Police Authority Chairs	0	25	100	75
Chief Constables	25	25	75	75
All police	20	24	80	76
Trades Unions heads of offices in Wales	21	-	79	-
Wales Trades Unions Congress Executive Committee	38	-	62	-
Heads of voluntary organisations	38	-	62	-
Newspaper editors	30	15	70	85
Chief executives, Welsh Assembly Government – sponsored public bodies	13	10	87	90
Chief executives of Wales's Top 100 private companies	-	0	-	100

Table 3.5. The proportion of women in key posts in Wales 2005–9[60]

Horizontal gender segregation is a further feature of the labour market. This refers to the clustering of women in certain employment sectors and types of job (see Table 3.6), for example health and social work (79 per cent) and education (72 per cent).

Employment sectors	Female		Male	
	'000s	%	'000s	%
Health and social work	149	79	39	21
Education	83	72	32	28
Hotels and restaurants	39	62	24	38
Banking, insurance and pension provision	25	59	17	41
Other community, social and personal	39	54	32	46
Public administration and defence	53	54	45	46
Wholesale, retail and motor trade	101	50	99	50
Real estate, renting and business activities	46	44	59	56
Manufacturing	45	25	133	75
Transport, storage and communication	15	19	65	81
All sectors[61]	611	48	663	52

Table 3.6. Horizontal gender segregation in the labour market (2005).[62]

Gender disparities are also evident when female employment is analysed by standard industrial sector (Table 3.7). Data covering the period 1981–2008 show that, despite a significant overall increase in the proportion of economically active women, two sectors – 'education, health, public administration and other services' (1981, 35.3 per cent; 2008, 51.4 per cent) and 'Distribution, transport, finance and business services' (1981, 32.6 per cent; 2008, 40.9 per cent) – constitute the vast majority of women's employment over the period.

As noted, there is a general dearth of official data relating to sexual orientation. However, recent research evidence[64] identified the way in which significant proportions of lesbian, gay and bisexual people face discrimination in the workplace. Thus, of those surveyed, 30 per cent reported feeling that they could not talk about their private life at work, 21 per cent reported being the butt of office jokes and 19 per cent said that they felt a lack of respect from their work colleagues or superiors.

Standard Industrial Classification	1981	1991	2001	2008	% Change
Agriculture Forestry and Fishing	3300	2500	6,920	3000	−9.1
Mining Energy and Water Supplies industries	3800	3300	3576	1000	−73.7
Manufacturing industries	54000	54800	49,269	35000	−35.2
Construction	2300	2900	6820	7000	304
Distribution etc., transport etc., finance and business services	64400	74600	223039	247000	383.5
Education, health, public administration and other services	69700	85500	260179	310000	445
Total	197,500	223,600	549,803	603,000	

Table 3.7. Changes in sectoral distribution of females in full-time employment in Wales 1981–2008[63]

3.4 Housing

When household type is analysed by sex and age, significant gender differences emerge. Many more women in Wales over the age of 60 years live alone than men; there are three times as many women over the age of 70 living alone than men, and four times as many over the age of 85.[65] With regard to gender and homelessness, recent Welsh government data reveal that there were 1,713 applications to local authorities from women (56 per cent) compared with 1,369 from men (44 per cent).[66] In terms of gender, criminal justice and homelessness, a recent study estimated that, of those on community sentences and released from prison, women have more complex housing needs compared to men and that in 2006 approximately 400 such women were homeless.[67]

In relation to differences between ethnic groups, official data on the percentage of households classed as overcrowded show clear differences between ethnic groups: white British, 5 per cent; Asian or

Asian British (including Bangladeshi), 32 per cent; Black or Black British (including African), 26 per cent; and Chinese, 23 per cent.[68] In relation to tenure, Muslim households in Wales are more than twice as likely as households overall to be living in private rented accommodation (20 per cent compared with 9 per cent). They are less likely than households in general to be owner-occupiers (59 per cent compared with 72 per cent overall) or council tenants (10 per cent compared with 14 per cent overall).[69] Differences in rates of home ownership were evident amongst ethnic groups. Whereas the home ownership rate for the population as a whole is 72 per cent; for Black or Black British (Caribbean) citizens it is 59 per cent; and for Black or Black British (other Black) individuals it is 44 per cent. For Black or Black British (African) the comparative figure is only 38 per cent.[70]

With respect to age, amongst the population as a whole 80 per cent of people over the age of 60 own their own home, compared with 70 per cent of people under the age of 60. Moreover, older people are much less likely to rent properties: only 5 per cent of people over the age of 60 rent, compared with one in seven people under 60.[71] In the face of sustained patterns of in-migration, affordable homes for local people in Welsh-speaking communities is a key contemporary issue in housing policy. Census data reveal that the number of communities where over 70 per cent of the population are able to speak Welsh declined from 92 in 1991 to 54 in 2001.[72] On other matters, a recent government-funded study of Lesbian, Gay and Bisexual (LGB) people and housing in Wales[73] identified a series of issues. These included the fact that homophobic harassment in and around the home was the most prolific cause of housing problems for those surveyed; it was the most significant factor in the need to move home. Problems of harassment were found to occur across all tenures, ranging from verbal through to physical abuse. The study also highlighted the effects of homophobia within the home:

> Particularly in the form of rejection from family members, being forced out of the family home, ostracised by family members or being physically attacked by a family member. This was shown to have particular implications for young LGB people who were dependent on their parental/guardian unit for housing as well as financial, material and emotional support. The data make clear that young LGB people are vulnerable in this regard.[74]

3.5 Health

Findings from the Welsh Health Survey reveal key gender differences. Contrasts in the incidence of health conditions between the sexes pose significant challenges for policy-makers and those charged with service delivery. Examples include arthritis (affects 17 per cent of women and 10 per cent of men) and back pain (14 and 10 per cent). Furthermore, men tend to have higher levels of lung cancer, stomach and colorectal cancer, heart disease and diabetes than women.[75] Notably, the Welsh Health Survey provides two summary measures of physical and mental health. These reveal worse health and well-being amongst women in respect of physical health, differences that apply across virtually all age groups.[76] In addition, there are much higher levels of mental illness for women (nearly twice as high as men), but there are approximately four times as many deaths from suicide for men than women.[77]

In terms of health, ethnicity and faith, Muslims – and particularly those from the Pakistani and Bangladeshi ethnic groups – have higher reported levels of long-term illness and poor health than the average for all people aged 50 to 64 years. This difference is more pronounced for women (for example, limiting long term illness affects 34.4 per cent of women in the population as a whole, compared with 48.2 per cent of Muslim women).[78]

Statistical measures from the Welsh Health Survey also confirm an intuitive fact; that older people's overall health (as measured by the physical health summary score) generally gets progressively worse as people get older. Measures focusing on mental health identified 80 years as the age at which deterioration was commonly reported.[79] In respect of the population as a whole, there are gender differences in life expectancy; 77 years for males and 81 years for females (the same as in Northern Ireland, marginally lower than in England, 77.5 and 81.7 respectively, and higher than in Scotland at 74.8 and 79.7).

In relation to socio-economic status, official data show that levels of ill-health increase from comparatively low levels for managerial and professional classes to higher levels experienced by routine and manual classes. However, it is people in the 'never worked and long-term unemployed' category, that report the worst health. For example, data on reported illness show that 21 per cent of people who have never worked reported a mental illness compared with 7 per cent of people with managerial or professional status; and 19 per cent of those who had never worked reported back pain, compared with 9 per cent amongst managers and professionals.[80] In relation to sexual orientation, recent research indicates that 21 per cent of LGB people surveyed report being dissatisfied/very dissatisfied with the service provided by NHS Wales (this compares with 13 per cent giving such a response in the Living in Wales Survey). Moreover, 8.4 per cent of LGB people felt discriminated against by their GP; 6.7 per cent felt discriminated against by their local hospital; and 4.5 per cent said that issues of prejudice meant they felt uncomfortable visiting their partner in hospital.[81]

3.6 Transport

Recent analysis reveals key gender differences in transport patterns in Wales. For example, women are over twice as likely to walk to work as men (16 per cent compared with 7 per cent), whereas men are more likely to drive to work (86 per cent compared with 77 per cent).[82] In addition, men travel approximately three times further than women in connection with their work. Just over eight out of ten men have a full driving licence compared with just over six out of ten women.[83] With regard to public transport, 56 per cent of women are frequent or occasional users of buses compared with just 39 per cent of men.[84] Moreover, research findings by the former Equal Opportunities Commission also underline the gendered nature of transport use and demand. Inter alia, they reveal that women are less likely to have choice in forms of transport that they use; men tend to do more commuting; women are more likely to work irregular shifts and to need to commute outside normal working hours; women are more likely to be carers and to take escort trips; women are more likely to travel with luggage, bags and pushchairs; and female bus users are twice as likely as male bus users to say they feel unsafe using the bus at night.[85] Gender differences are also evident in road casualty rates. For injuries of each severity type, the casualty rate for males was greater (55 per cent) than for females (45 per cent) (for example, in absolute terms, annual figures indicate the extent of gap as 526 male accidents per 100,000 population compared with 405 per 100,000 for females). Males also make up the vast majority of casualties who were pedal cyclists or users of two-wheeled motor vehicles.[86]

Official analysis reveals that 60 per cent of disabled people in Wales have the use of a car compared with 80 per cent of non-disabled people. Moreover, people with a long-standing illness or disability who are in employment are nearly twice as likely not to have the use of a car compared with non-disabled people.[87] In terms of ethnicity, there are key differences between different ethnic groups. Black households are least likely to have access to a car or van (17 per cent, with 41 per cent of such households having no access to cars or vans). Moreover, over 30 per cent of Indian, Pakistani, 'other Asian' and Chinese heritage households have access to 2 or more cars or vans, whilst just 15 per cent of Bangladeshi households had similar access.[88]

3.7 Summary: Gender and Inequality in Wales

As the foregoing discussion notes, in education there are major disparities between the sexes in attainment, subject choice and participation rates (in FE and HE). Such inequalities are crosscut by other social identities, as evidenced by the marked gender gap in educational attainment amongst Pakistani-origin pupils (boys attain just over two-thirds of the average score for girls). Official data and research evidence show that gender equality issues are not reserved to education but exist in all policy areas. Some gender disparities are pronounced (such as the comparatively low numbers of women holding senior employment posts); others are subtler (for example, the incidence of certain illnesses and diseases, or in relation to transport patterns). Yet, they all present key challenges to policy-makers. It must also be remembered that they need to be considered in an holistic way. For example, the low economic activity rates of women in some ethnic groups (such as 56 per cent for Bangladeshi women) is more than a discrete, labour market issue; it has wider equality policy implications for issues of potential child poverty or religious freedom, as well as equality in housing, pensions and household wealth in later life.

Equality indicators show that over recent decades there has been progress in relation to a number of gender equality issues. For example, whereas women were once marginalised in higher education (constituting just a quarter of university students in 1960), they now form the majority of students. There have also been major changes in the nature and extent of women's engagement with the labour market.

Today a significantly higher proportion of women are in employment compared to forty years ago (women's economic activity rate is currently 72.7 per cent[89] compared to 36.7 in 1971). However, major gender inequalities persist; many are related to the uneven allocation of caring activities within the household. Thus, for example, 44 per cent of women work part time, compared to 11 per cent of men. In employment, as with other policy areas, other social identities crosscut those of gender, presenting intersectional equalities issues. This is demonstrated by the different full-time employment rates of disabled women and men (63 per cent and 90 per cent respectively).[90] Further evidence of progress over recent years can be seen in the increase in the number of women employed in managerial positions (up from 10 per cent in the 1970s to approximately 33 per cent today); the growth in the number of women using some form of flexible working arrangement (currently 58 per cent of women);[91] and the decrease in girls leaving school without a qualification (down from 20 to 6 per cent since the 1970s). However, despite these advancements, the evidence shows the persistence of widespread and significant inequalities between the sexes. For example, despite numerous policy interventions and equality laws over past decades, the gender pay gap persists, as does occupational segregation or the clustering of women into certain types of employment such as administrative and secretarial posts (women make up 78 per cent of all employed in these areas). Overall, the current evidence shows that gender inequality continues to be an issue that crosscuts policy areas.

3.8 Prejudice versus Tolerance: Social Attitudes

A number of studies provide insight to Welsh people's views on, and experiences of, equality and discrimination issues.[92] Findings from the Living in Wales Survey[93] show that prejudiced and discriminatory attitudes still prevail (see Table 3.8).

Overall, the Survey found that 12 per cent of respondents had experienced discrimination, harassment or victimisation in the last five years. However, this varied in terms of age, affecting 17 per cent of those aged 16 to 24 years; 14 per cent of adults (aged 25–59/64); and five per cent of pensioners (60/65+). The reasons given for the discrimination experienced by respondents included 'race' (24 per cent), language (7 per cent), age (6 per cent), gender (5.5 per cent),

Statement	Agree %	Disagree* %
It would not matter to me if one of my close relatives married someone from a different ethnic background	77	12
This neighbourhood is a place where people from different backgrounds can live together harmoniously	76	10
It is better for a country if there is a variety of different cultures	58	20
On the whole, Muslims who live in Wales make a positive contribution to society	32	18
I would have no objection to a gypsy/traveller site being located near to my home	13	78
To be truly Welsh, you have to be white	11	81
It is better for a country if almost everyone shares the same customs and traditions	43	42
If a country wants to reduce tensions it should stop immigration	54	27

Table 3.8. Social attitudes survey results Wales (circa 2008)
*Table excludes 'neither agree nor disagree' responses).[94]

colour (4.9 per cent), disability (4.5 per cent) and sexual orientation (4 per cent). Of those who had experienced discrimination, harassment or victimisation, under a half (45 per cent) reported the incident (of the minority that did report the incident, they did so to the police, 62 per cent; local authority, 19 per cent; and employer or someone at work, 16 per cent). In addition, a recent study by Stonewall Cymru[95] found 22 per cent of the LGB people surveyed[96] reported experiencing homophobic harassment in the previous twelve months, with 5 per cent experiencing homophobic violence and 3 per cent homophobic property crime. A comparatively low proportion of those surveyed said that they would report homophobic violence (56 per cent) and harassment (23 per cent). Reasons given for not reporting crime to the police were that the victim did not think the incident was serious enough to warrant police involvement, or that it was felt the police would not take the incident seriously. A majority of respondents said they were offended by the portrayal of LGB people in the print media (63 per cent) and broadcast media (61 per cent). Official statistics show that homophobic incidents reported to the police in Wales totalled 429 in 2006 and 369 in 2007. However, there were just 29 successful prosecutions of offences with a homophobic element in Wales in 2006, 47 in 2007 and 58 in 2008.[97] The prevalence of domestic abuse incidents can be gauged from figures relating to the Wales Domestic Abuse Helpline; this took nearly 15,000 calls during its first two years, including 1,300 women who contacted the helpline wanting emergency refuge accommodation.[98]

Further insights into prevailing social attitudes on equalities are provided by the findings of the Welsh Perception Survey.[99] The first set of findings relate to the workplace. Just 42 per cent of respondents agreed that 'being treated unfairly at work because you are a woman is a thing of the past' whilst almost half (49 per cent) disagreed.[100] There were significant differences in the responses to this statement from different age groups; 49 per cent aged 16–34 agreed with it compared with 30 per cent of those aged 55–64.[101] In respect of age equality in the workplace, 94 per cent agreed that people should be able to continue working after the official age of retirement if they wish. On matters of Welsh language and workplace recruitment, views were divided, with 42 per cent agreeing and 43 per cent disagreeing that 'employers should favour those who speak both Welsh and English when filling jobs'. Just over a half of respondents viewed as fair positive action in the form of the provision of additional training for women (55 per cent) and Black or Asian people (54 per cent) in order to address their under-representation in senior positions such as managers and chief executives. However, significant proportions of respondents viewed such interventions as unfair (42 per cent and 43 per cent respectively).

On in-migration issues, considerable proportions of respondents said that they would be worried if there was more in-migration to Wales from people from Eastern Europe (32 per cent), Muslims (30 per cent), Black and Asian people (25 per cent) and English people (16 per cent); overall, 53 per cent said that they would be concerned by increased in-migration from these groups as a whole. In relation to the provision of goods and services, the majority of respondents (over 70 per cent) said that, in the hypothetical case of a bed and breakfast manager, she or he should not be allowed to discriminate against specific groups (such as homosexual or disabled people), although between 11 and 17 per cent of respondents felt such discrimination was acceptable.

When asked, 'who is suited to the role of primary school teacher?', a majority of respondents had positive attitudes towards gay men and lesbian women, and Black and Asian people, with 78 and 90 per cent respectively agreeing that they would be 'very' or 'fairly well suited' to the job. In contrast, someone who is transgender was deemed 'suitable' by just 48 per cent (and 'unsuitable' by 33 per cent). Other groups failing to get majority support were Gypsies and Travellers (deemed 'suitable' by 37 per cent and 'unsuitable' by 47 per cent) and people who experience depression from time to time (deemed 'suitable' by 40 per cent and 'unsuitable' by 46 per cent). With regard to social networks and relationships, the Survey concluded that 'Welsh society seemed well integrated',[102] as approximately three-quarters of those surveyed said that they knew someone who was from a different religion (80 per cent); from a different racial or ethnic background (77 per cent); and younger or older than them by 20 years or more (95 per cent). In addition, a significant proportion of respondents said that they were friends with someone who was younger or older than them by 20 years or more (75 per cent); disabled (74 per cent); and gay, lesbian or bisexual (74 per cent).

Further insight into prevailing social attitudes is provided by the responses to the Survey question, 'how would you feel if a close relative married or formed a long-term relationship with someone from . . . [list of social groups]?' The responses were as follows: someone who is transgender ('happy' 33 per cent; 'unhappy' 45 per cent); a Gypsy Traveller ('happy' 42 per cent; 'unhappy' 38 per cent); someone with a mental health condition ('happy' 38 per cent; 'unhappy' 37 per cent); an asylum seeker ('happy' 40 per cent; 'unhappy' 37 per cent); someone of the same sex ('happy' 54 per cent; 'unhappy' 26 per cent); someone who had a learning disability ('happy' 65 per cent; 'unhappy' 11 per cent); someone with a different religious belief ('happy' 71 per cent; 'unhappy' 21 per cent); and someone from a different ethnic background ('happy' 72 per cent; 'unhappy' 19 per cent).[103] On the issue of domestic violence, 97 per cent of respondents said that it is 'never ok to bully or hit a partner'. There was a similar response to this question across all demographic subgroups. Moreover, two thirds (67 per cent) of respondents disagreed with the proposition that 'domestic violence is best handled as a private matter instead of by the police'. However, a significant minority (19 per cent) felt that it *was* best handled as a private matter – those in agreement were more likely to be men, older adults and those from non-white ethnic groups.

3.9 Comparative Perspectives

3.9.1 Scotland

The diversity of Scotland's population is described by the following characteristics. The overall number of people reporting a disability and/or a long-term illness is believed to be 18 per cent of the population, or 914,400 people.[104] At the last Census, the size of the minority ethnic population was 101,677 (2.1 per cent), an increase from just over 60,000 in 1991 (1.2 per cent). Pakistani-origin people are the largest minority ethnic group (0.63 per cent), followed by Chinese-origin (0.32 per cent), Indian-origin (0.3 per cent) and those from 'mixed' backgrounds (0.25 per cent). In relation to faith, marginally over two-thirds of the Scottish population reported currently having a religion in the Census. Christians constitute the largest religious affiliation (65.1 per cent). The latter group is comprised of 42.4 per cent Church of Scotland, 15.9 per cent Roman Catholic and 6.8 per cent 'other Christian'. The second largest religious grouping was Muslims (0.84 per cent, or 42,600 people). As in Wales, the population is an ageing one, with the male population aged 65 years and over forecast to rise steadily from 341,000 (2004) to 581,000 (2031) (a potential increase of 71 percentage points), and the female over 65 years population estimated to grow from 486,000 to 727,000 over the same period (a potential increase of 50 percentage points). Estimates suggest that lesbian, gay, bisexual and transgender (LGBT) people make up 5 per cent of the Scottish population (Macpherson and Bond, 2009: v). With regard to the socio-linguistic profile of the country, in addition to other 'minority' languages, according to the 2001 Census 92,400 people aged three and over (1.9 per cent of the population) had some Gaelic language ability. The total number of people who could speak, read or write Gaelic fell by 3,800 (6 percentage points) between 1991 and 2001.[105] A review of existing data reveals the endurance of key inequalities; these are summarised in Figure 3.1.

- **Gender**: *Survey responses* – agreeing to following statements: 'Equal opportunities for women have gone too far' (6%); 'A man's job is to earn money, a women's job is to look after the home' (11%).[106] *Employment rate:* full-time – men 71%, females 43%; part-time – females 28%, males 7%.[107] *Gender pay gap*: full-time 13.5%, part-time 32.1%.[108] *Exclusions from schools*: male pupils account for 79%.[109] *Attainment gap:* achieving five+ grades 1–2 at Standard Grade or equivalent – girls 53%, 42% of boys.[110] *Gender and subject choice in HE*, % women students by subject: education 79%; biological sciences 68%; computer science 16%; engineering and technology 12%. Women's apprenticeships: <1% construction and plumbing; <2% in engineering. Only 1% of apprentices in early years care and education are men.[111] *Employment by sector*: women constitute 77% of all workers in health and social work, 75% education and 7% construction. *Glass ceiling:* women constitute 10% of senior police officers; 18% of secondary head teachers; 19% of local authority council leaders.[112] *Domestic abuse*: 2005–6, 45,796 incidents reported to the police (86.1% victims female – where gender recorded).[113]

- **Ethnicity**: *Survey responses* – agreeing to following statements: 'equal opportunities for black people and Asians gone too far' (18%); 'would mind inter-racial marriage' (17%); 'ethnic minorities take jobs' (20%); 'ethnic minorities don't contribute skills' (18%).[114] *Employment rates*: BME 58%; white ethnic groups 75%. *Economic inactivity rates:* BME 37%; white 20%.[115] *Educational attainment:* 14–16 years: percentage of pupils gaining 5+ standard grades at credit level (or equivalent) in 2004/5 – BME females 46%; white females 39%. S4 pupils gaining 5+ standard grades at credit level – Chinese pupils 52%; Black African pupils 28%.[116] *'Race crimes'*: 2007–8, Procurators Fiscal received reports of 4,394 charges.[117]

- **Sexual Orientation**: *Survey responses* – agreeing to following statements: 'equal opportunities for gay men and lesbians gone too far' (19%); 'would prefer an MSP who is not gay' (18%); 'male homosexual relationships are always wrong' (29%); 'gay men and lesbians unsuitable primary school teachers' (27%);

'gay couples should not be allowed to marry' (30%); 'gay male couple are not as good parents as a man and woman' (39%); 'councils should not fund support groups for gay men and lesbians' (60%).[118] Almost half of those surveyed found it acceptable for guesthouses to refuse accommodation to same-sex couples.[119] *Civil partnerships*: There were 688 registered in 2007 (339 male and 349 female couples).[120]

- **Disability**: *Survey responses* – agreeing to following statements: 'equal opportunities for disabled people have gone too far' (3%); 'wheelchair users not suitable primary school teachers' (31%); 'do not agree shops and banks should be forced to make themselves accessible' (21%).[121] *Employment rate*: non-disabled adults 82%; disabled adults 48%. *Economic inactivity rates*: disabled adults 48%; non-disabled adults 13%.[122] *Average median weekly pay*: estimated 5% higher for non-disabled adults than for disabled adults (full-time employees).[123] *Holding full driving licence:* disabled people 44%; non-disabled people 72%.[124] *Higher education:* 2004–5 disabled students 6% of all students;[125] proportion of HE graduates who are disabled is 5%.[126]

- **Faith**: *Economic activity:* of all faith categories, Muslims are least likely to be economically active (52%); have the highest unemployment rate (13%); are most likely to have never worked (30%).[127] *Proportion in full-time HE by faith*: Church of Scotland 2.5%; Roman Catholics 4.6%; Hindu 18.2%; Muslim 16%; Buddhist 15.6%.[128] *Sectarianism*: (2007–8), reports to Procurators Fiscal, 608 charges of an offence aggravated by religious prejudice (court proceedings initiated in 91% of charges).[129]

- **Age**: *Ageing population:* households headed by people aged 60+ years projected to increase by 33% (2004–24), from 730,000 to 990,000; number of households headed by 85+ year-olds projected to increase from 56,000 to 120,000.[130] *Higher education:* more than fourfold increase (1994–5) in HE students aged 50+ years, and doubling of those 40–9 years.[131]

Figure 3.1. Contemporary (in)equalities in Scotland

3.9.2 Northern Ireland

Results from the last Census showed that 44 per cent of the population of Northern Ireland described themselves as being brought up in a 'community background' that was Catholic, whereas 53 per cent of the population stated that they were brought up in a Protestant background. The Census also reported that the ethnic minority population of Northern Ireland stood at 14,279, less than 1 per cent of the overall population. With regard to in-migration from A8 countries, National Insurance number registrations from accession nationals increased from 1,657 to 10,177 between 2004/5 and 2005/6, with Poland being the largest accession country represented in these figures (over the same period, registrations in respect of non-accession nationals increased by 1,268 or 30 percentage points). With regard to disability, the Northern Ireland Survey of Activity Limitation and Disability reports that 18 per cent of the population resident in private households are limited in their daily activities for reasons associated with a disability or long-term condition.[132] Northern Ireland also has a changing age profile. In the decade 1996 to 2006, the population of pensionable age increased from 253,400 to 284,100, a rise of 12.1 percentage points. In the ten-year period between 1996 and 2006 the number of children in the population fell from 415,100 to 380,100, a fall of 8.4 percentage points.[133] Between the censuses of 1991 and 2001, the proportion of Irish speakers increased by 18 percentage points. The 2001 Census also showed that there were 167,490 people, or 10.4 per cent of the population, with some knowledge of Irish. Key equalities issues in Northern Ireland are summarised in Figure 3.2.

3.10 Conclusions

Demographic and social change means that Wales's population is characterised by unprecedented diversity when measured by a range of indices such as faith, non-belief, ethnicity, age, language and nationality. The drivers of this change include increasing longevity, migration, globalisation and socio-economic processes. Official data and research evidence show that within this heterogeneous society there exist key differences between people along lines of gender, ethnicity, disability, age, sexual orientation, caring responsibilities and language. Such differences are evident across all policy areas and relate to a range of matters including contrasting behaviour patterns,

- **Gender:** *Occupational profiles* – higher 'managerial' groups (1–3), males 32.1%; females 27%. Administrative/clerical occupations: males 6%; females 24%. *Gender pay gap:* (full-time) males earned 11% more than females; part-time pay gap is 30%. *Part-time employment:* 39% of female employees; 6% of male employees. *Caring:* women more likely to be informal carers than men; 34% of female carers report that they spend at least 30 hours per week caring (19% of those providing 50+ hours per week feel they are in poor health). *Abortion:* The Abortion Act (1967) that allows for NHS abortion with the consent of two doctors does not apply to Northern Ireland. *Pensions:* average weekly state retirement pension (March 2007) was £82.67 for women; £105.60 for men. *Suicide:* 76% were males. *Domestic abuse:* (2007–8) 23,076 domestic incidents[134] reported to police and 9,283 prosecutions for domestic crimes.[135] *Education:* school leavers, 45.3% of girls and 31.8% of boys entered HE.[136]

- **Ethnicity:** *Education:* pupils leaving school with no GCSEs: 'white' pupils 3.9%; BME pupils 8.6%. *Racist incidents:* (2007/8) police recorded 976 (conviction rate 11.4%).[137] *Bullying:* 8% of school pupils reported bullying about their race and/or colour.[138] *Education:* proportion of pupils achieving 5+ A*–G grade GCSEs (or equivalent) – white pupils 41.6%; BME pupils 14.5%.[139] Extremely poor educational performance of Traveller children ('the vast majority of Irish Travellers would be counted as having no formal qualifications').[140] *Economic Activity – BME women:* Chinese women 70%; Pakistani 25%; Gypsy Traveller 16%.

- **Sexual Orientation:** in 2007/8, police recorded 160 homophobic and 7 transphobic incidents.[141]

- **Disability:** *Poverty:* Over half (56%) of households with 1+ disabled people live in poverty (compared with 29% who have no one with a disability).[142] *Crime:* (2007/8) police recorded 49 incidents and crimes with a hate motivation against disabled people. During 2007/8 the number of disability hate crimes increased by 16 (+61.5%).[143] *Bullying:* 40.3% pupils in a recent study reported that they had been bullied about their disability 'at least once or twice'.[144]

- **Faith**: *(Un)employment:* (2001–6) the number of Protestant female employees rose from 132,106 to 136,989, an increase of 3.7%; Catholic female count increased from 98,719 to 115,829, a rise of 17.3%.[145] *Sectarianism:* (2007–8) police recorded 1,584 sectarian incidents.[146] The unemployment rate was higher for Catholic men (9%) compared with Protestant men (5%).[147] *Bullying:* 7.9% of school pupils in a study experienced some form of bullying in relation to their religion.[148] *Policing:* As of April 2007, 21% police officers in the Police Service of Northern Ireland were Catholic.[149] *Deprivation:* 20 most deprived wards with the worst health and social services outcomes, for all indicators the proportions of the population of those who are Catholic or who are Nationalist are higher than Protestant or Unionist.[150]

- **Age**: *Fear of crime:* highest perception of risk of victimisation of mugging/robbery amongst 60+ years age group (14%).[151] Highest proportion of households with no central heating: 65–9 years (6%), 70+ (5%) – overall population average (3%).[152]

Figure 3.2. Contemporary (in)equalities in Northern Ireland

needs and differential allocation of resources, wealth accumulation and access to services. Focus on the evidence base of contemporary inequalities reveals their widespread nature as well as complexity, not least the variation in the extent of inequalities within and between equality 'strands' and policy areas. This chapter highlights how social attitudes survey data form part of the evidence base on inequalities. They too offer a mixed picture. Whilst the vast majority of the population generally rejects sexist and racist attitudes, significant minorities still hold discriminatory attitudes, notably towards Gypsy Travellers, transsexual people, asylum seekers and people with mental illness. A further key fact is the endurance of inequalities. Whilst equality laws have existed for several decades in relation to gender and race, current data show such inequalities to be deeply entrenched. It is also the case that there are major shortcomings in the availability of appropriate data with which to measure and understand patterns and processes of inequality. Notwithstanding two official reviews (Walby et al., 2008; ONS, 2007a), three issues continue to be of concern: the lack of official data gathering relating to gay, lesbian, bisexual and transsexual people; in the wake of devolution, the failure of some official bodies to provide Wales-only statistics; and the absence of an annual series of comprehensive statistical equalities digests for Wales.

From a comparative perspective, there are commonalities between all three of the UK's devolved polities, as well as with patterns and processes at a British/UK level. The endurance, complexity and unevenness of inequalities across the breadth policy areas are evident in all territories. In each of the devolved nations there are country-specific equalities issues that need to be factored into the overall situation (the Welsh language in Wales; the Irish language and sectarianism in Northern Ireland; and the Gaelic language and sectarianism in Scotland). Overall, the evidence presented here shows that over recent decades there has been limited progress in tackling inequalities. Indeed, the increasing heterogeneity of contemporary society has extended the dimensions of inequality and discrimination and brought new challenges. Thus, as the foregoing review shows, inequalities are a major and enduring feature of society at the beginning of the twenty-first century.

4

Promoting Equality:
A Governance Perspective

4.0 Introduction

This chapter looks at the way that Wales is governed in the wake of devolution. Specifically, it explores the new institutional arrangements set out in the National Assembly's founding statutes that have the potential to promote equality by facilitating inclusive policy-making. Accordingly, initial attention is placed on the concept of new governance and related political theory. Developments are then contextualised by reference to the earlier period of administrative devolution in Wales and New Labour's Modernising Government programme (Cabinet Office, 1999), which included the creation of devolved legislatures in the UK. The characteristics of 'inclusive governance' mechanisms in the National Assembly's founding acts are then examined. A comparative perspective is introduced by reference to developments in Scotland and Northern Ireland. The chapter concludes by outlining the ongoing challenges associated with the new governance arrangements if they are to advance equality and deliver inclusive politics.

4.1 New Governance

From an equalities perspective new governance theory is suited to examining the impact of constitutional reform in Wales for, as Newman (2001: 11) observes, it is 'an analytical concept, giving rise to questions about what forms of power and authority . . . typify a particular approach to governing'. Rhodes (1997: 46) explains that it 'signifies a change in the meaning of government, referring to a new process of governing . . . or, a new method by which society is governed'. The most significant recent change in the UK is the shift away from the 'Westminster Model' of government that occurred as a result of constitutional reform in 1998–9. There are competing interpretations of the Westminster Model, yet its core characteristics are often described as its hierarchical and elitist nature; ultimate power or sovereignty vested in the UK parliament (and centralised in the Prime Minister and the cabinet); a strong central executive and clear lines of accountability; and the existence of centralised state control (Dearlove and Saunders, 1991; Hill, 2004; Bevir, 2008). Thus, the model's greatest utility is as an 'organising perspective' to describe the way in which the British government has traditionally been seen to operate. Its core features largely capture the situation following the Acts of Union when few aspects of state administration were concerned solely with Wales. However, over recent years, this long-established model of government has been subject to what Rhodes (1997) describes as a series of 'revolutions': the development of the welfare state and its institutions; Thatcherism; the rise of 'New Public Management' (Hood, 1991, 1995; Hughes, 2004); and membership of the EU (Carr and Massey, 1999; Compston, 2004; Bache and Flinders, 2004). As noted, constitutional reform and the (re-)establishment of legislatures in Wales, Scotland and Northern Ireland is the latest in a series of developments that has undermined the Westminster Model. As Meehan (2003: 4) emphasises, these changes reflect and reinforce, 'a lack of capacity on the part of governments, acting alone, to effect desired changes. Instead, public power manifests itself through increasingly blurred boundaries between different tiers of government, the public and private, and between the state and civil society'. According to Newman (2001: 79), new governance is part of a broader economic and social transformation that has seen the rise of networks and partnerships and the emergence of a plurality of interdependent actors and institutions. A key aspect of this shift is the increasing legitimacy of the 'horizontal dimension' of policy-making. As Colebatch (2002: 23) explains, this 'sees policy in terms of the structuring of action. It is concerned with relationships amongst policy participants in different organisations outside the line of hierarchical authority . . . It recognises policy work takes place across organisational boundaries as well as within them.' New governance is therefore concerned with:

> the changing nature of the policy process in recent decades. In particular, it sensitizes us to the ever-increasing variety of terrains and actors involved in the making of public policy. Thus, it demands that we consider all the actors and locations beyond the 'core executive' involved in the policy-making process'. (Richards and Smith, 2002: 2)

The shift to new governance has major implications for the promotion of equalities. Kooiman and Van Vliet (1993: 64) underline this point in the following terms:

> The purpose of governance in our societies can be described as coping with the problems but also the opportunities presented by complex, diverse and fragmented societies . . . governing in modern society is predominantly a process of coordination and influencing social and political interactions . . . [and] balancing social interests.

As Verba et al. (1987: 21) note, 'in the more developed societies the problem of participation . . . is less one of mobilizing an apolitical mass to life. Rather it is one of the unequal access to and unequal use of political opportunities.' For Squires (2005: 380), this is central to advancing equalities. She observes that 'enabling excluded groups to unsettle institutionally accepted conceptions of equality will require a parity of participation, which makes democratic inclusion central to both the meaning and realization of equality'.

A challenge for social scientists is how to evaluate the impact of new governance. In this regard Skocpol (1997: 136) argues for:

> Bringing the state back into a central place in analyses of policy-making . . . a complete analysis, in short, requires examination of the organisation and interests of the state, specification of the organisation and interests

of socio-economic groups, and into the complementary as well as conflicting relationships of state and societal actors.

Thus, state restructuring associated with new governance has seen a renewed interest in neo (or new) institutionalist theory. This provides a further theoretical framework to examine recent developments for it emphasises the need to locate policy-making in an organisational context (Selznick, 1996). As Wildavsky (1987: vii) observes, following the shift to new governance, 'the relationship between different institutional arrangements and the demand and supply of policy analysis will matter more and so should be subject to scrutiny'. Reflecting on constitutional reform in the UK, Laffin (2000: 534) emphasises that 'institutional or constitutional design . . . [can be seen] as a matter of overcoming, or at least recognising, a series of collective action problems: how to create institutional arrangements that will provide a check on individuals' pursuit of self-interest or factional interest, even to promote cooperative behaviour'. March and Olsen (1984: 738) share this viewpoint and emphasise that:

> Political democracy depends not only on economic and social conditions but also on the design of political institutions . . . [They] are arenas for contending social forces, but they are also collections of standard operating procedures and structures that define and defend interests. They are political actors in their own right.

Hall (1986: 231) also underlines the centrality of the design of political institutions to the promotion of equality: 'the organisation of policy-making affects the degree of power that any one set of actors has over policy outcomes . . . organisational factors affect both the degree of pressure an actor can bring to bear on policy and the likely direction of that pressure'. Two noteworthy branches of institutionalist theory relate to gender equality: state feminism and feminist institutionalism. The former gives precedence to structures, the latter to power relations. Thus, state feminism refers to 'government structures that are formally charged with furthering women's status and rights' (Stetson and Mazur 1995: 2; see also McBride, 1995; Rankin and Vickers 2001; Lovenduski 2005). Feminist institutionalism, on the other hand, explores 'the ways in which political institutions reflect, structure and reinforce gendered patterns of power' (Kenny, 2007: 23). Both underline the interconnectedness of the various theoretical strands around new governance and equalities for, as Lowndes and Wilson (2001) emphasise, 'institutional filters' (or the openness of the design of political institutions) are a key explanatory variable as to why participation rates in government institutions vary between different social groups defined by, for example, gender ethnicity, faith, language, disability and so on. Allied to such institutional perspectives is the concept of constitutionalism (Tully, 1995; Vile, 1969), or the idea that governments must act in accordance with a known constitution. As Laffin (2000: 534) alludes, devolution was an opportunity to re-write constitutional law so as to shape the future actions and priorities of government: 'constitutional design is a matter of building in incentives and sanctions likely to influence legislative behaviour to maximise the possible gains from cooperation'.

It should be noted that the shift to new governance is not a 'zero-sum game' in that elements endure of traditional forms of governing as described by the pre-existing Westminster Model. It is a point made by Kooiman and Van Vliet (1993: 252) who state that:

> instead of relying on the state or market, socio-political governance is directed at patterns of interaction in which political and traditional hierarchical governing and social self-organisation are complementary, in which responsibility and accountability for interventions are spread over public and private actors.

This combination of new and traditional forms of governance is captured in the 'asymmetric power model' of governance (Marsh, 2008). Its characteristics resonate with the current situation in Wales: namely, the predominance of governance rather than government; hierarchy of political organisation within the state; strong central government that is increasingly subject to challenge; power-dependence, involving asymmetric exchange relations between political institutions, sectors and interests; a dominant political tradition, but with increasing contestations; and enduring structured inequality in society.

Before examining selected features of new governance in contemporary Wales, attention is now placed on their immediate origins and the political context that led to constitutional reform.

4.2 New Labour's Modernising Government Programme

In the 1980s and early 1990s there was growing discontent with the prevailing mode of governance of the UK. In part, the concern was that an 'erosion of democratic accountability was linked to a possible decline in the legitimacy of decisions about public policy' (Newman, 2001: 59). A prevailing view was that government had become an increasingly exclusive process, one that did little to serve the plurality of social interests (Hirst and Barnett, 1993; Wright, 1996). This had territorial dimensions and was particularly evident in Wales and Scotland where significant sections of the population resented British government policies that were often seen as being imposed on, and contrary to the needs of, local people. Speaking in the mid-1990s, the leader of one opposition party complained that 'for the past 17 years Wales has been governed on the basis of the priorities of south-east England, not the priorities of the people of Wales'. He added, 'in short we do not have a meaningful democracy at the all-Wales level'.[1] According to one analyst, this was the result of the 'centralizing and anti-democratic tendencies of Conservative Party governments' (Bradbury, 1998: 127), whose support in Wales at general elections declined from 32.2 per cent of the electorate in 1979 to 19.6 per cent in 1997. During this period central government adopted statist solutions to circumvent and exclude local democratic opinion from the process of government in order to achieve its will. Thus, successive administrations in the Welsh Office were accused of adopting a 'cavalier approach' and of appointing 'many Conservatives rejected at the ballot box' to unelected quangos (Bradbury, 1998: 126) in order to ensure delivery of Conservative policies (cf. Griffiths, 1996; Morgan and Roberts, 1993; Ridley and Wilson, 1995; Gay 1996). Rawlings (1998: 466) describes the overall situation:

> By 1996 the Welsh Office was responsible for . . . the great proportion of identifiable general government expenditure in Wales. Yet there was limited territorial autonomy. The standard view is of a [government] department tightly constrained by the British constitutional framework, engaged for the most part in the humdrum business of implementing policies decided elsewhere.

According to Morgan and Mungham (2000: 65), the last years of the Welsh Office were characterised by a policy process that was 'dependent on the whims of the Secretary of State who was neither elected nor accountable to the people of Wales'. In the view of another observer, the Welsh Office ministers of the time 'lacked a . . . strategy for coherent national policy-making' (McAllister, 1999: 635). Within this administrative framework civil servants exercised considerable power in drafting and implementing policy. Yet, as Osmond states, (1999a: 3) they were 'not responsible to elected Members of Parliament or other representative organisations' in the country. Throughout the existence of the Welsh Office little was done to increase the participation of women in political decision-making (NAW, 2000). By 1997, just 28 per cent of its public appointments were filled by women and a mere 0.6 per cent by people from an ethnic minority background (Welsh Office, 1999) and none of the 452 appointees of the Secretary of State for Wales were 'non-white' (Hanson, 1995: 4). McKenzie (2001: 19) lamented that 'the development of policy [under the Welsh Office] . . . is not an area where there has been a substantial and coherent involvement from any section of the [Black and minority ethnic] community'.

In response to this exclusivist approach, a core strand of the political discourse of New Labour was concerned with the wider promotion of equality and the creation of 'an inclusive society' (Blair, 1998: 12). Beveridge et al. (2002: 389) outline the key nexus between 'inclusiveness' and equality: 'mainstreaming must enhance the inclusion and participation of women in the decision-making processes of society and, in particular, reduce or eliminate gendered barriers to inclusion and participation'. Inclusiveness was presented as a 'keystone' in Labour's Modernising Government White Paper (Cabinet Office, 1999) where it was defined as:

> Ensuring that policy-makers take as full account as possible of the impact the policy will have on different groups – families, businesses, ethnic minorities, older people, the disabled, women – who are affected by the policy. (Cabinet Office, 1999: 14)

Elsewhere in the document, it is given a more participatory interpretation and is defined as 'involving others in policy-making . . . [which] means developing new relationships between Whitehall, the devolved administrations, local government and the voluntary and private sectors; consulting outside experts, those who implement policy and those affected by it early in the policy-making process' (Cabinet Office, 1999: 24).

Government of Wales Act (2006)
Partnership Council (s72, Government of Wales Act, 2006): a forum comprised of Welsh ministers and representatives from county, county borough and community councils; national park authorities; and police, fire and rescue authorities. Purpose: to advise Welsh Ministers about matters affecting the exercise of any of their functions, or to advise and raise any matters that affect or are of concern to member organisations.

Local Government Scheme (s73): 'the Welsh Ministers must make a scheme setting out how they propose, in the exercise of their functions, to sustain and promote local government in Wales'.

Voluntary Sector Scheme (s74): 'the Welsh Ministers must make a scheme setting out how they propose, in the exercise of their functions, to promote the interests of relevant voluntary organisations . . . In determining the provision to be included in the voluntary sector scheme, the Welsh Ministers must consider how they intend to exercise such of their functions as relate to matters affecting, or of concern to, relevant voluntary organisations . . . The voluntary sector scheme must specify – how the Welsh Ministers propose to provide assistance to relevant voluntary organisations . . . [and] propose to consult relevant voluntary organisations about the exercise of such of their functions as relate to matters affecting, or of concern to, such organisations'.

The Business Scheme (s75): requires that 'Welsh Ministers make a scheme setting out how they propose, in the exercise of their functions, to take account of the interests of business'.

Regulatory Impact Assessments (s76): 'the Welsh Ministers must make a code of practice setting out their policy on – (a) the carrying out of regulatory impact assessments in connection with relevant Welsh legislation . . . a regulatory impact assessment is an assessment as to the likely costs and benefits of complying with relevant Welsh subordinate legislation'.

Equality of Opportunity (s77): 'the Welsh Ministers must make appropriate arrangements with a view to securing that their functions are exercised with due regard to the principle that there should be equality of opportunity for all people'.

The Welsh Language (s78): 'the Welsh Ministers must adopt a strategy setting out how they propose to promote and facilitate the use of the Welsh language'.

Human Rights (s81): 'the Welsh Ministers have no power – to make, confirm or approve any subordinate legislation, or do any other act, so far as the subordinate legislation or Act is incompatible with any of the Convention rights'.

Equality of Treatment (s35): '(1) The Assembly must, in the conduct of Assembly proceedings, give effect, so far as is both appropriate in the circumstances and reasonably practicable, to the principle that the English and Welsh languages should be treated on a basis of equality. (2) The Assembly must make appropriate arrangements with a view to securing that Assembly proceedings are conducted with due regard to the principle that there should be equality of opportunity for all people.'

Standing Orders of the National Assembly for Wales
Standing Order 6.1. Family-friendly working hours: 'Organisation of Business. Motions under [the timing of Assembly business] must have regard to the family . . . responsibilities of Members and their likely travel arrangements; and should normally seek to avoid timetabling business before 9.00 a.m. or after 5.30 p.m. on any working day.'

Standing Order 7.61. Provisions relating to plenary business: 'time must be made available in each Assembly year for debates on the following items of Assembly business . . . (iv) the annual report of the Equality and Human Rights Commission'.

Standing Order 17. There is to be a Committee on Equality of Opportunity to consider and report on the relevant duties contained in the Act placed on the Assembly, the First Minister, Welsh Ministers or the Commission

Standing Order 20. Makes provision for regional committees to be (re-)created should at least two-thirds of AMs back such a proposition in a vote of the Assembly.

Standing Order 28. 'The Assembly must consider, in accordance with the provisions of Standing Orders . . . any admissible [public] petition.'

Electoral System: 40 AMs elected under the first-past-the-post system. 20 elected from five electoral regions. The latter are chosen from party lists, with numbers decided according to the D'Hondt system. This relates to the support received by parties that get a large spread of votes in the country but not sufficiently concentrated to win constituencies outright. Thus, this electoral mechanism is widely held to be more representative of votes cast than first-past-the-post arrangements.

Figure 4.1. Inclusive governance: features of constitutional law in Wales

In turn, the prevailing discourse of 'inclusiveness' shaped the development of each of the UK's devolved legislatures. For example, in the mid-1990s the term was established as one of the three core principles of the Northern Ireland Women's Coalition in its attempts to span sectarian divisions (NIWC, 1998). Subsequently, it shaped the Standing Orders of the Northern Ireland Assembly (NIA, 1999). In Scotland, the Scottish Civic Assembly (*c.*1995) and other campaigning bodies advanced the need for an inclusive Edinburgh-based legislature (Lindsay, 1998) and, in turn, the principle influenced the structures of the Scottish Parliament.

In Wales, pro-devolution campaigners called for the creation of an 'inclusive and participatory democracy' (Welsh Office, 1997; Hain, 1998: 14) to address the exclusive administrative practices of the Welsh Office, to tackle enduring social divisions and to overcome the long-standing political marginalisation of women, disabled people, ethnic minorities and others (Chaney and Fevre, 2001). Prior to becoming Prime Minister, Tony Blair stated that:

a Welsh Assembly and a Scottish Parliament are good for Britain and good for Wales and Scotland. It will mean making people's vote count. It will bring government closer to the people, make our politics more inclusive and put power in the hands of the people where it belongs. (Blair, 1996: 9)

The devolution White Paper published in 1997 developed the theme by saying:

The Government is committed to establishing a new, more inclusive and participative democracy in Britain. Its proposals for a Welsh Assembly reflect these aims. An Assembly – which will work in partnership with local authorities and other public bodies in Wales, with the voluntary sector, with central government in Whitehall and with European institutions – will be at the heart of that new democracy. (Welsh Office, 1997: 3)

We now turn to explore the extent to which the political discourse around inclusion was translated into constitutional law and the design of the institutions of devolved governance.

4.3 'The Inclusive Exercise of Functions'

Examination of the devolution statutes of 1998 and 2006, as well as the procedural law (Standing Orders) of the National Assembly, reveals how the earlier debate around inclusivity has been applied to the institutional design of devolved governance. Under the heading 'The inclusive exercise of functions', the Government of Wales Act (2006) details a range of channels and procedures designed to foster civic engagement and promote equality. The majority of these updated earlier provisions in the 1998 devolution statute and are deserving of attention for they delineate key features of new governance in the wake of constitutional reform.

The devolution statutes require the creation of a range of statutory partnerships between government and local authorities, public sector bodies, the voluntary sector and business organisations. For example, Section 72 of the Government of Wales Act (2006) sets out the functioning of the Partnership Council. This forum is comprised of Welsh ministers and representatives from county, county borough and community councils; national park authorities; and police, and fire and rescue authorities. Under the terms of the Act, the Partnership Council has a wide brief and may give advice to Welsh Ministers about matters affecting the exercise of any of their functions or raise any matters affecting member organisations. As part of the arrangements (GOWA, 2006, s73), Welsh Ministers must publish and present to the National Assembly a scheme setting out how they propose, in the exercise of their functions, to sustain and promote local government (and the activities of other member organisations of the Partnership Council). Its potential impact on the promotion of equalities is evident, for the current Scheme states that 'the Partnership Council will provide a forum for collaboration by Welsh Ministers and local government in promoting major crosscutting themes such as equality of opportunity' (WAG, 2008(13), para. 3.1). Allied to the Partnership Council is the partnership agreement for public services. Entitled 'Partnership and Managing Change' (WAG, 2007a: 2), it too sets out a 'vision for public services that are . . . designed with citizens at the centre and promote social justice and equality'.

In addition to formalising links between government and public bodies, the devolution statute aims to embed new governance by establishing partnerships with the private and voluntary sectors. Thus, Section 75 of the 2006 Act requires that 'Welsh Ministers make a scheme ("the business scheme") setting out how they propose, in the exercise of their functions, to take account of the interests of business'. Importantly, Section 74 of the Act is aimed at engaging civil society and requires that ministers publish and present to the Assembly a Voluntary Sector Scheme setting out how they propose to promote the interests of voluntary organisations. The Scheme must also specify how ministers propose to consult relevant voluntary organisations about 'the exercise of such of their functions as relate to matters affecting, or [are] of concern to, such [voluntary] organisations' (see WAG, 2008(11), 2008(12)). Crucially, Section 2.7 of the Scheme states: 'the goal is the creation of a civil society which: has a duty to promote equality of opportunity to all its members regardless of race, colour, sex, sexual orientation, age, marital status, disability, language preference, religion or family/domestic responsibilities' (NAfW, 2000; 2008(12)).

In addition to the partnership clauses a series of equality duties are also set out in the devolution statute; these are discussed in chapter 6. Both the partnership arrangements and equalities duties have underpinned the development of institutional equalities mechanisms. A prominent example is the Assembly's cross-party Standing Committee on Equality of Opportunity. Standing Order 17 states that 'there is to be a Committee on Equality of Opportunity to consider and report on the relevant duties contained in the Act placed on the Assembly, the First Minister, Welsh Ministers or the Commission' (NAfW, 2007). Accordingly, a key function of the committee is to scrutinise ministers' compliance with the statutory equalities duties in the constitutional law associated with devolved governance. It also has a policy development role and publishes reports on equalities issues (e.g. Accessibility of Information Report, NAfW, 2008b) and conducts inquiries (e.g. the Accessibility of Polling Stations in Wales Inquiry, NAfW, 2007c).

A further example of institutional arrangements to promote equality is the dedicated Equality, Diversity and Inclusion Division in the Assembly Government civil service (an administrative department with no parallel in the former Welsh Office). Its mission statement refers to:

> Creating a world class Wales, where the richness of our culture is celebrated; a modern Wales, with a vibrant economy where every individual's unique contribution is enabled and valued; an inclusive Wales, where freedom, choice, dignity and respect are the cornerstones of the way we live (WAG, 2007e: 4).

In response to its statutory duty to promote equality for the Welsh language (GOWA, 2006, s78), the Assembly Government has also created a Welsh Language Unit within its administrative structures. It is tasked with overseeing the development and implementation of its Welsh Language Scheme.

Equality is also embedded in procedural aspects of the National Assembly. Thus, Section 35 of the Government of Wales Act (2006) states:

> Equality of treatment (1) The Assembly must, in the conduct of Assembly proceedings, give effect, so far as is both appropriate in the circumstances and reasonably practicable, to the principle that the English and Welsh languages should be treated on a basis of equality. (2) The Assembly must make appropriate arrangements with a view to securing that Assembly proceedings are conducted with due regard to the principle that there should be equality of opportunity for all people.

In addition to the foregoing duty, Standing Orders reinforce the principle of equality in Assembly proceedings. For example, Standing Order 7.61 covers 'Provisions Relating to Plenary Business' and asserts that 'time must be made available in each Assembly year for debates on the following items of Assembly business . . . (iv) the annual report of the Equal Opportunities Commission; (v) the annual report of the Commission for Racial Equality; (vi) the annual report of the Disability Rights Commission [now superseded by the Equality and Human Rights Commission]'. Moreover, Standing Order 8.9 covers the language used in political debate and states that 'The Presiding Officer is to maintain order in plenary meetings and must call to order any Member who . . . is using disorderly, discriminatory or offensive language or language which detracts from the dignity of the Assembly'. Family-friendly working hours are also provided for in Standing Order 6 – Organisation of Business. This states that 'Motions under Standing Order 6.1 [the timing of Assembly business] must have regard to the family and constituency or electoral region responsibilities of Members and their likely travel arrangements; and should normally seek to avoid timetabling business before 9.00am or after 5.30pm on any working day'.

A spatial dimension to the inclusive exercise of devolved functions was provided for under Section 61 of the 1998 devolution statute. This stated that 'the Assembly shall establish a committee for north Wales . . . [and] also establish a committee for each of the other regions of Wales to provide advice to the Assembly about matters affecting the region'. As a result, regional Committees were a feature of the first two Assemblies, 1999–2007. However, the 2006 Act contains no such requirement for regional committees and none have been established in the third Assembly. Yet, Standing Order 20 does make provision for regional committees to be (re-)created should at least two-thirds of AMs support such a proposition.

Another noteworthy institutional development that may further inclusiveness is the creation, at the outset of the third Assembly, of a public petitions procedure. This provides a new means of access to the policy process for the public and organisations outside government. Under Standing Order 28, 'the Assembly must consider, in accordance with the provisions of Standing Orders . . . any admissible petition'. In accordance with the new arrangements, the Presiding Officer refers eligible petitions to the cross-party Petitions Committee. In turn 'the Committee may: (i) refer the petition to the government, any other committee of the Assembly or any other person or body for them to take such action as they consider appropriate; (ii) report to the Assembly; or (iii) take any other action which the committee considers appropriate'.[2]

Overall, the foregoing developments are significant on a number of levels. The statutory partnerships require government to work with, and uphold the interests of, representatives of sectors outside government. They provide structures for issues to be raised with ministers and add transparency to such contacts through published minutes and transcripts. Their statutory footing means that non-compliance by government can be challenged by judicial review. In like manner, the statutory duties in relation to promoting equalities and the Welsh language require action on the part of government and also carry judicial review sanctions. A further key feature of the new governance arrangements is the way in which they afford statutorily-based access to the policy process for those outside government. This is a significant development, for under the former Welsh Office arrangements the Secretary of State and ministers often used executive procedures to determine policy. The foregoing institutional mechanisms oblige the cabinet to listen to external interests, provide legal checks on its actions and, in the case of the public petitions process, allow those outside the political classes to initiate policy proposals.

4.4 Comparative Developments in Scotland and Northern Ireland

4.4.1 Scotland

In the case of Scotland, constitutional law was also shaped by a concern for the promotion of equality, participation and inclusiveness. As Mitchell (2000: 610) observes, after the positive referendum result in 1997, a leading role was played by the all-party Consultative Steering Group (CSG) appointed by the Westminster government to finalise the institutional design of the Scottish Parliament. In its work the CSG emphasised four guiding principles. Namely, that:

- the Scottish Parliament should embody and reflect the sharing of power between the people of Scotland, the legislators and the Scottish Executive;
- the Scottish Executive should be accountable to the Scottish Parliament and the Parliament and Executive should be accountable to the people of Scotland;
- the Scottish Parliament should be accessible, open, responsive and develop procedures which make possible a participative approach to the development, consideration and scrutiny of policy and legislation;

- the Scottish Parliament in its operation and its appointments should recognise the need to promote equal opportunities for all (CSG, 1998: 3).

The CSG report also noted that 'it is important that our proposals for a more open political process are paralleled by the development of appropriate institutions at different levels in Scottish society, to ensure meaningful dialogue between the Parliament and civic society' (CSG, 1998: 7).

Reflecting the points raised by the CSG and others, the Scotland Act (1998) makes qualified provision for the parliament to legislate in relation to equalities. The devolution statute states that the Scottish Parliament may advance 'the encouragement (other than by prohibition or regulation) of equal opportunities, and in particular of the observance of the equal opportunities requirements' (Schedule 5, Section 22). Whilst the Scotland Act is less prescriptive than the Government of Wales Acts in terms of requiring statutory partnerships, institutional and structural innovations to promote participatory democracy have emerged in the wake of devolution. A number of these are set out in the Standing Orders of the Parliament.[3] For example, Rule 6.9 requires that there is a cross party Equal Opportunities Committee. It states:

1. The remit of the Equal Opportunities Committee is to consider and report on matters relating to equal opportunities and upon the observance of equal opportunities within the Parliament.

And it continues,

2. In these Rules, 'equal opportunities' includes the prevention, elimination or regulation of discrimination between persons on grounds of sex or marital status, on racial grounds or on grounds of disability, age, sexual orientation, language or social origin or of other personal attributes, including beliefs or opinions such as religious beliefs or political opinions. (Scottish Parliament, 2007)

In like fashion, Standing Orders (Rule 6.10) require a Petitions Committee to 'consider public petitions addressed to the Parliament . . . [and] decide what action should be taken upon an admissible public petition'.

As Carley (2006: 250) observes, 'partnerships underachieve if they are not integrated into, and supported by, mainstream governance structures'. It is therefore significant that the Scottish Government itself has legislated to put some cross-sectoral partnerships with government on a statutory footing. Thus, for example, the Local Government in Scotland Act (2003) establishes a duty on local authorities and other agencies to implement community planning in partnership with citizens and civil society (Communities Scotland, 2003). In addition, in terms of government–third sector working, the Scottish Voluntary Sector Compact was introduced in 1999 and subsequently revised in 2004. Although not statutorily based, it 'sets out the principles for Government and the voluntary sector to work together. Its aim is to develop robust relationships for the wider public good and acts as a concordat or code for both Government and the voluntary sector as a way of conducting business' (Scottish Executive, 2005: 36). The Scottish Government's latest action plan for the third sector re-emphasises partnership working and asserts:

> We will expect to see increased partnership working between third and public sectors. Building on the concordat with local government together with the work of Community Planning Partnerships (CPPs) and Local Social Economy Partnerships (LSEPs), we want to promote new relationships, especially around both the design and delivery of services . . . We will, in partnership with the Scottish Council for Voluntary Action, facilitate the third sector's input into the wider policy agenda for skills and workforce development in Scotland. (Scottish Government, 2008: 134)

4.4.2 Northern Ireland

With regard to governance in Northern Ireland, writing in the first months after the Good Friday Agreement Knox (1999: 326) concluded that 'the new Assembly has the opportunity to overhaul an inappropriate system of governance characterized by a high level of centralization and low level of accountability'. However, not all were supportive of the inclusive agenda. For example, Morison (2001: 291) questioned the ambition of the new arrangements:

> There seems to be a view that all possible political voices must be accommodated within some sort of idealized public space . . . the nature of the constitutional architecture of the settlement structures almost

seems to indicate a reckless abandon of concern over costs and convenience as every conceivable political viewpoint and relationship is factored into an ever more complex edifice of government.

Almost a decade on, Murphy (2007: 305) concludes that 'the instruments and tools of public policy at the sub-national level have changed significantly since the introduction of devolution. New actors have been introduced to the process . . . new forms of decision making have also emerged'. A key example is the statutory requirement for a civic forum as set out in the Northern Ireland Act (1998, s56). This stemmed from a commitment in the Belfast Agreement for a body to 'comprise representatives of the business, trade union and voluntary sectors, and such other sectors as agreed by the First Minister and the Deputy First Minister. It will act as a consultative mechanism on social, economic and cultural issues' (Northern Ireland Office, 1998). The Forum met for the first time in October 2000 and had 60 members drawn from ten sectors of civil society, namely voluntary and community; business; trade union; churches; arts and sports; culture; agriculture and fisheries; community relations; education; and victims.[4] At the time of writing, the future of the Forum is uncertain. Under the provisions of the Belfast Agreement,[5] the Civic Forum is currently subject to an official review to 'examine objectively the effectiveness and appropriateness of the current structure, operation and membership of the Civic Forum in consultation as necessary with a wide range of interests representative of society as a whole'.[6] In its submission to the ongoing Review, the official body representing the voluntary sector, the Northern Ireland Council for Voluntary Action's (NICVA), highlighted its potential value for boosting inclusiveness. It concluded that 'as a mechanism it extends participative democracy and can offer a range of additional voices to contribute to the process of making better decisions at a political level' (NICVA, 2008: 34). Moreover, it recommended that the civil forum be reconstituted in order to 'have clear relationships set down with the First and Deputy First Ministers, the NI Executive and the Assembly to ensure that any advice and evidence it puts forward will be understood and considered appropriately'. The NICVA also expressed concern that any reconstituted Forum: 'must be adequately resourced to carry out its agreed remit, including having an appropriate research capacity . . . [and] should embody the requirements of equality and inclusion and its membership should reflect this . . . there is a need to ensure parity of gender representation' (NICVA, 2008: 55).

Devolution in the province provides the foremost example of the growth of partnership working since constitutional reform in the UK. A recent official study of government partnerships at all tiers of administration in Northern Ireland identified no less than 584 partnerships; the majority of which had been established to improve service delivery (45 per cent) or to promote policy consultation, engagement and networking (29 per cent), particularly at district council level (OFMDFM, 2005). An indication of the extent of the input of voluntary organisations to the policy process can be seen in figures for 2006–7 when '1,207 people from 948 organisations participated in [NICVA] training sessions, policy fora, information seminars, conferences and roundtable meetings . . . [and] reviewed 181 policy documents' (NICVA, 2007: 6).

A further key feature of the new governance arrangements is the comprehensive equality and human rights clauses in the Northern Ireland Act (see the discussion in chapter 6). According to Harvey (2000: 61) they are 'useful examples of how law might be shaped to include the voices of affected groups in the process of enforcing change in public administration'. In addition, under Standing Order 22 of the Assembly, Members of the Legislative Assembly for Northern Ireland (MLAs) may introduce public petitions for consideration.

Notwithstanding these new participatory mechanisms, one study of the first years of policy-making by the Assembly (and the Northern Ireland Office during the periods of direct rule) underlined the scale of the challenge ahead if participatory democracy is to be realised. It reported that: 'housing policy has tended to converge with policies in England, rather than moving towards a distinctively local agenda. Local political agendas remain dominated by disagreements over constitutional status thus policy formulation is determined more by officials than by elected politicians' (Paris et al., 2002: 154). An additional concern related to inclusiveness and the policy process in the province is the strong dependence upon European Union aid programmes to fund and develop partnership structures. According to recent research, 'unless other sources of funding become available, in the longer term the sustainability of the input of the voluntary and community sector to local governance may be problematic' (Acheson and Williamson, 2007: 41).

Scotland

Rule 6.9 Standing Orders[7] require that there is a *cross party Equal Opportunities Committee.*

Rule 6.10 Standing Orders require the existence of a *Petitions Committee* to 'consider public petitions addressed to the Parliament . . . [and] decide what action should be taken upon an admissible public petition'.

Local Government in Scotland Act (2003) establishes a duty on local authorities and other agencies to implement community planning in *partnership with citizens and civil society*.

Scottish Voluntary Sector Compact, introduced in 1999 and revised in 2004, 'sets out the principles for Government and the voluntary sector to work together. Its aim is to develop robust relationships for the wider public good and acts as a concordat or code for both Government and the voluntary sector as a way of conducting business' (Scottish Executive, 2005: 36).

Legislating for equalities: The Scotland Act (1998) states that the Scottish Parliament may advance 'the encouragement (other than by prohibition or regulation) of equal opportunities, and in particular of the observance of the equal opportunities requirements' (Schedule 5, Section 22).

Electoral system: 73 members representing individual constituencies are elected under the first-past-the-post system. In addition, there are 8 Scottish Parliament Regions; each region has 7 seats in the Parliament. These 56 seats are elected by the proportional representation Additional Member System. (Proportional representation is a more responsive mechanism than first-past-the-post in terms of linking the total popular vote for each candidate to the profile of those elected.)

Northern Ireland

A statutory requirement for a *civic forum* as set out in the Northern Ireland Act (1998, s56). The Forum is comprised of 60 members drawn from ten sectors of civic society, namely voluntary and community; business; trade union; churches; arts and sports; culture; agriculture and fisheries; community relations; education; and victims.

Partnership working: A recent official study of government partnerships at all tiers of administration in Northern Ireland identified no less than 584 partnerships, the majority of which had been established to improve service delivery (45%), or to promote policy consultation, engagement and networking (29%) (OFMDFM, 2005).

Under Standing Order 22 of the Assembly, MLAs may introduce *public petitions* for consideration by the Assembly.

Equalities duty: Section 75 of the Northern Ireland Act (1998). This places an active duty to promote equalities on designated pubic bodies. Under Section 75, named public authorities are required to have due regard to the need to promote equality of opportunity: between persons of different religious belief, political opinion, racial group, age, marital status or sexual orientation; between men and women generally; between persons with a disability and persons without; and between persons with dependants and persons without.

Electoral system: The Single Transferable Vote (STV) system of proportional representation is used to elect Members of the Assembly. STV has a number of advantages over the simple first-past-the-post system used in the Westminster elections: it increases voter choice (voters can vote for more than one candidate and can choose between candidates as well as between parties); it ensures that more voters have an effect on the outcome (over 80% of all valid votes are used to elect the six members in each constituency); and it ensures an outcome that is more representative of the views of the electorate (a party's overall share of seats will better reflect their overall share of the vote, i.e. voters will be proportionately represented).[8]

Figure 4.2. Inclusive governance: features of constitutional/statutory law in Scotland and Northern Ireland

4.5 Discussion

The views of equalities groups about the effectiveness of the new governance structures in Wales are discussed in chapter 8, but prior to such an evaluation it is pertinent to highlight some general issues and challenges to realising inclusive governance. One early concern was the danger 'that the new Welsh legislature over-bureaucratises the voluntary sector' (Chaney and Fevre, 2001: 152). In response, the government asserts that the devolved structures are aimed at a situation where 'dialogue replaces top-down prescription' (WAG, 2006e: 35; WAG, 2007g). Yet, the bureaucracy required for voluntary sector organisations to effectively engage with government may result in their partial 'colonisation' by the political system; making them less able to articulate their own values in order to press for social change around issues such as equalities. A further concern is the effect of 'communication distortions' on levels of participation (Whipple, 2005). In other words, citizens' levels of awareness of the structures and processes of policy-making shape their propensity to get involved. Here, the mass media have a central role; yet, during the initial years of the Assembly, a major concern has been poor coverage and low levels of public knowledge about devolved policy and law making (Wyn Jones, 1998; BBC Trust, 2008).

With regard to practical matters, the new structures also raise issues as to whether some groups outside government possess the necessary organisational capability and resources to influence policy. This was highlighted in the Independent Commission Review of the Voluntary Sector in Wales (ICRVS, 2004: 18) which stated that 'parts of the voluntary and community sector, notably equality groups, lack sufficient capacity and support to enable them to make a real impact'. In response, government funding and support for voluntary organisations, networks and partnership working is a welcome development (see chapter 8). Yet, it is not without is potential dangers. As Verba et al. (1983: 87) observe, 'the impact of institutional interference on participation disparities amongst groups depends upon *who* is affiliated and *who* is unaffiliated' (original emphasis). In this way it raises the spectre of neo-corporatism or 'the exclusive relationship between a handful of privileged groups and the state' (Wilson, 1990: 69; see also Mansbridge, 1992).

Power asymmetries in the partnership arrangements with government pose further challenges. These arise from the fact that governments often have powers to veto, override or substantially amend proposals from other parties in the partnership; powers that co-participants do not possess (Klijn and Koppenjan, 1999; Skelcher et al., 2005, Davies, 2007). It should also be noted that the structures of new governance alone are no guarantee of greater levels of engagement with those outside government. This also depends on the prevailing level of 'social capital', or the social networks and norms that underpin civil society, and thus patterns of active citizenship (Putnam, 1993; Granovetter, 1985; Fukuyama, 1999; Portes, 1995; Chaney, 2003). The new governance arrangements also require knowledge, expertise and resources to operate in the new political landscape. As Newman (2002: 7) observes, 'in the new knowledge-based and networked economy "who you know" and whether you can access crucial networks is becoming highly significant. As the site of action shifts, so equality agendas must be renegotiated.'

Notwithstanding such concerns, from a comparative perspective, in each devolved polity, constitutional reform has resulted in a raft of governance mechanisms designed to foster inclusion and participation. For example, in Scotland, legislation has been passed by the Parliament to require intersectoral working between government and voluntary bodies. Furthermore, the Petitions Committee is a further conduit for engagement in policy work. In Northern Ireland, the requirement to consult with groups and interests covered by the Section 75 equality duty is a significant and enforceable mechanism for the inclusion of hitherto marginalised groups in public business. In addition, the past decade has seen the rapid development of partnership working between government and other interests in the province. In Wales, the devolution Acts set out a series of equality duties and put partnership working with government on a statutory footing. Thus, overall, constitutional reform in the UK has seen a major transformation in the structures of contemporary governance, one with the potential to significantly advance the promotion of equalities through inclusive approaches to policy-making. Yet, when viewing these developments, as Newman (2001: 26) warns, caution is also required in order prevent 'an over-simplified view of change . . . that tends to over-read the extent and embeddedness of change and underestimate important points of continuity with past regimes'.

5

The Equalities 'Infrastructure' in the Devolved State

5.0 Introduction

The following analysis examines the growing equalities 'infrastructure' in Wales and compares it to developments in the UK's other devolved territories. The term is used here to denote public bodies that, wholly or in part, have an official remit to advise on, monitor and enforce equality policies and law across a broad range of public functions. As the following discussion reveals, one consequence of the creation of the National Assembly for Wales has been the development of a Welsh 'proto-state' to support devolved administration. Constituent institutions include new dedicated Wales-only bodies (e.g. the Welsh Commissioners for Children and Older People); pre-existing organisations that, to varying extents, have reconfigured to adapt to devolution (e.g. the Welsh Language Board); and bodies with a remit across Great Britain that have quasi-federal structures (e.g. the EHRC). Whilst several of these are principally concerned with the promotion of equalities, others, such as the Wales Audit Office and the Care and

Social Services Inspectorate Wales, have equalities-related functions. Therefore, the purpose of the following discussion is to map the equalities infrastructure in the wake of devolution, explore the official remit and functioning of its constituent parts, and reflect on its existing work and potential for future development.

5.1 Equalities and the State

The state may be defined as 'a legally circumscribed structure of power with supreme jurisdiction over a territory' (Held, 1989: 11). As noted in chapter 2, the notion of power is central to the promotion of equalities in the modern state. Here, social power can be viewed as 'a form of causation that has its effects in and through social relations. In its strongest sense, it is an agent's intentional use of causal powers to affect the conduct of other participants in the social relations that connect them together' (Scott, 2001: 1). Thus, the state may use its powers of supreme jurisdiction to compel action and enforce prevailing laws through legal mechanisms, the allocation of resources and public policy programmes; even the use of physical force. However, the institutions of the state are not neutral. From a Gramscian perspective (Gramsci, 2007) they may further the hegemony of ruling elites such that 'political class domination is inscribed in the organization and institutions of the state system' (Jessop, 2007: 120; Poulantzas, 1978); in this way, they may reproduce inequalities and patterns of discrimination. Connell (2007: 138) develops this point by observing that 'the state is an issue in gender politics both because state institutions are deeply embedded in the gender order and because state power has capacity to shape gender relations on the large scale'. Over recent years, recognition of the power of state institutions to challenge discrimination and inequality has seen a growing role for public inspectorates. This has been underpinned by the introduction of 'fourth generation' equalities duties (see chapter 6), as well as EC directives, such as the European Race Equality Directive (2000/43/EC, Article 7(2)). The latter requires member states to 'designate a body or bodies for the promotion of equal treatment of all persons without discrimination on the grounds of racial or ethnic origin'. Such directives demonstrate how 'Europeanisation has played a significant role in the growth of equality bodies with a general mandate . . . [and in turn] their implementation has triggered reform of the national equality institutions' (Bell, 2008: 42). In the UK, domestic developments such as the Macpherson Report (cf. Macpherson, 1999; Recommendation 66) have also emphasised the need for robust equalities inspection regimes. Indeed, the present can be characterised as a period of transition demonstrating not only increasing functional specialisation (as constitutional reform has seen a significant growth in 'devolved' state bodies tasked with monitoring the quality of public services), but also the placement of increasing attention on monitoring and enforcing public sector compliance with new equalities laws. A recent UK government policy document summarised the situation:

> The public service inspectorates across England, Scotland and Wales have an important role to play in . . . monitoring performance against equality objectives and outcomes . . . in practice, various public service inspectorates . . . have taken on the role of assessing compliance as part of their wider responsibilities. Some inspectorates have also developed their own equality standards, some of which go beyond the requirements of the existing [British] public sector equality duties, against which they assess the performance of the bodies they inspect. (DLGC, 2007b: 104)

Against this background of change, we now look at developments in the devolved context. First, in relation to advice-giving bodies, and then in relation to those concerned with monitoring and enforcement.

5.2 Advice, Support and Strategic Coordination of Equalities in the Public Sector

With the political reprioritisation of equalities in the wake of devolution it is apposite to explore the extent to which it has been accompanied by appropriate developments in the extent and coverage of advice provision on equalities issues. In the case of municipalities, such a coordinating body was founded in the era of administrative devolution. The Welsh Local Government Association (WLGA) 'supports authorities in the development of policies and priorities which will improve public service and democracy' (WLGA, 2008: 1). In this sense it is a key strategic link on equalities and other issues. It not only represents the 22 local authorities in Wales, but also (as associate members) the four Welsh police authorities, three fire and rescue authorities, and three national park authorities. The WLGA's

Equalities and Social Justice Team is funded by the Welsh government's Local Government Division to support local authorities in improving their equalities practice; thus, it 'works to embed equality and social justice principles across the full range of work undertaken by Welsh local government'. It describes recent progress in the following terms:

> While efforts have been made, and targeted action in some key areas has been undertaken, difficulties in embedding such practice is a common factor and further support, guidance and direct assistance is required to facilitate change. Local authorities have responded positively to the new equality duties and some innovative examples of work are widely available, however, while processes are being developed, it is taking time to get them right and ensure that fairer outcomes are provided for all citizens. (WLGA, 2007, unpaginated)

The Equalities and Social Justice Team's main priority area of work is 'supporting authorities in implementing Equality Improvement Framework' (WLGA, 2008a: 3). This was launched in 2008 and, according to the WLGA:

> Links more closely to the wider improvement agenda through performance management and requirements under the Wales Programme for Improvement, for example, embedding equality through self-assessment processes and better collection and use of disaggregated performance data. The Framework also reflects the current requirements of equality legislation to take a joined up approach across all the equality strands. (WCVA, 2007c: 12)

In health, the NHS Wales Centre for Equality and Human Rights was founded in 1994. It describes itself as 'a national, strategic resource for NHS Wales', and its work as 'the delivery of organisational and cultural change to secure equality outcomes in employment and to address inequality in the planning, commissioning and delivery of services through a mainstreaming approach'.[1] Its ongoing work programme includes: a coordinating role ('working with NHS leaders to ensure that equality, diversity and human rights issues are mainstreamed throughout NHS Wales through inclusion on the agenda of Boards, advisory machinery, key groups, e.g. chief executives, medical, nursing directors'); a strategic input ('reframing the focus onto the patient delivery/service improvement agenda');

improving skills ('influencing the workforce development, education and training agenda'); and providing advice ('expert advice on equality, diversity and human rights issues . . . [and] bespoke support for organisations').[2]

Whereas the foregoing organisations pre-date devolution, a number have developed in its wake. At a strategic level, Public Services Management Wales (PSMW) provides support to public bodies. This government agency's work includes advice and training to managers on promoting equality and social justice (PSMW, 2008). A further key advice-giving body is the Children and Family Court Advisory and Support Service (CAFCASS) Cymru. Initially, in 2001 CAFCASS was established across England and Wales. In 2005, the service was devolved and became answerable to the Welsh government. As set out in the Children Act (2004) and Children and Adoption Act (2006), CAFCASS Cymru's remit is to provide expert independent advice to courts on the interests of children involved in family proceedings. Thus, its duties include safeguarding and promoting the welfare of children; giving advice to any court about applications made to it; and providing information, advice and other support for children and their families.

Advice and support on race equality issues is provided by a network of five race equality councils (RECs) across Wales: North Wales Racial Equality Network, Race Equality First (Cardiff), South East Wales Race Equality Council, Swansea Bay Race Equality Council and the Valleys Equality Council.[3] Although technically voluntary services, they are considered here as they form a key part of the equalities infrastructure and, to varying extents, are based upon state funding from sources such as local authorities, the Welsh government and the EHRC. In infrastructure terms, the RECs are unique in providing information, advice and support for individuals across the country, as well as policy work and initiatives to promote good community relations. However, whilst noting that RECs 'offer a vital localised service', Williams et al. (2003: 65) concluded that:

> there is by no means a seamless service for 'race' in Wales. The system that exists is characterised by conflicts/criticism/staff turnover and lacks integration and coordination . . . the service is inhibited in terms of providing the fullest range of services either because of legal, financial, procedural or political barriers.

The Arbitration and Conciliation Service (ACAS) is a non-departmental UK government body. It has a duty under the Employment Tribunals Act (1996, s18) to provide advice and conciliation to individuals or groups of workers in relation to employment protection legislation, including alleged cases of discrimination. In Wales, sex discrimination allegations comprise the majority of its caseload (see Table 5.1) (ACAS, 2007). According to Williams et al. (2003: 52), 'within ACAS, success is essentially measured in terms of [employment] tribunal avoidance. ACAS figures suggest that performance in Wales is broadly in line with that of England with a 77 per cent avoidance rate compared with a 75 per cent rate across England'. They offer a generally positive assessment of its work, noting that 'it is encouraging to report that ACAS Wales/Cymru is generally very well regarded amongst the key professional players. Indeed, the service may be well placed to respond positively to recent government initiatives that suggest the need for a more proactive approach in respect to dispute resolution with an increasing emphasis on early intervention' (ibid.). The Equality and Human Rights Commission Wales also provides advice and support on equalities. Moreover, as it develops, it promises to offer a more coordinated and bilingual advice service and, importantly, offer human rights information from a Commission in Wales for the first time.

	1999–2000	2000–1	2001–2	2002–3	2003–4	2004–5	2005–6	2006–7	2007–8[4]
Sex Discrimination	199	215	161	195	620	142	105	254	209
Race Discrimination	71	67	53	49	52	39	36	62	57
Disability Discrimination	126	139	210	79	129	114	129	171	-
Equal pay	58	203	49	14	10	12	8	673	-
Age Discrimination[5]	-	-	-	-	-	-	-	13	-

Table 5.1. Individual discrimination cases referred to ACAS in Wales from employment tribunals

Overall, as the foregoing indicates, devolution has seen some progress in institutional developments to provide support and advice on equalities in the public sector. Yet, there remain continuities with the pre-devolution era. The general picture that emerges is one of growing capacity, but it is also one of uneven provision. On this evidence, there is a need for further development of the advice infrastructure; a key issue is the extent to which this is coordinated across the sector to prevent duplication and ensure consistency.

5.3 Monitoring and Enforcing Equalities Law: Inspectorates, Tribunals and Commissioners

A broad range of state boards, commissioners and inspectorates play a role in the monitoring and enforcement of equalities laws. Not all of these are devolved, yet constitutional reform in Wales has seen the development of a series of new public agencies (see Figure 5.1 below). Moreover, a growing number of Westminster Acts of parliament give the National Assembly framework powers to set the standards to be applied by inspectorates when monitoring service delivery. For example, the Care Standards Act (2000, s23) empowers the Welsh government to determine the National Minimum Standards for fostering services to be applied by the Care and Social Services Inspectorate Wales. The latter state that 'the fostering service should ensure that children and young people, and their families, are provided with foster care services which value diversity and promote equality.'

At a British level, official policy documents associated with the government's Equality Bill (2009) set out the future role of public inspectorates:

> The public service inspectorates across England, Scotland and Wales have an important role to play in assessing compliance with the proposed single public sector equality duty and monitoring performance against equality objectives and outcomes. (DCLG, 2007: 104)

Against this trend of increasing monitoring and regulation of equalities, what features and components define the infrastructure in Wales? One prominent component that predates devolution is the Welsh Language Board (*Bwrdd yr Iaith Gymraeg*). It has regulatory authority under the provisions of the Welsh Language Act (1993). For

The Wales Audit Office	The Auditor General wishes to promote diversity, equal opportunities and human rights both as an employer and through his audit and inspection functions.[6]
Public Services Ombudsman for Wales	Principles of Good Administration . . . Treating people without unlawful discrimination or prejudice.[7]
Care Standards Inspectorate for Wales	*Handbook for analysing performance information* May 2008: 'Equality and diversity and Involving users and carers cover subjects that should manifest themselves across many of the domains'. 'Social Care – Children's Services, Indicator The percentage of initial assessments taking place during the year where the following is recorded: a) Ethnicity b) Religion c) First language choice . . . Success In Promoting Independence And Social Inclusion Local Authorities . . . Promotion of equality and diversity in your services, including hard to reach groups.[8]
Healthcare Inspectorate Wales[9]	'All inspection/investigation reports and other published material to contain specific reference to equality matters where appropriate.'[10] 'HIW will ensure that assessment of the extent to which NHS bodies promote diversity, comply with race equality legislation and the expected standards for fair access and treatment of patients irrespective of gender, race, ethnicity, age, religion, sexual orientation is integral to its inspection work.'[11]
Welsh State Schools Inspectorate Estyn	*The Common Inspection Framework for Education and Training in Wales* 'What are the principles of inspection? . . . focus inspection on priority areas of National Assembly policy, including tackling social disadvantage, equality of opportunity and sustainable development; apply the principle of equality for both Welsh and English to all our inspection work, providing bilingual services whenever they are appropriate . . . How will inspection teams make judgements? . . . Valuing equality of opportunity and diversity.'[12]
General Teaching Council Wales	*Statement of Professional Values and Practice* 'Teachers acknowledge the need for mutual accountability and commitment from all partners in achieving shared aspirations and goals. They are committed to providing equal opportunities to pupils, colleagues and others with whom they come into professional contact, regardless of gender, ethnicity, age, religion and beliefs, special needs, sexual orientation and linguistic background.'[13]

Social Services Inspectorate for Wales	*National Minimum Standards For Fostering Services* 'Standard 7 – Valuing diversity 7.1 The fostering service ensures that children and young people, and their families, are provided with foster care services which value diversity and promote equality.'[14] *National Minimum Standards For Boarding Schools* *Discrimination and Equal Opportunities* 'Standard 18 18.1 Within the school, there is no inappropriate discrimination on grounds of gender, disability, race, religion, cultural background, linguistic background, sexual orientation or academic or sporting ability. These factors are taken into account in the care of boarders, so that care is sensitive to different needs.'[15]
Children's Commissioner for Wales	'Equality of opportunity: It is essential that the Children's Commissioner's team is accessible and welcoming to all the children of Wales, celebrates diversity and embraces anti-oppressive practice.'[16]
Older People's Commissioner for Wales	*Commissioner for Older People (Wales) Act (2006)* Section 2. General functions (1) The Commissioner may – (a) promote awareness of the interests of older people in Wales and of the need to safeguard those interests; (b) promote the provision of opportunities for, and the elimination of discrimination against, older people in Wales; (c) encourage best practice in the treatment of older people in Wales; (d) keep under review the adequacy and effectiveness of law affecting the interests of older people in Wales.

Figure 5.1. Details of Welsh inspectorates and commissioners' offices and their equality work/remits

example, sections 17–19 of the Act set out statutory powers of investigation should a public body be non-compliant. Moreover, compelling remedial action by organisations is provided for in section 20 of the Act. This states that 'the Secretary of State for Wales [now superseded by Welsh government ministers] may give such directions to the public body as he [*sic*] considers appropriate . . . any such directions made under subsection (2) shall be enforceable, on an application made by him, by mandamus [or Mandatory Order]'.[17]

In respect of employment matters, employment tribunals covering Wales, Scotland and England undertake enforcement of British-wide anti-discrimination law. As Williams et al. (2003: 16) observe, the Tribunals Service Agency has been slow to adapt to devolution. Indeed, it only recognised Wales as a single administrative region in 1987. Unlike other cross-border agencies, the Tribunals Service has not fully developed its structures and practices to adapt to the distinctive policy context in Wales. Fundamental shortcomings exist in the provision of disaggregated data on discrimination cases in Wales. Williams et al. (2003: 16) conclude that 'in post-devolution Britain, there is an urgent need to recognise Wales as a distinct administrative entity. Existing arrangements not only add to constitutional and legal uncertainties but also hinder planning on a devolved regional basis.'

With regard to special educational needs (SEN), prior to 2003, appeals against Welsh local education authorities were made to the England and Wales SEN Tribunal. In 2003 a devolved body, the Special Educational Needs Tribunal for Wales (SENTW), was established.[18] Parents may appeal to SENTW against local education authority decisions about their child's education. A recent development is the Education (Wales) Measure (2009) that gives children themselves the right to appeal to the Tribunal (WAG, 2008(23)). Overall, since its inception, SENTW has dealt with over 700 appeals (including: 2005–6, 150; 2006–7, 118; 2007–8, 94; and 2008–9, 92). A total of 77 per cent of all appeals that went to a full hearing[19] were upheld (either fully or in part). SENTW also considers claims of disability discrimination against schools in Wales.[20]

The Welsh state education inspectorate Estyn is independent of, but funded by, the Welsh government. Established in the pre-devolution era, its latest framework for schools inspections sets out a range of criteria to measure the promotion of equalities, such as the quality and effectiveness of teaching, training and assessment; how well learning experiences meet the needs and interests of learners and the wider community; and the effectiveness of leadership and strategic management. Estyn also assesses the promotion of equalities by careers advisors, training providers and further education institutions, as well as local authority education services.

In relation to child protection, Fortin (1998: 479) underlines the need for statutory bodies to safeguard the rights of children on the grounds that they can independently scrutinise government policies and take a strategic overview of public services. The Children's Commissioner for Wales (the first independent statutory commissioner of its type in the UK) was established in 2001 and has powers to review the effect of policies on, and the delivery of services to, children and young people (Clarke, 2002; Hollingsworth and Douglas, 2002). Williams (2003: 215) points to the progressive stance taken by the devolved administration, observing that:

> The powers of the Commissioner are wide ranging in relation to matters affecting children where powers have been devolved . . . The Welsh Assembly Government also ensured that the UNCRC [United Nations Convention on the Rights of the Child] was enacted into secondary legislation [relating to the creation of the Commissioner's office] whereas the UK government had refused to include it in the primary legislation.

The powers of the Commissioner are extensive and include dealing with complaints, whistle blowing, advocacy and reviewing the operation of public bodies. Limitations in the Commissioner's role relate to her/his powers to take action on cross-border/non-devolved issues. A further key challenge is highlighted by Hollingsworth (2003: 77), namely the procedures available to the Commissioner

> to make robust representations about the failings and shortcomings of the body to which he is himself accountable, the Assembly [Government], when exercising his power to review the effect on children of the Assembly [Government]'s own actions under section 72B [of the Care Standards Act, 2000]. His independence from the Assembly [Government] becomes absolutely crucial in this regard.

Rees (2010: 165) summarises the current challenges facing the Commissioner in relation to her/his powers:

> WAG must ensure that the Commissioner's powers and functions are as strong as possible, and needs to respond appropriately to the Commissioner's work. Due to the Assembly's enhanced powers, this may prove easier than in the past. The Commissioner, meanwhile, must enhance the influence of the office, and build upon its credibility. Raising awareness, and developing an effective long-term work programme will facilitate this. As Wales moves further apart from England, one would hope that children's rights will become a central component of Welsh law and policy.

The first Older People's Commissioner for Wales was appointed in 2008 under the terms of the Commissioner for Older People (Wales) Act (2006), the first such post in the UK. The Commissioner's role is to 'be a source of information, advocacy and support for older people in Wales and their representatives; as well as looking at the interests of older people as a whole'.[21] Her/his statutory powers are wide-ranging and include examining the cases of individual older people (particularly when raising issues that may have a wider impact on older people in general); assessing the effect that public agencies (including the Welsh government) have on older people; issuing guidance on best practice in relation to regulated public services to ensure that they safeguard and promote the interests of older people; and helping individuals should they wish to make a complaint about public services. In addition, 'the Commissioner is able to look at the way in which a local authority, or health body, implements the policies and procedures that it has put in place for dealing with elder abuse'. If these are not being carried out effectively, the Commissioner can hold the relevant authorities to account.[22]

On other matters, the Commissioner for Public Appointments regulates the processes by which UK government ministers and, on devolved matters, Welsh government ministers make appointments to the boards of public bodies. At present, in the absence of a dedicated commissioner for Wales, the UK Commissioner oversees appointments to over 20 Welsh public bodies.[23] Under statute she/he is 'obliged to maintain the principle of selection on merit in the manner in which the Commissioner considers best calculated to promote equality of opportunity'.[24]

As the foregoing suggests, there are several notable aspects to the equalities infrastructure around the monitoring of anti-discrimination law following devolution. On one level, it is characterised by complexity. It is made up of a variety of bodies: Wales-only organisations that pre-date constitutional reform and who have adapted to the new context; cross-border agencies whose mode of operation has sometimes changed little from the era of administrative devolution; and new, devolved bodies. The speed and scale with which the latter have emerged is striking and underlines the emergence of distinctive Welsh state machinery in the twenty-first century. The organisational aims of the various bodies are diverse. Not all are solely concerned with the enforcement of equalities law. Organisations such as the Wales Audit Office have specific purposes (i.e. upholding financial probity) but also include equalities and discrimination within their general remit. In contrast, others are solely focused on protecting the rights of equalities-groups such as children and older people. A further striking feature of the infrastructure is the considerable variation in the way that equalities issues are addressed in their official reports. During the first decade of devolution, inspectorates and regulatory bodies (with notable exceptions such as Estyn) have not generally included a full-analysis of equalities matters in their official monitoring procedures. There has also been a lack of government coordination of equalities monitoring by these bodies. Given the Welsh government's powers to influence their remits and establish inspection frameworks, this is a missed opportunity. There is an indication that this is beginning to be addressed following the announcement by the government that in future the inspection reports of two devolved inspectorates, the Care and Social Services Inspectorate for Wales and the Healthcare Inspectorate Wales 'will include a section on compliance with equality legislation and will highlight improvements to be made by each body in order to improve their level of compliance. This will provide demonstrative information with regard to equality indicators and provide a citizen-centred regulation and inspection service' (WAG, 2007e: 20).

5.4 The Equality and Human Rights Commission

Established in 2007, the Equality and Human Rights Commission (EHRC) is a single equalities body founded under the terms of the Equality Act (2006). It has a key role in the provision of advice and enforcement of equalities law in Great Britain and is a non-departmental public body, funded by, but independent from, government. It replaces the pre-existing British equality commissions: the Equal Opportunities Commission; the Commission for Racial Equality; and the Disability Rights Commission. O'Cinneide (2002: v) describes the benefits of combining 'strand-specific' commissions in this way:

> Comparative experience demonstrates that single commissions can offer clear advantages in terms of developing effective cross-strand strategies, addressing overlapping and multiple forms of discrimination and emphasising the core principle of diversity that underpins all of the equality grounds.

However, he also warns that 'if established badly, a single commission could constitute a step backwards, diluting levels of expertise, creating a hierarchy of grounds and serving as an excuse for watered down resources' (ibid.). At the outset of its work the EHRC announced four interim strategic priorities: to build an independent and credible Commission; to target key inequality battlegrounds; to improve life chances and reducing inequalities; and to promote a new understanding of equality and human rights. In addition to providing advice and guidance, the monitoring and enforcement powers of the new Commission are extensive (see Figure 5.2). For example, it may conduct inquiries into any matter relating to its duties (and can compel evidence relevant to an inquiry); publish statutory codes of practice in respect of any area of equalities law; and provide legal advice, representation or assistance to individuals bringing legal proceedings under anti-discrimination legislation.

Inquiries	EHRC can conduct inquiries into any matter relating to its duties. Inquiries may be thematic (e.g. in respect of hate crimes) or may be specific into named organisations. The Commission will be able to compel evidence relevant to an inquiry.
Statutory codes of practice	The Commission can publish statutory codes of practice in respect of any area of equalities law. These will help businesses and the public sector to understand their responsibilities. It will not generally be unlawful if an employer or service provider fails to comply with a code of practice. However, courts and tribunals will take relevant codes of practice into account when deciding if discrimination has occurred.
Third-party interventions	The Commission will be able to seek leave to intervene in equality – and human rights – court cases (*Amicus Curiae*, or 'friend of the court') to provide the court with expert knowledge
Supporting cases	The Commission will have the power to provide legal advice or representation or any other form of assistance to individuals bringing legal proceedings under discrimination legislation. The intention is that such support should have strategic significance – such as testing equality law – rather than mass provision of legal aid.

(continued)

Dispute resolution	The Commission will have the power to arrange conciliation services in disputes related to discrimination in the provision of goods, facilities, services and education, and the exercise of public functions. (Employment matters will continue to be covered by the Arbitration and Conciliation Service, ACAS.)[25]
Unlawful Act Notice/ Statutory Investigation	If the EHRC decides that, after an investigation, unlawful discrimination or harassment has taken place, it will be able to serve an Unlawful Act Notice on the organisation that has committed the discrimination. The notice can involve the organisation or individual having to prepare an action plan, setting out the steps he or she will take to stop the discrimination occurring or recurring and the timescale in which the action will be taken. The Commission has the power to conduct a statutory investigation to find out whether unlawful act notices and binding agreements are being complied with. The Commission may apply to the courts for an injunction where it believes that there is persistent discrimination.
Binding agreements	Instead of enforcement action being taken by the use of Unlawful Act Notices/Statutory Investigations, the EHRC can enter into a binding agreement with companies or organisations. Ultimately, if the organisation in question does not stick to the plan, the Commission can apply to the courts to enforce it.

Figure 5.2. Selected equalities law enforcement and dispute resolution procedures of the Equality and Human Rights Commission

The pre-existing equality commissions had a variable record in tailoring their operations to the social and political specificities of Wales (the EOC was the most adapted and played a significant part in shaping the development of the Assembly; in contrast, the DRC was largely a centralised organisation, while the CRE opened an office in Wales as late as 1995). It is therefore significant that, under the terms of its founding statute, the EHRC has a quasi-federal structure. The Equality Act (2006) sets out a number of provisions relating to Wales. For example, in issuing statutory codes of practice (under s14.9) the EHRC[26] is obliged to consult with Welsh ministers. In addition, one of the EHRC's British board of commissioners shall be someone appointed with the consent of the Welsh government (Schedule 1 (3c)). However, the principal way in which the Commission is structured to operate in the post-devolution era is through its statutory Wales and Scotland Committees. According to the Act, the former should be strategic links between the Commission's operations at Wales and Great Britain levels. Thus, statute states that it 'shall advise the Commission about the exercise of its functions in so far as they affect Wales' (Schedule 1, 27) and, in turn, 'before exercising a function in a manner which in the opinion of the Commission is likely to affect persons in Wales, the Commission shall consult the Wales Committee' (Schedule 1, 28). The Commission also delegates to the Wales Committee: information, research, education, training, advice and guidance functions pursuant to the EHRC's core duties in relation to equality and human rights (sections 8–10 of the Act). Moreover, Section 11(2) of the Equality Act (2006) gives the EHRC the right 'to advise central or devolved government about the effect of an enactment' (i.e. lawmaking). With the growing legislative dimension to devolution in Wales, it is significant that Schedule 1 of the Commission's founding statute delegates entirely to the Wales Committee the 'giving of advice to devolved government about enactments which, in the opinion of the Commission, affect only Wales'.[27] Lastly, the Equality Act gives the Wales Committee a further mechanism to influence the public policy programme of devolved government for it is required to issue an annual report that 'shall, in particular, include the Commission's activities in relation to (a) Scotland and (b) Wales'. The Commission is obliged to send a copy to the Welsh government.[28]

Following the creation of a single equalities body structured to reflect constitutional change, a key issue is the nature of the emerging relationship between EHRC Wales and both the Welsh government and National Assembly. An early presentation by the Commission to the Assembly's Equality Committee gives some insight. According to the EHRC, there will be 'two key roles for the Commission in terms of our relationship with the Assembly and Government: advising and enforcing the law' (NAfW, 2007: 2). The Commission also affirmed its intention to advise on devolved policies with a bearing on equalities: 'the Commission can bring an equality and human rights dimension to the policy-making process . . . We found our membership of the Public Service Management Board to be a good way of raising equality issues at the highest level, complementing a plethora of other connections'. In terms of working with backbench and opposition AMs, the EHRC gave an indication of the developing relationship:

The Commission has a role in assisting the Equality of Opportunity Committee to scrutinise: the work of Ministers in delivering their programmes and compliance with the statutory duty to promote equality of opportunity for all people as set out in the Government of Wales Act. We could assist Assembly Members to scrutinise the equality and human rights impact of proposed legislation. The Commission's advisory role extends to other Assembly Committees and individual AMs will also be able to access advice. Advising the Assembly may involve partnership working . . . there may also be the opportunity for informal partnerships on key initiatives. (NAfW, 2007e: 4)

Overall, it is too early to fully determine the impact that the EHRC will make at the devolved level. Recent analysis (O'Brien, 2008: 32), concludes that it 'enjoys an historic opportunity' because of the 'fourth generation' duties that it is required to enforce, for they 'go beyond the negative notion of anti-discrimination towards a more positive, value-driven conception of equal participation [and this] offers the best chance of fruitful coalition with a human rights approach'. In addition, Mabbett (2008: 50) observes that 'the new modes of implementing equality policy provide a programme for an extended conception of legal rights'. But, he warns, 'they shift away from the mechanisms that have proved fruitful in the past. They are much more dependent on winning arguments through the main political and administrative channels of public policy-making'. Thus, he also notes such a move beyond traditional, predominantly anti-discrimination work will involve the EHRC in a new 'political phase': 'new modes of governance try to overcome the limitations of legal methods, but they draw the Commission back into a political domain where it will face all-too-familiar contests for attention and resources' (Mabbett, 2008: 54). Against government rhetoric of 'a step change in the battle against discrimination' (DTI, 2004: 2), Niven (2008: 25) asks 'how transformational will the EHRC be?'. He concludes that 'much will depend on the interplay between features of the EHRC that, on balance, tend to an integrationist and distinctive approach – and of its external context and environment, which, at present at least, appear to point on balance the other way and to a continuing emphasis on group-based priorities'. He continues, 'it is likely to take several years to resolve this seeming dislocation. Put crudely, the jury is likely to be out for some time on whether the EHRC is simply ahead of its time or out of step'.

5.5 Comparative Perspectives

5.5.1 Scotland

As in Wales, devolution in Scotland has seen the development of a number of new regulatory bodies with equalities remits. For example, Bòrd na Gàidhlig (the Gaelic Language Board) is funded by, but independent from, the Scottish Government. It was established in 2006 under the terms of the Gaelic Language (Scotland) Act 2005. The latter statute aims to promote the use of Scottish Gaelic, secure its status and ensure its long-term future. It tasks Bòrd na Gàidhlig to increase the number of persons who are able to use and understand the Gaelic language; to encourage the use and understanding of Gaelic; and to facilitate access, in Scotland and elsewhere, to the Gaelic language and Gaelic culture. The language board has a monitoring and quasi-enforcement role: 'when appropriate and reasonable, [it can] ask a public body to draft and implement a Gaelic language plan'. The Gaelic Language (Scotland) Act (2005) sets out evaluation criteria to be applied by the Board when assessing if a public body is meeting the aims of its Gaelic Language Plan. In terms of dispute resolution, Bòrd na Gàidhlig and public bodies can approach the Scottish Ministers when agreement cannot be reached on matters relating to Gaelic language plans and their implementation.[29]

Unlike Wales, Scotland has its own public appointments regulator: the Public Appointments and Public Bodies (Scotland) Act (2003) established the Office of the Commissioner for Public Appointments in Scotland (OCPAS). Its job is to create and regulate the process by which people are appointed to the boards of many of Scotland's public bodies.[30] As a result, it oversees the adherence to the Code of Practice for Ministerial Appointments to Public Bodies in Scotland. One of the Code's core tenets is that 'accessibility to appointments is a fundamental requirement and the appointments process will promote and demonstrate equality of opportunity and treatment to all applicants' (OCPAS, 2006: 3). In relation to public finances, Audit Scotland is a statutory body founded under the Public Finance and Accountability (Scotland) Act (2000) to provide services to the Auditor General for Scotland and the Accounts Commission (a statutory, independent body which monitors the finances of local authorities in Scotland). Audit Scotland aims to adhere to equalities principles and undertakes thematic evaluations on equalities such as its 2008 report, 'The Impact of the Race Equality Duty on Council Services'.[31]

Founded under the provisions of the Scottish Commission for Human Rights Act (2006), the Scottish Human Rights Commission (SHRC) is a key part of the post devolution equalities infrastructure. It has a duty to promote human rights and encourage best practice among public bodies. Its functions include disseminating information; providing advice and guidance; research; education or training; monitoring; and recommending changes in the law. The SCHR has extensive powers, including those to conduct inquiries into Scottish public authorities in connection with general human rights matters; to compel members of public authorities to give evidence or produce documents in relation to an inquiry; to enter places of detention in connection with an inquiry; and to apply to intervene in civil cases in the Scottish courts, and to intervene in any other court or tribunal where the rules of that court or tribunal allow.[32]

Future evidence of the developing nature of the equalities infrastructure came in the 2008 announcement by the Scottish Government of two new organisations (from April 2011): Social Care and Social Work Improvement Scotland (SCSWIS) and Healthcare Improvement Scotland (HIS). These new bodies will assume the functions of a range of pre-existing organisations such as the Scottish Commission for the Regulation of Care ('the Care Commission'), which has a duty to regulate and inspect all adult, child and independent healthcare services and ensure adherence to the National Care Standards (which include upholding the principle of equality). The new bodies will also assume the remit of the current Social Work Inspection Agency, which, under the terms of Inspection of Social Work Services (Scotland) Act (2006), inspects the standard and quality of social work services and assesses 'inclusion, equality and fairness in service delivery'.[33]

In terms of criminal justice, Her Majesty's Inspectorate of Constabulary for Scotland (HMICS) is responsible for inspecting the eight Scottish police forces and five police services. It carries out scheduled and thematic inspections that include equalities issues, such as the recent reports 'The Police Response to Domestic Abuse' (HMICS, 2008) and 'The Care of Detained and Arrested Children' (HMICS, 2008a).

In both Scotland and Wales, separate national education inspectorates have existed for over a century. HM Inspectorate of Education (HMIE) assesses the breadth of education and training in Scotland. As in Wales, it monitors the extent to which education and training providers promote equalities. For example, the current set of quality indicators for secondary schools inspection instructs inspectors to examine 'approaches to inclusion; promoting equality and fairness; and ensuring equality and fairness'. According to HMIE (2007: 37), the latter indicator

> relates to the steps taken by the school to promote and ensure a strong sense of equality and fairness through the curriculum and across all aspects of its work. It focuses on the parts played by staff in the school working with partner agencies to ensure that all learners are included in the life of the school. It ensures that diversity in the school community and beyond is valued.

5.5.2 Northern Ireland

Foremost in Northern Ireland's equalities infrastructure is the Equality Commission for Northern Ireland (ECNI). Founded in 1999 under the terms of the Northern Ireland Act (1998), it took over from the Commission for Racial Equality for Northern Ireland, the Equal Opportunities Commission for Northern Ireland, the Fair Employment Commission and the Northern Ireland Disability Council. The ECNI has a duty to oversee compliance with the legal framework around equalities in the province (see chapter 6), including in relation to accessing goods, facilities and services under the comprehensive Section 75 equality duty (whereby public authorities must have due regard for the need to promote equality of opportunity and good relations, equality-impact assess their policies and consult with those affected by their policies, including service users).

Another key, post devolution body is the Northern Ireland Human Rights Commission (NIHRC). It is an independent, statutory body set up in March 1999 under section 68 of the Northern Ireland Act (1998). Its role is to promote awareness of the importance of human rights, to review existing law and practice, and to advise the Stormont government.[34] Enhanced by the provisions of the Justice and Security (Northern Ireland) Act (2007), the Commission has extensive powers to conduct investigations, enter places of detention and to compel individuals and agencies to give oral testimony or to produce documents. On the contentious issue of public appointments, the Office of the Commissioner for Public Appointments for Northern

Ireland[35] is independent of government and, founded in 1995, it pre-dates the Good Friday Agreement. The Commissioner's role is 'to provide guidance for government departments on procedures for making public appointments; to audit those procedures and report on them annually; and to investigate complaints about appointment processes'. The aforementioned guidance is the Commissioner's Code of Practice. It prescribes the standards by which appointments should be made and has seven principles including the declaration that government departments (and subordinate bodies) 'should sustain programmes to promote and deliver equal opportunities principles' (OCPANI, 1995). Following criticism of the previous code, the latest version has stronger wording and states 'the need for diversity to be rigorously addressed' (OCPANI, 2008).

The Northern Ireland Social Care Council (NISCC) was founded under the Health and Personal Social Services (Northern Ireland) Act (2001). It is a regulatory body established to improve and regulate standards of social care, including the registration, regulation and training of the social care workforce and developing occupational standards.[36] Listed among the NISCC's core principles for conducting inspections is 'equity and fairness: supporting equality of opportunity and valuing diversity' (NISCC, 2008). The Care Council is a listed authority under the Section 75 equality duty and is therefore required to undertake equality impact assessments in relation to the exercise of its functions.

Established in 2003,[37] the Regulation and Quality Improvement Authority is the independent health and social care regulatory body for Northern Ireland. Through the Northern Ireland Executive's Quality Standards for Health and Social Care it is required to 'ensure implementation of the duty [s75] in respect of human rights and equality of opportunity for the people of Northern Ireland'. Thus, one of the healthcare standards is 'equality of opportunity and ensuring that positive outcomes for service users and staff are promoted; and that their background and culture are valued and respected'. The corresponding assessment criterion is that the organisation 'actively pursues equality screening and, where appropriate, equality impact assessment in compliance with section 75 of the Northern Ireland Act, 1998' (DHSSPSNI, 2006: 20–32).

5.7 Summary

Devolution has seen the comparatively rapid development of a state infrastructure around equalities in Wales. Over the past decade a series of new bodies has been created. They either have a dedicated equality remit (e.g. commissioners for children and older people) or include equalities within their general organisational aims (e.g. Health Inspectorate Wales). In terms of support and advice on equalities, there is some evidence of progress in the provision offered by state institutions. In the case of health and local government, pre-existing structures have adapted to the demands of devolution. In addition, new, post-devolution bodies such as the CAFCASS Cymru have incorporated advice and support on equalities into their wider remits. The EHRC also promises to offer more coordinated advice provision than seen in the past; importantly, this includes human rights information from a Commission in Wales for the first time. Thus, the overall trend that emerges is one of growing capacity, but it is also one of uneven provision. It suggests the need for further and sustained development to address the findings of an earlier study that concluded that support and advice on equalities was 'fragmented; disjointed and sparse, with few trained and experienced specialists in this complex area of the law . . . It is the few, and only those well equipped, who are using the system, but even for them the pathways are complex and the obstacles are many' (Williams et al., 2003: iv). In particular, there is a need for extending individual organisations' capacity and expertise to offer advice and support on equalities, as well as to improve coordination across the public sector.

In terms of the monitoring and enforcement of anti-discrimination law in Wales, the nascent equalities infrastructure is characterised by complexity. It is made up of a variety of bodies: Wales-only organisations that pre-date constitutional reform; cross-border agencies whose mode of operation has, to varying extents, changed from the era of administrative devolution; and new devolved bodies. The speed and scale with which the latter have emerged is striking and underlines the emergence of distinctive Welsh state 'machinery' in the twenty-first century. The creation of the Special Educational Needs Tribunal for Wales is part of the trend towards distinctive Welsh regulatory processes, ones that are more responsive (and accountable) to the situation in Wales.

A further feature of the equalities infrastructure is the considerable variation in the way that equalities issues are addressed in official monitoring and inspection activities. Despite the growing legal framework on equalities (see chapter 6), over the past decade inspectorates and regulatory bodies (with notable exceptions, such as the education inspectorate) have not generally included a full-analysis of equalities issues in their official monitoring procedures. There has also been a lack of government coordination of the devolved inspectorates and monitoring bodies. Given the Welsh government's powers to establish the inspection frameworks for a number of these, this is a missed opportunity.

The creation of a new single equalities body, the EHRC, structured to reflect constitutional change is a major discontinuity over the pre-existing situation. Founded in the pre-devolution era, the three former British equality commissions varied in their preparedness and willingness to deal with the devolved policy context. The provisions of the Equality Act (2006) effectively oblige the EHRC to structure its operations in the context of a quasi-federal Britain. Through the legal right to advise devolved government on the equalities implications of its lawmaking, as well as the activities of the Commission's Wales Committee, there is the potential for the EHRC to exert a strong and positive impact not only on devolved law but on policy as well.

From a comparative perspective there are similarities and contrasts in relation to developments in Wales, Scotland and Northern Ireland. In all three polities, pre-existing equalities-related organisations have to varying extents adapted to devolution. The separate legal jurisdictions in Scotland and Northern Ireland have seen the creation of standalone human rights commissions; over future years these are likely to have a major impact on equalities outcomes. All three territories have seen the comparatively rapid development of devolved state inspectorates, commissions and allied bodies. In addition, Northern Ireland has its own equalities commission (with powers over some cross-border agencies) and, as noted, the EHRC in Wales and Scotland is potentially a major driver of change.

Overall, comparative analysis underlines how devolution is leading to distinctive state 'machinery' to monitor and enforce equality policy and law determined by the Welsh, Scottish and Northern Irish administrations. This is a positive development. It offers the potential for more effective monitoring of the distinctive equalities agenda in each polity. Yet, it is also the case that significant issues remain over the enforcement powers of devolved bodies, as well as their institutional capacity. Moreover, the devolved governments need to address issues of strategic coordination between the component parts of the devolved infrastructures. If this is done, the new monitoring and regulatory bodies could make a significant contribution to securing equalities outcomes over future years.

6

Legislating for Equality in a Quasi-Federal UK

6.0 Introduction

The literature on policy 'delivery analysis' distinguishes between 'hard' and 'soft' policy enforcement responses. Policies backed by legal duties are characterised as the former type, for, as Parsons (1999: 513) asserts, 'policy is all very well, but without an enforcement or compliance capability, the delivery of public policy is unlikely and uncertain'. Thus, law is a key instrument for the promotion of equalities. Whilst the policy discourse around equalities can sometimes be declaratory and lacking in necessary detail, legal instruments can offer more precision and lessen the chances of an implementation gap. This is because state inspectorates are charged with overseeing compliance with legal duties, and failure to comply may result in legal proceedings and the imposition of sanctions. Moreover, equality laws may move beyond discrete measures of redress for individuals and impose legal duties that require systemic action on the part of public bodies, including government. In these various ways the law can convey rights to individuals, for, as Walker (1980: 1070) observes, 'the counterpart and correlative of a legal right is a legal duty, in that if one person has a legal right of a particular kind some other person or persons must be subject to a legal duty'. This is not to suggest that equality laws alone offer a panacea for the successful promotion of equality. Securing equalities outcomes also depends on combining effective laws with other factors such as securing political will amongst decision makers, developing a knowledge base through appropriate training programmes and deploying adequate resources. Notwithstanding this, examining the legal framework around gender and other modes of equality is central to understanding the effectiveness of state actions to tackle inequalities and discrimination. However, all too often contemporary analysis is principally aimed at the level of the unitary state (e.g. White, 2006; Hill and Kenyon, 2007; Bagilhole, 2009) with few studies offering combined examination of the legal framework emanating from the supra-, unitary and sub-state levels. This chapter addresses such lacunae by setting out a comparative perspective on the legal framework on equalities in Wales. Thus, initial attention is placed on the influence of the United Nations and European Union. Subsequent analysis centres on devolved lawmaking and the equality of opportunity clauses in the Welsh devolution statutes. The discussion then focuses on comparative developments in other devolved polities such as Scotland, Northern Ireland, the Basque Country and Catalonia. The chapter concludes with a critical evaluation of recent legal developments and the promotion of equality at the 'sub-state' level.

6.1 Multi-level Governance and the Legislative Framework on Equalities in Wales

The body of equalities law applying in Wales underlines the growing salience of multi-level governance to the promotion of gender and other forms of equality. Here the term 'multi-level governance' is used to describe the dispersion of authoritative decision-making, including lawmaking, across multiple territorial levels (Hooghe and Marks

2001b: xi). Bache and Flinders (2004: 58) see this as part of a 'reappraisal of the traditional dichotomy between 'domestic' and 'international' policy. They characterise it as 'the growth of the "intermestic" . . . [such that] national governments increasingly operate in a context shaped by the intersection of internal and external jurisdictions'. In some ways this represents continuity as well as change. As Keating (2002: 257) observes:

> The nation state never monopolized political action in Europe in the past . . . [and today] the new types of regionalism and of region are the products of th[e] decomposition and recomposition of the territorial framework of public life, consequent on changes in the state, the market and the international context.

Devolution in the UK can therefore be located within this wider trend of regionalisation, with equalities law in Wales increasingly the product of the interplay between the legislative outputs of different tiers of government.

6.1.1 The United Nations

At the supranational level, the United Nations has had a key role in shaping equalities law through codifying fundamental freedoms that may transcend the laws of sovereign states. The principal example is the UN Universal Declaration of Human Rights (1948) (UNDHR). Article One states that 'all human beings are born free and equal in dignity and rights', and Article Two states that 'everyone is entitled to all the rights and freedoms set forth in this Declaration, without distinction of any kind, such as race, colour, sex, language, religion, political or other opinion, national or social origin, property, birth or other status'. The rights and freedoms expressed in the Declaration include: 'all are equal before the law' (Article 7); 'everyone has the right to freedom of thought, conscience and religion (Article 18); and 'everyone, without any discrimination, has the right to equal pay for equal work' (Article 23(2)) (see Morsink, 1999). These have been elaborated in subsequent treaties and declarations; many have been described as 'second generation' human rights instruments because they relate to equality as applied to economic, social and cultural spheres (see Vasak and Alston, 1982). Accordingly, they advocate equal treatment in relation to social policy on matters such as housing, health and education. In terms of gender equality, the principal example of a second-generation human rights law is one established thirty-one years after the original UNDHR; namely, the UN Convention on the Elimination of All Forms of Discrimination Against Women (CEDAW). This commits member states to undertake a series of measures to end discrimination against women. It entreats governments:

> To incorporate the principle of equality of men and women in their legal systems, abolish all discriminatory laws and adopt appropriate ones prohibiting discrimination against women; to establish tribunals and other public institutions to ensure the effective protection of women against discrimination; and to ensure elimination of all acts of discrimination against women by persons, organizations or enterprises.[1]

Under article 18 of CEDAW, the UK in common with other UN member states is required to publish reports on the progress that it is making to meet the Convention's objectives. Whilst UN conventions are binding at the unitary state level, since 1999 the UK's progress reports have been adapted in light of constitutional reform:

> In Scotland, Wales and Northern Ireland, the women's agenda has been separately addressed, with devolved administrations in place. But while the policies may differ in detail across the UK, they are the same in their desire to improve the status of women by introducing the principles of the Convention in to every strata [*sic*] of society. (DTI, 2004: 3)

The UK's 2008 report gives details of devolved policy developments that address CEDAW goals. For example, under the heading 'Wales: Increasing the numbers of women with access to higher education', the report notes that 'widening access and participation is a key overall objective for the Welsh Assembly Government. Latest figures show that 56 per cent of Higher Education learners are female and 58 per cent at Further Education colleges . . . About 40 per cent of academic staff at Higher Education Institutions are female' (UNCEDAW, 2008: 97). The UN's assessment of the UK's progress continues to raise a number of issues including a lack of strategic coordination on adherence to CEDAW between devolved and central government; and the need 'to ensure the incorporation of all provisions of the Convention' in the Equality Bill (2009) (UNCEDW, 2008a: 8).

Further UN conventions on equalities that either directly or indirectly have shaped public policy in Wales (see chapter 7), as well as the UK more generally, include the International Convention on the Elimination of All Forms of Racial Discrimination (1965) and the UN Convention on the Rights of the Child (1990) (UNCRC). The former commits member states to the elimination of racial discrimination defined as:

> Any distinction, exclusion, restriction or preference based on race, colour, descent, or national or ethnic origin which has the purpose or effect of nullifying or impairing the recognition, enjoyment or exercise, on an equal footing, of human rights and fundamental freedoms in the political, economic, social, cultural or any other field of public life (Article 1).

More recently, the UNCRC obliges states to act in the best interests of the child. This has seen a shift from the pre-existing situation in a number of states whereby common law regarded children as possessions. Instead, the Convention sets out basic rights including the assertion that states 'shall take all appropriate legislative, administrative, social and educational measures to protect the child from all forms of physical or mental violence, injury or abuse, neglect or negligent treatment, maltreatment or exploitation, including sexual abuse, while in the care of parent(s), legal guardian(s) or any other person who has the care of the child'.

At the other end of the age spectrum, the UN International Plan of Action on Ageing (1982) encourages member states' governments 'to incorporate the following overarching principles into their national programmes on age equality': independence, participation, care, self-fulfilment and dignity.[2] Against each principle the UN sets out further and more specific aims. For example, under 'independence', 'older persons should remain integrated in society, participate actively in the formulation and implementation of policies that directly affect their well-being and share their knowledge and skills with younger generations'.[3] The most recent UN Convention on equalities is that on the Rights of Persons with Disabilities. Signed by the UK in 2007, it came into force in 2008. Article 3 asserts that states should uphold the 'independence of persons; non-discrimination; full and effective participation and inclusion in society; and equality of opportunity'. A key principle of the Convention is that of 'reasonable accommodation'. In other words, that service providers and others should undertake 'necessary and appropriate modification and adjustments . . . to ensure to persons with disabilities the enjoyment or exercise on an equal basis with others of all human rights and fundamental freedoms'. As with other UN conventions, quasi-judicial processes oversee member states' compliance with treaty obligations. In the latter case, the Committee on the Rights of Persons with Disabilities is part of the monitoring and enforcement framework and it may consider communications from individuals, or group of individuals, claiming to be victims of a violation of the provisions of the Convention by a state party to the Protocol; and it may conduct an inquiry on a state following information received 'indicating grave or systemic violations of the Convention'. Overall, however, the greatest impact of UN treaty obligations on the promotion of equalities is not their enforcement at a UN-agency level; rather, it is the way in which they become legally enforceable if and when they are incorporated into domestic legal codes.

6.1.2 The European Commission

In addition to UN treaty obligations, over the past six decades a European human rights framework has developed. Specifically, in 1953, the European Convention on Human Rights (ECHR) came into force for all Council of Europe member states. It was incorporated into the UK-wide Human Rights Act (1998) that came into effect in 2000 (1999 in relation to devolved functions in Wales and Scotland). From an equalities perspective a key aspect of ECHR is Article 14 that prohibits discrimination. Specifically, it protects against discrimination on a range of grounds including sex, race, language and religion. However, it only applies to rights under the Convention. Influenced by the Convention, the EC has been a key driver of equalities reforms (Rees, 1998; Walby, 2004; Waaldijk and Bonini-Baraldi, 2006). Thus, gender equality has been a core principle of the EEC/EU since the 1957 Treaty of Rome (Van der Vleuten, 2007) when the founding treaty introduced the principle of equal pay for men and women. Since then gender equality has been advanced through successive EU Treaties and no less than thirteen directives (see Figure 6.1).

Equal Pay Directive (1975)

Provides that sex discrimination in respect of all aspects of pay should be eliminated.

Equal Treatment Directive (1976)
Provides that there should be no sex discrimination, either direct or indirect, nor by reference to marital or family status, in access to employment, training, working conditions, promotion or dismissal.

Social Security Directive (1979)
Requires equal treatment between women and men in statutory schemes for protection against sickness, invalidity, old age, accidents at work and occupational diseases and unemployment.

Occupational Social Security Directive (1986)
Aimed to implement equal treatment between women and men in occupational social security schemes. Amended in 1996.

Self-employment Directive (1986)
Applies principle of equal treatment between women and men to self-employed workers, including in agriculture and provides protection for self-employed women during pregnancy and motherhood.

Pregnant Workers Directive (1992)
Requires minimum measures to improve safety and health at work of pregnant women and women who have recently given birth or are breast-feeding, including a statutory right to maternity leave of at least 14 weeks.

Parental Leave Directive (1996)
Provides for all parents of children up to a given age defined by Member States, to be given at least 3 months' parental leave and for individuals to take time off when a dependant is ill or injured.

Burden of Proof Directive (1997)
Required changes in Member States' judicial systems so that the burden of proof is shared more fairly in cases where workers made complaints of sex discrimination against their employers.

Equal Treatment in Employment Directive (2002)
Substantially amends the 1976 Equal Treatment Directive, adding definitions of indirect discrimination, harassment and sexual harassment and requiring Member States to set up equality bodies to promote, analyse, monitor and support equal treatment between women and men.

Goods and Services Directive (2004)
Applies the principle of equal treatment between women and men to access to goods and services available to the public. Extends gender equality legislation outside the employment field for the first time.

**Non-discrimination and Equal Opportunities for all –
A Framework Strategy (2005)**
The EU should consider how its experience of combating sex discrimination and promoting gender equality may be transferable to other grounds of discrimination . . . In some areas, it may be appropriate to consider the development of an integrated approach to the promotion of non-discrimination and gender equality. This integrated approach should take into account the fact that some people may experience multiple discrimination on several grounds.[4]

Recast Directive Equal Treatment in Employment and Occupation (2006)
To enhance the transparency, clarity and coherence of the law, a directive was adopted in 2006 putting the existing provisions on equal pay, occupational schemes and 'the burden of proof' into a single text.

Figure 6.1. European gender equality directives and communications

These have required, among other things, equal treatment concerning access to work, training, promotions and working conditions, including equal pay and social security benefits as well as guaranteed rights to parental leave. Notably, in 1996, the European Council of Ministers adopted the Fourth Action Programme (1996–2000) on Equal Opportunities for Women and Men. This was formally ratified in the 1997 Amsterdam Treaty that restated equal opportunities for men and women as a central objective of the EU. Importantly, Article 13 of the Treaty, the Directive on Employment, broadened the focus of equality initiatives beyond gender, and set out to prevent discrimination in the workplace on the grounds of age, sexual orientation, religion, race and disability. Such developments at a EU level required member states to incorporate the Directive on Employment into domestic law. As a result, in 2003, the Westminster government passed UK-wide Employment Equality Regulations on Religion or Belief, and sexual orientation, followed in 2006 by the Employment Equality (Age) Regulations. In the absence of a European constitution, recent analysis of case law relating to enforcement of the EC's gender equality instruments by the European Court of Justice revealed that this legal framework has had a key role in the incremental creation of women's rights (Cichowski, 2004).

According to its own assessment, gender mainstreaming is now 'a central feature of European Union policy-making in all sectors' (Commission of the European Communities, 2000: 30). Academic analysis, although more cautious, also makes a positive overall assessment. It concludes that 'the policy outcomes of gender mainstreaming have varied starkly across issue-areas in the EU . . . [nevertheless] the spread of gender issues across the policy arena is impressive, and merits further monitoring in the years to come' (Hafner-Burton and Pollack, 2002: 296). More recently, the EC has published an official Communication setting out a framework strategy on 'non-discrimination and equal opportunities for all'. This is significant in that, whilst giving primacy to sharing and applying the knowledge gained from combating sex discrimination to other equality spheres, it also signals a shift of emphasis in official EU anti-discrimination practices by emphasising the need to move away from discrete, strand-based strategies (e.g. sex, 'race' or disability discrimination etc.) towards intersectional, cross-strand approaches to equalities (EC, 2005: 2–4). It remains to be seen how comprehensively the Framework Strategy will be embedded in EU policies and practices, including those at the 'sub-state' level via the EU Committee of the Regions. Nevertheless, this legal underpinning to a more holistic approach to equalities is a potentially significant advancement.

6.1.3 UK/British Equalities Law

Over recent decades, the UK government has passed a series of Great Britain, or UK-wide, equalities laws. These may, as in the case of the Disability Discrimination Acts (1995, 2005), impact on the private and voluntary sectors. Yet, as in the case of the Race Relations Amendment Act (2000), it is the public sector that is the principal focus of such enactments, including the requirement to promote equality in the exercise of 'public functions'. The latter are defined as 'the activities of public authorities . . . [and crucially] this includes the policy decisions of Ministers . . . and the policy-making decisions of government organisations' (DLGC, 2007b: 51). Currently, discrimination in the exercise of public functions is unlawful on the grounds of race, disability, sex, religion or (non-) belief and sexual orientation. Details of the principal British equalities statutes are presented in Figure 6.2.

Statute	Provisions
Equal Pay Act 1970 (and amendments)	This statute outlaws discrimination between male and female employees in the same job in respect of pay and terms and conditions. It establishes the principle of equal pay for work of equal value.
Rehabilitation of Offenders Act 1974	This Act stipulates that, in set circumstances, the convictions of offenders will become 'spent'. Thus they do not have to be disclosed when applying for employment or training.
Sex Discrimination Act 1975	This statute makes it unlawful to treat a woman or a man less favourably in employment and training. In addition, it proscribes sex discrimination in the provision of education and the provision of goods, facilities and services.
Race Relations Act 1976	This Act makes it unlawful to discriminate against an individual on the grounds of race, colour, nationality, ethnic or national origins in employment, training, education and the provision of goods, facilities and services.

(continued)

Statute	Provisions
Public Order Act 1986	Racial hatred is defined by s17 of the Public Order Act 1986 as 'hatred against a group of persons in Great Britain defined by reference to colour, race, nationality or ethnic origins'. Incitement to racial hatred is governed by section 21 of the same Act.
Employment Rights Act 1996	This legal instrument Act is significant in establishing maternity rights.
Human Rights Act 1998	Incorporates the European Convention on Human Rights into UK law and introduces a range of political and civil rights such as the right to life, personal freedom, the Right to a fair trial etc.[5]
Crime and Disorder Act 1998	Part 2 of this Act defines a racial incident as 'any incident in which it appears to the reporting or investigating officer that the complaint involved an element of racial motivation; or any incident which includes an allegation of racial motivation made by any person.'
Sex Discrimination (Gender Reassignment) Regulations 1999	These regulations extend the Sex Discrimination Act (1995) to cover discrimination on the grounds of gender reassignment.
Article 13 of the Treaty of Amsterdam 1999	This Treaty allows the European Council to prosecute Member States for failing to give equal opportunities in terms of freedom of movement of persons, social security/welfare and employment.
The Race Relations (Amendment) Act 2000	This statute places named public authorities under a general duty to promote race equality. In the exercise of their functions they must aim to eliminate unlawful discrimination, promote equality of opportunity, promote good relations between people of different racial groups.
Special Educational Needs and Disability Act (2000) SENDA	This Act requires that post-compulsory education does not treat disabled learners less favourably for a reason related to their disability, and to provide reasonable adjustments for those students.
Employment Equality (Sexual Orientation) Regulations 2003	These regulations make it unlawful to discriminate on grounds of sexual orientation in employment and vocational training. The regulations include protection against direct discrimination, indirect discrimination, victimisation and harassment.

(continued)

Statute	Provisions
Employment Equality (Religion and Belief) Regulations 2003	These came into force on 2 December 2003 and make it unlawful to discriminate on grounds of religion or belief – or lack of religion or belief – in employment and vocational training. The regulations include protection against direct discrimination, indirect discrimination, victimisation and harassment.
The Disability Discrimination Act 1995 (Amendment) Regulations 2003	These came into effect in October 2004. Inter alia, they extend the provisions of the original Act to cover all employers, no matter how small, no matter how few employees they have in their organisation.
The Gender Recognition Act 2004	This statute means that transsexual people can marry in their acquired gender, obtain a birth certificate recognising the acquired gender and obtain welfare benefits and pension rights of the acquired gender.
Civil Partnership Act 2004	This statute allows same-sex couples to enter into a formal legal civil partnership through a statutory civil registration procedure.
Disability Discrimination Act 2005	This legislation enhanced the Disability Discrimination Act 1995 (DDA). It placed a duty on public sector bodies to promote disability equality.
Employment Equality (Sex Discrimination) Regulations (2005)	Inter alia, these regulations include a new definition of indirect sex discrimination and make less favourable treatment of women on grounds of pregnancy or maternity leave unlawful.
Employment Equality (Age) Regulations 2006	These came into effect from 1 October 2006 and make it unlawful to discriminate on the basis of age in all aspects of employment, including recruitment and training.
Equality Act 2006	This statute introduced a range of measures including a positive duty on public bodies to promote equality between men and women, and extended protection on the grounds of religion and belief to provision of goods, facilities and services.
The Equality Act (Sexual Orientation) Regulations 2007	These regulations made it unlawful to discriminate on the grounds of sexual orientation in the provision of goods, facilities and services, in the disposal and management of premises, in education and in the exercise of public functions.

(continued)

Statute	Provisions
Equality Act 2010	Harmonises pre-existing equalities law. Inter alia it extends the circumstances in which a person is protected against discrimination, harassment or victimisation because of a protected characteristic.

Figure 6.2. Principal UK/British equalities statutes

If enacted, the Equality Bill (2009) represents the greatest revision in equalities law yet seen in Britain. It has two main aims: to harmonise anti-discrimination legislation and to strengthen the law on the promotion of equalities. It will largely end the current patchwork of legal protections on equalities. Notably, most of the existing British/UK legislation will be repealed. Importantly, the Bill will strengthen the law in a number of areas. For example, it will:

- place a new duty on named public bodies to consider socio-economic disadvantage when making strategic decisions about how to exercise their functions;
- extend the circumstances in which a person is protected against discrimination, harassment or victimisation because of a protected characteristic;
- extend the circumstances in which a person is protected against discrimination by allowing people to make a claim if they are directly discriminated against because of a combination of two relevant protected characteristics;
- create a duty on listed public bodies to consider how their policies, programmes and service delivery will affect people with the protected characteristics;
- allow an employer or service provider or other organisation to take positive action so as to enable existing or potential employees or customers to overcome or minimise a disadvantage arising from a protected characteristic.[6]

Against this backdrop of a complex and developing framework of UN, European and British/UK equalities-related law applying to the Welsh polity, we now focus attention on the equality clauses in the constitutional law associated with devolution in the UK.

6.2 Constitutionalising Equality: The Welsh Statutory Duties

As the foregoing suggests, state promotion of gender and other modes of equalities currently takes place within the complex and shifting structures and processes of multi-level governance. This presents both opportunities and challenges for 'regional' government. On the one hand supranational and national tiers of government may impose restrictions that act to constrain regional initiatives (e.g. EC directives on competition limit the scope for positive action in promoting equalities in public procurement). On the other, devolved law making and policy development present significant political opportunity structures for challenging gender and other forms of discrimination, not least through their ability to target specific issues and patterns of inequality through tailored policy initiatives more attuned to local needs than those emanating from elsewhere. As discussion later in this chapter (see section 6.5, below) reveals, the situation in Wales is one where the contemporary legal framework around equalities is increasingly shaped by the development of Welsh law following devolution. In part, this stems from the role of constitutional law, and the catalysing effect of the equalities clauses in the Welsh devolution statutes.

Writing at the outset of devolved governance, Lambert (1999: 69) underlined the fact that the general equality duty in the devolution statutes (GOWA, 1998, s120; superseded by GOWA, 2006, s77) has 'no parallel in any other devolution legislation'. It is singular in its non-specific phrasing and all-embracing scope and is an imperative that applies to all people and all functions of government. It marks a significant divergence in the equality law applying in Wales compared with elsewhere in the UK for it modifies all Westminster Acts of Parliament where the Assembly/Welsh government has powers in their exercise and implementation. According to Clements and Thomas (1999: 10–11), the government 'has a duty to put in place a clear and known process to guarantee due regard to the principle of equality of opportunity, applicable to all of its decisions including the possibility of it having to take positive action to ensure equality, otherwise a legal challenge, via judicial review, is likely to be successful'. The duty is an example of a 'fourth generation' equality law. These require that 'even though not responsible for creating the problem in the first place . . . duty bearers become responsible for participating in its eradication . . . Positive action is required to achieve change, whether by

124

encouragement, accommodation, or structural change' (Fredman, 2000: 162). Section 77 of the Government of Wales Act (2006) reflects the Assembly's post-May 2007 parliamentary structure and states that 'Welsh Ministers must make appropriate arrangements with a view to securing that their functions are exercised with due regard to the principle that there should be equality of opportunity for all people'. Clause 2 of s77 sets out the mechanisms by which the duty will be monitored:

> (2) After each financial year the Welsh Ministers must publish a report containing –
> (a) A statement of the arrangements made in pursuance of subsection (1) which had effect during that financial year, and
> (b) An assessment of how effective those arrangements were in promoting equality of opportunity, and must lay a copy of the report before the Assembly.

It is likely that legal challenges to the Welsh government under s77 will be necessary before the exact meanings are attached to the key terms in the equality clauses such as 'due regard', 'principle that there should be equality of opportunity for all people', and 'appropriate arrangements'. A shortcoming of the duty is that the main enforcement mechanism is judicial review. This is usually an extended and expensive process and one not likely to be viewed as affordable by many individuals and civil society organisations. Another limitation is the lack of a requirement for government to publish an anticipatory scheme setting out how it will address its equality duty. Rather, the s77(2) clause is concerned with government reporting on what it is currently doing, or has done in the past. To some extent these issues are dealt with in the Equality Act (2006) which gives to the Equality and Human Rights Commission monitoring and enforcement powers in respect of the Welsh government's adherence to Great Britain-wide equality statutes, such as those on race, gender and disability (see chapter 5). However, the Section 77 duty makes no requirement for government to publish an equalities scheme relating to the broader provisions of the general equality duty in the devolution statute.

From an equalities perspective, a notable feature of the devolution statute is Section 76, entitled 'Regulatory Impact Assessments' (RIA). It requires that Welsh Ministers 'must make a code of practice setting out their policy on . . . the carrying out of regulatory impact assessments in connection with relevant Welsh legislation'. Published in 2008, the Code states: 'Welsh Ministers' Statutory Functions. (5.2) In compiling any RIA, Welsh Ministers will have due regard to . . . Section 77 – Equality of opportunity [and] Section 78 . . . the English and Welsh languages should be treated on a basis of equality' (WAG, 2008(17): 6). Thus, regulatory impact assessments are a useful mechanism for anticipating the impact of devolved legislation on equalities.

It is likely that as devolved governance develops, the human rights clause in the Government of Wales Act (2006) will also exert an increasing influence on the actions of government and devolved public sector. The relevant clause is explicit. Section 81 states that 'Welsh Ministers have no power – (a) to make, confirm or approve any subordinate legislation, or (b) to do any other act, so far as the subordinate legislation or act is incompatible with any of the Convention rights'.

As noted, the Government of Wales Act (2006) also requires a proactive and strategic approach in respect of language equality. Section 78 of the statute asserts that 'Welsh Ministers must adopt a strategy ("the Welsh language strategy") setting out how they propose to promote and facilitate the use of the Welsh language'. Alongside this provision sits the Welsh Language Act (1993). It obliges all public sector bodies providing services to the public in Wales to publish a Welsh Language Scheme setting out how they propose to treat Welsh and English on an equal basis. As of the end of 2006, the number of approved schemes in operation totalled 342 public bodies, 50 voluntary sector organisations and three private sector businesses (the latter in relation to privatised services).[7] However, the Welsh Language Act does not convey to the citizen comparable rights nor set out similar mechanisms and provisions, as the Great Britain-wide 'race', gender and disability Acts. As a result, the Act has been strongly criticised with campaigners variously calling for the legal right not to be discriminated against for speaking Welsh, and the right to receive goods and services in Welsh when dealing with the public, voluntary and private sector.[8] The proposed Welsh Language Measure (2010) may give equal status to the Welsh language, create the office of language commissioner and convey additional legal rights to Welsh speakers.

6.3 Government and Equalities Law: Comparative Developments in the UK

6.3.1. Northern Ireland

Whilst some equalities laws in the province are local enactments of UK statutes, others are distinctive and apply solely to that jurisdiction. For example, the Fair Employment and Treatment (NI) Order (1998) (subsequently amended) makes unlawful discrimination on the grounds of religious belief and/or political opinion in the fields of employment, the provision of goods facilities and services, the sale or management of land or property, and further and higher education. The Sex Discrimination (NI) Order (1976) and later amendments make discrimination unlawful against an individual on the grounds of her or his sex and marital status in relation to employment, training, education, the disposal and management of premises, and the provision of goods, facilities and services. Furthermore, the Gender Reassignment Regulations (Northern Ireland) (1999) make it unlawful to discriminate on grounds of gender reassignment in employment and training. In terms of 'race' equality, the citizens of Northern Ireland had to wait 21 years before comparable legislation to British statutes were introduced via The Race Relations (Northern Ireland) Order (1997). This (and subsequent enactments)[9] makes unlawful discrimination on the grounds of colour, race, nationality or ethnic or national origin in the fields of education, employment, the disposal and management of premises, and the provision of goods, facilities and services. With regard to disability, the Disability Discrimination Act 1995 (Amendment) Regulations (Northern Ireland) (2004), and subsequent amendments, provide protection for disabled persons against discrimination on the grounds of disability and require reasonable adjustments in relation to employment and access to goods, facilities, services and premises. The law on homosexuality in Northern Ireland has also lagged behind that in the rest of the UK (homosexuality was decriminalised in 1967 in Wales and England; in 1980 in Scotland; and in 1984 in Northern Ireland). Recently, the Equality Act (Sexual Orientation) Regulations (Northern Ireland) (2006) built upon earlier enactments and made it unlawful to discriminate on grounds of sexual orientation in the provision of goods, facilities, services, education and the exercise of public functions. However, the most significant piece of equalities law in the province is Section 75 of the Northern Ireland Act (1998). This places an active duty to promote equalities on designated pubic bodies. Under its provisions named public authorities are required to have due regard to the need to promote equality of opportunity:

- between persons of different religious belief, political opinion, racial group, age, marital status or sexual orientation;
- between men and women generally;
- between persons with a disability and persons without;
- between persons with dependants and persons without.

Each authority must thus have an equality scheme in place, a plan for performance on the duty and must assess (and publish a report on) the equality impact of their policies. If a public authority's assessment shows a possible 'adverse impact' on any protected group, it must consider how this might be reduced, and how an alternative policy might lessen any adverse impact that the policy may have (ECNI, 2007). In addition, consultation with those affected by public policy decisions is at the heart of the Section 75 duty. It has been subject to two official reviews in 2004 and 2007. The first highlighted how, in a strategic sense, the duty relates to the operation of the overall system of governance in the province and that:

> one of its principal strengths, namely its somewhat rigid and prescriptive approach (one that requires action), is at the same time overly bureaucratic. This raises concerns about what has been termed the 'tick box approaches to mainstreaming'; namely, the danger that mainstreaming achieves procedural, but little by way of substantive, improvement in equalities. (Chaney and Rees, 2004: 30)

A further issue was that, in its early years, Section 75 lacked an overall strategic focus. According to McCrudden (2004: 121) there was a particular need to pay attention to strategic objectives such that a 'much stronger approach' was required from the Northern Ireland Equality Commission on enforcing compliance and monitoring policy outcomes. The latest review published in 2007 identified both strengths and shortcomings:

> That Section 75 has had an impact is beyond question. What is less clear is whether that impact has been universal, in terms of extending across

the entire public service, and consistent, in terms of being applied with equal energy in all cases. What is also unclear is whether the application of Section 75 has had results as positive as might have been expected. What seems certain is that there is unrealised potential for good within the legislation as currently framed. (ECNI, 2007: 2)

The Review continued, 'over a relatively short period, it has effected substantial change in how policy is made. The result is more informed and evidence-based policy that reflects the needs of individuals, in terms of equality of opportunity and good relations' (ECNI, 2007: 7). Greater emphasis on avoiding overly bureaucratic procedures, the need for a strategic approach to equalities and the need to secure a more effective monitoring and compliance regime were also key themes in the Review's recommendations (ECNI, 2007: 14).

If implemented, the proposed Single Equality Bill for Northern Ireland will address some of the issues raised in relation to Section 75 and strengthen and simplify the existing framework of equalities legislation. As it currently stands, the Section 75 duty presents a number of key contrasts and commonalities with the Welsh government's general equality duty (GOWA, 2006, s77). Foremost of these is that the Northern Ireland clause is more prescriptive in that it focuses on specified strands; it also has more robust enforcement 'machinery' and, crucially, it requires that public bodies produce equality schemes and undertake impact assessments. In common with the Welsh duty, its initial years have led to over-emphasis on process at the expense of achieving outcomes.

6.3.2 Scotland

The Scotland Act (1998) states that the Scottish Parliament may advance: 'the encouragement (other than by prohibition or regulation) of equal opportunities, and in particular of the observance of the equal opportunities requirements' (Schedule 5, Section 22). Here equal opportunity is defined in broader terms that in British-wide statutes, specifically it denotes:

The preservation, elimination or regulation of discrimination between persons on grounds of sex, marital status, on racial grounds, or on grounds of disability, age, sexual orientation, language or social origin, or other personal attributes, including beliefs or political opinions (Scotland Act 1998, Schedule 5, section L2).

O'Cinneide (2009: 46) summarises the current situation regarding devolution and equalities law in Scotland: 'the devolution settlement is complex and has grey areas and built-in ambiguities. As a mix of reserved and devolved competencies, the allocation of competencies in the area of equal opportunities is particularly complex'. Moreover, as Mackay (2009: 54) notes, 'the question of whether or not EO/equalities powers should be devolved is part of the ongoing discussions of the National Conversation and the Calman Commission on the future of devolution'. Notwithstanding such developments, as in the Welsh case, the enforcement mechanism of the Scottish equalities clause is judicial review. Breitenbach (2005: 12) summarises its impact by stating that 'while equal opportunities clauses have been attached to some Acts passed by the Scottish Parliament, in general the approach to promoting equality in Scotland has been more voluntaristic'. However, the annual reports of the Equality Committee of the Scottish Parliament do reveal a systematic approach to reviewing parliamentary Bills and advising on their equality implications (an average of five Bills per year are reviewed by the Committee).[10] Moreover, a survey of recent legislation shows a general trend to place equalities duties on public bodies, regulators and commissioners. Within a British context this is significant because of the broader range of equality strands listed in the equality clause of the Scotland Act (1998). Thus, *de jure*, such Acts require ministers and public sector managers in Scotland to encourage the promotion of equality in respect of social origin, and 'other personal attributes . . . including political opinions' – a wider framework than applies to comparable public bodies in England. Figure 6.3 outlines examples of Scottish Acts that contain equality clauses; in most cases, the text of the Act refers to the enabling powers set out in Schedule 5 of the Scotland Act (1998).

Disabled Person's Parking (Scotland) Act (2009)
outlaws the abuse of disabled parking bays.

Sentencing of Offences Aggravated by Prejudice (Scotland) Act (2009)
legislative proposal that 'hate crime' legislation in Scotland is to be strengthened to protect disabled people and those from the lesbian, gay, bisexual and transgendered communities.

Adult Support and Protection (Scotland) Act (2007)
contains provisions in relation to elder abuse.

Prostitution (Public Places) (Scotland) Act (2007)
has created, for the first time, offences which target those who purchase sex on the streets.

Bankruptcy and Diligence etc. (Scotland) Act (2007)
s50 Scottish Civil Enforcement Commission – The Commission must, in the exercise of its functions, act – (a) in a manner that encourages equal opportunities and in particular the observance of the equal opportunity requirements.

Housing (Scotland) Act (2006)
s185 Equal opportunities (1) The Scottish Ministers and local authorities must perform the functions given to them by this Act in a manner which encourages equal opportunities and in particular the observance of the equal opportunity requirements.

Police, Public Order and Criminal Justice (Scotland) Act (2006)
s100 Equal opportunities. This section requires all persons (including organisations) who carry out their functions under this Act to do so in a way which encourages equal opportunities and, in particular, the observance of the equal opportunities requirements.

Further and Higher Education (Scotland) Act (2005)
s21 Equal opportunities (1) The Council must exercise its functions in a manner which encourages equal opportunities and in particular the observance of the equal opportunity requirements.

National Health Service Reform (Scotland) Act (2004)
s4 Equal opportunities (1) Health Boards, Special Health Boards and the Agency must discharge their functions in a manner that encourages equal opportunities and in particular the observance of the equal opportunity requirements.

Education (Additional Support for Learning) (Scotland) Act (2004)
sets out support measures and duties on education providers that
are broader in scope than previous 'Special Educational Needs'
legislation.

Local Government in Scotland Act (2003)
Section 59 Equal Opportunities – inter alia – places a duty on
local authorities mentioned in section 16(1) and any other person
discharging a function under the Act to carry out their functions
in a way which encourages equal opportunities and observes
equal opportunity requirements.

Transport (Scotland) Act (2005)
regional transport strategies . . . shall include provision about
each of the following matters . . . how transport in the region
will be provided, developed, improved and operated so as . . . to
encourage equal opportunities.

Sexual Offences (Proceedings and Evidence) (Scotland) Act (2002)
to prevent the accused in a sexual offence case from personally
cross-examining the complainer, and to strengthen the existing
provisions restricting the extent to which evidence can be led
regarding the character and sexual history of the complainer.

Protection of Abuse (Scotland) Act (2001)
this Act extended the legal powers open to police and addressed
an earlier shortcoming in the law that meant that, unless a criminal offence had been committed, the police had no power to
arrest an abusive person (including domestic abuse) who was in
breach of an interdict.

Standards in Scotland's Schools etc. Act (2000)
s5 Education authorities' annual statement of improvement
objectives . . . shall include an account . . . of the ways in which
they will, in providing school education, encourage equal opportunities and in particular the observance of the equal opportunity requirements.

Figure 6.3. The promotion of equalities in Scottish Acts

From a comparative perspective the Scottish equalities clause differs from the Welsh 'section 77' provisions (GOWA, 2006), foremost, because it is not a duty (rather it describes the parliament's legislative competence). It is also specific, detailing nine equality of opportunity 'strands'. Yet, as in the Welsh case, it too has a broader scope than British-wide equalities statutes and is enforceable via judicial review.

6.4 International Examples of 'Regional' Equalities Duties

The inclusion of equalities clauses in the constitutional law relating to regional government within unitary states is not a phenomenon restricted to the UK. Examples are to be found in states such as Germany, Canada, Spain and Australia. Thus, in the German case, for example, the Constitution of the Free State of Saxony contains the following edicts:

Article 8 [gender equality]
The promotion of the legal and actual equality of women and men shall be a duty of the Land

Article 18 [equality before the law]
(1) All persons shall be equal before the law.
(2) Women and men shall have equal rights.
(3) No one may be discriminated against or favoured because of gender, parentage, race, language, homeland and origin, faith, or religious or political opinions.

Article 19 [of faith, conscience and creed]
(1) Freedom of faith and conscience, and freedom to profess a religious or philosophical creed, shall be inviolable.
(2) The undisturbed practice of religion shall be guaranteed.

In Australia, state governments may legislate in relation to the promotion of equalities as evidenced by the New South Wales Anti-Discrimination Act (1977). This sets out protection on the following grounds: race, sex (including pregnancy and sexual harassment), marital status, disability, homosexuality, age, transgender, and carers' responsibilities. Schedule 5 of the Act covers the actions of the state government and the public sector. Likewise in Canada, provincial legislatures have powers to pass laws in relation to equalities matters (such as the Nova Scotia Married Women's Property Act, 1989).[11] This trend is not restricted to Commonwealth countries. Since 2002, the Basque Parliament has passed five equality laws. The most recent and comprehensive is the 'Law for the Equality of Women and Men'. This instrument is notable in a number of respects, including its wide-ranging and detailed nature, acknowledgement of the intersectionality between gender and other strands of equality, and its emphasis on training and equal representation. Its principal features are described in Figure 6.4. A further example is provided by Catalonia's Statute of Autonomy (see Figure 6.5), which also embeds the principle of equality in constitutional law. Specifically, it requires government and public bodies to promote equalities in the exercise of their functions, 'regardless of background, nationality, gender, race, religion, social condition or sexual orientation'. Furthermore, it states that public bodies 'shall also promote the eradication of racism, anti-Semitism, xenophobia, homophobia, and of any other manifestation that may constitute a violation of the equality and dignity of the individual'. In addition, Article 41 of the Statute of Autonomy sets out comprehensive provisions in respect of gender equality.

* Gender equality is framed within the principle of equality between women and men, and the expressed prohibition of any kind of sex discrimination.
* The law's preamble refers to the key role of the feminist movement in advancing the progress towards equality – and that sex discrimination intersects with other kinds of discrimination linked to ethnicity, language, age, disability, wealth, sexual orientation, etc. It also makes an explicit appeal to men's co-responsibility in the domestic realm.
* The Act sets out eight general principles, which have to guide public actions: equal treatment, equal opportunities, respect for diversity and differences, a general integration of gender perspectives in all areas, positive action, sex roles and stereotypes, balanced representation, and coordination/collaboration.
* Title I of the Act defines the different functions and competencies of each administrative level – regional and local – and establishes a basic institutional organisation, the coordination

mechanisms among institutions and the criteria for financing gender equality policies in the Basque Country – including the creation of 'Equality Units' in the different departments of the Basque government.

- Title II details a set of measures for integrating a gender per-spective in Basque public administration. Inter alia: 1) elabo-rating gender equality plans in the regional and local levels; 2) securing the adequacy of studies and statistics; 3) gender training for Basque civil servants; 4) measures for promoting equality in administrative norms and actions, including gender impact assessment, and positive discrimination in civil servant selection and promotion (in levels and areas with less than 40 per cent of women representation), and a balanced representa-tion in selection committees.
- Title III includes measures for promoting equality in the fol-lowing areas: 1) socio-political participation (2 articles and 5 sub-articles); 2) culture and mass media (3 articles and 9 sub-articles); 3) education (6 articles and 10 sub-articles); 4) work (with a section in domestic work – 2 articles – and another one in employment – 7 articles and 13 subarticles); 5) other basic social rights, with one article in health (4 sub-articles), one in social inclusion (4 sub-articles) and one in environment and housing (2 sub-articles); 6) reconciliation of personal life, family and labour (3 articles and 10 sub-articles); 7) violence against women, with one section on research, prevention and training and a second one in assistance and protection to vic-tims of sexual aggressions (13 articles and 22 sub-articles).
- Title IV of the Act specifies the creation of an independent equality body (Defensoría para la Igualdad de Mujeres y Hombres). This body is defined in respect of type, functions, organization and budget, working and reporting procedures – through a total of 13 articles and 33 sub-articles).
- Title V establishes the infringements and sanctions regime in cases where the law is broken.

Figure 6.4. The principal characteristics of the Basque law for the equality of women and men[12]

ARTICLE 4. RIGHTS AND GOVERNING PRINCIPLES

3. The public authorities of Catalonia shall promote the values of freedom, democracy, equality, pluralism, peace, justice, solidarity, social cohesion, gender equity and sustainable development.

ARTICLE 6. CATALONIA'S OWN LANGUAGE AND OFFICIAL LANGUAGES

1. Catalonia's own language is Catalan. As such, Catalan is the language of normal and preferential use in public administration bodies and in the public media of Catalonia, and is also the language of normal use for teaching and learning in the education system.

ARTICLE 40. PROTECTION OF THE INDIVIDUAL AND THE FAMILY

4. The public authorities shall promote public policies to encourage the emancipation of young people, by facilitating access to work and housing, so that they may develop their own lives and participate with equal rights and obligations in social and cultural life.
5. The public authorities shall guarantee the legal protection of people with disabilities and shall promote their social, economic and occupational integration.
6. The public authorities shall guarantee the protection of the elderly so that they may lead a decent and independent life and be able to participate in social and cultural life. They shall also strive for full integration of the elderly in society by means of public policies based on the principle of inter-generational solidarity.
7. The public authorities shall promote the equality of the different stable forms of union established between couples, bearing in mind their characteristics, regardless of the sexual orientation of the partners. The law shall regulate these unions and other forms of cohabitation and their consequences.
8. The public authorities shall promote the equality of all individuals, regardless of background, nationality, gender, race, religion, social condition or sexual orientation, and shall also promote the eradication of racism, anti-Semitism, xenophobia, homophobia, and of any other manifestation that may constitute a violation of the equality and dignity of the individual.

ARTICLE 41. THE GENDER PERSPECTIVE
1. The public authorities shall guarantee adherence to the principle of equal opportunities for women and men in access to work, training, professional promotion, working conditions, including salary, and in all other circumstances, and shall also guarantee that women will not be discriminated against as a consequence of pregnancy or motherhood.

Figure 6.5. Selected extracts of the equality clauses of the Statute of Autonomy of Catalonia[13]

6.5 Lawmaking in Wales

Given the growing salience of 'regional' legislation to the contemporary promotion of equalities it is appropriate that we turn to the processes of lawmaking in Wales. A striking feature of the first decade of devolution has been the increasing use of legal instruments passed by the National Assembly to promote equalities. It is part of a growing body of Welsh law that gives the lie to a widely held view that equality of opportunity is a reserved, non-devolved matter (Livingstone, 2001; Bagilhole, 2009). This erroneous belief persists at the highest levels, for example, the preamble to the Equality Bill (2009) notes 'under the Welsh devolution settlement the subject matter of equal opportunities is not devolved to Wales' (it then proceeds, in contradictory fashion, to list additional legislative competencies in the field of equalities to be conveyed to Welsh Ministers). Thus, devolved enactments either contain explicit equality clauses or deal with substantive topics that have a strong bearing on issues of equality, such as mental health services or education (see Figure 6.6). Between July 1999 and May 2007 this legislative dimension was based on executive lawmaking powers previously exercisable by the Secretary of State for Wales. Lambert and Navarro (2007: 15) describe the complexity of this process:

> Such powers were mostly derived from specific ministerial functions set out in over 350 Acts of Parliament. The listed Acts come within some 18 subject areas, but the Secretary of State for Wales was not responsible

for all functions in any subject area. Overall functions in each subject area were the shared responsibility of both the Secretary of State for Wales and a Whitehall-based government department and applied to both England and Wales.

Under this arrangement, the National Assembly has generally gained additional legislative powers on an incremental, case-by-case basis as Westminster Acts set out powers exercisable by the National Assembly or Welsh government (as well as those retained by central government). Notwithstanding the convoluted nature of these arrangements, the amount of 'devolved' secondary legislation for Wales not only increased significantly but, as noted, after July 1999 it also impacted on the notionally 'reserved matter' of equality.

The Special Educational Needs (SEN) Code of Practice for Wales provides an example of this and illustrates the way in which the Assembly uses its secondary legislative powers under Westminster Acts to shape the prevailing legal equalities framework. In relation to state education for those with SEN, after 1999 the National Assembly assumed the powers the Secretary of State for Wales under Section 313 of the Education Act (1996) to issue (and from time to time to amend), a code of practice giving practical guidance in respect of the discharge by local education authorities (LEAs) and governing bodies of maintained schools of their functions under the Act. Following an initial consultation process in 2000 with LEAs, schools and SEN voluntary bodies, a new Code of Practice was approved unanimously by a plenary session of the Assembly and became law in April 2002 under Statutory Instrument No. 156 (W.22), the Special Educational Needs Code of Practice (Wales) Order 2002.[14] The detailed guidance set out in the Code requires education providers to adhere to a range of general principles, including that 'the special educational needs of children will normally be met in mainstream schools or settings' (NAfW, 2000c: 2). A further example is provided by the statutory guidance issued in 2007 by Welsh ministers under the provisions of the Countryside and Rights of Way Act (2000). Thus, in relation to the estimated 33,000 kilometres of public rights of way in Wales, new guidance was issued to local highway and National Park authorities requiring them to have regard to the needs of people with mobility problems 'when authorising the erection of stiles, gates or other works on public footpaths and bridleways'.[15]

Policy Area	Scope of Legal Equality Requirements	Details of Welsh Legislation
Education	Provision of grants to teachers of personal and social education to fulfil curriculum requirements relating to education on equal opportunities	The Special Educational Needs and Disability Tribunal (General Provisions and Disability Claims Procedure) Regulations (2002)
	's3 – (1) Each authority must prepare and publish a Single Education Plan . . . The plan must contain a statement of the overall strategic vision and values that the authority apply in discharging their education responsibilities, having regard to their responsibilities under equality legislation . . .'	The Single Education Plan (Wales) Regulations (2006)
	A new requirement that equal opportunities information must be included in the school prospectuses	The Education (School Information) (Wales) (Amendment) Regulations (2001)
	Greater consideration of maternity leave, ordinary adoption leave (as well as parental leave or paternity leave) in respect of the induction arrangements for school teachers	The Education (Induction Arrangements for School Teachers) (Amendment) (Wales) Regulations (2004)
	Imposition of duties on the National Council for Education and Training for Wales to have due regard to the promotion of equality of opportunity	The Learning and Skills Act (2000) (Commencement No. 2) (Wales) Order (2000)
	'To enable persons to undertake courses of further or higher education designated for the purposes of that Scheme, by providing financial assistance in or towards meeting the cost of books, equipment, travel or childcare incurred in consequence of their attending such a course.'	The Education (Assembly Learning Grant Scheme) (Wales) (Amendment) Regulations (2002)

(continued)

Policy Area	Scope of Legal Equality Requirements	Details of Welsh Legislation
Education (contd)	Places legal duties on governing bodies and head teachers to exercise their respective functions with due regard of the need (a) to eliminate unlawful discrimination on grounds of race or sex; and (b) to promote equal opportunities and good relations, between (i) persons of different racial groups and (ii) males and females	School Government (Terms of Reference) (Wales) Regulations (2000)
Health	Provision of comprehensive cervical screening by contractors to NHS Wales	The National Health Service (General Medical Services Contracts) (Wales) Regulations (2004)
	Greater regulatory protection for women having an abortion	Abortion (Amendment) (Wales) Regulations (2002)
		Private and Voluntary Health Care (Wales) Regulations (2002)
	Enhanced disability premiums in means tests for determining the amount of housing renovation grant and disabled facilities grant	The Housing Renewal Grants (Amendment) (Wales) Regulations (2001)
Local Govt./ Public sector	Section 4. You must – (a) carry out your duties and responsibilities with due regard to the principle that there should be equality of opportunity for all people, regardless of their gender, race, disability, sexual orientation, age or religion	The Local Authorities (Model Code of Conduct) (Wales) Order (2008)
	Amends the procedures regarding settling equal pay claims ('back payments') in local authorities	The Local Authorities (Capital Finance and Accounting) (Wales) (Amendment) Regulations (2007)

(continued)

Policy Area	Scope of Legal Equality Requirements	Details of Welsh Legislation
Local Govt./ Public sector (contd)	Insertion of equality clauses into existing legislation, e.g. Section 20, 'Insert . . . "the Assembly Government remains committed to changing the profile of the workforce in Fire and Rescue Authorities within Wales to reflect the diversity of the communities that Fire and Rescue Authorities serve, and this will be reflected in the Human Resource Strategy currently being developed".'	The Fire and Rescue National Framework (Wales) (2005) (Revisions) Order (2007)
	A new ethical framework for local government and public authorities in Wales – employees of relevant authorities must comply with policies relating to equality issues	The Code of Conduct (Qualifying Local Government Employees) (Wales) Order (2001)
	Incorporating equality as a public sector performance indicator	The Local Government (Best Value Performance Indicators) (Wales) Order (2001)
	The number of domestic violence refuge places per 10,000 population which are provided or supported by the best value authority	The Local Government (Best Value Performance Indicators) (Wales) Order (2001)
Housing	Inter alia, adds to those persons with priority need for accommodation: 'a person fleeing domestic violence or threatened domestic violence – a person without dependant children who has been subject to domestic violence or is at risk of such violence, or if he or she returns home is at risk of domestic violence'.	Homeless Persons (Priority Need) Wales Order (2001)

(continued)

Policy Area	Scope of Legal Equality Requirements	Details of Welsh Legislation
Childcare	'Payment to a member of the authority who is a councillor of an allowance ("care allowance") in respect of such expenses of arranging for the care of children or dependants as are necessarily incurred in the carrying out of that member's duties as a member.'	Local Authorities (Allowances for Members of County and County Borough Councils and National Park Authorities) (Wales) Regulations (2002)
	Duty on local authorities to broaden nursery education and prepare and submit childcare plans to the National Assembly for approval	Education, Wales, The Education (Nursery Education and Early Years Development and Childcare Plans) (Wales) Regulations (2003).

Figure 6.6. Examples of equality clauses in secondary legislation passed by the National Assembly for Wales

A further aspect of the devolved lawmaking arrangements is the significant increase in the number of Acts of the UK parliament that have been concerned solely with matters relating to Wales (hitherto, this was something of a rarity). Recent examples include the Public Services Ombudsman (Wales) Act (2005) and the Commissioner for Older People (Wales) Act (2006). Crucially, some UK Acts of parliament convey 'framework powers' to the Assembly. This means that, on a given topic, rather than apply similar provisions to those relating to England, the devolved legislature may specify singular legal arrangements for Wales. Overall, critics have argued that this somewhat opaque system of lawmaking undermines democratic accountability and is subject to a number of serious shortcomings, including its lack of clarity and the limited opportunities for the Welsh government and National Assembly to influence Bills as they passed through the UK houses of parliament (Sherlock, 2000; Richard Commission, 2004; All Wales Convention, 2009).

Arguably, the Government of Wales Act (2006) has gone some way to addressing the earlier problems. Yet, critics claim that the failure to grant full lawmaking powers to the Assembly has had the effect of compounding the existing shortcomings (see Pratchett, 2005; Richard

Commission, 2006; All Wales Convention, 2009; Chaney, 2009). Still, key features of the present processes are worth noting here because of their potential to shape the promotion of equalities. As noted, one of the main impacts of the second devolution statute has been to create a parliamentary structure for the National Assembly with legal separation of the legislative (National Assembly for Wales) and executive (Welsh Assembly Government) branches of government. Under the new arrangements the functioning of the devolved body is described as 'primarily legislative' (Wales Office, 2005: 56). Welsh ministers (rather than the National Assembly) have generally taken over the powers to make statutory instruments and the National Assembly has gained powers to make primary laws for Wales – known as Measures. The latter are derived from the complex process of Legislative Competence Orders (LCOs). As the 2005 White Paper explains, these:

> Give the Assembly powers, in specified areas of policy, to modify – i.e., amend, repeal or extend – the provisions of Acts of Parliament in their application to Wales, or to make new provision. This power of modification would apply to Acts currently in force and also to any Acts which Parliament might make in the future in the specified areas (unless a particular Act contained a specific prohibition precluding use of the Assembly's modifying powers). (Wales Office, 2005, para. 3.16)

Lambert and Navarro (2007: 14) underline the significance of this change:

> Once the Assembly has an enabling power given to it by an Order in Council [i.e. LCO], it is then master of its own house. The main requirement is that the Measure must come within the provisions of the Order. The making of a Measure by the Assembly will require no prior consent or debate in Parliament. Within the parameters of the Order and without Parliament's further consent, it can make as many of its own laws as it wishes . . . the measure making power raises the National Assembly for Wales to the status of a quasi-parliament.

It should be noted that, under the provisions of the Government of Wales Act (2006), setting the legislative agenda is not the sole preserve of the executive. Under Standing Orders 22.47 and 23.99 *Y Llywydd/* the Presiding Officer holds periodic Legislative Ballots to select an

AM who may submit proposals for legislation either through a Legislative Competence Order or a Measure.[16]

The potential of the new lawmaking arrangements to the promotion of equalities can be seen by reference to the Welsh government's legislative programme for 2008–9, the first full year of the enhanced powers. Each of the five proposed Measures dealt explicitly with an equality-related topic (that is, an issue where there is a recognised need to increase the rights or resource allocation to historically marginalised or discriminated-against groups). Thus, the proposed Measures were in the following areas: child poverty (placing a duty on public agencies to demonstrate their contribution to ending child poverty); additional learning needs (to extend the range of individuals who may appeal to the Special Educational Needs Tribunal for Wales); charging for non-residential social care (to establish a fairer and more consistent approach to charging for specified services levied by local authorities across Wales); better local services (to introduce a Measure for local government, which will require local partners to co-operate in effective and joined-up community planning and service delivery); and affordable housing (the introduction of a Measure giving the power to suspend the 'Right to Buy' under the Housing Act 1980, thereby safeguarding stocks for, inter alia, older people and disabled people). In addition, the Welsh government asserts that 'the 14–19 Learning and Skills (Wales) Measure (2008) sets out to achieve equality of opportunity and experience for 14–19-year-old learners across Wales' (WAG, 2008(33): 25). Importantly, through the use of Measures and secondary legislation, the Welsh government can impose duties, standards and regulations on the devolved public sector in relation to equalities issues. For example, the Improving the Health of Homeless and Specific Vulnerable Groups' Standards 2008–9 issued by the government state that:

> Every Local Health Board and Local Authority should already be analysing and considering how to address the needs of these groups as part of their work on preparing and implementing their Health Social Care and Well-being Strategy and Children and Young People's Plan, in accordance with published Guidance. (WAG, 2008(7): 1)

In addition, ministerial circulars are a further means of formally placing requirements on public sector bodies in respect of equalities issues in areas such as specialist provision for learners with learning

144

difficulties and/or disabilities;[17] student support arrangements in respect of childcare;[18] and national standards for the health and social care of older people.[19] Moreover, remit letters from Welsh ministers to the managers of subordinate public sector bodies, local government and other agencies set out strategic priorities required by government. For example, one such letter to the chair of the Sports Council for Wales states:

> this remit letter sets out your role in relation to . . . [WAG's] strategic agenda including the priorities, key Performance Indicators and outputs that I expect the Sports Council to deliver . . . [there are] four key priority outcomes, and the underpinning priorities of sustainable development, social justice and equality of opportunity.

6.6 Evaluating the Legal Framework Around Equalities in Wales

The legal framework on equalities in Wales is effectively composed of UN treaty obligations and EC directives incorporated into UK law, other Westminster statutes, and laws passed by the National Assembly for Wales. In respect of Westminster statutes, recent developments have led to the most comprehensive set of Great Britain-wide laws yet seen. They prohibit discrimination on the grounds of race (including ethnic and national origins, colour and nationality), sex (including gender reassignment), disability, religion or belief (including lack of religion or belief), sexual orientation, and age. Furthermore, they will be updated by the Equality Act (2010). The Wales-specific part of the framework derives from Wales-only statutes (e.g. the Welsh Language Act, 1993), constitutional law (e.g. GOWA, 2006, s77, the Welsh government's general equality duty), and laws passed by the National Assembly (e.g. Special Educational Needs and Disability Tribunal (General Provisions and Disability Claims Procedure) Regulations (2002)). Prior to May 2007, the latter consisted of secondary legislation. Subsequently, primary legislation (in the form of Measures) covers key equality-related topics such as the Welsh language, additional learning needs, education, and mental health. Significantly, under the provisions of the devolution statute (GOWA, 2006, s76) Regulatory Impact Assessment procedures are required to assess the equality implications of all Wales-only primary legislation (e.g. the Social Care Charges (Wales) Measure (2010)). Such developments underpin moves towards the (re-)emergence of a Welsh jurisdiction and the transition from 'soft' to 'hard' policy instruments around the promotion of gender and other modes of equality in the Welsh context.

Overall, it is clear that the present marks a significant yet transitional phase in the development of equalities law in Wales. 'Transitional' in the sense that in the case of non-devolved matters, as with the rest of Britain, the fragmented set of British-wide equalities statutes are largely being replaced by the Equality Act (2010). In addition, we are witnessing the 'bedding-in' of new post GOWA (2006) lawmaking processes (with the prospect of a forthcoming referendum on full primary lawmaking powers). In terms of evaluating whether these developments mark a positive advancement for achieving equalities outcomes, cautious reading of the evidence suggests that they do. As noted, the equality duties in the devolution statutes and the Assembly's growing legislative powers have led to the development of an increasingly distinctive body of law covering the promotion of equality. With the bulk of the devolved functions of the Welsh government concerned with social policy it is apparent and appropriate that, as devolution matures, there is an increasing emphasis on legislation as a 'hard' policy delivery instrument to decrease the likelihood of an implementation gap. Increasingly, codes of practice, service delivery standards and duties on the public sector are monitored and enforced by Wales-specific inspectorates, commissioners and tribunals (see chapter 5). This marks a key progression from the early years of the Assembly when public policy often contained declaratory statements around the promotion of equality but lacked appropriate legal mechanisms to ensure that they were fully applied. However, with little time elapsed since the provisions of the Government of Wales Act (2006) came into effect, it is too early to assess the full impact that the Assembly's primary law making powers will have on the future promotion of equalities. Nevertheless, it is clear that devolution has an increasingly legislative dimension. This presents an unprecedented opportunity to innovate and use legal instruments to back the promotion of equality in public policy and service delivery.

7

Analysing the Devolved Governments' Public Policy Approaches to the Promotion of Equality

7.0   Introduction
7.1   Promoting Equalities in Public Policy?
    7.1.1   Children, Education, Lifelong Learning and Skills
        – Compulsory Phase Education
        – Further and Higher Education
        – Additional Learning Needs
        – Children and Young People
        – Childcare
        – Asylum Seekers
        – Careers
    7.1.2   Economy and Transport
        – Economic development
        – Transport
        – Work Life Balance
        – Gender Pay Gap
        – Science
    7.1.3   Social Justice and Local Government
        – Child Poverty and Inclusion
        – Strengthening and Regenerating Communities
        – Youth Justice
        – Domestic Abuse
        – - Forced Marriages and Honour Based violence
    7.1.4   Environment, Sustainability and Housing
        – Housing
        – Homelessness and Rough Sleeping
        – Environment and Sustainable Development
        – - Gypsy Travellers

7.0 Introduction

In this chapter attention is focused on developments in equalities
policy since the creation of the National Assembly for Wales. Such a
focus is appropriate for, as Mooney et al. (2008: 483) observe, 'through
critical social policy analysis we can both evaluate and explain the
complex interrelations between devolved governance and the
continuing reproduction of inequalities and social divisions
throughout the UK'. Thus, the following discussion draws principally
upon policy discourse analysis (DeLeon, 1998; Edelmann, 1977,
1988). This is part of a post-empiricist, interpretative approach that
places an emphasis on the language of policy documents in order that
'ideas thus move to the centre of policy evaluation' (Fischer, 2003b:
223). This methodology allows an appreciation of how policymakers
formulate and construct problems; it enables focus on their claims and
rhetoric; it acknowledges that policy documents are complex exercises
in agenda-setting power; and it means that policy issues like equality
of opportunity may be framed in particular forms of language
reflecting the political viewpoints of those in power (Fischer and

Forester, 1993: 5–7). Where available, policy evaluations are also discussed, thereby providing instrumental analysis of the developing equalities agenda.

Necessarily, given the plethora of policies launched by successive governments, what follows is not an exhaustive account of all initiatives spanning the past decade. Rather, the objective of this chapter is to selectively map the aims, language and scope of policies in each Major Expenditure Group (MEG) in the government's budget (WAG, 2008(30): v). Rather than offering a 'strand-based' view (i.e. one with a discrete focus on gender, 'race', disability etc.), and reflecting this book's concern to present an holistic perspective, the chapter is principally organised by policy area. At the end of the chapter, a comparative perspective is provided by analysis of developments in the UK's other devolved polities.

7.1 Promoting Equalities in Public Policy?

Successive Welsh governments have published their strategic policy agendas, overarching documents that set out the framework for detailed policies across the range of devolved competencies. For example, published in 2003, the Welsh Labour administration's 'Wales: A Better Country' asserted that:

> We will promote gender equality, good race relations and race equality and tackle discrimination on grounds of age and disability. We want to see people in public life reflecting the diversity in the population as a whole. (WAG, 2003b: 12)

The most recent example, 'One Wales', the 2007 Welsh Labour-Plaid Cymru coalition government's strategic policy agenda, also asserts the aim of promoting equalities. Under the heading 'A Fair and Just Society' it states:

> Our ambition is a Wales where everyone achieves their full human potential and everyone can live free from poverty, discrimination, fear or abuse . . . Our programme of government involves: promoting equality . . . we recognise that if some individuals and groups are discriminated against arbitrarily, this damages their life chances. We aim to foster cohesive, plural and just communities where people, regardless of

physical ability, gender, sexual orientation, race, creed or language, can feel valued. (WAG, 2007k: 26)

The latter statement clearly signals a broadening of focus in relation to equalities. Overall, such documents are significant for they identify the promotion of equalities as a core overarching theme, a priority to be applied to all policymaking. We now turn to assess the extent to which this is being realised.

7.1.1 Children, Education, Lifelong Learning and Skills

Education policy has a singular and important role in the promotion of equalities (Ahonen, 2002). As Lynch and Lodge (2002: 1) assert, 'formal education plays a foundational role in determining the character of the political, economic and socio-cultural life of any given society . . . it is a key player in legitimating and ordering socio-cultural relations'. This means that policy can challenge pre-existing and contemporaneous social norms that may discriminate, de-legitimise, marginalise and oppress social groups. It can also break the intergenerational transmission of prejudice passed on by socialisation within families and other social structures. In this way education may equip one generation with knowledge to challenge discriminatory or prejudiced views held and deemed acceptable by forebears and peers alike. As Cole (2000: 4) notes, the overall purpose of equal opportunities policies in education is 'to enhance social mobility within structures which are essentially unequal . . . they seek a meritocracy, where people rise or fall on merit'.

Education is one of the key devolved areas of policy making. The total Departmental Expenditure Limit for 2008–9 under the MEG for 'Children, Education, Lifelong Learning and Skills' totalled almost £2 billion, the third largest in the government's budget. Analysts are clear about the impact of devolution on education policy; for Jones (2000: 64), it has resulted in 'an entirely new element in the system of control', whereas Rees (2004: 28) concludes that it 'has led to the emergence of a distinctive regime of educational provision in Wales'.

Compulsory Phase Education

In 2001, the government set out its vision for compulsory-phase education in its ten-year strategy 'The Learning Country' (WAG, 2001a). This stated that policy 'will be actioned with due regard to the Assembly's consistent commitment to . . . promote equality of opportunity' (WAG, 2001a: 8) and outlined plans to 'provide guidance on the scope within the National Curriculum for Wales for promoting equal opportunities'. The latter guidance set out detailed direction on the advancement of equalities in schooling (ACCAC, 2001). However, three years later, a review by the Schools Inspectorate (Estyn, 2004) highlighted mixed progress and the need for a further strengthening of policies. Among its main findings was the fact that 'a minority of schools ha[d] embedded the promotion of race equality and diversity within the ethos, philosophy and day-to-day life of the school'. The successor strategy, 'The Learning Country: Vision into Action' (WAG, 2006h), signalled a notable broadening of the equality aims with, inter alia, references to tackling child poverty and the implementation of an Offender Learning Strategy.

The UK Equalities Review (DLGC, 2007a: 47) called for policies in early years education, 'to prevent the start of a cascade of disadvantage' (see also Phillips, 2007: 2). The phased revision between 2008–11 of the schools curriculum in Wales through the introduction of the Foundation Phase for 3 to 7-year-olds (see Siraj-Blatchford et al., 2007; WAG, 2008(36)) introduces a new approach, one that focuses on experiential learning. Analysis reveals a broadening and deepening of the level of instruction to education providers on the promotion of equalities (see Figure 7.1).

'The Foundation Phase curriculum promotes equality of opportunity and values, and celebrates diversity.' (4)

'Under the United Nations Convention on the Rights of the Child and the Welsh Assembly Government's overarching strategy document Rights to Action, all children and young people must be provided with an education that develops their personality and talents to the full. Settings/schools should develop in every child a sense of personal and cultural identity that is receptive and respectful towards others. Settings/schools should plan across the curriculum to develop the knowledge and understanding, skills, values and attitudes that will enable children to participate in our multi-ethnic society in Wales. Settings/schools should develop approaches that support the ethnic and cultural identities of all children and reflect a range of perspectives, to engage children and prepare them for life as global citizen.' (7)

'The equal opportunities legislation which covers age, disability, gender, race, religion and belief and sexual orientation further places a duty on settings/schools in Wales towards present and prospective children to eliminate discrimination and harassment, to promote positive attitudes and equal opportunities and encourage participation in all areas of setting/school life.' (7)

'The Welsh Assembly Government is committed to developing and promoting the Welsh language. All settings/schools will implement a Welsh language educational programme in the Foundation Phase for children 3 to 7 years.' (12)

'Personal and Social Development, Well-Being and Cultural Diversity – The Foundation Phase supports the cultural identity of all children, to celebrate different cultures and help children recognise and gain a positive awareness of their own and other cultures. Positive attitudes should be developed to enable children to become increasingly aware of, and appreciate the value of, the diversity of cultures and languages that exist in a multicultural Wales.' (15)

'Personal and Social Development, Well-Being and Cultural Diversity: Skills – Social Development. Children should be given opportunities to: develop an awareness of different cultures and the differing needs, views and beliefs of other people in their own and in other cultures. Treat people from all cultural backgrounds in a respectful and tolerant manner. Begin to question stereotyping.' (15)

'Language, Literacy and Communication Skills – They should be helped to develop an awareness of Wales as a country with two languages, and to show positive attitudes to speakers of languages other than Welsh and English.' (19)

'Creative Development – Children should be given opportunities to: experience traditions and celebrations of different cultures.' (40)

Figure 7.1. Examples of the equalities provisions in 'Foundation Phase: Framework for Children's Learning for 3 to 7-year-olds in Wales' (WAG, 2008(24))

In terms of secondary education, existing studies point to pivotal role of the schools curriculum in challenging prejudice and promoting equality (Riddell, 1992; Osler, 2000; Dunkwu, 2001). Here, major change is also ongoing with the introduction (between late 2008 and 2010) of a revised National Curriculum for 11 to 19-year-olds. For all subjects the legally binding Curriculum Orders specify the skills, programme of study and outcomes to be adhered to by education providers, the following statement prefaces each:

> The equal opportunities legislation which covers age, disability, gender, race, religion and belief and sexual orientation further places a duty on schools in Wales towards present and prospective learners to eliminate discrimination and harassment, to promote positive attitudes and equal opportunities and encourage participation in all areas of school life . . . (WAG, 2008(9): 3)

Analysis of the new curriculum reveals that the policy discourse is one of promoting pupils' understanding of diversity, tolerance and, challenging prejudice, racism and stereotyping (see Figure 7.2).

Art and design	'In art and design, learners explore and express their ideas and feelings concerning personal, social, environmental, moral and spiritual issues through their creative activities. Through art and design activities they become aware of other cultures and ways of life, and develop the concept of global citizenship' (8)
Welsh	'Welsh contributes to learners' personal and social education by developing their awareness of the role and differing contributions of minority and global languages within society. By developing their appreciation of two cultures, they are better able to appreciate other cultures, and be sympathetic to them.' (8)
Geography	'In geography, learners have opportunities to study their role as local and global citizens and appreciate the diversity of communities in Wales and other countries . . . They learn to use information about places and peoples to counter stereotyping, make well-informed judgements about issues, develop their own views and opinions, and appreciate the values and attitudes of others.' (9)
English	'Pupils should be given opportunities to develop their oral skills through: increasing their confidence in language use by drawing on their knowledge of English, Welsh and other languages.' (12)

(continued)

English (contd)	'Pupils should be given opportunities to develop their reading/viewing skills through reading/viewing extracts and complete texts: that reflect the diversity of society in the twenty-first century . . . [and] texts with a Welsh dimension and texts from other cultures.' (13)
Music	In music, learners perform and listen to the music of Wales, from the past and present. This includes music from the classical tradition, folk and popular music, and other traditions and cultures, which represent the communities of Wales. Music also contributes to learners' spiritual and emotional development, and promotes awareness and valuing of their own and other cultures.' (8)
	'[study] . . . should link with and extend pupils' musical experiences and include examples taken from the European 'classical' tradition, folk and popular music, the music of Wales, and other musical traditions and cultures.' (13)
History	'History contributes to learners' personal and social education by developing their skills of enquiry and critical thinking; their understanding of different views and interpretations of people and events; and of the way in which people have affected their environment in the past. It gives learners an historical context in which to set their lives.' (8)
	'PSE prepares learners to be personally and socially effective by providing learning experiences in which they can develop and apply skills, explore personal attitudes and values, and acquire appropriate knowledge and understanding. Specifically the aims of PSE are to . . . promote self-respect, respect for others and celebrate diversity. . .' (4)
Personal and Social Education	'Learners should explore their rights in a democratic society as underpinned by the United Nations Convention on the Rights of the Child. They have a right to be involved in making decisions, and planning and reviewing any actions that might affect them.' (11)
	'Positive attitudes should be developed to enable children to become increasingly aware of, and appreciate the value of, the diversity of cultures and languages that exist in a multicultural Wales.' (16)
	'Learners should be given opportunities to understand: their rights, e.g. the UN Convention on the Rights of the Child, and responsibilities how injustice and inequality affect people's lives • what is meant by disability • the challenges learners might have in accessing learning opportunities in school' (11)

(continued)

Personal and Social Education (contd)	'Learners should be given opportunities to understand how to recognise and challenge effectively expressions of prejudice, racism and stereotyping . . . [and] how to challenge assertively expressions of prejudice, racism and stereotyping.' (20–2)

Figure 7.2. Examples of the equalities provisions in the Revised National Curriculum Orders by Subject Area – to be implemented 2008–10[1]

In addition, the 'School Effectiveness Framework: Building effective learning communities together' (WAG, 2008(14): 7; see also WAG, 2008(24)), places new requirements on education providers and restates 'the government's commitment to promoting equality of opportunity . . . and [ensuring] that children and young people are listened to, treated with respect, and are able to have their race and cultural identity recognised' (WAG, 2008(22): 14).

In terms of gender equality in education, Delamont (1980: 3) highlights the way that 'schools develop and reinforce sex segregation, stereotypes and even discriminations which exaggerate the negative aspects of sex roles in the outside world, when they could be trying to alleviate them'. As noted in chapter 3, gender segregation in subject choice is a feature of both compulsory and post-compulsory education in Wales and beyond (Francis, 2000; Whitehead, 1996). It is an issue that was targeted by policymakers shortly after the Assembly was founded. Almost a decade on, the government has re-emphasised that these early policies 'still provide relevant guidance for schools' (WAG, 2008(22): 27).

A growing literature (cf. Cole and Virdee, 2006; Gillborn, 2005; Tomlinson, 2008) attests to what Crozier (2005: 585) refers to as 'young people of African Caribbean and mixed 'race' backgrounds' cumulative negative experiences . . . [and] academic underachievement', such that they 'become demotivated to learn by a system that they feel has rejected them, or imposed exclusion' (see also, Bhattacharyya et al., 2004; and Wright et al., 2004). Addressing this issue, the government's core education policy (WAG, 2006h: 6) sets out the aim of 'deliver[ing] a strategy for ethnic minority achievement that ensures the needs of all ethnic minority groups, including Gypsies and Travellers, refugee children and asylum seekers are met more effectively'. This has resulted in the Minority Ethnic Achievement Grant (WAG, 2003c) that provides additional funding to local education authorities for pupils from 3 to 18 years for teaching English or Welsh as an additional language; extra teaching and support; teacher training initiatives and, classroom aids.

Further and Higher Education

The transition phase as pupils begin to consider their options after compulsory education is also an area where there is evidence that the promotion of equalities has begun to be addressed. For example, Learning Pathways is a policy designed to promote 'the need for a more flexible and balanced approach to the education of 14 to 19-year-olds, providing a wider range of experiences which will suit the diverse needs of Wales's young people'.[2] It has legislative force via the Learning and Skills (Wales) Measure (2009) and its aim is to increase the proportion of 16-year-olds progressing to further learning in education and training, and to realise the goal of '95 per cent of young people by the age of 25 to be ready for high skilled employment or higher education by 2015'. The Pathways are intended to offer a programme of study tailored to individual needs, a key element of which is the assignment of a Learning Coach to each pupil to give personal support, careers advice and guidance. The remit of the coach includes responsibility 'to ensure that all individual learners have equality of opportunity; to be aware of the additional needs of ethnic minority individual learners in relation to language and equal opportunities and those needing additional support; and to be aware of the need to avoid stereotyping' (NAfW, 2004b). If effectively implemented, such a targeted approach to individual needs offers the potential to address gender stereotyping in career and further education subject choices, as well as advancing the education of groups with traditionally low levels of engagement and attainment in post-16 education.

Devolution has also seen the development of policies to promote equalities in higher education. These have stemmed from the government's strategy 'Reaching Higher' (WAG, 2002a: 5), which asserted that 'we want a sector that takes its rightful place in the delivery of the Assembly's wider priorities and principles, including those of sustainability, social inclusion, equal opportunities and the development of bilingualism'. Notably, it sets out a number of equality targets, including 'the proportion of young people with a disability attending HE to match the proportion of those in Wales with a disability by 2010'. 2007/8 figures suggest that with 8.3 per cent of disabled students in Welsh HEIs (compared with 7.8 per cent of the population in receipt of Disability Living Allowance), on this measure at least, the target has been met (HEFCW, 2008). Subsequent policy development has resulted in the introduction of further targets. For example, 'the proportion of Welsh domiciled students in Welsh HEIs undertaking some element of their courses through the medium of Welsh to increase to 7 per cent by 2010' (WAG, 2006h: 25). At 5.4 per cent, or 3,977 individuals, the latest available figures for 2007/8 indicate that it is uncertain whether this will be achieved.[3]

Since 2006, university tuition fees have varied between UK countries. The Independent Study into the Devolution of the Student Support System and Tuition Fee Regime in Wales (2005) underlined the need for equality considerations to be mainstreamed into student support measures. These have been introduced through the government agency, Student Finance Wales. In particular, Special Support Grants provide funding for assistance with the costs of registered or accredited childcare during term time and short vacations, and the Parents' Learning Allowance contributes to the support of dependants in a learner's household (Student Finance Wales and WAG, 2007). Against the background of the government's ongoing review of fees, its 2009 '21st Century Higher Education Strategy and Plan for Wales – For Our Future', reasserts the need to 'ensure improved accountability for the measures funded from fee income that promote equality of opportunity' (WAG, 2009: 19).

As noted, major challenges remain in relation to language equality in higher education. The current policy solution set out in the 'One Wales' government policy agenda is to establish a Welsh-medium higher education network, *Y Coleg Ffederal* (The Federal College), 'in order to ensure Welsh-medium provision in our Universities' (WAG, 2007k). Ministerial agreement to funding the Federal College was announced in late 2009. According to a preliminary report, the new college will

> Be a new and independent legal entity with a Constitution . . . It will not be a single geographical entity and it will not be a degree awarding body in its own right, but will work with and through the existing higher education institutions in Wales (the Federal concept). Its Mission will be to maintain, develop and oversee Welsh medium provision in higher education in Wales . . . it will create appropriate conditions for promoting

and expanding Welsh medium scholarship in a wide range of disciplines. (Williams, 2009: 6)

In the wake of the Leitch Review into the UK's long-term skills needs (H. M. Treasury, 2006), further education in Wales continues to be the subject of ongoing review and policy development. Among the stated 'guiding principles' underpinning the government's 'Skills That Work for Wales' (WAG, 2008(22)) are equality of opportunity and Welsh language skills. This policy is indicative of a more sophisticated approach to the promotion of equality in government policy, not least through its use of equality impact assessment techniques (WAG, 2008(22): 9–10).

Special Educational Needs (– Additional Learning Needs)
Special Educational Needs are defined in the following terms:

> Children have special educational needs if they have a learning difficulty, which calls for special educational provision to be made for them.
> Children have a learning difficulty if they:
> (a) Have a significantly greater difficulty in learning than the majority of children of the same age; or
> (b) Have a disability which prevents or hinders them from making use of educational facilities of a kind generally provided for children of the same age in schools within the area of the local education authority
> (c) Are under compulsory school age and fall within the definition at (a) or (b) above or would so do if special educational provision was not made for them.[4]

The SEN Code of Practice for Wales (NAfW, 2002) provides advice to LEAs, maintained schools and others bodies on how to meet their statutory duties to identify, assess and make provision for children's SEN. It is comprehensive and founded on a number of core principles including that 'special educational needs should normally be met in mainstream early years settings, or schools' (NAfW, 2002: 6). The state education inspectorate's reports give an insight into the effectiveness of SEN policy. It concluded that 'most children and young people with special educational needs [were] receiving good provision and achieving good standards in learning and behaviour in mainstream and special schools . . . [and that] effective support [was] provided for pupils with severe and complex needs and disabilities'. However, it also highlighted some shortcomings including that 'most local authorities: do not monitor the quality of provision well enough for those pupils educated in other authorities or in independent special schools' (Estyn, 2007b: 15).

Following a three-part review of Additional Learning Needs (ALN) undertaken by the Assembly's Education, Lifelong Learning and Skills Committee (NAfW, 2007a), future policy is likely to become more distinctive compared with that applying elsewhere in the UK. Through the Additional Learning Needs Legislative Competence Order (LCO) (2008) the Assembly has secured the powers to pass primary legislation in this field. In recent years the government has committed itself to producing 'an action plan in response to the recommendations of the Assembly Education, Lifelong Learning and Skills Committee Review of SEN'.[5] In the meantime, the Committee's recommendations indicate the possible nature of future policy. For example, they include a call for 'new statutory assessment arrangements based on a continuously assessed record of need' (NAfW, 2006: 16–22). In addition, late 2009 saw primary legislation proposed in the Assembly to give greater rights in the workplace for adults with ALN.

In the wake of devolution new measures have also been implemented to ensure that equality of opportunity is addressed in teacher training programmes. The literature of the General Teaching Council for Wales outlines how this should be achieved (GTCW, 2006a, 2006b, 2007). This is complemented by the statutory inspection arrangements covering teacher training courses that require inspectors to assess 'how well the training promotes equal opportunities' (Estyn, 2004: 28).

Overall, there is mixed evidence in terms of the effectiveness of the policy framework around equalities in education. An international comparative study of compulsory phase education concluded that Welsh policies had seen 'progress across the board in children and young people's achievement. However, in relation to the age, ability, gender and socio-economic circumstances of children and young people, this progress is uneven and needs to be advanced further'.[6] Reviewing schools' compliance with the Disability Discrimination Act, the education inspectorate found that 'very few local authorities have developed effective partnerships between mainstream schools and special schools to support and develop the curriculum and teaching . . .' (Estyn, 2007: 2). In an earlier report, the inspectorate also found that 'many head teachers show a high level of commitment to meeting the needs of ethnic minority pupils' (WAG, 3003f). Yet, a government-commissioned independent study highlighted the fact that 'future . . . policies will need to be more specific in articulating diversity issues . . . [and] should refer explicitly to removing barriers faced by people with disabilities, minority ethnic people, gender, sexual orientation and religion or belief, in order to demonstrate the promotion of equality', and that 'the use of equality and diversity baseline data is essential to measuring the effectiveness of policy strategies and action plans' (NAfW, 2007b: 7).

Children and Young People

The government's commitment to applying the United Nations Convention on the Rights of the Child (UNCRC) was set out in 'Children and Young People: Rights into Action' (WAG, 2004a); it also articulated the aim of 'valuing diversity and promoting equality of opportunity' (WAG, 2004a: 15). A raft of policy measures has emerged that link to these aims, including those promoting the participation of children and young people in public decision-making (see Figure 7.3) (WAG, 2004a: 33). For example, at a national level, 'Funky Dragon' (the Children and Young People's Assembly)[7] has been developed to give children and young people the opportunity participate in decision making and meet with government ministers. Whilst at the local level, the Assembly has passed legislation creating Children and Young People's Partnerships in each local authority area. School councils are a further development in the 'participation agenda' designed to involve pupils in the day-to-day running of all schools (including the development of school policies).

Policy	Details
Funky Dragon, the Children and Young People's Assembly for Wales	'Funky Dragon's main tasks are to make sure that the views of children and young people are heard, particularly by the Welsh Assembly Government, and to support participation in decision-making at national level.'[8]
The Children and Young People's Participation Consortium for Wales and the Participation Unit	'The Participation Consortium is a multi-agency strategic body. It is working at a national level to develop capacity and practice in terms of the participation of children and young people (0–25 years) in decision-making in Wales.'[9]

(continued)

Policy	Details
Youth forum	Examples: The Welsh Youth Forum on Sustainable Development[10] and the Minority Ethnic Youth Forum ('objective is to bridge the gaps in engagement between the Assembly Government and minority ethnic young people').[11] In addition there are 22 local youth forums, one in each local authority area ('peer-led representative groups of children and young people').[12]
Participation in the children and young people's voluntary sector	The Third Sector Partnership Council (TSPC) is a body that maintains regular dialogue between the voluntary sector and the Welsh government. Two dedicated networks on the VSPC represent children and youth organisations respectively.
Statutory requirement for schools councils in all primary, secondary and special schools	'Commitment to ensuring that all children and young people can contribute to decisions that affect them . . . WAG has introduced a statutory requirement that all primary, secondary and special schools in Wales have a school council . . . Wales is the only country in the UK where such legislation is currently in place.'[13]
Statutory requirement for associate pupil governors in schools	*Associate Pupil Governors* 7.(1) The head teacher of a school must ensure that the school council has the opportunity to nominate up to two pupils from years 11 to 13 (inclusive) from its membership to be associate pupil governors on the school's governing body. Established under The School Councils (Wales) Regulations 2005, No. 3200 (W.236).[14]
Young people's plans – statutory guidance (2007) on partnership, local cooperation and lead roles	Places legal duty on local authorities and their partners to prepare 3-year strategic Children and Young People's Plans.[15] Statutory guidance requires that children and young people participate in the work of the Children and Young People's Partnership.[16] Established under The Children and Young People's Plan (Wales) Regulations 2007, No. 2316 (W.187).

Figure 7.3. Examples of Welsh government policies to promote children and young people's participation in public decision-making.[17]

In terms of social services for children, government policy requires that each local authority be evaluated against set service delivery targets. The latter include advocacy and complaints; integrated children's systems; children with disabilities; looked after children;

161

and care leavers.[18] Writing in the first years of devolved governance, Williams (2003: 252, op. cit.) highlighted that 'the key challenge is to meet the gap between the admirable principles and aspirations of the Welsh Assembly Government and the reality for children and young people at local level'. She emphasised a number of issues that continue to resonate today, including the fact that the funding given to local government for children's services is not always hypothecated, and that there are 'few apparent sanctions for failure to use the money appropriately'.

Action on child poverty is the shared responsibility of the UK and Welsh governments. Research has highlighted that:

> The proportion of children in Wales living in low-income households is now the same as the average for Britain as a whole. A decade ago, by contrast, the child poverty rate in Wales was well above average. However, despite this progress, one in every four children in Wales still lives in a low-income household. (Kenway et al., 2005)

The government's Child Poverty Strategy was launched in 2005[19] (with the accompanying Implementation Plan published in 2006). The overarching policy aim is to eradicate child poverty by 2020. From an equalities perspective, the Implementation Plan is an example of good practice in that it sets out targets and policy outcomes to be achieved alongside implementation methods.[20] Assessing these developments, one independent study concluded that 'the Assembly Government's actions to tackle child poverty are laudable in many ways' (Save the Children et al., 2008: 11). Adamson (2008: 64) broadly concurs with this, yet offers a note of caution: 'their eventual success will depend on the long-term determination of government and a commitment to heavy expenditure . . . Whether such policies can survive the inevitable political cycle . . . remains to be seen'. Recent research (McCormick and Harrop, 2010) affirms this point and raises questions about the rate of progress achieved thus far.

Childcare

As Rees (2000: 186) observes, 'childcare, [is] so often a neglected feature of regional economic development'. Following devolution, the government's approach to this issue has primarily been driven by a concern with child poverty and there is some emerging evidence of positive policy outcomes. In 2004, in the wake of its Childcare Action

Plan (WAG, 2002g), the government formed a Childcare Working Group, tasked with implementing the plan. A subsequent report by the Group included a series of recommendations some of which were adopted in the Childcare Strategy for Wales (WAG, 2005a: 5). Included in the latter was the provision of free part-time childcare places for all 2 and 3-year-olds, and measures to address the childcare needs of Welsh-speaking children and ethnic-minority communities. As a result, '19 specific and timed actions on meeting the needs of disabled children . . . Welsh-speaking children and ethnic-minority communities' were introduced (NAfW, 2007c: 8). However, further progress is needed in implementing the Strategy, including measures to address ongoing shortages in Welsh-medium and bilingual childcare provision (NAfW, 2007d). Critics also point to the need to expand state childcare provision in Wales for 'the majority of care provision is . . . left to the private and voluntary sector' (Bevan Foundation, 2005: 8). A further fundamental issue, one that policy interventions have generally failed to address, is the fact that the domestic division of unpaid work, including childcare, has remained relatively unchanged (see Gershuny, 2000; Lewis, 2006). Thus, Rees's (1999: 85) assessment of the pre-devolution situation holds true for today: 'after twenty years of equality legislation and dramatic industrial restructuring, more women have taken up paid work but they appear still to have the majority responsibility for domestic work and childcare'.

Asylum Seekers and Refugees

Analysis of existing welfare policies (Griffiths et al., 2006: 881) illustrate how 'far from promoting the integration of refugees . . . [such] frameworks may rather perpetuate a condition of institutionalised marginality for refugee groups'. In a similar vein, Squire (2008) also charts 'the development of restrictive asylum policy since New Labour came into power in 1997'. Notwithstanding this, there is some evidence that post-devolution policies have taken a slightly different trajectory (WAG, 2004b). For example, an early initiative to support asylum seekers was the decision taken by the Assembly in 2000 to use its powers (under the Local Government Finance Act, 1988, s88)[21] to extend grant eligibility to individuals seeking asylum (NAfW, 2000a). Subsequently, in 2006, the government published its Refugee Housing Action Plan (WAG, 2006a). Its objectives included raising awareness of refugee housing and support needs, and developing an effective response to language and communication barriers (WAG, 2006a: 84). In response to a 'One Wales' commitment (WAG, 2007k: 12), the government has published its Refugee Inclusion Strategy (WAG, 2008(34)). Citing its general equality duty (GOWA, 2006, s77) it 'aims to foster cohesive, plural and just communities where people, regardless of physical ability, gender, sexual orientation, race, creed or language, can feel valued' (WAG, 2008(34): 69). It is a notable document in a number of respects, not least for its use of the language of mainstreaming equalities (e.g. 'we will mainstream refugee inclusion across the work of the Welsh Assembly Government', WAG, 2008(34): 70). Overall, these policy developments signal a welcome use of equalities legislation to coordinate services for asylum seekers. Future outcomes will depend on detailed policy development in the wake of the Refugee Inclusion Strategy, such as measurable targets and effective monitoring.

Careers

As Esping-Andersen et al. (2002) highlight, tackling gender segregation in the labour market is a key challenge for social policy makers. The official remit of the government-funded body Careers Wales acknowledges this fact. It states that services should be 'designed to meet individual needs regardless of race, gender, marital status, age, disability, beliefs, sexual orientation, social or economic background'.[22] According to the organisation, 'equal opportunities is central to all guidance activities and all Careers Wales advisers are trained to challenge any inequality and stereotypical views' (Careers Wales, 2006: 4). Nevertheless, the agency asserts that:

> Although Careers Wales is making strides in tackling gender stereotyping in the workplace, the issue is the result of a multitude of lifelong socio-cultural influences. We will continue to work closely with key partner organisations . . . to share best practice and develop positive approaches to tacking inequality.[23]

Assessing these developments, the Welsh state education inspectorate offered a positive appraisal. It highlighted the role of political will and leadership in the promotion of equalities and observed that:

> Careers Wales has developed policies to challenge gender perceptions of career choice . . . there are examples of good practice in each of the

Careers Wales companies . . . [involving] setting challenging targets and putting robust monitoring and reporting processes in place to take forward equality and diversity, including gender stereotyping'. (Estyn, 2007a: 5)

7.1.2 Economy and Transport

Economic development and transport are 'devolved' issues with a combined annual spending allocation of £1.2 billion per annum. However, key parts of these portfolios are shared with other tiers of government.

Economic development
An international comparative study of over one hundred economies by Morrison et al. (2007: 32) highlights the 'business case' for equalities. They conclude that 'economic growth appears to be positively correlated with gender equality'. In like fashion, the Equalities Review (DLGC, 2007a: 20) asserted that 'removing barriers to women working in occupations traditionally done by men, and increasing women's participation in the labour market, would be worth between £15 billion and £23 billion: equivalent to 1.3 to 2.0 per cent of Gross Domestic Product (GDP)'. Against this background, equality of opportunity was one of the crosscutting themes of the multi-billion pound European Structural Fund economic aid programmes in Wales 2000–6 administered by an executive agency of the Welsh government. The policy document that set out the targets for the 'Objective One' programme stated that 'gender is a major cause of inequality of opportunity . . . and the labour market is characterised by horizontal, vertical and contractual segregation. A key to addressing this issue is to pursue gender mainstreaming in projects' (WEFO, 1999: 5). In accordance with EC Directives, the strategy document also made detailed provisions for 'race' and disability equality. The Welsh language was another of the crosscutting themes. The Single Programme Document that set out the detail of the policy was notable for the way in which it published targets and outcomes in relation to equalities. While some observers question the economic impact of the programme (e.g. Boland, 2004) formal evaluations have generally given it a positive assessment in terms of equalities outcomes. For example:

- *Objective 1 target 30 per cent of start up Small Medium Sized Enterprises (SMEs) assisted to be owned by women.* 'Some indication of progress in this area can be obtained from wider labour market data. For the Objective 1 region in 1999/2000, 32.7 per cent of the self-employed were female; this had risen to 34.4 per cent in 2003/4. As a comparator, the all-Wales measure had a larger increase from 32.3 per cent in 1999/2000 to 36 per cent in 2003/4.'

- *Objective 1 target 50 per cent of higher level training places to be taken up by women.* 'Enrolments in Higher Education Institutions (HEIs) in Wales (undergraduates and postgraduates) in 1998/9 included 51,890 women (52.8 per cent), which in 2002/3 had risen to 65,576 women (56.1 per cent). This represents an increase of 26.4 per cent of women across Wales.'

- *Objective 1 target to increase female participation rates in the labour market to 70 per cent.* 'The Economic Activity Rate of the Working Age Population of women in the Objective 1 area in 1999/2000 was 67.1 per cent; in 2004/5 this had risen to 71.1 per cent.' (ECOTEC, 2006: 34–56)

In contrast to the EC aid programme, launched in 2002, the Welsh government's economic development strategy adopted the more familiar declaratory approach to equalities. Limited details were provided in the Strategy document in respect of policy targets or implementation (WAG, 2002d). In like fashion, the Entrepreneurship Action Plan For Wales (WDA, 2000: 34) and Action Plan for Innovation (WAG, 2002e) also make generalised reference to equalities. Little improvement was evident in the subsequent economic strategy, 'Wales: A Vibrant Economy' (WAG, 2005d, 2006c).

New European Structural Funds (or 'Convergence Funds') are providing further economic aid over the period 2007–13. Under these arrangements, the government is responsible for allocating assistance amounting to a total of £3.2 billion. The overall strategy document, or Operational Programme, identifies equality as one of its four main priorities (WEFO, 2007: iv). Accordingly, a detailed series of equality indicators relate to 'training and targeted interventions for previously excluded groups, particularly Black and Minority Ethnic people and disabled people . . . and, activities to challenge gender stereotyping, support women . . . into non-traditional areas of work, and encourage work life balance' (WEFO, 2007: 91).

Overall, as a recent review concluded, there are some positive aspects attached to economic policy in the wake of devolution: 'at a high level . . . [there is evidence of] coherent commitment to equality and recognition of the mutual interdependencies between economic performance/growth and participation/social justice issues' (NAfW, 2007: 31). However, with the exception of European aid policy documents, there has been a worrying dearth of equalities indicators and analysis about how different equality strands will be affected by the various policy initiatives. Moreover, equalities targets are seldom articulated in full.

Transport
Contemporary research highlights the wide range of equalities issues that apply to transport policy. For example, gendered aspects of daily mobility and associated social risks (Camarero and Oliva, 2008; Greed, 2006: 267); meeting the needs of older people (Fiorio and Percoco, 2007); and applying the social model of disability to deliver socially inclusive transport (Aldred and Woodcock, 2008; Falkmer, 2001; Marin-Lamellet et al., 2000). There is evidence that devolved transport policy has begun to acknowledge some of these issues. Thus, the cross-party Assembly Environment, Planning and Transport Committee's Policy Review of Public Transport asserted that it 'should also act as a positive lever in improving equality of opportunity for all . . . [including] significantly improved levels of accessibility for disabled people' (NAfW, 2001c: 6). Subsequently, the promotion of equalities was identified as a priority by the 2000–3 Welsh Labour-Liberal Democrat coalition government's 'Transport Framework for Wales' (NAfW, 2001d). Whilst, as noted, aspects of transport policy are shared with Westminster, the government's powers have been enhanced significantly by the Transport (Wales) Act (2006) and the Railways Act (2005). Both have contributed to what Cole (2007: 195) refers to as 'a radical change process in the governance of transport'. The latest key policy development, 'Connecting the Nation: The Wales Transport Strategy' (WAG, 2008(18): 59) 'sets out the long-term outcomes for transport in Wales [based on] strategic priorities . . . [that] will provide the focus for the national and regional plans which will follow'. It is notable for its espousal of an holistic approach to equalities and refers to 'mainstreaming the commitment to equality' as a strategic priority (WAG, 2008(18): 33). Reflecting on such developments, Bradbury and Stafford (2008: 82) refer to 'a

fundamental distinctiveness of the Welsh approach to transport policy'. Yet, whilst the Transport Strategy embeds the promotion of equalities as one of its core objectives and, encouragingly, articulates this using the language of mainstreaming, it remains to be seen whether subsequent policy development will apply equalities indicators, targets and appropriate monitoring mechanisms to secure equalities outcomes.

Work-Life Balance

The social welfare policies of the twentieth century were largely based on the male breadwinner model (Lewis, 1992, 2006). However, as Gershuny (2000) outlines, in all developed economies there has been a major shift with women entering the labour market in unprecedented numbers. Wales is no exception. In 1971, just a third of women of working age were economically active; by 2006 their economic activity rate was 71 per cent (the figure for men remained broadly constant over the same period, at approximately 80 per cent) (EOC, 2006: 7). However, on some measures, gender inequality has been deepened by this transformation in women's employment profile for it has not been matched by a commensurate increase in men's household or domestic work, including caring for children. As Lewis and Campbell (2008: 524) explain, prior to 1997, 'the UK trailed the rest of Western Europe with regard to policies to help individuals balance employment and family care responsibilities . . . [However] since the election of the Labour Government in 1997, the issue of 'work and family' has received considerable attention from several government departments'. Examples of such policies include the right to request flexible working, the extension of paid maternity and paternity leave, and the introduction of the childcare element in Working Tax Credits. The fact that benefits and taxation are matters reserved to Westminster limits devolved government's scope to promote work-life balance in employment practices. Yet, it has undertaken partnership working to reform the practices of public sector bodies and private businesses. Starting in 2002, the government and *Chwarae Teg* (a 'professional agency for the economic development of women in Wales')[24] launched the 'Work Life Balance in Wales' initiative with the aim of encouraging public sector organisations and small and medium sized enterprises (SMEs) to introduce flexible working practices (Chwarae Teg, 2007). According to *Chwarae Teg* (2007: 2), '31,551 employees at all levels now have access to work-life balance initiatives across 10 public sector organisations. *Chwarae Teg* has trained 150 public sector managers in how to successfully manage a flexible work force, and 55 SMEs (1,670 employees) in total have been directly supported in adopting smarter working practices'. Notwithstanding this progress, there is considerable scope for expanding policies in the public sector (which currently employs 23.7 per cent of the working population in Wales).[25]

Gender Pay Gap

Reviewing contemporary evidence relating to the gender pay gap in the UK, Mumford and Smith (2007: 653) highlight 'that stronger enforcement of equal pay legislation is likely to be the most appropriate policy response'. Whilst the Welsh government does not have an enforcement role, from the outset of devolution it worked closely with the regulatory body, the (former) Equal Opportunities Commission (EOC) Wales. Initial attention was placed upon the Assembly's own pay practices; its equal pay audit was cited as best practice by the EOC. Following this, the policy focus was broadened and a three phase Close The Pay Gap Campaign was launched in 2001. Government, EOC Wales and the Wales Trades Unions Congress undertook it jointly. Its primary objective was to tackle discrimination in pay systems, raise awareness of the pay gap and secure commitments from employers to undertake pay reviews (NAfW, 2005a). An interim evaluation concluded that, as a result of the Campaign, 'a significant number of employers, mainly based in the public sector, are planning or have carried out equal pay reviews and [it has] led trades unions in Wales to place a renewed focus on discrimination in pay systems' (Chaney, 2004: 106). Whilst noting further progress, an independent evaluation of the latest phase of the campaign concluded that 'the issue of financial support to assist in settlements/back pay will be an important question for the next phase of the campaign and for the Assembly Government . . . there is considerable work still to be done' (Fitzgerald, 2007: 9). One weakness of the policies adopted to date is their limited impact upon the private sector.

Science

The under-representation of women in science, technology, engineering and mathematics careers (SET) is a phenomenon that exists in most industrialised countries around the world. Causal factors include the dearth of female scientists and engineers as role models; the pedagogy of science classes (which, research suggests, favours male students); cultural pressure on girls and women to conform to traditional gender roles; and an inherent masculine worldview in scientific epistemology (Blickenstaff, 2005: 371). Against this background, 'A Science Policy for Wales' (WAG, 2007q: 24) states that:

> It is well-documented that there are proportionately too few women entering careers in many aspects of SET, the Welsh Assembly Government has provided funding and support for some time to Women Into Science and Engineering (WISE) in Wales. We will continue that support.[26]

The latter organisation describes its aim as being 'to promote science and engineering as a suitable career among girls and women, helping them to progress in their careers and ensuring their retention in the profession'.[27] In addition, 'A Science Policy for Wales' details work done by Careers Wales in supporting 'activities run as part of the teacher training programme and adult guidance', and providing 'taster programmes for women who are interested in opportunities in science engineering and technology' (WAG, 2007q: 56). At present, the percentage of professional women engineers in Wales totals just 5 per cent.[28] The scale of this gender segregation suggests the need for policy interventions across the school curriculum, teacher training, careers advice and through positive action policies such as WISE. Key challenges for future success include the extent to which they are adequately resourced, coordinated, supported over the medium to long-term and monitored in an effective manner.

7.1.3 Social Justice and Local Government

Strengthening and Regenerating Communities

The Equalities Review (DLGC, 2007a) highlighted that 'the links between equality and social cohesion are well documented. Violence, conflict, insecurity and political instability are all more likely to occur in more unequal societies' (DLGC, 2007a: 21). Such concerns resonate with Communities First (WAG, 2007j; WAG, 2007m), a predominantly area- based policy programme to regenerate the most disadvantaged communities in Wales. Additional 'projects of special interest' are also included in the programme, some of which relate to equalities issues (e.g. those targeting disabled people, victims of domestic violence and minority ethnic groups) (WAG, 2007m: 3). Listed among Communities

First's key principles is 'the promotion of a culture in which diversity is valued and equality of opportunity is a reality' (WAG, 2007m: 1). The programme aims to achieve a range of goals in the areas covered by the scheme, including to ensure public services are delivered in ways that are more responsive and more locally accountable, and to encourage active citizenship. A number of national organisations have been funded to help support Communities First Partnerships in 'mainstreaming equality, diversity and human rights issues and engag[ing] with excluded groups'.[29] A systematic review of the programme (WAG, 2006e) identified the need for further support to achieve the desired equality outcomes. Notably, it concluded that 'we have not come across much evidence of the involvement of physically or mentally disabled people on partnerships as representatives' (WAG, 2006e: 50). In response, direct funding was allocated to each Communities First Partnership from 2008/9 onwards in order that they could determine ways in which to mainstream equalities into local action plans (WAG, 2007j: 145).

The aim of promoting equality is also set out in the planning and community development policy, 'Local Vision: Statutory Guidance from the Welsh Assembly Government on Developing and Delivering Community Strategies' (WAG, 2008(9), 2008(19)). This instructs local authorities and organisations engaged in the community planning process to 'ensure that all communities are able to participate on an equal basis, by taking account of their different needs and interests' (WAG, 2008(19): 4). As with Communities First, the policy guidance allows local partnerships to determine local priorities within a national framework. It is a further example of equalities policies being backed in law, in this case by Wales-only regulations that are binding on local authorities (WAG, 2007j). Both Communities First and Local Vision clearly link to the government's strategic crosscutting equalities agenda. However, a key issue in both cases is the need for ongoing and effective monitoring of equalities outcomes.

Youth Justice

Youth justice is an area where inequalities persist. For example, the Youth Justice Board's research into the treatment of young people from an ethnic minority background in the criminal justice system reveals that 'the chances of a case involving a mixed parentage young male being prosecuted is 2.7 times that of a white young male with similar case characteristics' (DLGC, 2007a: 83). In response, the government's All Wales Youth Offending Strategy (WAG, 2004d: 12) states:

> All strategic planning work concerned with youth offenders and those at risk of offending needs to take full account of diversity, disability, culture and language issues ... [Furthermore] the provision of bilingual services, information and advice at all stages of a young person's involvement with the criminal justice system is critical.

The Strategy highlights the monitoring and compliance role of the Children's Commissioner for Wales (WAG, 2004d: 32). It is also noteworthy in the way in which it articulates equalities aims in terms of universal entitlements. For example, stating that 'every young person in Wales aged 11–25 has a basic entitlement to: participate in decision-making on all matters which concern them or have an impact on their lives . . . [and] education, training and work experience – tailored to their needs' (WAG, 2004d: 32).

This distinctive policy framework around equalities and youth justice in Wales presents particular challenges to cross-border agencies. The comments of a former Welsh Social Justice minister indicate that some bodies have been slow to respond to the realities of devolution (WAG, 2007n); it is an issue also highlighted by the Children's Commissioner. A recent report notes that:

> It has become clear that there are circumstances when the Children's Commissioner for Wales's powers are insufficient . . . in areas of policy and legislation that are not devolved to WAG such as youth justice actions of the police and courts and most functions of the Home Office. (Children's Commissioner for Wales, 2007a: 17)

Notwithstanding the Youth Offending Strategy's espousal of the need for bilingual service delivery, research by Hughes and Madoc-Jones (2005: 374) highlights significant shortcomings. They conclude:

> Either the current Youth Justice Board for England and Wales needs to engage more proactively with the bilingual context of Wales, or a new Youth Justice Board for Wales should be constituted. Such a Board would be specifically concerned and focused on Welsh issues and might therefore be more committed towards making equal opportunities a reality for Welsh speaking young people in custody.

Domestic Abuse

Dubnova and Joss (1997: 79) note how 'sensitivities and stigma associated with domestic violence, the conceptualization of it primarily as a judicial and legal issue, and the lack of data on the dimensions of abuse have hampered understanding and the development of appropriate policy interventions'. The government's 'Tackling Domestic Abuse: The All Wales National Strategy' (WAG, 2005k: 3–9) aims to address such shortcomings. As with policy on asylum seekers, it is a notable example where devolution has resulted in national policy frameworks where previously none existed. The aims of the strategy are threefold: to protect victims; to hold abusers to account; and to prevent domestic abuse happening in the first place. It asserts that 'the principle of equality is central to this strategy'. However, Charles and Mackay (2008) have criticised the way in which such an equal treatment model fails to fully address the gendered aspects of domestic abuse, thereby preventing the development of a complete range of specialist services for women. A core aspect of the strategy is the need to develop partnership working to tackle abuse. It also stresses the need for co-working between government departments and emphasises the role of state education in preventing abuse:

> children/young people need to know how to form supportive and respectful relationships; they need to be able to identify with basic values: equality, value of cultural diversity, dignity, respect, mutual support and responsibility for actions.

The policy also emphasises the need for a coordinated network of services related to social diversity, one 'that meets the needs of all victims including children and young people, people with disabilities, men, people who live in a rural part of Wales, people who do not speak English and those from BME communities'. As with youth justice policies, it is an example of the government trying to develop effective policies with the added complication that criminal justice, central to such an issue, has yet to be devolved. As Charles and Mackay (2008, op. cit.) observe, this has created a 'Westminster drag' effect; in contrast to more innovative policies seen in Scotland, the Welsh government has been constrained by having to follow the dominant Whitehall policy frame on criminal justice.

Forced Marriage and Honour Based Violence

Phillips and Dustin (2004: 531) observe how, on the issue of forced marriage, 'the literature on feminism and multiculturalism has identified potential conflicts between the recognition of cultural diversity and securing women's equality'. The Forced Marriage (Civil Protection) Act (2007) has seen the adoption of a regulatory approach that provides civil remedies for those faced with forced marriage. Against this background, the government's Forced Marriage and Honour Based Violence Action Plan (WAG, 2008(16)) sets out a series of objectives and related actions. These are centred on inter-agency coordination, data gathering, raising awareness, challenging attitudes, support and, education. Examples include: developing a coordinated network of services that meet the needs of all victims 'including children and young people, people with disabilities, men and people who do not speak English'; and 'to improve the capacity of education, social service and health professionals working in the community to handle forced marriage cases and the provision of victim-centred services'. The Action Plan is a further example of post-devolution policy development in an area previously not covered on an all-Wales basis. It sets out an agenda for future policy work. A key issue will be the extent to which clear policy outcomes are defined, as well as the allocation of responsibility for implementation and related timescales.

7.1.4 Environment, Sustainability and Housing

Environment

The government's Environment Strategy for Wales (WAG, 2006n) states that climate change, degraded ecosystems and loss of biodiversity 'will vary in how they impact on different people and in different places . . . the action we take. . . will reflect our duty to promote equality of opportunity' (WAG, 2006n: 7). As a result, the policy details environmental issues with particular relevance to one or more equality strand. However, the associated Environment Strategy Action Plan 2008–11 (WAG, 2008(35)) lists few actions that could be considered as addressing equalities issues and represents an example of a significant disconnect between the espousal of equalities in the overarching strategy document and the detailed action plan that is supposed to secure its implementation.[30]

Sustainability

The government's Sustainable Development Scheme, 'Starting to Live Differently' (WAG, 2004e), asserts that the 'vision of sustainable development remains a broad one, embracing commitments to improving quality of life, promoting equality and tackling disadvantage and poverty'. The accompanying Sustainable Development Action Plan (WAG, 2004f) outlines implementation details and refers to the need 'to tackle inequality for reasons of race, gender and disability'. However, both fail to include policy indicators that fully relate to promoting equalities. Thus, the statutory review of the Sustainable Development Scheme pointed to 'confusion [on] the issue of whether sustainable development should be given 'primacy' over the other issues such as equality, social justice, [and] bilingualism (Flynn et al., 2008: 37). Overall, the extent to which policy on the environment and sustainability addresses equalities issues compares poorly with other areas and illustrates the variability of approach between government departments.

Housing

The government's Housing Strategy (NAfW, 2001: 6) notes that 'Wales should be a place where diversity is celebrated, and where equality of opportunity is a reality for all. We are committed to making all BME housing matters mainstream to ensure equality of opportunity and the empowerment of all people'. The Housing Strategy Action Plan (WAG, 2006m) outlines the progress made against these aims. It shows that positive progress has been made in a number of areas, including improved data gathering, official guidance on equalities issued to local authorities and funding of services for targeted groups such as refugees and older people.

In reviewing recent developments in housing policy, Netto (2006: 581) refers to the need for contemporary approaches that provide 'mainstream and specialist BME service provision and multi-agency working; culturally sensitive allocation policies . . . and mechanisms for providing culturally responsive services to diverse communities'. In these regards there is evidence of some progress in the devolved context. 'Race' equality has been the subject of successive government strategies, including the first Black, Minority Ethnic Housing Action Plan for Wales (WAG, 2002c: 22). However, whilst noting some advancement, an evaluation of the policy (WAG, 2005g: 32) identified a significant implementation gap. It concluded that many social landlords' strategies had 'no timescales, no clear actions, no clear allocation of responsibility'. Addressing some of these concerns, a successor policy, the Minority Ethnic Housing Action Plan 2008–11 (WAG, 2008(20): 9) places greater emphasis on 'key issues, desired outcomes, responsibility [for implementation/monitoring], milestones/ action, and date of completion'. Overall, it evidences good levels of consultation and engagement with citizens and NGOs, as well as underlining the need for partnership approaches to policy implementation. The latter is an aspect that is central to the 'good relations' duty in the Equality Act (2006, s10.1).

Homelessness and Rough Sleeping
The government's first Homelessness Strategy (WAG, 2003d) was superseded by the National Homelessness Strategy For Wales 2006–8 (WAG, 2005c: 3); the latter stated that 'services must be designed in accordance with the equality and diversity needs of the community'. It set out specific measures for women, refugees, Gypsy Travellers and, respectively, older, BME, lesbian, gay, bisexual and disabled people (WAG, 2005c: 26). An official evaluation of the strategy (WAO, 2007: 7) found that 'the downward trend in homelessness is positive but not conclusive', and that the strategy 'has encouraged a more joined-up approach to preventing homelessness'. However, it observed that 'evaluating the extent to which the Strategy's objectives are being delivered will be difficult, especially where the objectives involve outcomes without quantifiable targets, for example, on better service planning' (WAO, 2007: 10). The review also concluded that further progress is needed to improve coordination and local service delivery. The Ten Year Homelessness Plan for Wales 2009–19 aims to address earlier shortcomings. Based upon an equalities impact assessment, the new plan includes 'ensuring social inclusion and equality of access to services' among its aims (WAG, 2009b: 1, WAG, 2008(15)).

Gypsy Travellers
Focusing on Gypsy Travellers within the British legal system, Bancroft (2000: 41) refers to:

> The function of the law in establishing moral and social norms and pathologising aspects of Traveller life . . . [whereby] a variety of legal principles, discourses and bureaucratic agencies combine to construct Travellers as deviant with regard to the moral and social order.

Given this context, it is significant that the constitutional law associated with devolution in Wales has seen the development of policies promoting equality for Gypsy Travellers. In 2003, the cross-party Assembly Equality Committee's Review of Service Provision for Gypsies and Travellers stated: 'delivering equality of opportunity to Gypsies and Travellers in Wales should be considered in the light of the Assembly's statutory equality duty, which we believe is a powerful mechanism for improving their circumstances' (NAfW, 2003c: 6). Subsequent policy reviews have also highlighted a range of issues, including that 'very few Gypsy Traveller learners attend a secondary school . . . many have low levels of basic skills' (Estyn, 2005b: 14); and that there is 'an estimated additional need for permanent accommodation for 275–305 Gypsy Travellers over the next five years . . . [a minimum of] 150–200 local authority site places' (WAG, 2005f: 8). In response, government initiatives include: capital funding of £1 million per annum under the Gypsy Traveller Site Refurbishment Grant and, new official guidance to local authorities on best practice in Gypsy Traveller site management (WAG, 2008(4)). However, despite being promised in the government's current policy agenda (WAG, 2007k), an All-Wales Strategy on Gypsies and Travellers is still awaited.[31]

Rural Affairs
A diverse range of equalities issues relate to rurality. These include meeting the needs of carers in rural localities (Arksey and Glendinning, 2008); securing effective community-based, long-term care services for older people (Kolodinsky, 2001); gender equality in farm decision-making (Hall and Mogyorody, 2007); understanding the challenges and barriers faced by rural female entrepreneurs (Merrett and Gruid, 2000); and sustaining the independence of disabled people (Gant and Walford, 1998). Against this background, the Rural Development Plan (RDP) for Wales 2007–13 (WAG, 2007o) sets out a range of grants and training schemes that have been administered in a way that may incentivise the promotion of equalities in the private sector because applicants are assessed as to whether they 'can demonstrate that they have addressed and targeted the measures under the crosscutting themes', including 'evidence of equal opportunity . . . and that Welsh Language related issues are reflected and costed into the project' (WAG, 2007o: 161). Among other initiatives in the RDP is 'Farming Connect', described as 'a bespoke range of services

specifically targeted at women'. According to the policy document, these 'aim to empower women within agricultural and forestry businesses' (WAG, 2007o: 166). Overall, the RDP exhibits strategic commitment to the promotion of equalities and states the need for all related measures to be compliant with the government's general equality duty. In contrast to many policies, the plan also sets out details of technical support and guidance on equalities; in part, this is due to the need to comply with EC requirements. However, the official evaluation of the first RDP (2000–6) was critical. It concluded that 'the monitoring of financial progress has failed to provide transparent and meaningful management information' (Ekos Ltd, 2009: 92). It also raised issues about measurability of policy outcomes. With regard to equality and other crosscutting themes, it offered a somewhat contradictory assessment: these 'have been sufficiently addressed by the programme, but the scale and the extent to which they have is unclear' (Ekos Ltd, 2009: 68). Improved monitoring criteria are a feature of the successor RDP (WAG, 2007o).

7.1.5 Heritage

Sport

The academic literature highlights a broad range of equalities issues in sport, including gender inequalities and cultural diversity issues in sports management (Dowling, 2006; Moore et al., 2001; Hargreaves, 1997); tackling gender stereotyping (Clark, and Paechter, 2007); challenging heteronormativity and homophobia (Caudwell, 2007; Blanc et al., 2006); and understanding experiences of disability discrimination (Hayley, 2005; French and Hainsworth, 2001). 'Climbing Higher', the government's initial Sports Strategy, attempted to address some of these issues. It asserted that 'all funded activity must comply with acceptable standards of fairness, transparency, accountability, equality, respect and bilingualism in Wales' (WAG, 2005h: 2). In a similar vein, the successor document refers to the need to 'address the gender, disability and minority ethnic imbalances in sports participation'; to ensure that 'issues of equality will be mainstreamed through all the programmes receiving investment'; and to 'mainstream the Welsh language' (WAG, 2006i: 5). Ministerial remit letters to the government agency, the Sports Council for Wales, require it to implement these aims. A recent example is unequivocal and states that 'the Welsh Assembly Government's duties towards . . . equality and promoting the Welsh language should be mainstreamed into the way you do your business, including through your estate management, procurement processes and programme activities' (WAG, 2008(1)). In turn, the Sports Council summarises key aspects of its equalities work as:

> Encouraging female participation in sport; promoting sport amongst disabled people, working extensively with the Federation of Disability Sport Wales, the establishment of Disability Sport Cymru; and . . . develop[ing] a network of contacts in BME communities to encourage higher levels of participation in sport. (Sports Council for Wales, 2007: 5)

There is some evidence that such policies are having an impact. For example, Federation of Disability Sport Wales data show an increase in the number of those participating in its programmes (a rise from 14,271 in 2004 to 134,988 in 2007, Sports Council for Wales, 2007: 6). There has also been a narrowing of the gender participation gap in sports (cf. West et al., 2002). In 1989/90, data on those recording 'any participation in sport in the previous four weeks' showed a 15 percentage point gap between women (46) and men (61). By 2004/5, the gap had fallen to 6 percentage points, with the participation rate for women at 56 per cent and men at 62 per cent (Sports Council for Wales, 2007: 6). Notwithstanding this progress, a fundamental weakness in the government policy framework is the absence of equality-specific targets in its sports strategy (Sports Council for Wales, 2007: 8). Despite this shortcoming, the Sports Council is a notable in its attempts to apply gender budgeting to public administration. The latter is a policy tool highlighted in the mainstreaming literature (Verloo and Roggeband, 1996; Budlender and Sharp, 1998). It is based upon the use of sex disaggregated data and gender analytical information to explore the differential gender impact of budget allocations (see Budlender, et al. 2002; Elson, 1998). The Sports Council project provided clear evidence of gender inequalities in public spending on sport and raised a number of issues, including the need for better communication and accountability between politicians, policy-makers and public agencies. It also underlined a key concern, namely that official government data gathering was generally not geared to gender budgeting because sex disaggregated statistics were often unavailable (Baumgardt, 2005). This point is one that has wide resonance in the devolved context and beyond; whilst policies may espouse the promotion of equalities, shortcomings in official statistics and other forms of data may prevent the use of equalities indicators thereby undermining the effectiveness of policies (see Breitenbach and Galligan, 2006).

Culture

A survey of the academic literature reveals a series of ongoing issues in relation to the promotion of equalities in the arts and cultural activities. These include the role of theatre in disabled people's identity-development (Hellier-Tinoco, 2005); older people's engagement with the arts (Keaney and Oskala, 2007); effective provision of cultural activities in ethnically diverse communities (Syson and Wood, 2006); and tackling experiences of homophobia in the arts (Breen, 2001). Reflecting such concerns, the first post-devolution Culture Strategy (WAG, 2002f: 56) stated that 'by 2010 Wales will be, and be known to be, a nation whose culture . . . is both diverse and shared; treasures its bilingualism as a growing reality; ensures equality of access for all to participate'. In turn, it set out a series of initiatives including the production of 'plans to promote cultural diversity . . . [and] to consider how the cultural Assembly Sponsored Public Bodies can encourage funded organisations to take steps to ensure that Black and ethnic minority communities and the disabled are fully represented in all aspects'. One such policy initiative was 'Moving On: An Arts and Disability Strategy for Wales' (WAG/ACW, 2006). Among its aims were to increase 'the diversity of artistic development and opportunities to build audiences more representative of communities across Wales' (WAG/ACW, 2006: 14–15). An evaluation report highlighted some progress: for example, between 2003/4 and 2006/7 the number of disabled artists and arts organisations accessing Arts Council Wales (ACW) grant funding schemes had increased by 38 percentage points and the value of grants awarded had increased by 48 percentage points. In addition, over the same period there was a 70 percentage point increase in attendances at events funded by the strategy (Arts Wales, 2008). However, the need for further work was also identified, including the fact that 'equality impact assessment should be incorporated into ACW's disability action plan and [that] more work should be undertaken to increase the number of disabled people employed by, or advising ACW' (Arts Wales, 2008: 23).

Welsh Language

With an overall growth in the number of Welsh speakers recorded in the 2001 Census, Williams (2007, 2008) claims that 'coordinated policies in education, the media and public life' have stabilised earlier decline (see also MacKinnon, 2004). Against this background, the government's national strategy for the Welsh language, *Iaith Pawb* ('Everyone's Language') (WAG, 2003e: 3), states that 'the Assembly Government will mainstream consideration of the Welsh language into the policy-making processes of all Assembly Ministerial portfolios'. To this end, it has issued written advice to all government departments. One example says that mainstreaming means:

> Reflecting the Assembly Government's vision for a bilingual Wales as an integral part of everything you do. The aim is to ensure that every opportunity is taken to: promote and support the Welsh language; contribute to the Assembly Government's vision of a truly bilingual Wales; and plan, provide and evaluate services in Welsh and English. (Cited in Arad Consulting and Evans, 2007: 9)

Whilst identifying some progress, an interim evaluation of *Iaith Pawb* (Arad Consulting and Evans, 2007) also pointed to the need for more alignment between the strategy's principal aims and some of the initiatives that have developed over recent years. It concluded that '*Iaith Pawb* actions and projects link only indirectly to the strategic targets . . . there appears to be insufficient coordination across actions and projects. New initiatives being developed need to demonstrate complementarity with other actions and priorities' (Arad Consulting and Evans, 2007: 9). The report also pointed to the need for updating language policy with more strategic coordination between government and the Welsh Language Board. The interim evaluation also examined the way in which Welsh was referred to in the government's key policy documents (see Figure 7.4). This raised issues that resonate with other equality strands, particularly in relation to the government's earlier policies and strategies; namely, how to evaluate progress against generalised, declaratory statements of intent. For example, referring to one of the aims in 'Wales: A Better Country – The Strategic Agenda of the Welsh Assembly Government' (WAG, 2003b), the evaluation questioned 'how to measure/assess progress towards being a 'truly bilingual nation'. What consideration has been given to this at a senior level within the Welsh Assembly Government/senior civil service in Wales (Arad Consulting and Evans, 2007: 46, see also WAG, 2008g)?

In respect of language equality in education, official evaluations have variously concluded that 'there is a need for radical and innovative approaches to improving and expanding Welsh for Adults provision in ways that meet the needs of students in the 21st century' (Estyn, 2004: 18); and that, in relation to compulsory phase education, there is 'weak strategic planning' (Estyn, 2007b: 39). Notwithstanding these challenges, Williams (2004: 24) highlights the way in which the strategy reframes the traditional policy discourse around language equality. He notes:

> *Iaith Pawb* seeks to deliver us from that old prejudice that the Welsh language belongs by birthright to a shrinking minority alone. For all its lacunae, *Iaith Pawb*'s declared act of political ambition in creating a bilingual Wales can serve as a binding promise to which we, as citizens, can hold government to account, as we . . . press for the urgent systemic reforms whereby rhetoric is turned into reality.

Policy Area/ Strategy Document	Examples of References to Welsh Language
Crosscutting Policy Wales: A Better Country (WAG, 2003)	'We are moving towards becoming a truly bilingual nation . . . 'strengthening Wales's cultural identity and helping to create a bilingual country'; investment to support the 'vision of a truly bilingual Wales'.
	Evaluation issue: how to measure/assess progress towards being a 'truly bilingual nation'?
Public Service Delivery Making The Connections (WAG, 2004) and Delivering The Connections (WAG, 2005)	Vision: 'excellent public services are essential to a prosperous, sustainable, bilingual, healthier and better-educated Wales'; 'all public bodies in Wales . . . should develop the capability to: communicate effectively in English, Welsh and other languages of the communities they serve'.
	Evaluation issue: there appears to be comparatively little detail on what the particular challenges and opportunities are for better public service delivery within the context of a bilingual nation.

(continued)

Policy Area/ Strategy Document	Examples of References to Welsh Language
Planning People, Places, Futures – The Wales Spatial Plan (WAG, 2004)	Planning that respects distinctiveness: 'develop Wales in line with the vision in *Iaith Pawb*, as a modern bilingual society with increasing opportunities for people in all areas of Wales to use Welsh in all aspects of their lives'; another action mentioned with particular relevance to the language is 'the review of TAN20 providing guidance on the implementation of planning policy on the Welsh language'.
	Evaluation issue: what arrangements are in place to monitor the impact of Spatial Plan developments on the language?
Education, Lifelong Learning and Skills The Learning Country: Vision Into Action (WAG, 2006)	Links to *Iaith Pawb*: 'recognising the crucial role which education at all levels has in helping us achieve the vision and aspirations of *Iaith Pawb*'; schools and Learning: 'require local authorities to assess demand for Welsh medium schools places in order to ensure that provision matches needs'.
	Evaluation issue: there is a wide range of activities and actions . . . to what extent can it be said that these are these linked actions within a common strategy for Welsh medium education?
Economic Development Wales: A Vibrant Economy, W:AVE (WAG, 2005)	'joining up policy agendas across the Assembly Government and meeting our corporate commitments to social justice, sustainable development, equality and the Welsh language'.
	Evaluation issue: there are numerous references to the Welsh language. How can WAG demonstrate that these commitments are being met? Are the arrangements to consider the impact of new activities on the Welsh language sufficiently robust? The W:AVE document does not include specific references to economic and community development initiatives that will target support for individuals in Welsh-speaking communities
Sport Climbing Higher (WAG, 2005)	'Participation in sport and physical activity also offers many opportunities to promote our vision of a bilingual Wales as set out in *Iaith Pawb*.'

(continued)

Policy Area/ Strategy Document	Examples of References to Welsh Language
Sport Climbing Higher (WAG, 2005) (contd)	Evaluation issue: although the link is made, noting that participation in physical activity can help promote a bilingual Wales, this is touched upon only very briefly in Climbing Higher.
Culture Cymru Greadigol – Creative Future: A Culture Strategy For Wales (WAG, 2002)	'Bilingualism is a jewel in our national crown. We want the living reality of bilingualism to be reflected across the range of our cultural and sporting life.'
	Evaluation issue: what are the implications of the earlier merger between WAG's Culture and Language Department with Education and Lifelong Learning? Could this facilitate better strategic planning in relation to the Welsh language across the two policy areas?
Health and Social Care Designed for Life (WAG, 2005)	Effective Welsh and English bilingual services are essential to providing quality care
	Evaluation issue: what evidence exists of specific increases/improvements in capacity to be able to deliver additional health and social care services through the medium of Welsh?

Figure 7.4. Mainstreaming language equality in public policy? Policy aims and evaluation criteria.[32]

As noted, further legal and policy developments are scheduled; ones that have the potential to address the inadequacies of the Welsh Language Act (1993) (Lynch, 2008), such as the forthcoming Welsh language Measure (2010) (see chapter 6). However, a key issue for the next generation of language rights will be the extent to which they relate to the private sector.

Tourism

Contemporary equality issues in relation to tourism include gender, labour-market flexibility and equal pay (Flacke-Neudorfer, 2007; Santos and Varejão, 2007); lesbian tourism geographies (Johnston, 2007); the dearth of older people in tourism advertising (Patterson, 2007); and travel constraints and access to tourism facilities experienced by people with disabilities (Shaw et al., 2005; Yates, 2007). Against this background, the national tourism strategy 'Achieving Our Potential 2006–13' (WAG, 2006o: 7), states that 'the tourism industry should be open to all . . . such as older people and females who are not well represented in other industry sectors'. The policy document also notes that, 'care must be taken to avoid any potential negative effects of tourism on the Welsh language'. Yet the strategy does little to address the findings of research on the tourism industry in Wales that concluded: 'significant [gender] inequalities still exist in the tourism workplace . . . [whereby] women are quiescent and feeling powerless to act' (White et al., 2005: 37). The strategy does, however, contain an action plan that details 'action', 'lead' and 'timescales' against a range of 'strategic issues', but those that relate to equalities are limited in number and generalised in nature.

7.1.6 Health and Social Services

The burgeoning international academic literature around equalities in healthcare points to a range of ongoing issues including a dearth of gender-comparative research (Annandale, 2007); tensions between equality and politically-defined entitlement in state healthcare provision (Harris, 1999); training needs to address homophobia in the healthcare environment (Gill and Hough, 2007); institutional barriers to sexuality in later life (Bauer et al., 2007); resistance to workplace diversity (Johnstone and Kanitsaki, 2008); the need to transform the healthcare experience of disabled people (Boyles et al., 2008); and the need to end cultural racism, language prejudice and discrimination in hospital contexts (Johnstone and Kanitsaki, 2008). In addition, Bywaters and McLeod (1996: 3) underline the salience of intersectionality: 'issues of (in)equality and discrimination in the health service manifest themselves in a variety of forms . . . People occupy not one but multiple social positions with consequences for health'.

Against this backdrop, health and social services is the largest major expenditure group in the Welsh government's budget, currently totalling £5.7 billion per annum (WAG, 2008(30)). Over the past ten years, devolution has ushered in some significant discontinuities in health policy (Greer, 2005). The government's principal health strategy 'Designed for Life' (WAG, 2005e: 13) states that 'we will promote the active participation of citizens and communities in service development. We will engage all, irrespective of their race, language, religion, disability, age, gender and sexual orientation'. Linked to the overarching strategy, individual health policies that address specific aspects of healthcare provision vary in the amount of attention that they devote to equalities. At the more comprehensive end of the scale, the NHS Wales human resources policy (WAG, 2006b: 13) asserts that, 'equality and human rights strategies will be developed to mainstream the promotion of diversity into all elements of organisational activity, ensuring compliance with legal requirements and best practice'. This is accompanied by a series of action points and details of those required to lead on implementation, as well as the timescale for their achievement (WAG, 2006b: 23). At the opposite end of the scale, other health policies are less specific. For example, the latest Emergency Care Service Strategy (WAG, 2008(2): 36) asserts that 'people accessing unscheduled care services will be treated as individuals with dignity and respect, regardless of age, disability, gender, race, sexual orientation, language or religion/belief'; yet, absent are the specified means to achieve this aim. Despite this, there have been areas of progress, such as the announcement of an end to mixed wards in NHS Wales hospitals (Anon, 2008). Notwithstanding this, other studies point to further problems. One stated:

> The literature suggests that language sensitive healthcare practice is central to ensuring high quality care. However, it is evident that language barriers continue to compromise the quality of care within nursing and other health services . . . one issue that has received little attention is the level of language awareness that healthcare professionals currently demonstrate. (Irvine et al., 2006: 442)

Overall, post-devolution health policies espouse a strategic vision for equality of opportunity, one that links to other government strategies. Moreover, there is evidence of targeted funding, special projects and discrete initiatives to promote equalities. However, there is much scope for a more systematic approach, one based upon coordinated actions, clear implementation plans and robust monitoring of outcomes.

Mental health
'Raising the Standard' (WAG, 2005i) is the government's National Service Framework (NSF) for mental healthcare. A number of its service-delivery standards (and associated 'key actions' and performance targets) have explicit equalities dimensions: for example, 'social inclusion, health promotion and tackling stigma' (standard 1); 'service user and carer empowerment' (standard 2); and 'providing

equitable and accessible services' (standard 4). The framework document sets out in detail the requirement to monitor equalities outcomes, noting that 'all agencies must ensure compliance with recent legislation to ensure that the rights of minority groups are considered . . . [this] should be built into implementation monitoring arrangements' (WAG, 2005i: 29). However, there is mixed evidence in terms of the impact of the developing policy framework. Research by Madoc-Jones (2004: 216), undertaken during the early years of devolution, referred to 'the destructive effects of linguistic oppression, and the difficulties of second language communication for mental health service users . . . insufficient attention is being paid to the linguistic needs of Welsh speakers'. In contrast, an official review (AOiW, 2004) concluded that 'progress in some areas is encouraging . . . health and social care agencies have made progress in some important areas in developing mental health services for older people' (AOiW, 2004, unpaginated). However, the latter noted the need for further improvements, including more measures 'to support GPs in making decisions that may lead to an early diagnosis of mental health problems'. A subsequent review of mental health services for adults (WAO, 2005) also offered a mixed assessment, stating that there are 'several examples of good practice'. Yet, overall, it found that agencies 'responsible for planning and delivering mental health services need to work together to develop a more comprehensive range of services to meet the diverse and complex needs of service users' (WAO, 2005: 6). Notwithstanding this, there has been recent progress in relation to the gathering of equalities data in relation to mental health (NAfW, 2006a: para 17.24).

Older People's Services
Fredman and Spencer (2003: 21) highlight the complexities of applying age equality to public policy. They note that, unlike other equality 'strands', age does not define a discrete group. A key issue is the way in which older people often experience multiple forms of inequality (e.g. based on age *and* disability, race, gender etc.). Following devolution, there has been significant policy development in relation to services for older people. In 2002, an Advisory Committee was tasked with producing evidence-based policy recommendations that would lead to the government's future Strategy for Older People. Significantly, one of its recommendations was the adoption of the UN's Principles for Older Persons (WAG, 2002b: 12).

The resulting report, 'When I'm 64 ... and more' (WAG, 2002b), set out over 100 policy recommendations, including that the 'government should consider the case for the appointment of an Older People's Commissioner for Wales' (WAG, 2002b: 14). The subsequent 'Strategy for Older People 2003–8' (WAG, 2003a) defined 'older people' as those aged 50 years and over. It articulated its purpose as being to 'challenge and change attitudes to older people'. It continued, 'they must get a fair deal and be able to contribute to society as equal citizens' (WAG, 2003a: 15). The strategy was notable for its ambition; it set out a raft of initiatives for improving public services for older people across the range of devolved policy portfolios. Subsequently, the Commissioner for Older People (Wales) Act was passed in 2006, and the first Commissioner appointed in January 2008 (see chapter 5). Overall, policy development in this area has been characterised by its broad scope, attempts to integrate age equality across a breadth of policy areas and, through the creation of the Commissioner's Office, legally-backed independent monitoring mechanisms.

The outcomes of the strategy include the introduction of free swimming, free bus travel and access to heritage sites for those aged over 60 years; and an initiative to ensure that older people claim all their pension and benefit entitlements (Link-AGE Wales). Two related policies are the National Service Framework for Older People (WAG, 2005l) (this established national standards and services in health and social care); and the Healthy Ageing Action Plan (WAG, 2005m) (that provides guidance at a local level on interventions to promote the health and well-being of older people). To date, policy evaluation has been provided by an advisory group report (AGSTOPW, 2007) and an independent interim review (AWARD, 2007). In all, these identified mixed progress:

- the strategy 'is widely recognised for its achievements and progress . . . [and] has made considerable progress . . . We recognise that health, well-being and independence is an area where perhaps the most progress has been made to date';
- putting the strategy into action: 'All local authorities had a coordinator in place, as well a local Champion ... [however] reports and plans produced by authorities varied greatly in terms of size, detail and terminology used';
- innovative practices: 'Several innovative projects were identified across Wales tackling a range of issues including intergenerational

activities, increasing police training, health promotion ... [and] engaging with minority ethnic groups';
- support organisations – some difficulties were identified in allocating resources according to need across Wales;
- performance measures: 'Current use of performance measures in relation to the Strategy is weak; the integration of older people's views into local authority strategic planning needs to be further embedded and widened' (AWARD, 2007: 121).

Against this background, the Strategy for Older People in Wales 2008–13 (WAG, 2008(6): 3–4) sets out four principal strategic themes that, the Strategy asserts, 'embody the "mainstreaming" of older people's concerns across all policy areas'. They are: 'Valuing Older People' – maintaining and developing engagement; 'Changing Society' – supporting the economic status and contribution of older people; 'Well-being and Independence'; and 'Making it Happen' – the effective implementation of the strategy. Reflecting issues identified in the earlier evaluation reports about a dearth of performance measures, a significant development in terms of assessing equality outcomes is the latest strategy's inclusion of 'indicators of change'. According to the government, 'in most instances changes can be charted over the period of the Strategy and beyond' (WAG, 2008(6): 51). One of the notable commitments in the strategy was the publication of the Intergenerational Strategy (WAG, 2008(8)). This states that 'we need to move from our current programmatic approach to a strategic approach where we identify where intergenerational considerations can strengthen existing strategies and propose an action plan to translate these opportunities into practice' (WAG, 2008(8): 9).

Overall, as noted, policy developments on age are characterised by their ambition and, in some respects, pioneering nature (such as the adoption of the UN Principles for Older People and the creation of the office of Older People's Commissioner). These factors, together with the engagement from older people's organisations, and detailed monitoring and equalities indicators (now being put in place), make the Older People's Strategy an example of good equalities practice. Yet, the latter assessment does not deny significant and ongoing challenges – a point advanced by the new statutory regulator: 'the [Older People's] Commissioner has already indicated her intention to use her legal powers should she believe that older people are being put at risk . . . [she] will be examining, among other matters, the services they [public agencies] provide, handling of complaints, whistle-blowing and availability and effectiveness of advocacy services' (OPCfW, 2008: 9).

Social Services
Social services in Wales support 150,000 people; account for nearly £1.1 billion in public spending; employ over 70,000 people; and are delivered by around 1,800 statutory, private and voluntary organisations (WAG, 2007p: 12). 'Fulfilled Lives, Supportive Communities' (WAG, 2007p) is the government's ten year strategy for social services. Its principal focus is local authorities. Significantly, it articulates the need to promote a rights-based approach to equalities. It states that 'services will be provided with personal dignity, privacy and with full regard to equality in all settings . . . and, carers' needs will be recognised and supported'. It continues,

> Our vision is firmly rooted in both the social model of disability, and in a rights based approach. This is derived for children from the UN Convention on the Rights of the Child. For older people the UN Principles for Older People promote independence, participation, care, self-fulfilment and dignity. Our Learning Disability Strategy sets the framework for people with learning disabilities. The social model promotes rights, equality and choice for all disabled people. The real problems for disabled people tend to come from people's attitudes to disability, as well as physical and organisational barriers. Social services must help to tackle these issues through their own actions and by influencing others. (WAG, 2007p: 14)

A key issue in social service provision over recent years has been the 2003–7 Welsh Labour government's widely perceived reneging on its earlier 2003 manifesto commitment to introduce free home care. 'Home', or domiciliary, care refers to health care provided in the individual's home by healthcare professionals or by family and friends; in other words, non-medical and non-custodial forms of care. The earlier manifesto commitment was broadly similar to policy goals that were implemented in Scotland.[33] Following accusations of betrayal from disabled people's organisations, and indicating the salience of equalities issues in post-devolution electoral politics (see chapter 8), the government of the time introduced a three year, £75M package of initiatives as a 'workable way of taking . . . [its] original policy forward' (Morgan, 2007: 34). These were significant and included increasing the level of household income that can be retained before charging for domiciliary care, and increases in the ring-fenced Carers' Grant Scheme. Subsequently, policy development in this area has centred on a consultation exercise on the future funding of services designed to promote independent living (e.g. meals on wheels, home adaptations, occupational therapy and day care).[34] As a result, a government 'green paper' on funding care was published in late 2009 to inform an upcoming Westminster Bill and future legislative competence of the National Assembly on this issue.

Overall, whilst the 'Fulfilled Lives' Strategy document espouses the core aim of promoting equalities there is a need for comprehensive use of equalities targets supported by robust monitoring mechanisms. A further concern is that the annual reports of Care and Social Services Inspectorate Wales (and predecessor organisations) have in the past paid scant attention to equalities outcomes.[35] The commitment made in 2007 that future reports will cover compliance with equality legislation marks a potentially positive development (WAG, 2007e: 20).

Carers

The international academic literature on caring identifies a broad variety of equalities issues, including the need for greater understanding of the consequences of the gendered positioning of carers (Ussher and Sandoval, 2008); promoting cultural competence when caring for non-English speakers (Garrett et al., 2008); addressing the needs of young carers of adults (Grey et al., 2008; Warren, 2007); the need to make provision for carers with different faiths in respite care (Chou, 2008); tackling institutionalised homophobia among social care practitioners (Carr, 2008); and creating effective policies to help carers combine work and care (Arksey, 2007). As Pascall and Lewis (2004: 373) observe, across Europe 'policies for supporting unpaid care work have developed modestly compared with labour market activation policies'.

Against this backdrop, the 'Carers' Strategy in Wales: Implementation Plan' was published just months after the Assembly was founded. It asserted the need for, 'the promotion of a culture in which diversity is valued and equality of opportunity is a reality' (NAfW, 2000b: 6). It has been superseded by the Carers' Strategy for Wales Action Plan (WAG, 2007i). The action points listed in the plan include the need to 'consider with existing Black and Minority Ethnic networks and other minority groups, how to improve communication with carers' (WAG, 2007i: 3–4). A further action point is a review of the implementation of the provisions of the Carers (Equal Opportunities) Act (2004) (WAG, 2007i: 23) (this places a duty on local authorities to inform carers of their right to an assessment of support needs). Overall, the carers' strategy demonstrates appropriate policy aims in accessible language and contains elements of good practice, such as information on how Black and minority ethnic issues and young carers' needs are being addressed. Much will depend upon the future quality of the monitoring of the action plan, and the awaited revised carers' strategy. Further policy development in this area is ongoing with the Proposed Carers' Strategies (Wales) Measure (2010) currently proceeding through the Assembly. If passed it will place a new requirement on NHS Wales and local authorities to work in partnership to prepare, publish and implement a joint strategy in relation to carers.

Learning Disabilities
Research into the inequalities experienced by people with learning disabilities reveals that many face problems in relation to gaining access to public services, and the prejudiced attitudes of staff in public agencies, as well as difficulties in obtaining appropriate treatment and support (DRC, 2006). Studies of the labour market also identify their low employment rates (Berthoud and Blekesaune, 2007). The 'Statement on Policy and Practice for Adults with a Learning Disability' (WAG, 2007r) aims to address such issues. It sets out initiatives in six areas, including the provision of accessible information and advocacy, and community living (defined as 'living at home and within the communities of which they are a part'). The policy is notable for the collaborative way in which it was co-written by government, the Learning Disability Implementation Advisory Group (LDIAG) (a body comprised of people and organisations working with people with learning disabilities), and All Wales People First (an alliance of self-advocacy groups of people with learning disabilities). The policy discourse in the statement is one of empowerment and rights, for example: 'all people with a learning disability have . . . the right to a healthy, useful, independent life . . . control over their lives . . . to be part of their community . . . and the right to use local services' (WAG, 2007r: 14).

The 'Policy and Practice for Adults with a Learning Disability: Action Plan' (WAG, 2007r: 3) links to the earlier statement and details implementation measures, monitoring and targets in relation to the six areas of policy and practice. This addresses shortcomings identified in an earlier Disability Rights Commission policy review (DRC, 2007) that referred to 'a lack of coordination between the organisations and groups working on this agenda across Wales' (DRC, 2007: 42). The DRC study also highlighted positive aspects of policy development, observing:

> In Wales we are pleased to note that regular health checks for people with learning disabilities have been introduced through the General Medical Services (i.e. General Practitioner) contract . . . and that GPs in Wales have also been incentivised to write an Annual Health Report for individuals with mental health problems who are assessed as receiving 'Enhanced' support under the 'Care Programme Approach. (DRC, 2007: 44)

Overall, the government's Learning Disability Action Plan is significant as an example of the participatory approach to policy development and its attention to engaging people with learning disabilities. It is too early to judge the impact of the Plan; much will depend on the monitoring and delivery of the policy aims over the next five years.

7.1.7 Public Services and Performance

Public Services

Making the Connections: Delivering Better Services for Wales (WAG, 2004c), the government's initial strategy document for public services stated that the 'government is committed to promoting equality of opportunity for all . . . [and] the principle of equality between the Welsh and English languages, and meeting all other equality duties'. 'Making the Connections: Delivering Beyond Boundaries' (WAG, 2006f) sets out the government's updated framework; one that responds to an earlier review of local service delivery (WAG, 2006d) that highlighted the need for citizen-centred services. Reflecting the revised approach, the strategy asserts that its vision 'places citizens at the centre of services which are efficient, driven by a commitment to social justice and equality' (WAG, 2006d: 7). As an overarching strategy document, 'Delivering Beyond Boundaries' embeds equality as one of the principles to be applied in specific policy areas such as health, education and housing. Yet, as the forgoing analysis reveals, there is significant variation in the extent to which this is being realised. Key areas of public service delivery are provided or commissioned by local authorities in Wales. An insight into the effectiveness with which they promote equalities is provided by reports on statutory compliance undertaken in 2007 by the (then) Disability Rights Commission and the Commission for Racial Equality. The principal findings included that 'all authorities had relevant [equality] schemes in place and efforts had been made to meet the specific requirements of the legislation; [moreover, there was progress] . . . in relation to the involvement of disabled people in identifying priority issues for action . . . [and] opportunities to ensure elected members and staff understand their responsibilities and the steps to be taken to promote equality practices'. Yet, crucially, the reviews noted that 'further work is required to ensure that authorities have the necessary "arrangements" in place [to] . . . better inform service planning and delivery and undertake equality impact assessments'; moreover, there was a need for 'more transparent support from senior management to demonstrate how managers will be involved in developing and delivering the [statutory disability and "race" equalities] Schemes' (WLGA, 2008: 9).

A further and often overlooked aspect to the promotion of equalities is public procurement. As Broadnax (2000) highlights, this is the purchase of goods and services by state institutions used as an affirmative action mechanism to promote equality. Thus, state suppliers and contractors are encouraged to adhere to good equalities practices – a factor that is looked upon favourably when determining which organisations receive government contracts. In the devolved context it has considerable potential for influencing equalities practices in the private sector, for each year the government spends £300 million and the Welsh public sector as a whole over £4 billion, on buying goods and services from suppliers. As a result, devolution has seen government introduce revised procurement procedures, including a Voluntary Code of Practice on Equalities for suppliers, and resources and advice on equalities via the National Procurement Website (WAG, 2006l: 55). In accordance with EC law, most contracts are still awarded on the basis of open competition but, under the arrangements, suppliers who support the Voluntary Code will be assisted with positive action such as guidance on ways to improve their practices, and constructive feedback on unsuccessful tenders. It is likely that there is further potential for policy development to maximise future equalities gains through this process.

Public Appointments
In the 1990s, the limited diversity of those holding public appointments, particularly in regard to quangos, featured in the arguments of pro-devolution campaigners. A report on the situation in early 2000 showed the extent of prevailing inequalities: 'just over 30 per cent of appointments [were] held by women and 1 per cent [were] held by ethnic minorities, younger candidates [were] scarce and disabled people [were] extremely under-represented' (NHS Wales, 2001: 2). There have been a number of policy initiatives to address this issue. Building on the Nolan Committee inquiry into standards in public life (Committee on Standards in Public Life, 1995), the government has used its equality duty to go 'beyond what is laid down under the Nolan principles in terms of making transparent and open the procedures of making public appointments' (Chaney and Fevre, 2002: 34). A new Code of Practice for Ministerial Appointments to Public Bodies was introduced that led in a raft of measures including information dissemination strategies to reach under-represented groups and targeted advertising of posts. The Code of Practice also set out how management procedures would be changed to promote gender equality. It stated that the 'Public Appointment Unit [of the Welsh Government] will have discretion to look for the next man or woman on the list [of available assessors] in order to ensure gender balance on a[n appointments] panel' (NAfW, 2004: 62). A further move designed to increase the representation of women was the requirement that 'for all posts there should be provision for reimbursement of receipted childcare or carer costs' (NAfW, 2002: 8). Perhaps the most radical step in this area was the decision, taken at the end of 2000, to dismiss all the existing independent assessors involved in making public appointments (Chaney et al., 2007). As a result of this 'equality *coup d'état*', following advertising and interviewing against criteria, 55 new assessors were appointed, thereby signalling a clear break with past practices and putting in place assessors with greater equality competencies. Importantly, 56 per cent of the new assessors were women (NAfW, 2003b). More recently, a 'communications toolkit' has been developed to ensure effective communication with minority ethnic communities in public appointment campaigns. Figures for 2006–7 show that 180

appointments and re-appointments were made and, while the diversity of those appointed is gradually improving, major challenges remain. The percentage of females appointed was 48 per cent, the percentage of people from the minority ethnic communities appointed was 4 per cent and the percentage of disabled people appointed was 7 per cent.

7.2 Comparative Developments

One of the principal themes of constitutional reform was for devolved governments to deliver 'policies more in tune with the views of their electorates, [and to] be more responsive to "local" needs and aspirations' (Cornford, 2002: 32) – in other words, to 'generate substantive differences in public policy across the component parts of the United Kingdom' (Keating, 2002: 3). With this in mind, we turn to look at equality policy developments the UK's other devolved polities.

7.2.1 Scotland

In the wake of devolution, the Scottish government stated its intention to adopt a mainstreaming approach to equalities in public policy. 'Working Together for Equality' (Scottish Executive, 2000: 14)[36] states that 'mainstreaming equality is the systematic integration of an equality perspective into the everyday work of government involving policy-makers across all government departments'. This commitment was accompanied by institutional mechanisms to promote equalities, including the equality clause in the Scotland Act (1998, Schedule 5; see chapter 4) and the creation of an equality unit in government. Referring to the progress made in promoting gender equality Breitenbach (2005: 15) concluded that 'there is a need for . . . identifying policy goals, policy actors, and measures for evaluating success'. She highlighted progress in developing the participation of civil society and other groups in equality policy-making, but noted that 'its full potential has yet to be realised' (ibid., 2005:15). It is a viewpoint shared by McKay and Gillespie (2005: 127). They found evidence of 'progress towards equality proofing and . . . positive progress in terms of processes and reinforcing the commitment to mainstreaming'. However, they also conclude:

By examining a number of policy areas we did not identify specific outcomes that demonstrated how the new approach to policy-making, implied by the commitment to mainstreaming, was transforming the lives of women working and living in Scotland. (2005: 127)

Topic	Examples
Education	Schools will have lesson ideas for mainstreaming equality into the curriculum over a range of subjects including English and Maths. School staff will be provided with training materials on equality, inclusion and anti-discrimination, including case studies (launched early 2008).[37]
Social services	Funding of the Children, Fathers and Fatherhood project to raise awareness of issues affecting children in their relationships with their fathers and to encourage all fathers to develop their fatherhood skills.
Health	Improved access for people with a disability to independent advocacy;[38] NHS Scotland has been working in partnership with the Equality and Human Rights Commission through our Fair for All – Disability initiative to raise awareness of disability issues and deliver more responsive services for people with a disability.[39]
Public sector	Best Value in Public Services. Refreshed guidance issued in May 2006 – greater attention to equalities indicators;[40] government support for the 'Close the Gap' campaign and to encourage other employers to put their pay structures to the test.[41]
Transport	Concessionary travel for older and disabled people. It was estimated that there were approximately 1.2m people eligible to access Scotland-Wide Free Bus Travel. At 31 October 2006, 957,200 had been issued with National Entitlement Cards.[42]
Older people	Older People's Strategy – All Our Futures: Planning for a Scotland with an Ageing Population (2007). Creation of National Forum on Ageing; tackling the issue of elder abuse through the implementation of the Adult Support and Protection (Scotland) Act; provide support for services and grants that enable older people to make changes and improvements to their homes so that they can remain there wherever possible.[43]

(continued)

Topic	Examples
Criminal justice	Commitment to extend existing hate crime legislation to cover disabled people;[44] National Strategy on Domestic Abuse (Scottish Government, 2007), £40 million funding over three years, to address domestic abuse and violence against women, further supplemented by £10 million over three years to Education to take forward work specifically in relation to the National Domestic Abuse Delivery Plan;[45] a domestic abuse court service pilot (to October 2008) to fast track cases of domestic abuse;[46] 'the Government considers street prostitution to be a form of abuse of women. Prostitution (Public Places) (Scotland) Act 2007 came into effect on 15 October 2007. This legislation has created, for the first time in Scotland, offences, which target those who purchase sex on our streets'.[47]
Housing	Affordable Housing Investment Programme – fund a further 7,100 houses for social rent and low cost home ownership 95+ per cent new homes will be built to accommodate people with varying needs.[48] Communities Scotland's regulation and inspection of Registered Social Landlords is to ensure that social justice and equal opportunities exist across all aspects of social housing. The performance standards include a specific equal opportunities standard.[49]
Sport	Supporting the Scottish Executive in implementing and monitoring the strategy – Quality assure and equality impact assess sports governing body plans.

Figure 7.5. Selected examples of the promotion of equalities in the development of Scottish public policy

Published in 2007, the Scottish government's Gender Equality Scheme begins to address some of these issues. It set out nine gender equality objectives, including tackling the gender pay gap; ending violence against women; and promoting transgender equality. Furthermore, the government's statutory equality scheme reports on gender, 'race' and disability (Scottish Government, 2008a, 2008b, 2008c) show that there is generally good strategic commitment to the promotion of equalities, supported by a plethora of related policies across the breadth of devolved functions. As in the Welsh case, there is considerable variability in the extent of equalities work between policy areas. In general, there is scope for greater use of quantifiable equalities targets accompanied by implementation details and monitoring mechanisms. Notwithstanding this, there is some evidence of progress in relation to a number of policy initiatives (see Figure 7.5) such as tackling domestic abuse; the Children, Fathers and Fatherhood Project (to raise awareness of issues affecting children in their relationships with their fathers); concessionary travel for older and disabled people; and initiatives on tackling elder abuse. A notable development in respect of faith and community relations was the publication of the 'Action Plan on Tackling Sectarianism in Scotland' (Scottish Executive, 2006). This introduced a range of measures including an anti-sectarian education resource for schools; the requirement for the education inspectorate to produce a report on the effectiveness of schools' efforts to tackle sectarianism; the production (with the Scottish Football Association and Sport Scotland) of a strategy for tackling sectarianism; the introduction of Football Banning Orders (as part of the Police, Public Order and Criminal Justice (Scotland) Act 2006); and greater statutory powers for local authorities to regulate marches and parades. In terms of disability policies, the Equality Committee of the Scottish Parliament has given a cautious assessment of post-devolution developments, noting 'the progress that the Scottish Government is making' (ECSP, 2007: 9). However, it also expressed concern on a number of grounds, including limited advancement in promoting good practice in the provision of accessible information, and the pace of policy development on independent living for disabled people.

De Lima (2005: 152) offers a mixed assessment of the difference that devolution has made to the way that public policy addresses 'race' equality. She states that 'the gap between policy statements and policy action continues, and is apparent in areas such as social inclusion'. A further shortcoming is 'the lack of disaggregated data by ethnicity across all priority areas'. She continues, 'despite the limitations, it is important to acknowledge that devolution has opened up new opportunities in Scotland to address racism and discrimination in ways that did not occur previously' (2005: 158). Examples of the latter include increased consultation with BME communities, commissioned research to shape policy, and targeted policy initiatives in health, housing and education. In the latest evaluation of the Scottish equalities agenda, Fitzgerald (2009: iii) notes that 'the overall impact of the Scotland Act equal opportunities duties [*sic*] has been generally positive as they are seen to support a distinctively Scottish approach to equality policy and practice' (see Figure 7.6).

- Positive benefits have been seen in relation to changes in processes including data collection, research, policy design and consultation.
- There has also been greater awareness and understanding of equality issues and capacity building through, for example, equality training and secondments across the public sector.
- The move to a more equality sensitive culture within public authorities and greater accountability for meeting the requirements of equality legislation is also seen as an important positive benefit of this activity.
- Mixed benefits are more evident where the policy area is not fully devolved or where there is significant private sector provision of services.
- A lack of follow-through in respect of reporting and monitoring on equality matters, and a lack of clarity on what is required, are the key factors that lead to limited benefit from equal opportunities powers.

Figure 7.6. An evaluation of the Scottish equalities agenda (Fitzgerald, 2009).

As in the Welsh case, there is evidence of an increasingly sophisticated approach to promoting equalities. A key development has been the application of an equalities policy tool, the Equality Impact Assessment Toolkit (EIAT), to the work of government. This is significant and is indicative of the increasingly systematic manner in which equalities considerations are embedded in policy. Overall, however, when weighed against the publication of the (then) Scottish executive's mainstreaming policy in 2000, progress in mainstreaming equalities in policy has been frustratingly slow – and work is still ongoing. A further significant development is the recent emphasis on strengthening the lines of accountability for mainstreaming in the policy process. New practices introduced in 2008 should lead to more effective monitoring of the equality impact assessment process across government. In particular, as part of the government's internal assurance process, senior officials will be required to set out how the requirement to undertake impact assessments is being met in those areas for which they are responsible (Scottish Government, 2008b: 30).

In summary, the promotion of equalities in Scottish public policy exhibits a number of commonalities with the Welsh experience, including government espousal of the concept of mainstreaming equalities in the policy process, yet with a protracted implementation period; ongoing and increasingly systematic application of some mainstreaming techniques in policy work; continuing efforts to address shortcomings in the availability of equalities-related official data; and the need for greater use of quantifiable equalities targets accompanied by effective implementation and monitoring mechanisms. Thus, Fitzgerald (2009: 20) concludes that 'equality considerations are embedded in public policy discourse in Scotland ... [however] there is a lack of clarity about how this commitment and how these requirements fit together and how equality can be delivered in practice'. Mackay (2009: 55) offers a broadly similar conclusion:

> EO is not always central, it is often marginalized ... despite shortfalls, slippages and setbacks, overall there is a relatively positive story to tell. EO remains a principle with mobilizing power in the parliament ... there is still distance to travel ... and concerns about faltering commitment and competing priorities as the parliament enters its second decade.

7.2.2 Northern Ireland

The singular nature of the civil conflict in Northern Ireland has shaped policy approaches to equalities in the province. According to Wilson (2007: 154), 'the phrase "equality agenda" joined Northern Ireland's crowded political lexicon in the early 1990s, as the "republican movement" (the IRA and Sinn Féin) sought to legitimise its belated political "turn", reflected in the change of slogan from "Brits out" to "an Ireland of equals"'. In turn, Republicans have long questioned the discrimination faced by Catholics in service provision, the labour market and many other facets of life (Cameron Report, 1969; Palley, 1972; Whyte, 1983; Bew et al., 2002: McEvoy and Morison, 2003). Whatever its political provenance, the espousal of equalities in public policy was evident when devolved governance was restored in 1998.

For example, 'Strategy 2010: A Report by the Economic Development Strategy Review Steering Group' (EDSRSG, 1999: 12) referred to:

> A commitment by the public and private sectors to build an economy based on the principles of equality of opportunity and social inclusion. We seek an economy which is fair between the two communities but also offers equal opportunities for under-represented groups including women, ethnic minorities and people with disabilities.

It continued: 'the Steering Group concluded that there are a number of key principles which should underlie and shape the economic development strategy. It should . . . promote equality and social cohesion' (EDSRSG, 1999: 55). Yet, the promotion of equalities in public policy in Northern Ireland has subsequently been hampered by the suspension of the Assembly on a number of occasions, including the extended period between October 2002 and May 2007. This has resulted in less evidence against which to assess progress. However, a potentially significant policy developed during the latter period of direct rule is 'A shared Future' (OFMDFM, 2005). This sets out a range of initiatives to address its aims of:

> The establishment over time of a normal, civic society, in which all individuals are considered as equals, where differences are resolved through dialogue in the public sphere, and where all people are treated impartially. A society where there is equity, respect for diversity and a recognition of our interdependence. (OFMDFM, 2005: 10)

It was accompanied by a Triennial Action Plan (OFMDFM, 2006) setting out specific aims for respective government departments. However, as Hadden et al. (2007: 6) report, the policy provoked a mixed reception, welcomed by some bodies for integrating diverse communities, yet criticised by others as not being enforceable in law as part of the statutory provisions under Section 75(2) of the Northern Ireland Act (1998) (these require government and public bodies to have due regard to the desirability of promoting good relations between persons of different religious belief, political opinion or racial group). Moreover, the Northern Ireland Council for Voluntary Action questioned its vague policy targets and dearth of funding to address its aims (Hadden et al., 2007: 6). In addition, the Committee on the

Administration of Justice (2006) went as far as to suggest it was counter-productive.

A subsequent example of the way in which equalities have been addressed in public administration is the anti-poverty and social inclusion policy, 'Lifetime Opportunities' (OFMDFM, 2006). This makes repeated reference to the need to comply with the Section 75 equality duty (see chapter 6) and highlights the 'importance of creating employment opportunities as primary routes out of poverty and of the promotion of equality of opportunity as key to tackling labour market inequalities' (OFMDFM, 2006: 11). It also provides an example of the application of Section 75 strategic equality impact assessments to policy (see Figure 7.7). In terms of evaluating the executive's policy, the cross-party Committee for the Office of the First Minister and Deputy First Minister (2008) gave 'a general welcome for the strategy's framework, its life-cycle approach, its long-term objectives and goals . . . and the proposed Ministerial-led Forum to oversee the strategy's implementation'. Yet, it identifies a number of shortcomings and areas for improvement, including the need for 'more emphasis . . . [to] be placed on the specific needs of certain groups who are at high risk of disadvantage and poverty . . . [and] the need for the strategy to be linked more effectively with supporting strategies and proposals on children, older people, health, mental health and learning disabilities, neighbourhood renewal and welfare reform' (COFMDFM, 2008: 11).

Strategic Objective: all people; work towards the elimination of poverty and social exclusion in Northern Ireland by 2020		
Section 75 Group	**Poverty positive reduce differentials for:**	**Rationale**
Religious belief	Roman Catholics	Greater risk of poverty for Roman Catholics than Protestants
Political opinion	Nationalists and those not stating a political preference	The Poverty and Social Exclusion Survey NI (PSENI) indicated that the persons with the referenced political affiliations had the highest rates of poverty

(continued)

Strategic Objective: all people; work towards the elimination of poverty and social exclusion in Northern Ireland by 2020		
Section 75 Group	**Poverty positive reduce differentials for:**	**Rationale**
Racial group	Ethnic minorities/Irish Travellers	Data from Britain indicates that ethnic minorities are at high risk of poverty. There are no comparable NI data
Age	Younger people (with children)	Have a high risk of poverty
Marital status	Divorced/single/ separated (with children) Divorced/single/ separated	Association with lone parenthood and high risk of poverty; family breakdown is also an indicator of future financial hardship
Sexual orientation	Unclear; however, equality impact is likely to range from neutral to positive	Data for poverty by sexual orientation not available
Men and women generally	Females	Evidence suggest that females have a higher risk of poverty
Persons with a disability and persons without	Persons with a disability	Persons with a disability have among the highest risk of poverty, significantly higher than those persons without a disability
Persons with dependants and those without	With dependants	Larger families and lone parents have higher risks of poverty

Figure 7.7. Strategic equality impact assessment of the Northern Ireland Executive's anti-poverty and social inclusion policy 'Lifetime Opportunities' (OFMDFM, 2006).

In education, a revised schools curriculum introduced in 2007 gives prominence to citizenship education with an emphasis on diversity, inclusion, equality, social justice, human rights and social responsibility. In addition, the executive is conducting a policy review 'to ensure that Irish-medium education is fully and appropriately supported as an integral part of the educational system and contributes to the building of a shared future for all our citizens based on equality' (DENI, 2008: vi). A further key development has been the publication of the 'Equality, Good Relations and Human Rights Strategy and Action Plan' (DHSSPSNI, 2008). The aim of which is 'to promote and mainstream equality, good relations and human rights within a health and social care system that values diversity and is accessible to all those who need it' (ibid., 2008: 5). It sets out detailed strategic priorities, associated actions, 'key indicators of success' and 'outcomes sought'.

In terms of institutional mechanisms to promote equalities in policy, as noted, strategic equality impact assessments have been used to secure compliance with Section 75. This has been supported by new administrative practices, including an Inter-departmental Equality and Social Need Steering Group chaired by a senior official in OFMDFM, described as the 'principle mechanism for coordinating, monitoring and evaluating across departments and Agencies' (OFMDFM, 2006: 50).

A limited number of official reports allow an assessment of the developing equalities agenda in public policy. For example, McLaughlin and Faris (2004: 45) found that 'the statutory basis of the [Section 75] duty is proving effective in moving authorities towards compliance and mainstreaming of equality within the public sector'. However, another found that the impact of Section 75 was largely process-driven rather than focusing on outcomes (Chaney and Rees, 2004). A subsequent evaluation of Section 75 (ECNI, 2007: 37) was more sanguine, concluding that it 'has transformed the policy-making process, making it more inclusive, more evidence-based and, as a result, more informed'. However, it added that 'despite this . . . public authorities are generally poor at demonstrating policy outcomes arising from the mainstreaming processes'. The latter point was supported by an independent audit of public bodies' compliance with Section 75 (Reeves, 2007). This found that they were generally failing to demonstrate compliance with the equality duty in their policy work. In turn, Bridge (2007) has questioned whether this was, in part, related to the earlier policy guidance issued by the Equality Commission for Northern Ireland, for it did not require authorities to give full accounts of policy outcomes in relation to equalities. Overall, the review concludes in positive terms, stating that:

In a relatively short period of time, it [s75] has, indeed, been effective in achieving something of a transformation in the development and delivery of public policy. Section 75 has effected substantial cultural change in the institutions of government and, in particular, in how public policy is made. (ECNI, 2007: 80)

In response to the identified shortcomings, the Equality Commission has determined to 'amend its approach to progress reporting to require public authorities to measure the impact of mainstreaming on policy outcomes'. In addition, it asserts that 'future improvements to the consultation process must ensure that public authorities seek the views of the public and those directly affected by the policy' (ECNI, 2007: 46).

In terms of gender equality, ECNI's contribution to the UK report to the UN Committee overseeing member states' progress in relation to the Convention on the Elimination of Discrimination Against Women (CEDAW) highlights a number of ongoing issues and calls on the government of Northern Ireland to implement specific policy initiatives, including: measures to increase the number of childcare places; ensure a sustainable positive trend in the earnings of part-time working women; undertake a sectorally-focused strategy to reduce the gender pay gap; make changes to equal pay legislation to make pay audits mandatory; develop initiatives to increase the numbers of women in science and technology; and ensure that the Careers Strategy is gender proofed (ECNI, 2008: 23).

Overall, Northern Ireland presents a singular case, not least for the link between the civil conflict and the issue of equalities, but also because of distinctive features of governance in the province (such as qualified devolved competence over welfare benefits and oversight of some cross-border public agencies). Also, as noted, the extended periods when the Northern Ireland Assembly was suspended make it difficult to make a full assessment of the promotion of equalities in public policy. However, there is emerging evidence (e.g. anti-poverty and social inclusion policy, revised schools curriculum, etc.) of a strategic awareness of the need to comply with the Section 75 equalities duty. More importantly, equality impact assessments are being applied to public policy in order to identify actions to secure equality outcomes. As in the other two UK devolved polities, there remains much scope for a greater detailing of measurable equalities outcomes in all of the executive's policy documents. Further changes in the way that public policy addresses equalities are likely when (and if) the proposed single equality Bill for Northern Ireland becomes law.[50]

7.3 Conclusion

Analysis of almost a decade of public policy outputs reveals a stark discontinuity with the pre-existing period of administrative devolution in Wales. Prior to 1999, with the possible exception of Welsh language matters,[51] equalities were not generally seen as the responsibility of the territorial ministry for Wales. As a result, although a crosscutting issue, equalities considerations did not normally feature in the policy outputs of the Welsh Office. Analysis reveals that the creation of the National Assembly has led to the political prioritisation of equalities. All of the major policies and strategies issued by successive governments refer to the promotion of equalities as a key theme. This strategic commitment to equalities is a major transition; at a symbolic level at least, it points to the increasing realisation of one of the arguments of pro-devolution campaigners that constitutional reform would deliver inclusive public policy, which would further the promotion of equalities (Welsh Office, 1997; Chaney and Fevre, 2001). Inclusive approaches to policy also resonate with the literature on mainstreaming equality; specifically, the need to engage with groups targeted by the policies (see Beveridge and Nott, 2002; Donaghy 2004). The majority of key strategies that have emerged in the wake of devolution have been founded on consultation with those outside government, including hitherto marginalised groups traditionally targeted by equalities initiatives.

Previously absent, the foregoing analysis reveals that equality policy concerns now feature across the range of government portfolios (MEGs), from economic development to culture. On matters such as asylum seekers, forced marriage, honour based violence and domestic abuse, national Welsh strategies now exist for the first time. In areas of shared policy responsibility with Westminster (on topics such as child welfare and youth justice) there is some evidence of the Welsh government pursuing a more advanced equalities approach than the UK government (such as pressing for a ban on corporal punishment in public care settings in accordance with the UN Charter on the Rights of the Child). The result is policy that is specifically tailored to the social, economic and cultural specificities of Wales, rather than the pre-existing 'one size fits all' approach evident in policy outputs from Whitehall. A further notable aspect of change is the overall growth of government's policy-making capacity.

The present post-empiricist, interpretative focus on the language, scope and aims of policy documents reveals that the promotion of equalities in public policy has been characterised by a diversity of approaches and policy instruments. These include legal duties on public bodies, positive action, incentives to promote equalities in the private sector, and measures to develop the capacity of equality organisations in civil society (see Figure 7.8). In instrumental terms, the emerging evidence from a growing number of evaluative studies is that policies are beginning to achieve equalities outcomes (e.g. increase in numbers of disabled people participating in sports;[52] increasing diversity of those holding public appointments; greater attention to equality and diversity in the post-2008 schools curriculum, GPs obliged to write an annual health report for individuals with learning disabilities, etc.).

Instrument	Example(s)
Redistribution of resources and support for specific groups.	Student funding for higher education – Special Support Grants for assistance with the costs of registered or accredited childcare during term time (also Parents' Learning Allowance); Gypsy Traveller Site Refurbishment Grant Scheme; local authority grants for asylum seekers.
Promotion of equalities in accredited professional training.	Teacher training framework of the General Teaching Council for Wales.
A rights-based approach to equalities.	Government subscription to UN Convention on the Rights of the Child, and United Nations Principles for Older Persons; creation of Social Care Charter for service users with learning disabilities.
Changing the nature of public service delivery for targeted social groups.	Black, Minority Ethnic Housing Action Plan for Wales (2007l) requires BME Housing Action Plans from local authorities.

(continued)

Instrument	Example(s)
Conveying rights to citizens by placing legal duties on devolved public bodies to promote equalities.	Children and Families (Wales) Measure (2010) places a duty on public agencies to demonstrate their contribution to ending child poverty, and duties on public, voluntary and private sectors in the proposed Welsh Language Measure (2010).
Raise public awareness of equalities issues.	Close the pay gap campaigns.
Promote consultation and participation with groups targeted by equalities initiatives.	The introduction of schools councils: 'Funky Dragon' – the Children and Young People's Assembly.
Changing social attitudes around equality and discrimination.	Forced Marriage and Honour Based Violence Action Plan. (WAG, 2008(16)); the revised National Curriculum and Foundation Phase in schools education, with emphasis on tolerance and respecting diversity.
A broadening of focus on equalities to include economic status.	Child Poverty Strategy; Reaching Higher (higher education strategy), aim to increase the proportion of young people accessing HE from low participation neighbourhoods.
Legislating to back equalities policies in law.	Education (Wales) Measure (2009) gives children themselves the right to appeal to the Special Educational Needs Tribunal for Wales; greater rights for Welsh speakers in proposed Welsh Language Measure (2010).
Change the procurement practices of public services.	'Winning Our Business' policy of encouraging good equalities practice amongst suppliers to government and the public sector.
Promoting 'good relations'.	School Government (Terms of Reference) (Wales) Regulations (2000) places legal duties on governing bodies and head teachers to exercise their respective functions with due regard to the need to promote good relations between persons of different racial groups, and between males and females.
Promote Welsh language/bilingualism.	Iaith Pawb (WAG, 2003e): 'the Assembly Government will mainstream consideration of the Welsh language into the policy-making processes of all Assembly Ministerial portfolios'.

(continued)

Instrument	Example(s)
Advocacy of an intersectional/multi-strand approach to equalities.	Tackling Domestic Abuse: The All Wales National Strategy (WAG, 2005k).
Promoting equalities in the private sector.	General Medical Services (i.e. General Practitioner) contract incentivises GPs to write an annual health report for individuals with mental health problems; Rural Development Plan (WAG, 2007o) grants and training schemes.
To develop the capacity of equality organisations in civil society.	The government's Promoting Equalities Fund that extends grants to NGOs and policy networks.
Hypothecation of funding for the promotion of equalities.	Ring-fenced aspects of the Carers' Grant Scheme.
Encourage partnership working on developing equalities policies.	Statement on Policy and Practice for Adults with a Learning Disability (WAG, 2007r).
The creation of new monitoring arrangements to oversee the promotion of equalities.	Creation of the offices of Children's and Older People's Commissioners for Wales, respectively.
To embed equality as an evaluation/approval criterion for public sector reform.	Collaborative working plans between learning providers in the Delivering Skills that Work for Wales Strategy (WAG, 2008(22)ii).
Secure improvements in official data-gathering.	Carers' Strategy for Wales Action Plan (WAG, 2007i).

Figure 7.8. Contrasting policy instruments used to promote equalities in Welsh public policy (1999–2008)

However, despite these positive developments, ongoing problems and challenges remain. Whilst the majority of policies are integrated into the government's strategic vision and cite the aim of promoting equalities, a number do little more that offer a declaration of intent around equalities (e.g. Environment Strategy Action Plan 2008–11, WAG, 2008(35)). Analysis of the policy outputs of the past decade also reveals that there is a high level of variability in the way that different government departments address equalities issues. Generally absent in a number of policy areas (e.g. economic development, sustainable development and tourism) is a systematic approach that is based upon the use of equalities indicators and impact assessments. This was particularly evident in the early years of devolved governance.

From a comparative perspective, and notwithstanding the distinct socio-economic contexts, it is striking that the 'mainstreaming agenda' in each devolved polity shares key commonalities including: the need to move beyond the unsupported, declaratory espousal of equalities in policy documents; to overcome a preoccupation with administrative processes; and to ensure the systematic use of mainstreaming tools (such as impact assessments and equalities training). Indeed, these are issues that continue to resonate across the UK as reflected in a recent UN report: 'many public bodies, including government ministries, have faced difficulties in developing results-based and action-oriented equality schemes and in mainstreaming equality into all policies and processes' (UN Committee on the Elimination of Discrimination against Women, 2008: 4). Yet, encouragingly, as detailed in this chapter, these issues are starting to be addressed with the application of more sophisticated approaches to promoting equality. However, much work remains before effective mainstreaming is a feature of all policy work.

8

Lobbying and Electoral Competition on Equality Matters in the Devolved Polity

8.0 Introduction

Both the literature on mainstreaming equalities and new governance theory emphasise a participatory, democratic dimension to public policy-making. Lobbying is a key component of this and refers quite simply to 'the practice of attempting to influence the decisions of government' (Rosenthal, 2001: 11). This chapter relates to a stark reality: without engagement from organisations and networks outside government there is little hope for securing the 'new pluralism' in post-devolution public policy-making alluded to by former First Minister Rhodri Morgan (Morgan, 2002). Accordingly, here we explore the evidence for a developing 'equalities lobby'. First the discussion delineates the membership of the lobby and examines the interactions between agencies and groups in the Welsh policy domain. As Hill (2005: 76) observes, such a focus on networks and policy communities 'offers an important corrective to accounts of the political system and the operation of the state'. However, it is argued that to overlook completely the role of institutional structures would preclude an holistic account of the policy process. Accordingly, we build on the earlier discussion of the institutional aspects of devolved governance (chapter 4), and explore how organisations outside government have used 'inclusive governance' mechanisms to advance equalities claims. Thus, attention is placed on the National Assembly's Equality and Petitions Committees, as well as the Third Sector Partnership Council. The analysis concludes with a focus on a new dimension to the lobby; electoral competition around equalities as political parties and civil society organisations advance policy proposals in the context of elections to the Assembly. We first turn to consider theoretical perspectives on lobby development.

8.1 Lobbies, Interest Groups and Policy Theory

In policy terms, a burgeoning literature explores the relationship between those outside government and those on the 'inside', namely, officials and elected politicians. The classic 'Downsian' paradigm in political science emphasises that the primary objective of politicians is to win electoral support (Downs, 1957). Thus, in contrast to the contested notion of 'conviction politics' based on uncompromisable principles (Sykes, 2000), political candidates are held to adapt their policy platforms to maximise support at the ballot box. Grossman and Helpman (1996) develop this dualism and outline how lobbying leads to political candidates adopting policies founded upon a compromise between the policy preferences of lobbies and those of 'ordinary' voters. More sophisticated perspectives are presented by 'menu-auction' theory and 'transaction' models (Epstein and O'Halloran, 1999). These describe how lobbies incentivise and offer policy-makers a range, or 'menu', of 'payments' (e.g. in the form of votes, offers of expertise and so on) should the elected representative adopt the policy that they advocate. Policy theory also emphasises how lobbying can be an elitist process owing to the power and agency of elected representatives to act as 'gatekeepers' – 'the elected policy-maker chooses the lobbies that participate in the policy-making process . . . [thus] policy is the outcome of efficient bargaining between the elected policy-maker and a coalition of lobbies selected by the policy-maker' (Felli and Merlo, 2004: 23). In contrast, neo-pluralist accounts (e.g. Hilmar, 2005; Lowery and Gray, 2004) have drawn on the classic work of Robert Dahl (1951) and point to power and access to decision-making being widely (if unevenly) distributed throughout the political system and not limited to a political elite. Importantly, according to this perspective, a multiplicity of organisations may enter lobbying communities, thereby reflecting a diversity of social interests (including equalities constituencies historically marginalised in the conduct of public business). Whilst elitist and neo-pluralist conceptions offer opposed perspectives on the jostling for access and influence that defines the lobbying process, Lowery (2007: 53) also emphasises that cognisance is required of more mundane factors related to the actions of NGOs and others outside government, such as:

> Maintaining membership rolls or securing access from political elites on other issues the organization cares about, or changing the salience and popularity of the issue over the long haul, or blocking rival organizations from relying on a shared issue agenda, membership base, or patrons; or any number of other goals, all of which help the organization survive.

In contrast, Smith (1993: 67) offers a critical view of traditional theory stating that it offers a 'stark state/civil society dichotomy', when in reality things are not so clear-cut. He underlines how 'state actors [politicians, officials, etc.] are also actors in civil society; they live in society and have a constant contact with groups that represent societal interests. Therefore the interests of state actors develop along with the interests of the group actors.' A similar view is presented by the 'advocacy coalition approach' advanced by Sabatier and Jenkins-Smith (1993, 1999). This emphasises how, on specific policy issues, alliances may develop involving actors from different parts of the political system, including those inside and outside government.

As noted, such theories resonate with debates on the promotion of equality, not least because the degree of autonomy and influence of those seeking to influence public decision-making depends on the way that interest collectivities are organised and, crucially, how they connect to those in power. Policy network theory provides a framework for analysing this key aspect of the lobbying process. Here, work by Jordan and Richardson (1987) and Marsh and Rhodes (1992) usefully conceives of two 'ideal types' of network. At one extreme 'issue networks' are groups of organisations focused on a particular policy area or issue. These are dynamic entities generally characterised by a large and diverse membership; fluctuating levels of contact between members; some conflict and disagreement over issues; varying resources; unequal power among members; and limited capacity to regulate all network members. In contrast, 'policy communities' are seen as stronger, more rigid types of network. They are characterised by a relatively limited, sometimes exclusive, membership; a tendency to be comprised of professional interests; possessing shared values; having frequent interaction between network members; having hierarchical leadership that can 'deliver' members' support and agreement on issues; and exhibiting a relative balance of power between network members.

We now shift focus to apply some of these conceptual perspectives to an analysis of contemporary developments in equalities lobbying. First, we turn to look at the origins, nature, size and principal components of the post-devolution lobby.

8.2 Mapping the Lobby: NGOs, State Sponsored Policy Networks and Organisations

The origins of an 'equalities lobby' in Wales can be linked to past campaigning, notably in the 1960s and 1970s, by members of the women's movement (Chaney et al., 2007) and Welsh language pressure groups (Williams, 2008). Respectively, these social movements challenged enduring gender inequality (Inglehart and Norris, 2003; Walby, 1989) as well as what has been described from a socio-linguistic perspective as the 'cultural homogenisation of British society' (Sharpe, 1993: 293). As far as other equalities strands are concerned, Williams (2006: 191) writes that 'the black voluntary sector has a long tradition in Wales, characterised by a high degree of civil autonomy and radicalism and the development of alternative forms of welfare provision beyond the mainstream'. This contrasts with the experience of disabled people. As Betts et al. (2001: 74) observed, when reflecting on earlier patterns of civic engagement, 'historically the stress has been on care and on the representation *of* disabled people, not representation *by* disabled people'.

Overall, prior to 1999, lobbying opportunities for equalities groups were limited. Largely owing to central government's hegemony over much of public administration, Wales possessed a weak national policy-making capacity. This was reflected in the thinness and fragility of the policy lobby centred on the Welsh Office. Thus, at the outset of devolution, the First Minister observed: 'I don't think that we have the wealth of think tanks . . . and professional associations, organised interest groups, corporate lobby bodies and political consultancies' (Morgan, 2000). This was not a problem unique to Wales, as Adams and Robinson (2002: 204) state: 'each of the devolved administrations . . . has been very concerned at the dearth of policy-making capacity in their respective territories'. Yet, the situation was particularly acute in the case of equalities-oriented organisations' ability to engage with the new structures of governance, for their history was one of longstanding marginalisation.

When the Assembly began its work, women's organisations comprised 8 per cent of the country's 25,000 voluntary organisations. Views towards the 'new politics' from these organisations were mixed. As Betts et al. (2001: 70) noted, several organisation spoke of:

> their high expectations and excitement and looked forward to significant changes. Others were more cautious; they had no 'contacts in high places' and little or no understanding of the political process or channels of communication. They were concerned not so much about being forgotten as about getting to be known.

BME groups were also characterised by a fragile infrastructure. Black voluntary sector activity in Wales was sparse, comprising little more than 1 per cent of the sector as a whole (Chaney and Williams, 2003: 97). Thus, at the beginning of devolved governance, Williams and Chaney (2001: 80) observed that:

> The 'ethnic' population is relatively dispersed so that 'community', a concept dear to the heart of policy-makers, as a locus of intervention may be difficult to find. Indeed, little is known about the pattern of ethnic mobilisation in Wales, about diverse identities, community politics or the politics of recognition.

In terms of BME attitudes, many had 'an overriding sense that the Assembly lacked meaning and relevance for them' (Williams and Chaney, 2001: 85). Similarly, disabled people's groups were highly diverse in nature. They represented those that had acquired, rather than inherited, a disability, as well as those with restricted mobility, sensory impairment and learning difficulties. For some, these factors were openly acknowledged, for others they were hidden. Disabled people's organisations involved not only disabled people themselves but also carers, family and professional workers. Their views of devolution were mixed. Some said it presented 'a wonderful opportunity to influence the Assembly'; for others there was a mixture of uncertainty tinged with apprehension, or outright hostility (Betts, Borland and Chaney, 2001: 76). The principal umbrella body for disabled people's organisations highlighted that, in future, successful policy outcomes depended upon effective lobbying:

> Will there be a real change in our lives after May 6th [1999, the opening of the National Assembly]? The short answer is 'no'. It will take time for the Assembly to map out its agenda and to start the process of change. In the long term it could bring real changes to Wales but that will depend on disabled people engaging in the debate and communicating ideas. (Disability Wales, 1998: 23)

Almost a decade on, reference to the Wales Council for Voluntary Action database of 28,754 third-sector bodies reveals a proliferation equalities-related organisations, including those representing gender, ethnic 'minorities', religion, disability and age (i.e. children and families and youth) (see Table 8.1). Together they constitute almost half (47.1 per cent) of the sector, a total of 13,550 NGOs.[1] As such, they can lay claim to being the largest potential interest grouping in the third sector. However, a note of caution is necessary; many of these organisations do not engage directly in policy work. The reasons for this vary. Some are solely concerned with service delivery. Others lack the resources to lobby government, are unaware of participatory structures, or are unwilling to take on policy work (sometimes seen as too 'political'). In addition, some may not view their work as overtly equalities-orientated (e.g. some religious organisations, or various bodies working with youth offenders would not necessarily see themselves as respectively working for age and faith equality).

Referring to the first years of devolution, Adams and Robinson (2002: 204) explain that in the face of concerns over policy-making capacity 'each of the devolved administrations felt obliged to open the circles of decision-making in order to bolster their policy-making capacity'. An early example of this was the Promoting Equality Fund (PEF), a formal grant mechanism used by the Assembly Government to back equality policy networks. Established in 2000, in its first year

Forum heading	WCVA classification	Scope of operation					Total (number of organisations)	% of whole sector[1]
		National	Regional	Local	Branch	Project		
Gender		**60**	**72**	**1689**	**25**	**9**	**1855**	**6.5**
		0.2%	0.3%	5.9%	0.1%	0.0%		
	Men	21	20	238	3	2	284	1.0
		0.1%	0.1%	0.8%	0.0%	0.0%		
	Women	53	67	1476	24	7	1627	5.7
		0.2%	0.2%	5.1%	0.1%	0.0%		
Ethnic minorities		**62**	**43**	**232**	**15**	**11**	**363**	**1.3**
		0.2%	0.2%	0.8%	0.1%	0.0%		
	Refugees	20	2	11	4	0	37	0.1
		0.1%	0.0%	0.0%	0.0%	%		
	Ethnic minorities	55	43	226	14	11	349	1.2
		0.2%	0.2%	0.8%	0.1%	0.0%		
Religion		**113**	**123**	**3512**	**17**	**7**	**3772**	**13.1**
		0.4%	0.4%	12.2%	0.1%	0.0%		
	Religious organisations	113	123	3512	17	7	3772	13.1
		0.4%	0.4%	12.2%	0.1%	0.0%		

(continued)

[1] 28,754 organisations as at 1 July 2008.

Forum heading	WCVA classification	Scope of operation					Total (number of organisations)	% of whole sector[1]
		National	Regional	Local	Branch	Project		
Disability		**154** 0.5%	**168** 0.6%	**1143** 4.0%	**151** 0.5%	**63** 0.2%	**1679**	**5.8**
	Physical disabilities	132 0.5%	132 0.5%	873 3.0%	98 0.3%	42 0.2%	1277	4.4
	Learning disabilities	86 0.3%	97 0.3%	630 2.2%	107 0.4%	40 0.1%	960	3.3
Children and Families		**163** 0.6%	**140** 0.5%	**2724** 9.5%	**116** 0.4%	**110** 0.4%	**3253**	**11.3**
	Family welfare	76 0.3%	55 0.2%	415 1.4%	72 0.3%	86 0.3%	704	2.5
	Children	133 0.5%	119 0.4%	2524 8.8%	68 0.2%	84 0.3%	2928	10.2
Youth		**140** 0.5%	**142** 0.5%	**2227** 7.8%	**58** 0.2%	**61** 0.2%	**2628**	**9.1**
	Youth	140 0.5%	142 0.5%	2227 7.8%	58 0.2%	58 0.2%	2628	9.1
TOTAL		692	688	11527	382	261	13550	47.1

Table 8.1. Details of equalities-related voluntary organisations from the All Wales Database of Voluntary Organisations (WCVA, 2008a)

it allocated £150,000 to develop the capacity of policy networks representing women, Black and ethnic minority communities and disabled people (WAG, 2007d: 3). The low starting point of equalities policy-making capacity has meant that such government intervention continues a decade on. In 2008–9 the annual value of the Fund was just under £2M (Figure 8.1).[2]

Name	Network/Organisation Aims
All Wales Ethnic Minority Association (AWEMA)	To develop a good practice guide on race equality, 'devise tools which lead to increased participation amongst the minority ethnic communities in Wales . . . undertake a mapping exercise of the minority ethnic communities of Wales, develop information and help systems to support minority ethnic communities, identify numbers of minority ethnic applicants for public appointments in Wales'.[3]
Wales Women's National Coalition (WWNC)	'Women's Voice aims to impact on policies that affect women in Wales. We endeavour to vocalise the needs, opinions and struggles of women in Wales. Women's Voice provides a vocal point for women of all ages, ability and ethnicity living in Wales; consultation . . . involves members in Assembly consultative activities.'[4]
LGB Forum Cymru/ Stonewall Cymru	'Lobbying local authorities, public service providers and government for inclusion, and legislative and policy improvements for LGB people in Wales . . . we will focus on the following key strategic objectives for the next 3 years . . . Community development, Education, Employment, Fair life chances, Changing attitudes, Community safety.'[5]
Minority Ethnic Women's Network Cymru (MEWN)	Aims are 'to change the position of BME Women in Welsh society; to provide a platform for the views of BME women in Wales; to enable BME women to extend their knowledge and skills, and to encourage them to participate fully in local and national affairs as well as in voluntary activities and employment . . . To represent the needs of BME women in policy forums and campaign on issues affecting them.'[6]
Cardiff Women's Workshop	'We provide a range of services that promote gender equality and aim to improve the lives and role of women in society. Services include training, consultancy and support to individual women, groups and organisations.'[7]
Disability Wales	'We occupy a unique position within Wales by championing the rights and equality of all disabled people regardless of physical or sensory impairment, learning difficulty or mental health condition . . . We work with all areas of government – local, Assembly, Westminster and Europe – developing policy, campaigning, lobbying, challenging.'[8]

(continued)

Name	Network/Organisation Aims
Black Voluntary Sector Network Wales	Strategic objectives: to raise awareness of the needs of the Black Voluntary Sector Communities; to build the capacity of the Black Voluntary Sector; to develop the membership of the organisation; to represent, support and campaign for Wales's BME voluntary organisations, community groups, volunteers and communities in Wales; to play a strategic role to incorporate the needs of BME communities within policy and strategy.

Figure 8.1. Welsh Assembly Government funded equality policy networks/organisations

In addition to the PEF, other Welsh government departments continue to extend support to forums and networks of civil society organisations clustered around specific equality strands, as well as funding individual organisations. Over the past decade, examples of this support include that given to BAWSO (an all Wales, voluntary organisation, providing specialist service to Black and minority ethnic women and children made homeless through domestic violence); the All Wales Saheli Association (that 'seeks to develop positive futures to enrich and maximise the quality of the lives of Asian and Muslim children and families') (MEWN, 2007: 3); and the Welsh Refugee Council. Other prominent examples include the Wales Council for the Blind[9] and Children in Wales.[10] The latter organisation provides a striking example of how equalities-related NGOs can themselves act as catalysts to the formation of policy networks; a recent report listed no fewer than sixteen networks associated with this NGO (see Figure 8.2). Further government funding for standalone organisations has been extended via the Grass Roots Fund[11] that provides small grants[12] via County Voluntary Services 'designed to build capacity in small voluntary and community groups formed by communities of interest'. The funding is targeted at what it terms 'disadvantaged groups'. These include ethnic minorities; disabled people; lesbian, gay and bisexual people; women; those homeless or working for homeless people; refugees and asylum seekers; gypsies and travellers; and language communities' (WAG, 2007s: 12).

Accompanied and Unaccompanied Asylum Seekers Network	Made up of a range of professionals, including policy-makers from the Welsh government and its aims include: • allowing workers in this field to network and share good practice • contributing to the development of policy in this area
All Wales Children and Young People's Advocacy Providers Network	Aims include: • promoting partnership work and developmental strategies between organisations • facilitating problem solving and resolve potential conflicts of interest • promoting the UNCRC and Children's Rights • linking this group to broader issues of children and young people's participation in Wales
Children's Rights Practice Exchange Groups	To enable practitioners to exchange expertise and information; an e-briefing service for these groups continues to be utilised by way of circulating information and enabling communication between quarterly events
The Disabled Children Policy Group	Brings together those with a policy brief on disability to work together to highlight issues and concerns about services to disabled children
The Forum on Issues for Disabled Children	A multi-agency group that shares information and good practice, and lobbies for issues relating to disabled children and young people
The Early Years and Childcare Advisory Group	Concentrates specifically on the needs of the under-eights and their families; the group aims to raise public awareness of the needs and entitlement of all young children and their families and to influence public policy and bring about change
End Child Poverty Network Cymru	A coalition of organisations concerned with child poverty; a steering group consists of representatives from Children in Wales, Barnardo's Cymru, Save the Children Cymru, NCH Cymru, NSPCC Cymru, etc.
Fatherhood Wales Forum	Meets four times a year to exchange practice and provide an opportunity for members to respond to consultations, and to promote the importance of fathers in the lives of their children
Fatherhood Wales Policy Group	A multi-agency network recognising the important role fathers play in raising their children; the group works in partnership with Fathers Direct and has close links with . . . the Office of the Children's Commissioner for Wales, concentrating on specific policy issues to set the agenda for work in Wales

(continued)

Fforwm Magu Plant/Parenting Forum	A multi-agency network of parenting organisations; the forum promotes the sharing of good practice, dissemination of relevant information, training and quality standards, and communicates the views of parents, carers and children to policy-makers in Wales.
Looking After Health Exchange	A multi-agency group which aims to help guide policy across Wales to promote the health of children looked after
The Sure Start Network	The network has developed into a Flying Start/ Sure Start Network to reflect the direction of Welsh Assembly Government policy
The Young Disabled Persons' Network	The network brings groups of young disabled people together from across Wales to discuss issues relating to their rights
Young Carers Workers' Network	The network holds three one-day meetings to share issues, concerns and develop good practice, and also holds a two-day meeting and training event in September each year; the network supports young carers who can submit their views to the Carers Strategy Review Panel.
Children and Young People's Participation in Cymru Network	It affords representatives from Councils for Voluntary Services to improve knowledge, offer mutual support and understanding and discuss issues in order to enhance their work within Children and Young People's Partnerships; the network also aims to provide a national perspective, an opportunity for joint lobbying and to promote the benefits of Wales-wide coordination
Participation Workers' Network Wales	A multi-agency strategic body building capacity for the development of participation in Wales; the network supports workers and organisations interested in or actively promoting children and young people's participation.

Figure 8.2. The proliferation of policy networks around equality and rights for children[13]

In addition to the foregoing, devolution has seen the development of a plethora of state-sponsored policy networks covering the spectrum of equalities interests; government has established some, others have a different history. The effect has been a rapid increase in network density, giving some credence to the idea that devolution has supported the development of 'network governance'. It has also seen the rise of increasingly complex alliances of organisations engaged in policy work. The following examples illustrate this, and also highlight the extent to which government has been concerned to fund the strengthening of policy-making capacity in civil and civic society.

- *The Minority Ethnic Youth Forum*: set up to address 'the concern of many minority ethnic young people that they were not being involved in the political processes' (WAG, 2008(10): 27).
- *Age Alliance Wales*: 'an alliance of [older people's] voluntary organisations working in Wales . . . representing the concerns of its members as well as disseminating information to the voluntary sector' (WAG, 2008(6): 7).
- Better Government for Older People Cymru is 'a national network of coordinators, champions and 50+ Forums, to act as a channel of communication between the networks, the Welsh Local Government Association (WLGA) and the Welsh Assembly Government' (WAG, 2008(6): 9).
- *The Disabled Children and Young People's Network in Wales*: funded to act as 'the main national conduit of the views of disabled children and young people into a range of national initiatives . . . It also offers the opportunity for Ministers and officials to access their views on a range of policy initiatives'.[14]
- *Fforwm Iaith* ('Language Forum'): founded following the recommendation of the joint Policy Review of the Welsh Language conducted in 2002 by the National Assembly's Culture, and Education and Lifelong Learning committees. This called for a language forum to be established, one that 'should play a crucial role in improving coherence in strategic planning' (NAfW, 2002: 14).
- *The All-Wales Refugee Policy Forum*: founded in 2003 and 'made up of senior-level decision makers and key stakeholders from across Wales'.[15] Examples of its policy role include work with NHS Wales to develop the Welsh Asylum Seekers and Refugee Doctors Group (that receives Assembly Government funding for a re-qualification programme for refugee doctors) (WAG, 2004b).
- *Refugee Voice Wales*: a network of 29 refugee community organisations.[16]
- *Migrants Forum*: founded in 2007 by the Minister for Social Justice and Local Government who noted that 'although immigration matters are non-devolved functions, the Welsh Assembly Government has a responsibility to migrants resident in Wales

under its health, education and social services functions, and to a limited extent community cohesion . . . [the Forum] will provide targeted information of national importance'.[17]

- *The Faith Communities Forum*: aims to 'promote a dialogue between the National Assembly for Wales, Welsh Assembly Government and the major faith communities on any matters affecting the economic, social and cultural life of Wales'.[18] The Forum involves representatives of the following faiths: Baha'I, Buddhism, Christianity (Church in Wales, Churches Together in Wales (CYTUN), Evangelical Alliance Wales, Free Church Council, Roman Catholic Church in Wales), Hinduism, Judaism, Islam and Sikhism.

- *The Voluntary Sector Equality and Human Rights Coalition*: describes itself as 'a network of more than 80 voluntary sector organisations and networks in Wales working across all equalities and human rights issues. The coalition exists to further the equality and human rights agenda in Wales from a third sector cross-strand perspective of shared visions and mutual respect' (WCVA, 2008: 6).

- *National Partnership Forum for Older People*: a leading network for on age matters (see Figure 8.3).

Forum's Aims	Expert and informed advice to the Welsh Assembly Government on the development of its policies for older people (older people defined as aged 50+ years); acting as an effective channel of communication from older people and their representatives to local government and Welsh Assembly Government and, thorough the Assembly Government, to the UK Government.
Forum's Mission Statement	The forum's ambition is to involve all older people, pledging to ensure the voice of older people is heard; to engage with older people and their representative organisations; to advise and influence all levels of government; to evaluate the effectiveness of policies that impact on older people; to seek the fulfilment of aims and objectives within the WAG Strategy; to support the work of the Commissioner for Older People in Wales; and to support initiatives that relate to the aims of the forum.[19]
Membership	Five appointed lay members, and 13 nominated members (representing older people's organisations, local government, care, education, health, housing, transport, employment and voluntary sectors).

(continued)

Context of the Forum's work	Relates closely to the Strategy for Older People in Wales that was launched in 2003, following extensive consultations throughout Wales. The main aims of the Strategy for Older People in Wales are as follows: 1. tackle discrimination, promote positive images and give older people a stronger voice; 2. develop scope for working, learning and making an active contribution; 3. promote, improve health and well-being, and better and more integrated services; 4. promote high quality services, independent living and responsive services; 5. promote Strategy as 'catalyst for change' across sectors'.
Frequency of meetings	Biannual
Participants in Meetings	Forum members, Welsh government ministers, senior government officials, officials from other government departments and public bodies (e.g. the Pensions Service, UK government Department of Work and Pensions), staff from Age Concern Cymru (an independent organisation that acts as the Forum's secretariat) and 'observers' (a blanket term for anyone invited to be present/participate in the meetings) and participants in an annual 'open' meeting, with 'older people locally invited to participate in relation to discussions on key topics'.
Examples of the Forum's policy work 2006–7	Access to learning opportunities for older people; 'Age proofing' (auditing) services to assess their impact on older people; and the role of and procedures for appointment of the Commissioner for Older People in Wales.
Transparency/ independence from government	Thirteen nominated members from organisations outside government; annual 'open' meetings; minutes of meetings published on the Worldwide Web.

Figure 8.3. The National Partnership Forum for Older People[20]

Two further examples illustrate the extent and complexity of the nascent equalities lobby; one network is based around a single issue, the other is an alliance, or umbrella body, itself made up of component networks. Thus the Coalition on Charging Cymru is a lobby group campaigning for free home care provision for disabled people. It is comprised of organisations representing the interests of older people, disabled people and carers. In contrast, the Wales Disability Reference Group represents disabled people on the Voluntary Sector Partnership Council and is made up of five umbrella bodies: Disability Wales, Learning Disability Wales, Mind Cymru, Wales Council for the Blind and Wales Council for Deaf People (Disability Wales, 2007: 9).

As well as state-funded networks, government has supported individual equality projects in order to foster engagement with the policy process. A recent example is the Muslim Women Talk Project. Its aims were to 'establish a valuable communications link between the policy-makers and the Muslim community',[21] and its work focused on improving community relations and policy issues such as health and education). A further example is the Disability Equality in Action Project whereby the disabled people's network, Disability Wales, was commissioned to assist public sector bodies, including the Welsh government, with implementing the social model of disability (Disability Wales, 2006: 2).

A further, less prominent, element in the equalities lobby is the trades unions. Wales has one of the highest rates of union membership in the UK, with around a third of employees being members. In total, half a million people belong to approximately 50 Trades Union Congress (TUC) affiliated unions (Bevan Foundation, 2008). As an umbrella body, the Wales TUC has engaged in policy work with the Welsh government (examples include co-sponsorship of the Close the Pay Gap Campaigns, attendance at the Assembly's Equality Committee and representation on the statutory Business Partnership Council that forms a nexus between government and business interests). However, a recent study (Bevan Foundation, 2008) found that individual unions had yet to fully engage with devolved government on equalities issues, noting 'they are actively promoting equality at work, [but] they mostly do so on a UK-wide basis which can make it difficult for them to engage with Wales-specific issues and organisations'. The report warned that 'there is a strong risk that the Welsh Assembly Government and EHRC Wales will develop different priorities to unions and have different expectations of unions' roles. There is an urgent need for dialogue between the organisations' (Bevan Foundation, 2008: 25).

When weighed against the uncertainty over the implications of devolution expressed by many equalities-related organisations when the Assembly was created, a significant development is the way in which lobbying and policy work has become written into, or formalised in, their organisational aims. For example, those of Help the Aged Cymru state:

> Our priorities for influencing the Welsh Assembly Government centre on the following principles: Listening to and involving older people so that their needs and opinions are at the centre of all decisions on policies and strategies that affect them; [and] Working with the Commissioner for Older People in Wales to make sure that the interests, dignity and rights of older people in Wales are protected.[22]

Likewise, the official remit for Refugee Voice Wales is 'to raise awareness of refugee issues, influence policy, and campaign for refugee and asylum seekers rights'.[23]

A further key aspect in understanding the developing equalities lobby is the extent of the desire of 'ordinary' members to engage in policy work. This is important for it indicates whether the post-devolution lobby is characterised by 'executive modes' of engagement with government, whereby policy work is undertaken by organisations' management teams and policy officers, rather than through consultation with 'ordinary' members. At the end of the Assembly's first term an insight into this issue was gained by a survey of nine hundred members of eleven organisations designed to reflect the diversity of women's NGOs in Wales (Chaney et al., 2004). Analysis of the responses revealed a significant political dimension to their activities. When asked why members participated in the activities of all the voluntary organisations to which they belonged, over a quarter (27 per cent) said that they did so because they wished to influence the views of politicians and decision-makers, and 11 per cent said their membership was 'politically motivated'. Importantly, almost a half of women participated in order to 'promote the rights of women' (45 per cent). The survey also asked about the effectiveness of women's NGOs in interest mediation; in other words, in listening to members, lobbying and taking part in policy consultations. The surveyed organisations scored well on this measure. Overall, only 4 per cent of respondents said that they were never asked for their opinions in meetings (57 per cent said they were 'often' asked); more than three-quarters (78 per cent) said that the local branch of their NGO influenced policy in the organisation as a whole; and just under a quarter said it exerted a strong influence on the parent organisation (23 per cent). When asked how organisations such as their own should work with government, just under a half (41 per cent) of respondents agreed with the statement that devolved government would be better if women's NGOs engaged with it. Strikingly, just under a third (32 per cent) said that women's NGOs 'had a responsibility' to work with the Welsh government. When asked if they agreed or disagreed that they could influence political decisions affecting Wales, over a third (36 per cent) of all respondents either 'definitely agreed' (7 per cent) or agreed 'to some extend' (29 per cent). The study also revealed significant levels of participation by women's NGOs in the policy process. Almost a half (49.1 per cent) of those surveyed said that their organisation had lobbied the Assembly during its first term on at least one issue. Overall, such findings are striking, for they indicate significant levels of engagement in the policy work of the Assembly in the first years of devolution and, for those that had yet to be involved in policy work, a significant demand from grassroots members to do so.

Overall, as the foregoing indicates, the nascent equalities lobby in Wales is characterised by its low starting point, this has necessitated extensive and ongoing government support and funding over the first decade of devolution. Moreover, the funding arrangements, configuration and patterns of co-working between various interest groupings and networks constituting the lobby' are characterised by their density and complexity. Alliances of organisations may variously operate and receive state funding in relation to a policy area (e.g. health), a policy issue (e.g. independent living for disabled people), a single equality 'strand' (e.g. Disability Reference Group), two or more 'strands' (e.g. age and disability; the Disabled Children and Young People's Network), a specific project (e.g. Muslim Women Talk), or around the overall promotion of equalities (e.g. Wales Equality Reference Group). In addition, some equalities networks have emerged from civil society, whereas others have been created through government intervention. Furthermore, some are comprised of individual organisations, others of individual organisations and umbrella bodies. Adding to the complexity, organisations may variously choose to lobby within the proliferation of networks and alliances, or undertake 'standalone' lobbying of government. Moreover, some have a Wales-only remit; others may operate on an England and Wales, British or UK basis. Thus, the emerging evidence suggests that whilst initial concerns about the capacity of NGOs to engage in policy-making on equalities are being addressed, a key issue for the future will be whether the equalities lobby can continue to develop if state support for policy networks is scaled back.

8.3 Scotland and Northern Ireland

8.3.1 Scotland

Lynch (2002: 121) describes the impact that constitutional reform has made to lobbying in Scotland: 'before devolution, pressure group politics was a relatively closed environment. The main focus of pressure group attention was Scottish Office ministers and civil servants. Westminster offered limited opportunities for pressure group action.' In contrast, according to this analysis, the (re-)establishment of the Scottish Parliament has:

> Introduced a much more promising political environment for pressure group Scotland. It offered an open parliamentary system, with commitments to open government and participatory democracy. It produced a lengthy legislative process of guaranteed pre-legislative consultation. Multiple access points for discussing legislation with MSPs in committees and in plenary, and opportunities for further consultation with committees. (Lynch, 2002: 121)

Over the past decade this shift has also seen government funding for policy networks. A prominent example was the Scottish Civic Forum designed to be 'facilitative, recognise the plurality of voices and groups and take an active role in ensuring the effective involvement of groups traditionally excluded from the decision-making process' (CSG, 1999: 7). However, the former director of the forum has described the decline of this body: 'following early funding by the Scottish Executive, a change of government Ministers led to a shift in government priorities in the participation agenda and a decision was given, in February 2005, not to core fund the Forum'.[24] Whilst this organisation may have ended, government money has been used to found and aid other networks, such as the Scottish Women's Convention (SWC), that aims 'to support the women's agenda in Scotland . . . [and] provide a systematic way for women's voices to be included in policy development work'.[25] SWC is a network of over 300,000 women throughout Scotland drawn from business, churches, trades unions and voluntary organisations. Amongst women's NGOs, Engender is another prominent example. A membership organisation, it aims to 'increase women's power and influence and . . . improve women's lives by making government aware of what women need and want'.[26] It is a participant in the Scottish Women's Budget Group (SWBG), an alliance of organisations brought together in 2000 to lobby for gender responsive budgeting to become a mainstream feature of the policy process (Breitenbach, 2003). As Mckay and Gillespie (2006: 117) conclude, 'all of this activity demonstrates how a group of women acted collectively and embraced the opportunity presented by the devolution settlement to engage with the new institutions in attempts to promote a more gender equal Scotland'. Yet their assessment also highlights concerns and shortcomings, including 'frustration about the slow pace of change in the budget process . . . the work of the SWBG has failed to secure any significant gains in terms of more gender equitable outcomes' (p. 117). It is a view that participants in the SWBG shared: 'the Cabinet Secretary for Finance and Sustainable Growth made a number of positive commitments, pointing to the possibility of ongoing commitment to [gender budgeting] in Scotland . . . not much progress has followed' (Engender, 2008: 6). Following evident frustration at the rate of progress it should be noted that 2009 saw the publication of an Equality Statement to support the Scottish Government's draft Budget 2010–11. According to the government this is an ongoing process and there will be 'equality analysis with regard to the budget for 2011/12 . . . to ensure that public money contributes to greater equality in Scotland' (Scottish Government, 2009: 7).

In relation to the impact of devolution on BME groups, De Lima (2005: 137) highlights a dearth of research on race equality, and notes that 'getting racism on the policy agenda has been problematic, as it undermines and challenges the egalitarian myth that underpins a great deal of Scottish political and policy discourses'. Indeed, she observes that 'Scotland is no different to the rest of Britain and devolution has yet to make real difference to policy formulation by 'mainstreaming' into the process the complex ways in which ethnicity interacts with other social factors' (De Lima, 2005: 140). Nevertheless, there evidence of some progress:

> Despite the limitations, it is important to acknowledge that devolution has opened up new opportunities in Scotland to address racism and discrimination in ways that did not occur previously. It has led to . . . greater involvement of minority ethnic people in consultative activities . . . what is now needed are more radical measures to address the deficit in areas such as political representation, for example, by building the capacity of minority ethnic communities to engage in meaningful debate and participation. (De Lima, 2005: 153)

A prominent disabled people's organisation, Capability Scotland, also sees some evidence of progress since the Parliament was reinstated in 1999:

> It has been a decade of huge social and political change and we as an organisation have had to consider the implications those political, legislative and social changes have had and to adapt to them . . . The Scottish Parliament has always been accessible and committed to change and we will continue to work with it to influence policy. (Capability Scotland, 2007: 2)

Overall, how can the post-devolution development of an equalities lobby in Scotland be evaluated? A Joseph Rowntree Foundation/Civic Forum report offers the view that:

> The Scottish Parliament has created new ways for people to participate in the democratic process. The committees, particularly the Public Petitions Committee, provide people with direct ways of getting involved. These structures are potentially powerful, but need more resources. (JRF/Scottish Civic Forum, 2003: 87)

The report continued, 'the Executive collects views on its policies through consultations ... [and it] is consulting widely, but needs to do more to demonstrate that it takes consultation responses seriously and that they do influence the way policies develop' (JRF/Scottish Civic Forum, 2003: 88). Subsequent analyses have presented mixed conclusions. For example, a survey of voluntary organisations found that 'around 75 per cent of participants had no contact at all with the Scottish Parliament'; it also concluded that in the policy development meetings of the Parliament's Committees, 'on the whole, it is the already well-networked, more established, better resourced who are represented . . . A fundamental issue raised consistently is the need for much more effective feedback and explanation of the rationale for particular policy decisions taken' (Wilkie, 2004: 43). In terms of lobbying on equalities issues, Lindsay (2006: 17) affirms the idea of variability, noting 'real progress' in LGBT and gender equality, and anti-sectarianism. On disability, she notes how 'previously support was unavailable and issues were not recognised. Now, a plethora of specialist care and resources are available to those with a disability that were not available before.' Overall, she concluded that 'in some areas there had been negative progress': for example, in relation to race and ethnicity; refugee and asylum seekers ('in the Scottish Parliament, asylum seekers have been discussed in a negative tone and this notion has prevailed with the public'); travellers ('some support projects exist, but prejudice is rife against this group of people'); older people ('progress here has been made, but not a huge amount'); and mental health ('real change can only happen when there are resources available') (Lindsay, 2006: 17–18).

8.3.2 Northern Ireland

Fearon (1996: 2) described women's marginalisation prior to the opening of the Northern Ireland Assembly, observing that 'what remains constant is that women, while no less likely than men to be politically active, have much less access to political activities associated with power'. McDonough (1996: 25) concurred, saying that gender and social policy issues were 'still largely absent from the political agenda. The lack of recognition of the contribution of women . . . [is] a product of the power relations within . . . society generally: a deformed polity, post civil rights, has had its own atrophying effect'. Analysis following the establishment of the Assembly shows that of the 4,500 third sector organisations in the province, there were '280 organisations with women as their primary beneficiary group' (6.2 per cent of the total). Just over a third of these were small organisations with an annual income less than £1,000 per annum (NICVA, 2005: 45). Of women's NGOs, 14.1 per cent described their primary purpose as advocacy or gender equality. A key part of the gender equality lobby is the Women's Policy Forum formed by the Northern Ireland Council for Voluntary Action (NICVA) in 2004. It is comprised of NGOs 'from across the voluntary and community sector and is open to any organisation with an interest in women's policy issues'.[27] The minutes of its meetings detail its lobbying of ministers and officials on issues such as violence against women, childcare, health, social exclusion, the rights of ethnic minority women and trafficking.[28]

In terms of other equality strands, in the province there are 291 organisations comprised of, or working for, disabled people (6.5 per cent); 250 that are involved in the older people's sector (5.6 per cent); 926 NGOs involved in the young people and children's sector (20.6 per cent); and a 'limited number' of organisations representing LGB people. A prominent example of an LGB network is the Coalition on Sexual Orientation which has an active role in lobbying and policy development work.[29] As in the other two UK devolved polities, comparatively few organisations exist to represent the interests of Black and minority ethnic groups.

There are mixed views on the development of the Northern Ireland equalities lobby. An early assessment (Kearney, 2003: 61) offered a generally optimistic view, concluding that:

> We have a large and diverse voluntary and community sector . . . tackling inequality and exclusion . . . working across Northern Ireland providing vital services, acting as advocates, lobbying for change, contributing to the economy and bringing communities together to articulate their own needs and to advance participatory democracy and social justice.

However, a more cautious standpoint was presented by Hadden et al. (2007: 13):

> There remains a concern about the resources and capacity of the voluntary sector bodies in this area. A recent report of the 'Task Force on Resourcing the Voluntary and Community Sector'[30] recommended that specific funding should be made available for this purpose and that authorities and voluntary sector bodies should approach consultation on a more strategic basis.

Views gathered from focus groups as part of a recent evaluation of the impact of the Section 75 duty (Reeves Associates, 2007: 23–57) included the following assessments as to how equality, participation and engagement had changed in the wake of devolution:

- Gender: there is a 'gap between interpretation of Section 75 by civil servants and women's groups'; a 'lack of positive action', an 'emphasis on gender neutral approaches; [it is] a "tick box" exercise with emphasis on process'; accordingly, women's NGOs 'wanted a greater focus on the issues affecting women'; and a feeling that government 'needs to act as a role model'.
- Age: 'for young people there was the issue of inaccessible information in that much was over-complicated and too detailed'; 'over reliance by public authorities on technology'; 'easy access to Internet assumed'.
- Disability: 'resources not always available when required'; 'inaccessible information in that much was over-complicated and too detailed'.

- Ethnicity: 'there is some evidence that targeted consultation has enabled individuals and user groups from minority ethnic communities to engage in policy development'.

However, in relation to BME organisations, the Northern Ireland Council for Ethnic Minorities (2008: 22) identified a range of issues currently affecting political participation, including 'concerns on the accountability of those who represent the [BME] sector' and, delays in meetings with policy-makers. In general, it concluded:

> Discussions with the communities highlighted that all the groups testify to numerous barriers with government. Often, faith groups are thought of as 'a bit of an add-on' when the government is considering issues around religious belief; there was also a deep sense of tokenism, and a telling lack of capacity. However, all of the groups expressed unreserved openness to formal and informal ways of collaborating with government and civil society. (NICEM, 2008: 38)

Overall, after the extended period of suspension, the resumption of devolved governance in 2007 led to the assessment by NICVA that NGOs' participation in policy-making is beginning to gain momentum. It reported that 'during the year 1,207 people from 948 organisations participated in training sessions, policy fora, information seminars, conferences and roundtable meetings ... [and] reviewed 181 policy documents' (NICVA, 2007: 19). This evidence suggests that, notwithstanding the extended period of direct rule, devolved government is attempting to open the circles of decision-making and that, in a sometimes faltering and uneven manner, the Northern Ireland executive is an increasing locus for the lobbying activities of equalities-related organisations. Yet, it is also clear that much further work is necessary before an organised, and well-resourced equalities lobby is in place, one with the capacity to advance its claims on the policy process and represent all equality 'strands'.

8.4 Consultative Structures and Lobbying

In reviewing the political science literature on gender and politics Childs and Krook (2006: 16) highlight the need for contemporary study into 'factors that might constrain or enable women to influence policy-making, including ... the presence of gender machinery and links with women's groups in civil society'. Here we heed this call and turn to examine how equalities organisations have used the structures of devolved governance to lobby for the promotion of equality. First we look at the workings of the National Assembly for Wales's cross party Standing Committee on Equality of Opportunity.

Analysis of transcripts of committee meetings during the second Assembly 2003–7 (Chaney, 2008) reveals that it has provided discursive opportunities for the promotion of equality and acted as a nexus for NGOs and others to lobby policy-makers. Examination of the incidence of key gender equality terms (such as 'equal pay', 'gender budgeting' etc.) in the transcripts also revealed the importance to the promotion of equalities of securing the descriptive representation of women in decision-making structures (that is women present as elected representatives). It showed that women AMs and advisers to the committee were probabilistically more likely than their male counterparts to refer to the gender equality terms studied,[31] thereby placing them on the policy agenda (they accounted for 78 per cent of all such incidences).[32] As noted, the evidence shows that the committee is acting as a nexus linking elected representatives and gender equality advisers drawn from organisations outside government. The latter include trades unions officers, local authorities officials and members of civic and civil society groups.[33] The data show that these 'invitees' to the committee made a significant contribution to advancing the substantive representation of women (that is the situation whereby women's interests and concerns are reflected in the policy process) (Table 8.2). They accounted for 34 per cent of all references to the key equality terms analysed. When female and male invitees are compared, again, a gender-split is evident; women accounted for 71 per cent of the references to the gender-equality terms in the transcripts.[34]

Notwithstanding this positive development, a number of issues and challenges can be identified, including the capacity of the committee to offer effective scrutiny of government policies. This issue has become more noticeable in the third Assembly, as the post-2007 quasi-parliamentary status of the Assembly has placed increased demands on the under-size 60-member legislature (it comprises just 45 AMs if members of the cabinet are excluded). This has meant that the committee's membership has been scaled back; usually just five AMs attend (as opposed to ten, as seen in the first two Assemblies). Moreover, since May 2007 the pre-existing practice of representatives

Key Debating term	Female			Male		
	AMs	**Adviser**	**(All)**	**AMs**	**Adviser**	**(All)**
Domestic abuse	1.4	0.6	(2.1)	0	0.1	(0.2)
Equal pay	5.7	6.7	(12.4)	0.5	0.4	(0.8)
Childcare	8.3	0.7	(9)	0.5	1.1	(1.7)
Public appointments	1.3	5	(6.4)	0	0	(0)
Gender	8	6.6	(14.7)	2.3	3	(5.3)
Women	10.4	10.6	(20.9)	3.7	7.3	(11)
Girls	0.4	0.4	(0.8)	0.1	0.6	(0.7)
Gender budgeting	0.9	0.7	(1.6)	0.3	0	(0.3)
Mainstreaming	7.1	2.4	(9.6)	1	1.3	(2.4)
All	43.7	34		8.4	14	
N	422	328	(750)	81	135	(216)

Table 8.2. The incidence of key terms in the Equality Committee transcripts during the Second Assembly 2003–7 (percentages)

of the statutory equality commissions attending all meetings as 'standing invitees' has ended, thereby further reducing the scrutiny capacity. Another issue is the breadth and diversity of organisations engaging with the committee. Compared with the thousands of equalities-related NGOs on the Voluntary Sector Database (WCVA, 2008a), analysis of the invitees to the committee during the second Assembly shows that approximately fifty civil and civic organisations contributed to proceedings. The danger here is that engagement is restricted to a new political class, one that is not wholly representative of the interests that the committee is concerned to represent, and that limited further action is taken to broaden the circles of those engaged in policy work.

As noted in chapter 4, the Welsh government's statutory partnership with the voluntary sector has led to the formation of the Third Sector Partnership Council (TSPC). This participatory structure allows representatives of the sector to lobby and consult government; biannual meetings between sector representatives (including those representing organisations concerned with equalities) and government ministers are a key feature of the arrangements. Analysis of the transcripts of the ministerial meetings held during the Assembly's second term reveals that this institutional mechanism is significant to the promotion of equalities; discussion of such matters took place in the majority of meetings (Figure 8.4). Gender equality issues received

Key topic	Examples of policy discussions around each topic in ministerial meetings	Meetings when key topic discussed	
		No.	%
Disability	Concerns from voluntary sector about the availability of funding for implementation of new Strategy on Disability and the Arts;[39] discussion of implementation of recommendations around disability in WAG 'Climbing Higher' Sports Strategy;[40] 'discussion of National Sports Strategy 'voluntary members . . . highlighted areas for development such as the barriers in achieving targets for disabled children'.[41]	16	36
Gender	Minister updates voluntary sector representatives on WAG's equal pay campaign;[42] gender balance in the arts, 'the Minister assured the group that he would ensure that gender balance issues would be addressed in ASPB's remit letters, including the collection of relevant gender statistics';[43] paper presented by Wales Gender Budget Group highlighting how 'gender budgeting would greatly assist in fulfilling' the gender equality duty;[44] call for gender balance on the Review Panel for the Arts Council of Wales.[45]	18	40
'Race'/ ethnicity	The voluntary sector expressed concern over schools awareness of diversity, 'especially within schools with a low number of BME pupils who sometimes refuse to report racial bullying when it occurs';[46] discussion of funding for the North Wales Race Equality Network;[47] discussion of WAG's Race Equality Scheme;[48] discussion of initiatives taken to address race equality in the Wales Eye Care Initiative;[49] 'the voluntary sector raised concerns about the lack of access to health visitors and primary care for Gypsy and Traveller families, particularly in rural areas'.[50]	13	29

(continued)

238

Key topic	Examples of policy discussions around each topic in ministerial meetings	Meetings when key topic discussed	
		No.	%
Faith	It was reported that WAG is represented on the Office for National Statistics Census Topic Group;[51] discussion of faith in the Statistical Focus on Diversity.[52]	3	7
Language	Questioning minister whether EHRC will be covered by the Welsh Language Act;[53] discussion of how the Welsh language could be better represented in the guidance for Communities First economic aid programme;[54] 'voluntary sector expressed an interest in how the principles expressed in "Iaith Pawb" [WAG's Welsh Language strategy] are integrated into the Minister's portfolio'.[55]	15	33
Sexual orientation	Minister discusses policy around homophobic bullying in schools;[56] discussion of WAG support for sexual orientation amendments to UK Equality Bill (2005);[57] Stonewall Cymru lobbying the Office for National Statistics for the collection of Sexual Orientation data.[58]	8	18
Age	The Minister 'expressed concerns that the formalised structures of volunteer work and representation may not be the most appropriate for many of the children and young people in Communities First areas';[59] discussion of WAG's Statistical Focus on Older People;[60] voluntary sector representatives call for abuse of the elderly to be addressed.[61]	10	22
Generic equalities	Government minister outlines departmental cross-stand equality action plans;[62] discussion of the need for improved equalities data covering Wales;[63] discussion of equalities assessment tool in relation to EU structural fund aid.[64]	26	58

Figure 8.4. A nexus for the advancement of equalities? Details of a sample of ministerial meetings with voluntary sector representatives (2003–7)

the greatest attention (and were discussed in 40 per cent of meetings), followed by disability (36 per cent) and language (29 per cent). Examples of the deliberation over equalities issues included questioning ministers on the extent to which government had embraced gender budgeting techniques;[35] raising shortcomings in equalities data;[36] and calls for funding to address equal pay issues,[37] as well to support equality policy networks.[38]

As well as the TSPC meetings, the Assembly's Petitions Committee has emerged as a significant conduit for individuals, civil society organisations and others to advance equalities claims on government. Although it has only been in operation since mid-2007, seven out of the committee's first thirteen meetings[65] considered petitions with an equalities dimension. These called on government to take action to lay specific responsibility upon local authorities to identify and support young carers;[66] to review screening systems for sex-specific cancers;[67] and to extend the legal powers of the office of Children's Commissioner for Wales.[68]

In addition to the foregoing participatory structures, the emerging evidence reveals how equalities organisations are using standard policy consultations to lobby for the promotion of equalities. Thus, a summary of responses received on the government's draft economic strategy stated 'a number of issues on the importance of mainstreaming have been raised through the consultation process'. Examples included transport (issues around accessibility); education and skills (tackling occupational segregation and the gender pay gap); and raising earnings and the quality of jobs (the need to address gender stereotyping and occupational segregation) (WAG, 2006c: 21). A further example is provided by responses to the Refugee Inclusion Strategy (WAG, 2008(34)). This states that 'respondents requested specific recommendations be developed for issues which have a particular gender dimension, such as childcare provision, language support and domestic abuse ... [as a result, the strategy] now highlights how women's experiences may differ from the experiences of male asylum seekers and refugees' (WAG, 2008(33): 3).

8.5 Participants' Views of the Lobbying Process

Whilst the advent of the National Assembly has seen a substantial growth in participatory structures and policy networks, how do those outside government regard the new arrangements? The aforementioned survey of women's NGOs (Chaney et al., 2004) revealed that the majority of respondents (61 per cent) gave a positive assessment; just over a quarter (25.6 per cent) of those surveyed felt that their organisation had a 'good' working relationship with the Assembly and government. A further 13.8 per cent felt that the relationship was 'strong', and a fifth (21.3 per cent) said the relationship was 'fair' (just 8.5 per cent said it was 'poor').[69] When asked how government could improve its working relationship with women's NGOs, the responses pointed to issues of communication effectiveness between government and civil society. Just under a half (43 per cent) said that the government should provide better information on its policy work; whilst the majority (56 per cent) said that they would favour more opportunities to meet AMs locally; and over a third (38 per cent) said that there should be local 'workshops' on engaging in policy work. This point was also evident in the views of managers of women's NGOs. One reflected that:

> We've had problems in trying to establish any meaningful communication with the [Civil Service] Divisions within the Assembly [Government] . . . as an organisation that deals with a diverse range of issues ... [we] do not fit neatly into any one Division and, as a result, the organisation is constantly overlooked and passed around . . . leading to the loss of knowledge, rapport and ultimately funding. (NAfW, 2008c: 29)

Another echoed this concern, saying that 'the lack of clear communication with the voluntary sector has created further difficulties in forward planning. The sector needs to be involved at the very heart of these decisions' (NAfW, 2008c: 28). A mass membership women's NGO also highlighted concerns of a geographical nature and called on government 'not to neglect mid and north Wales, as it is easy to do this from the perspective that there are so many more resources and funding opportunities available in south Wales' (NAfW, 2008c: 28).

Financial support was a common anxiety amongst the NGOs surveyed. One observed that 'women fared badly in terms of funding . . . there are still concerns that funding for women's organisations is not easily available or accessible (NAfW, 2008c: 28). Gender budgeting was seen by some as a way to address these shortcomings. One manager explained:

We suggest that all funding allocations require evidence of differential benefits in both application and outcome . . . For example, the Department for Enterprise, Innovation and Networks provided £19.6M funding to the voluntary sector in Wales in 2005/6. It is not known how many women benefited, or what qualitative difference to their lives they derived from this budget. (NAfW, 2008c: 32)

More positive views were forthcoming in respect of how government had consulted on developing its own Equality Scheme (WAG, 2009c); one said it had 'successfully engaged with the voluntary sector and individuals during the development of the Scheme ... engagement events were organised to establish the key issues, and information was fed directly into the Scheme and action plans' (NAfW, 2008c: 27).

Mixed views of the lobbying process were also held by disabled people's organisations. The manager of a visually impaired people's NGO said:

One of the most effective ways of achieving our aims has been contributing to developments that are happening as a result of devolution . . . [we have] been ensuring at every possible opportunity that visual impairment is on the agenda, taking part in the task forces and working groups . . . there is now a comprehensive structure for the voluntary sector which ensures access to all Ministers on a regular basis. There is no doubt in my mind that the attitude and commitment of the Assembly to equality and social inclusion is making a major difference to Wales. The principle of considering disability and how policies impact on people with disabilities is a very strong one.[70]

Yet, other disabled people's organisations questioned whether government was placing sufficient emphasis on assessing the impact of its policies. For example, one said:

Equalities monitoring has been process-driven and assessed by volume, and not necessarily outcome of actions. The implementation/outcome gap is an issue across the public sector. Clear, evidenced-based evaluation methods need to be devised and operated jointly by both the public and voluntary sector. The additional costs of effective monitoring should be factored into budgets. (NAfW, 2008c: 32)

Again, funding was a major concern for disabled people's NGOs. One stated:

It is urgent that cross-sector funding be established and that there are opportunities for both funder and fundee to plan work realistically and sensibly. This could be achieved by more joint working by the Divisions within the Assembly [Government] or by more flexibility or by a special pot of funding. (NAfW, 2008c: 15)

Another developed this theme, saying:

The place of work on equality issues and on rights and entitlements has not yet been properly seated in Assembly [Government] funding. Through the National Assembly's Third Sector Partnership Council, requests have been made for an open and transparent grant scheme for work in this area. So far this has resulted in the excellent Disadvantaged Groups scheme[71] but this travels through local authorities so fulfils only a part of the need. (NAfW, 2008c: 30)

Other disabled people's organisations were keen to highlight positive outcomes from their lobbying activities. One stated that 'as a result of massive lobbying led by [our organisation] . . . and local societies, we have seen a major victory for people with wet age-related macular degeneration ... We asked the minister to stand up for people with this condition and today she has'.[72] However, others expressed a cynical view, stating that 'our leaders and organisations have been drawn closer and closer to the intoxicating flame that is the political process . . . mistakes must be corrected. The disabled people's movement must re-connect with the grassroots and be driven by their needs.'[73] In contrast, a more equivocal view was offered by a leading disabled people's policy network:

Although some people may still think that it [public policy] is still overly driven by a Westminster agenda, the Assembly is established as part of the life of Wales. It has already had a real impact on the lives of disabled people, both positive – the adoption of the Social Model of Disability – and negative – the dropping of the commitment to free home care by the Welsh Assembly Government.[74]

The organisation's manager continued:

We strive always to work in partnership with the Assembly government and on such issues as Direct Payments this has proved effective. Free Home Care has become a less harmonious area of joint working, following the Assembly [Government]'s abandonment of its manifesto pledge. This led inevitably to taking a critical stance towards government action on this particular policy. Whilst not a comfortable position for any party involved ... [we] seek to engage constructively with the Assembly and maintain dialogue on what remains a matter of crucial importance for thousands of disabled people.[75]

In respect of 'race' equality, as noted, BME groups faced a combination of factors, including a lack of capacity and resources, and the fragmentation of the BME sector.[76] A further concern expressed by one BME policy network was that:

When consultations are undertaken and the exercise is complete, no attempt is made to feed back on the findings. When civil servants and funding bodies undertake consultation work, it must be a part of their remit to disseminate their draft reports before they are sent to politicians or policy-makers for further consideration. This is absolutely necessary to ensure transparency and accuracy of reporting.[77]

Another BME organisation expressed a critical view of attempts at co-working by government:

'Partnership' has become rhetoric for the Welsh Assembly Government, key funders, and other key organisations, in order to justify control and the distribution of limited funding. It seems to also be fashionable to talk about 'partnership work'. However, effective partnerships are not evidenced, resulting in disillusion and apathy of smaller community groups. Key policy and decision-makers must realise the reality of community work through effectively listening to those from a grassroots level and ensure effective evaluation of all partnership work.[78]

The foregoing point was made by another NGO worker, who observed: 'there is insufficient support afforded to local groups. Through practical engagement with local groups we see them struggling to survive simply because they are neglected and marginalized because of the lack of resources and support mechanisms.'[79] This issue was again highlighted by an independent study commissioned by the government:

It was pointed out . . . that because many BME organisations are comparatively small, some of the capacity issues . . . apply disproportionately to them. The experience of BME organisations in dealing with the Assembly Government was mixed, with the work of the

Housing Directorate being singled out by two contributors as an example of good practice.[80]

Another concern expressed by BME groups was the dearth of official data on ethnicity. One said:

> There has been limited or no statistical information relating to ethnic minority women and the number of women who have accessed, and are continually benefiting from, the ethnic minority women's voluntary sector and the services provided in Wales. It is therefore argued that greater efforts must be made by the Welsh Assembly Government, Local Authorities and other statistical bodies to provide information by ethnicity, gender and faith.[81]

The view of some groups in the Muslim community was that there needed to be closer working with government. One said that it was imperative that WAG should 'play a key role in determining the direction of future activities and directives in relation to developing a stronger engagement with Muslim communities'.[82] The spokesperson for this organisation continued:

> If WAG is going to develop inclusion policies aimed at young people, a greater effort needs to be made to reach them through the people that they turn to – local project workers and community members who take the time to listen. The age gap is evident within the community. WAG needs to reassess the way it reaches Muslim communities and consider alternative and non-traditional methods of engagement.[83]

A further view from the Muslim community was that 'it is imperative that WAG take a leading role in the provision of accurate information and policy to the statutory service sector . . . [and undertake] further and more comprehensive work with policy-makers and service providers to raise awareness of the social behaviour and cultural attitudes toward domestic abuse and violence 'in the name of honour'.[84]

Some lesbian, gay and bisexual (LGB) organisations were positive about the change that devolution had brought: 'we have been a voice for LGB people at key decision making bodies, such as the Welsh Assembly Government . . . and at discussions about the single equality commission, new powers for the Assembly and the review of the voluntary sector scheme'.[85] Reference was also made to the government's statutory equality duty:

245

The National Assembly for Wales is in the vanguard of modern best practice with its founding duty to have due regard to equality of opportunity for all people . . . We recognise the commitment to equality shown by the Welsh government in helping to establish [our organisation] . . . and by funding it as a consultation partner ... we are mandated to support the Assembly in developing policies and services.[86]

On matters of language equality, despite a clear government commitment to bilingual service provision, one organisation complained:

As a voluntary organisation that works through the medium of Welsh we often find it difficult to discuss our needs or worries with someone through the medium of Welsh; there are many discrepancies . . . we would ask [for] fairness for both the Welsh and English languages and that both are treated equally.[87]

Moreover, an official report highlighted a number of issues related to Welsh medium 'groups' engagement with government. It found 'evidence [that] the Welsh speaking community did not have the capacity to meet the demands of the [consultative processes set out in the Voluntary Sector] Scheme'. Accordingly it:

Called on the Assembly Government to develop a national policy on the local provision of translation and interpretation services, and to put in place training, mentoring and IT [information technology] provision to support the Scheme. Otherwise, there would be instances of both English and Welsh speakers being unable to participate in some groups and forums through the language of their choice.[88]

Age equality organisations were generally positive about the new levels of engagement with government. A manager with one reflected that:

There were many opportunities for us to influence policy development . . . including through membership of various task and finish groups addressing specific issues affecting older people, and through involvement in a range of developments generated by the [government's] Strategy for Older People.[89]

Similarly, another recounted her organisation's lobbying work, saying:

> We have worked with Government and other agencies, including the Wales Equality Reference Group and the National Partnership Forum for Older People. We have brought pressure to bear in our campaigning, on such issues as the introduction of legislation against age discrimination in the provision of goods, facilities and services . . . All these events move us closer to the full rights and citizenship of older people in Wales.[90]

Yet, critical views were also evident: for example, '[we] responded to the Welsh Assembly Government consultation on "fairer charging guidance" to local authorities. We emphasised that these charges fell well short of the previously promised "free home care"'.[91] Elsewhere, an older people's policy network summarised the scale of the challenges faced by its members, stating:

> The position for far too many older people is one where their value within communities and the workplace is regularly overlooked; their status is diminished through negative portrayals and ageist attitudes; and where far too many older people experience varying extremes of poverty and social isolation. Much, therefore, remains to be done. And . . . [this organisation] is consistent in the emphatic representations it makes to the Welsh Assembly Government in order for them to use appropriate power and influences to address such issues.[92]

Organisations representing children and young people also offered mixed views of the policy process. One perspective was that 'organisations working with children often have to "translate" policy documents into accessible language and consider innovative ways of attracting the interest of young people'.[93] Another reflected that 'we lobby the WAG to put children's issues at the heart of its policy-making. During the past year the WAG has taken some welcome steps towards eradicating child poverty and protecting the rights of vulnerable children. However, there is still much to be done.'[94] Another policy network highlighted its most significant lobbying outcomes:

> Following representation from [us] . . . and our members, the Welsh Assembly Government formally adopted the Convention [United Nations Convention of the Rights of the Child] as a foundation of principles for dealings with children in 2004. This means that all of the

Welsh government's work in relation to children must follow these principles.[95]

Generally positive views were held by organisations representing refugees and asylum seekers. One underlined the role of new policy forums, noting that 'we are part of the All Wales Refugee Policy Forum, chaired by the Assembly's Minister . . . [the forum is] an important vehicle for policy change in Wales, it aims to ensure that devolved policy takes full account of refugees in our communities'.[96] Another detailed the impact of its campaigning: 'as a result of our lobbying, the WAG has issued a Refugee Inclusion Policy. This includes provisions that meet many of our demands. Among them are improved methods of collecting data regarding the children, and better social services for them . . . This is a direct result of our lobbying.'[97]

Away from organisations' views of the new equalities lobby we now turn to consider a new dimension to policy and politics ushered in by devolution, electoral competition around equalities as both civil society organisations and political parties advance equality policy proposals in the context of elections to the National Assembly.

8.6 Manifestos, Electoral Competition and the Promotion of Equalities

As the burgeoning literature on electoral competition highlights, adapting party policy programmes to maximise the support from targeted groups underlines the increasing salience of party competition in heterogeneous electorates (Franklin et al., 2004; Bischoff, 2005). From an equalities perspective, this means tailoring parties' policy programmes to engage with the diversity of society as defined by gender, ethnicity, faith, disability and other characteristics. A core strand of this body of work is concerned with the analysis of party election manifestos (Budge et al., 1987, 2001) and understanding gender differences in political activity related to the specific context of electoral campaigns (Atkeson, 2003; Hansen, 1997; Sapiro and Conover, 1997). Thus, in setting out substantive details of prospective policies, including the extent to which they embrace equality concerns, party manifestos are key data sources that do more than attempt to appeal to women voters. Rather, they perform a multiplicity of functions. At one level they provide useful snapshots of the progress made towards, and future aspirations for, equality between the sexes (Pelizzo, 2003). As Pradhan Malla (2000) highlights, they also provide a benchmark by which to check parties' delivery on earlier promises for gender equal politics, whilst work by Tamale (1999: 342) offers the cautious view that manifesto commitments to greater equality can sometimes be just rhetorical devices. Nevertheless, manifestos do reflect the outcome of collective intra-party negotiations and provide some insight into power relations between different groups and interests, thereby providing valuable indices of women's role in political agenda setting. Overall, contemporary research suggests that the rise of electoral competition over equality issues is part of a process whereby left-of-centre political parties in Europe have attempted to offset the decline in traditional support by competing for the vote of electoral constituencies defined by gender, ethnicity, sexual orientation and other characteristics (Kitschelt and Rehm, 2005).

As noted, equalities were not seen as part of the responsibility of the Welsh Office. For this reason little, if any, Wales-specific attention was paid to equality issues in the Welsh versions of manifestos issued by the main political parties standing in UK general elections. The creation of the National Assembly with a statutory duty to promote equalities across the breadth of its policy functions has changed matters and introduced a new directness in the electoral arrangements. Those forming a government in the Assembly have received endorsement of their Wales-specific policy proposals at the ballot box; as the following discussion reveals, these now include initiatives to promote equality. Related to this, election study data show the emergence of post-devolution electoral politics characterised by subtle differences in political behaviour of the sexes (Chaney et al., 2007a; Chaney, 2007). This arises from gendered responses to political factors such as party ideology and party leadership style, but also gender differences in voters' attitudes to the devolved policy agenda.

Notwithstanding the new electoral context, limited reference was made to the promotion of equalities in the manifestos for the first Assembly elections in 1999. Rather, they tended to include a general declaration indicating that the parties knew that they had to respond to the new political situation relating to equalities. Yet such statements were not generally accompanied by detailed policy proposals. For example, the Welsh Labour manifesto asserted that 'Labour is also determined to ensure that the National Assembly is a modern political institution. We will ensure it is committed to . . . equal opportunities' (WLP, 1999: 3). Similarly, Plaid Cymru declared that 'the Assembly has a crucial statutory responsibility to promote . . . equal opportunities and . . . th[is] require[s] action in all policy areas' (Plaid Cymru, 1999: 8). Against this low starting point, the emerging evidence shows that parties have increasingly recognised the potential link between manifesto commitments on equality and the electoral support that they receive from targeted groups. Not only did the 2003 and 2007 Welsh manifestos devote more attention to equalities than those of 1999, they also contained more detailed policy proposals (Chaney, 2007). It is a pattern that is also evident in the devolved elections in Scotland and Northern Ireland (see Table 8.3)

During the past two elections there has also been a broadening of the scope of equalities policy proposals. Whereas the 1999 manifestos referred to 'race', gender, language and disability, subsequent ones have also advanced equality proposals linked to age, sexual orientation, faith, carers and LGBT people. Notably, these elections saw parties produce 'mini-manifestos' solely dedicated to equalities policies (for example, Welsh Labour, 2003), or a series of themed mini-manifestos targeted at specific groups (for example, Plaid Cymru, 2007; manifestos for younger people, older people and people with learning difficulties). Overall, it is noticeable that the 2007 manifestos set out a variety of approaches to promoting equalities. For example, proposing redistributive practices, such as targeting state aid to certain groups ('we will further reform charging for home care services, making 10,000 disabled people better off'; Welsh Labour, 2007: 13–19), or creating new structures (for example, 'the 'Welsh Conservatives would encourage the EHRC to form regional partnerships with voluntary organisations to promote equality and diversity in local communities'; Welsh Conservatives, 2007: 25). Others set out plans for increasing the Welsh government's powers to promote equalities (for example, 'we will seek devolution of statutory responsibility for equality and full legislative powers over the child protection system'; Plaid Cymru, 2007: 31). Some proposals went beyond the usual targeting of the public sector (for example, 'to promote the role of managers, entrepreneurs and business leaders in promoting equality of opportunity and tackling discrimination in the workplace'; Welsh Liberal Democrats, 2007: 31).

A further notable development in the wake of devolution is the growing trend of civil and civic society organisations issuing their own

Country/ Province	Party	Incidence of 'equality'/ 'equal opportunities'		Incidence of 'women'/ 'gender'[98]		Examples of Gender Equality Policy Statements – 2007
		2003	2007	2003	2007	
Scotland	Scottish National Party†	15	10	3	5	'In government we will pull together the different strands of equality legislation under our control to deliver an integrated equality strategy' (p. 66).
	Scottish Conservative Party	1	0	0	1	–
	Scottish Liberal Democrats†	3	14	3	6	'Mainstreaming equality across every area of government is an important agenda that must move forward. We are committed to producing an annual report on the progress on mainstreaming equality as part of this process' (p. 57).
	Scottish Labour*	2	16	4	8	'A commitment to social and economic equality is perhaps the most fundamental of Scottish Labour's values. Tackling prejudice, intolerance and discrimination will always be one of our main priorities' (p. 80).
Northern Ireland	Sinn Féin*†	102	69	48	43	'Use public procurement contracts to deliver equality and inclusion' (p. 7).
	Northern Ireland Women's Coalition*[99]	5	–	8	–	–
	Democratic Unionist Party	15	2	4	0	'We will strive to ensure genuine equality for all including equality in funding' (p. 6).

(continued)

Country/Province	Party	Incidence of 'equality'/'equal opportunities'		Incidence of 'women'/'gender'[98]		Examples of Gender Equality Policy Statements – 2007
		2003	2007	2003	2007	
Northern Ireland (contd.)	Ulster Unionist Party*	2	4	1	13	'Ulster Unionists want to create opportunities for women of all ages, providing them with genuine choices, and equipping each to reach their potential' (p. 25).
	Social Democratic and Labour Party (SDLP)	68	26	2	5	'Equality and Human Rights are not just slogans – they are a part of our founding philosophy' (p. 42).
Wales	Plaid Cymru – the Party of Wales*†	23	8	5	9	'We will give a new impetus to the National Assembly's duty to promote equal opportunities and will seek devolution of statutory responsibility for equality and full legislative powers over the child protection system' (p. 31).
	Welsh Conservatives	2	10	1	1	'Welsh Conservatives would look at the feasibility of ending compulsory retirement in the public sector by 2011' (p. 25).
	Welsh Labour*†‡	24	3	19	1	'Action will be taken to address inequality in performance [in education], particularly by boys and some ethnic minority groups' (p. 22).
	Welsh Liberal Democrats*†	11	14	5	13	'The commitment to equality of opportunity is intrinsic to our approach to public policy, and building a fairer, better-educated, inclusive and prosperous Wales' (p. 40).

Table 8.3. Gender equality: content analysis of party manifestos in the devolved elections 2003 and 2007
Key: † Manifesto has dedicated section on equality and/or women, or ‡ separate, dedicated 'mini-manifesto' on equalities issued.

equalities manifestos at the time of Assembly elections in order to influence the policy programmes of the various parties and candidates (see Figure 8.5). The adoption of NGOs' policy demands in this way supports 'transaction' models of lobbying (Epstein and O' Halloran, 1999), because, by adopting such external claims, political parties may gain support from hitherto marginalised constituencies (a prime consideration when attempting to maximise electoral support).

'Strand'	Policy Demands
Gender	Developing a comprehensive, integrated approach that addresses gender-related abuse such as domestic violence and forced marriages;[100] closing the gender pay gap across the public and private sector in Wales;[101] getting more women into public life – women in Wales are under-represented in the corridors of power and this wastes talent and leads to wrong decisions in terms of public service delivery.[102]
'Race'	Taking a stand against racism and other forms of discrimination and leading by example;[103] tackling the low pay and economic exploitation of migrant workers;[104] the provision and availability of accessible and well-funded independent advocacy support for separated children seeking asylum in Wales; and continue working to ensure that Black and Minority Ethnic (BME) people are not disproportionately disadvantaged in comparison to others, in terms of access to good quality housing advice, services and accommodation.[105]
Disability	Improving the process of transition for disabled young people to enable them to take up opportunities such as college or training courses;[106] establish a working group to investigate further education and higher education opportunities for school leavers with complex impairments and additional support needs in Wales with a view to establishing a co-located specialist college;[107] a system that ceases charging for all non-residential services agreed through a community care assessment.[108]
LGBT	Make public spaces safe for lesbian, gay and bisexual people in Wales;[109] tackling the blight of bullying, including homophobic bullying, in our schools and colleges; making it safe for lesbian, gay and bisexual people who are harassed by neighbours to complain instead of being forced to move from their home.[110]

(continued)

'Strand'	Policy Demands
Religion, belief/ non-belief	Find out how gender, disability, race, religion age and sexual orientation affects those living in poverty in Wales and their ability to get out of it;[111] a National Centre to celebrate the Religious Heritage of Wales; a Church Social Action Fund to help churches with their good works; give 0.1 per cent of [WAG £14 billion budget] it to the poor (£14 million).[112]
Language	Promoting awareness of the Welsh language and encouraging individuals moving to Wales to learn Welsh;[113] implement their [Welsh Assembly Government's] strategy to promote and support the Welsh language and assess the impact of the strategy on an annual basis.[114]
Age	Banning use of sonic boom technology as a means of dispersing young people;[115] removing arbitrary age limits on volunteering and extending age discrimination legislation to cover all volunteers and unpaid workers;[116] implementing the commitment in the National Service Framework for Older People to remove all forms of age discrimination from the health service [in Wales];[117] the Welsh Assembly Government should lead the way in Wales by doing all it can to end the practice of forced retirement for all workers in Wales; the Welsh Assembly Government should ensure that all public and private care providing bodies integrate and apply the Human Rights Act into all standards of care for older people.[118]
General	Ensuring that health and social care services are planned and commissioned, bearing in mind the need to promote independent living, tackle health inequalities and provide those services in Welsh, English and relevant minority languages, and in a way that respects an individual's religion, belief, race, sexual orientation, gender, impairment;[119] to bring forward legislation – for example, a measure to enhance independent living for older and disabled people, including people from ethnic minority and lesbian, gay and bisexual communities;[120] to use performance indicators to measure equality in Assembly processes and outcomes;[121] to use targeted resources to address the paucity of voluntary sector advice and information services on equality.[122]

Figure 8.5. Examples of equalities organisations' policy demands in their Assembly election manifestos 2007

Unprecedented numbers of civil and civic society organisations' manifestos were issued in the 2003 and 2007 Welsh general elections. They spanned the breadth of the equalities lobby. Whilst the extent to which the grassroots membership of NGOs had been consulted in drafting the manifestos was not always obvious, one disabled people's organisation explained how it had produced its policy demands by stating that they had:

> Been compiled from the views expressed by visually impaired people and groups together with those of some professionals and visually impaired organisations. It is the result of a comprehensive consultation throughout . . . [which] began with members at the AGM . . . and was then widely notified to over 600 contact points in Wales. Telephone conferences were also organised to facilitate the input of visually impaired people across Wales.[123]

This document also gave an insight into the complexity of the equalities lobby, for it stated:

> Some issues are common to all disabilities and these have been laid out in the Disability Manifesto prepared by the Wales Disability Reference Group in which ... [we] represent visual impairment. But there are, in addition, concerns which relate particularly to visual impairment which do not always get effective attention and this Manifesto aims to highlight those specific issues'. [124]

Examples of equalities NGOs' manifestos include one prepared by an organisation representing children and adults with cerebral palsy, which called on government to 'banish disablism' and 'be the first to commit to the basic human right of disabled people with communication impairments to speak for themselves, by providing £10 million per year to fund a model joined-up communication aids service'.[125] Another example is that of an organisation of older people, which called on government to 'ensure that all public and private care providing bodies integrate and apply the Human Rights Act into all standards of care for older people'.[126] An organisation representing 'all who experience mental distress' called on the government to 'appoint an independent Commissioner for Mental Health ... [and] to introduce appropriate and responsive mental health legislation for Wales'.[127]

In addition to the manifestos of individual organisations, those issued by alliances of NGOs on single policy issues are increasingly common in the context of Assembly elections. One such coalition launched a manifesto on free home care for disabled people demanding the end of 'charging for all non-residential services agreed through a community care assessment'.[128] Another was issued by bodies concerned to end child poverty. Amongst its proposals was one for the Welsh government to 'to reduce the costs of education, particularly school trips and materials for GSCE courses'.[129] A further example was issued by an alliance of refugees' and asylum seekers' organisations that called for government action to 'empower refugees to rebuild their lives . . . [and] provide fair and equal access to services'.[130] Another, issued by an alliance of twenty equalities organisations drawn from the civil and civic society, called upon government to undertake a range of measures including 'identify[ing] the equality outcome for every pound of the £14 billion the Assembly Government spends each year ... [and] us[ing] performance indicators to measure equality in Assembly [Government] processes and outcomes'.[131]

Following the 2007 election, a number of organisations stated that their manifestos had an impact on the policy agendas of the political parties. One concluded that 'the leaders of the four main political parties in Wales all signed up to the pledges . . . and committed to implementing the actions through the next Assembly term. It went on to be supported by over 100 candidates from across different political parties and over half of the successfully elected members'.[132] Another stated that 'we were pleased, therefore, that some of . . . [our] manifesto calls were included in parties' election manifestos and to hear from some politicians that our work had directly influenced their party's policy positions'.[133] In like fashion, an older people's organisation described their experience in the following way:

> Ahead of the elections in May 2007 ... [we] worked with older people's forums to highlight the power of the so called 'grey vote' and launched our message for the forthcoming government, 'The Agenda for Older People in Wales'. This called on the new Assembly to listen to and involve older people, combat poverty, challenge home care charges, promote independence and equality, and to work with the Commissioner for Older People in Wales . . . this partnership with older people directly influenced candidate manifestos. Next year we will continue to work with older people to ensure that the pledges made by the politicians are honoured.[134]

8.7 Conclusions

Devolution has created a nascent equalities policy lobby. Its potential membership, and therefore political influence, is significant, on some measures involving almost half of the organisations on the third sector database. This is a powerful corrective to those who choose to style equalities as a 'minority', 'politically correct' undertaking. Furthermore, over the past decade there has been a significant increase in the number of member organisations and the degree of networking between the lobby's component parts. With this has come increased competition between organisations and 'strands' as its focus has broadened out from an initial concern with gender, 'race', language and disability, to faith, sexual orientation, age, refugees, carers, Gypsy Travellers, asylum seekers and other groups. Despite its comparatively rapid development, major challenges and issues remain, not least the issue of identity politics and the extent to which members of NGOs mobilise around social identities associated with equalities, as well as the extent to which there is coordinated action around a collective notion of equality. The lobby has been assisted in its development by continuing and extensive government support. This has been a necessary strategy to increase policy capacity. It remains to be seen whether, in the current fiscal climate, any scaling back in government funding will have a significant impact on the effectiveness of the lobby.

The fact that the National Assembly has yet to secure full parliamentary powers also presents a challenge for equalities organisations because the complex division of policy responsibilities between Cardiff and Westminster. This necessitates a dual lobbying focus. A further fundamental issue for some organisations is how they interpret their own role and whether they see it as having a policy dimension, or whether their *raison d'être* is service delivery or other non-lobbying activities. Unevenness is a further defining feature; comparatively strong networks exist around gender, children and older people, yet other interests lack comparable mobilising structures and, as a consequence, are weaker and more fragmented – such as those representing ethnic minority groups and faith communities. This in turn raises questions about the ability of such groups to make their voices heard against the background of increasing competition between equalities strands as they compete for access to policy-makers.

A further challenge arises from the fact that, whilst survey data indicates a willingness on the part of many NGOs to engage in policy work, a significant number lack the skills and knowledge to fully engage with the structures of devolved government. This situation is compounded by 'communication distortions' (Whipple, 2005) that sometimes result in a limited awareness of the policy process. In part, this stems from the often woeful network media reporting of devolution during its first years (BBC Trust, 2008).[135] As noted, in response to these concerns, government has attempted to boost lobby formation through core funding of equalities networks; whilst a necessary intervention, this has immanent dangers. Inter alia, it may potentially undermine organisations' independence and raise the spectre of co-option and neo-corporatism. A further key question relates to the representativeness of the new policy networks and whether they are actively concerned to extend and broaden their memberships. Inviting new players into established networks offers the benefit of greater legitimacy and political 'clout', yet for established players it also presents the prospect of increased competition in setting lobbying priorities, as well as access to scarce network resources. The internal practices of equalities-oriented organisations also present a potential challenge. In the face of limited time and resources, the temptation is sometimes to opt for an 'executive approach' to lobbying; in other words, agenda setting by managers rather than grassroots members.

Overall, it is clear that equalities organisations are using the structures of devolved governance to lobby and place their policy demands before government and engage in its policy work. Compared with the pre-devolution situation, this points to increased system openness and accessibility. For example, study shows that the Assembly's Equality Committee is acting as nexus between equalities organisations and elected representatives. It has also been the setting for the formation of 'advocacy coalitions' as NGOs, public bodies and AMs undertake policy reviews and campaigns around issues such as additional learning needs and tackling the gender pay gap. Moreover, the Committee's work underlines the importance of gender balance amongst decision makers, for, as discourse analysis reveals, women AMs and invitees are probabilistically more likely to advance gender equality claims in proceedings than their male counterparts. In addition, the records of Third Sector Partnership Council meetings with government ministers, and the work of the Petitions Committee, show that these mechanisms are increasingly being used by NGOs to press equality claims on those in power. A further notable development is the way in which devolution has introduced electoral competition around equalities in the context of Assembly elections. The emerging evidence shows how civil society organisations have seized the political opportunity structures to publish manifestos advancing equality policy demands. In turn, these are shaping the content of political parties' manifestos as they seek to maximise support at the ballot box from a range of social groups in an increasingly heterogeneous electorate.

From a comparative perspective, Scotland and Northern Ireland exhibit a number of commonalities with Wales. Following devolution in 1998–9, all three polities were subject to concerns about limits in the capacity of indigenous policy communities. Subsequently, they have all witnessed variability in the political participation rates of different equality strands. For example, whilst gender, LGBT and disability organisations generally note aspects of progress, ethnic minority and faith organisations have often struggled to participate in policy work. Frustrations are also evident to the extent that, for many NGOs, the increased access to government has been process-oriented and has not always translated into clear policy outcomes. In all three polities, too, there are concerns about the need to broaden the circles of those engaged in lobbying beyond the well-networked, more established, better resourced organisations. In part, the latter issue points to a growing 'professionalisation' of equalities lobbying – one based on media skills, political consultants and policy officers. Reflecting the low starting point and histories of exclusion and marginalisation, government intervention (such as the sponsorship of policy networks) continues to support the development of the nascent lobby in each country.

In summary, notwithstanding significant ongoing issues and challenges, the evidence of the past few years suggests a qualitative change in policy-making with the creation of a more open system of government, one that affords significant lobbying opportunities and presents an environment in which the promotion of equalities has become an established feature of the political bargaining between civil society organisations and devolved government.

9

Conclusion:
Equalities and Public Policy

Social diversity is a significant feature of contemporary Welsh society. In part, it is driven by factors like longevity, migration and globalisation. The result is a heterogeneous society comprised of multiple social identities such as gender, ethnicity, nationality, faith, non-belief, disability, age, sexuality and language. Such diversity reinforces the need to secure equality of opportunity for all. Its advent has also coincided with the rise of multi-level governance and the increasing role of the EU and 'regional' government in the promotion of equalities. It also comes at a time of advancement in equalities theory and an unprecedented expansion in anti-discrimination law. These factors mean that the present is a propitious time for studying the promotion of equality in public policy. However, as noted in chapter 1, traditional accounts have tended to focus on issues and developments at the unitary-state level, or in relation to European Union. In the era of multi-level governance, the present focus on the promotion of equalities in the devolved contexts of Wales, Scotland and Northern Ireland marks an initial contribution to the analysis of key changes at a 'sub-state' level. It is argued that such a 'governance-oriented' approach is necessary because the international trend of state restructuring and (quasi-) federalism points to the increasing 'territorialisation' of policy-making in ways that present both challenges and opportunities for the promotion of equalities – not least because, when compared with the 'one-size-fits-all' policy prescriptions of central government, 'regional' governments have the potential to better tailor their policy outputs to address local patterns and processes of inequality and discrimination.

At a conceptual level, as outlined in chapter 2, past decades have seen major and ongoing developments in equalities theory. These are currently shaping the way that governments, including the UK's devolved administrations, address equalities issues. Traditional enlightenment-era thinking around equal treatment has gradually been replaced by an emphasis on positive action measures. Yet, the most significant conceptual shift is marked by the widespread adoption of gender mainstreaming and, subsequently in many cases, generic mainstreaming of equalities. The latter has been described as 'the (re)organisation, improvement, development and evaluation of policy processes, so that an equality perspective is incorporated in all policies at all levels and at all stages' (CoE, 2004: 23). It is an ambitious strategy based upon a series of policy tools that includes disaggregated statistics, equality impact assessments, equality indicators, monitoring and auditing techniques, gender balance in decision-making, and equalities budgeting. Despite its widespread adoption, its full transformative potential has yet to be realised. Nevertheless, its ongoing application in policy work is a major discontinuity with earlier practices.

Chapter 2 also charted significant new developments in equalities thinking, including ongoing work on intersectionality, an approach that emphasises the need to move beyond a discrete focus on equality 'strands' and to examine issues of (in)equality related to multiple, simultaneous identities (such as gender *and* ethnicity). Attention was also given to Amartya Sen's 'capability approach' to equalities (Sen, 1984). This advances the notion of freedoms in the form of 'human capabilities', defined as 'the central and basic things in life that people can actually do and be'. They include individual substantive freedoms such as having access to adequate education and participating in public life. At the devolved level, as elsewhere, the full potential of these new conceptual 'turns' is, as yet, unknown. Whilst these comparatively sophisticated conceptualisations may offer the potential to address the shortcomings of earlier approaches to promoting equality in public policy, the main challenge lies in operationalising them in manageable and effective ways. Otherwise, as Squires (2008: 60) warns, they 'may require a policy response that may be too complex to be viable'.

The starting point for the empirical analysis in this volume was the examination of demographic and research data in chapter 3, in order to assess the nature and scale of inequalities in Wales. This confirmed the existence of equalities issues across the breadth of devolved functions, as well as considerable variation in the extent of inequalities within and between equality 'strands' and policy areas. In addition, social attitudes survey data presented a mixed picture. Whereas the vast majority of those surveyed generally rejected sexist and racist attitudes, other discriminatory views were found to prevail with regard to Gypsy Travellers, transsexual people, asylum seekers, and people with mental illness. Reference to gender equality indicators showed that over recent decades there has been some limited progress, such as in women's participation rates in higher education and the number of women employed in managerial positions. Yet, notwithstanding major changes in the nature and extent of women's engagement with the labour market, significant inequalities persist, as evidenced by the gender pay gap and occupational segregation. Overall, the contemporary evidence base reveals that inequality is a major and enduring feature of Welsh society at the beginning of the twenty-first century.

From a comparative perspective there are commonalities between all three of the UK's devolved polities, such as the endurance and complexity of equalities issues spanning all policy areas. Yet, there were also country-specific issues that need to be factored in: the Welsh language in Wales; the Irish language and sectarianism in Northern Ireland; and the Gaelic language and sectarianism in Scotland. Moreover, the indices of discrimination and inequality in each polity revealed significant contrasts in their scale and nature, thereby underlining the appropriateness of having 'regional' legislatures equipped to address local policy issues. Variations were also evident in the nature and extent of data coverage in the devolved nations. Northern Ireland shows most progress with the founding of the Equality Research and Information Service of the Northern Ireland Statistics and Research Agency, a body tasked with providing up to date information on equality strands defined in Section 75 of the Northern Ireland Act (1998).

In chapter 4, aspects of political equality were explored (cf. Verba et al., 1978) – in other words, the extent to which governance structures promote equality through participation. This is important for, as Squires (2005: 380) observes, 'enabling excluded groups to unsettle institutionally accepted conceptions of equality will require a parity of participation, which makes democratic inclusion central to both the meaning and realization of equality'. Accordingly, the analysis explored the extent to which earlier calls by feminists and Welsh language activists for devolution to deliver an inclusive and participatory democracy have been realised. Examination of the Government of Wales Acts (1998, 2006) revealed that extensive 'inclusive governance mechanisms' have been embedded into constitutional law. This is a major discontinuity, for whilst the pre-1999 mode of governance was largely exclusive in the way that it operated, devolved government is now *legally obliged* to promote inclusion and participation, not least under the terms of the principal equality clause in the devolution statute. The clause states that 'Welsh Ministers must make appropriate arrangements with a view to securing that their functions are exercised with due regard to the principle that there should be equality of opportunity for all people' (GOWA, 2006, s77). The latter duty has led to a series of institutional measures to promote equality, such as the Assembly's cross-party Standing Committee on Equality of Opportunity, the Equality, Diversity and Inclusion Division in the civil service, and the statutory requirement to uphold equality in Assembly proceedings (GOWA, 2006, s35). There is also evidence of innovation in the new governance arrangements, for they include a series of statutory partnerships between government and the public, private and voluntary sectors. These are noteworthy in that they require government to consult and co-work with NGOs, and are accompanied by statutory schemes setting out how government will meet its legal obligations with regard to partnership working (including its general duty to promote equalities). Underlining Hazell's (2007) observation about the dynamic and developing nature of devolution in Wales, the Assembly's Public Petitions Committee is a further nexus allowing a diversity of social interests to engage in policy-making. Overall, these new arrangements are evidence of a greater system openness that affords better opportunities to influence the conduct of public business. Importantly, many of the 'inclusive governance mechanisms' effectively offer a 'constitutional guarantee' of access to the policy process. For hitherto marginalised groups this is significant; it means that if government reverts to exclusivist practices, it may be subjected to legal challenge (via judicial review).

Comparative analysis reveals parallel 'inclusive governance' developments in Scotland and Northern Ireland. As in Wales, pro-devolution campaigners in Scotland were concerned that the new parliament should be founded on 'a participative approach to the development, consideration and scrutiny of policy and legislation . . . [and] its operation and its appointments should recognise the need to promote equal opportunities for all' (Consultative Steering Group, 1998: 3). Thus, the Standing Orders of the Parliament require that there is a cross party Equality Committee, as well as a Petitions Committee. Unlike Wales, the Scotland Act does not prescribe statutory cross-sectoral partnerships, yet the Scottish parliament has legislated to put some partnerships on a legal footing. In the case of Northern Ireland, Murphy (2007: 305) concludes that 'the instruments and tools of public policy at the sub-national level have changed significantly since devolution. New actors have been introduced to the process . . . new forms of decision making have also emerged'. The foremost example is the comprehensive equality clause in the Northern Ireland Act (1998, s75). Devolution in the province also provides the primary example of the growth of partnership working. A recent official study of government partnerships at all tiers of administration identified no less than 584 examples, the majority of which had been established to improve service delivery (45 per cent) or to promote policy consultation, engagement and networking (29 per cent) (OFMDFM, 2005).

Overall, the comparative analysis presented in chapter 4 shows that constitutional reform in the UK has introduced significant changes over the pre-existing 'Westminster model' of government. A decade on, it is evident that pro-devolution equalities campaigners in each territory were largely successful in their efforts to ensure that participatory governance mechanisms were embedded in the institutional blueprints of the devolved legislatures. However, as the discussion emphasises, major challenges remain before these institutional developments achieve major and lasting advances in the promotion of equalities, not least because of the straightforward reality that the new aspects of governance need time to develop and become embedded, as do revised practices of working.

It is not just the creation of the UK's devolved legislatures that underlines the significant scale of institutional change witnessed over the past decade. Analysis in chapter 5 revealed that devolution has seen the comparatively rapid development of a 'state infrastructure' around equalities in Wales, Scotland and Northern Ireland; in other words, public bodies that, wholly or in part, have an official remit to advise on, monitor and enforce equality policies and law across a broad range of public functions. This is noteworthy, for the institutions of the state have a key role in issues of equality. At worst, they may further the hegemony of ruling elites (Gramsci, 2007), sustain outmoded practices of public administration, or have a negative impact in shaping gender relations (Connell, 2007). However, when properly configured they may effectively challenge prevailing inequalities and patterns of discrimination. Thus, over the past decade in Wales, the new bodies have included the Commissioners for Children and Older People (with forthcoming legislation that will establish the office of Welsh Language Commissioner), as well as other institutions that include equalities within their remits (for example, Care and Social Services Inspectorate for Wales). Such developments signal the growing capacity of the devolved state to monitor and regulate equalities, yet the current picture is one where the nascent equalities infrastructure is characterised by complexity. It is made up of a variety of bodies, including Wales-only organisations that pre-date constitutional reform; cross-border agencies whose mode of operation has, to varying extents, adapted to devolution; and, as noted, new devolved institutions. The speed and scale with which the latter have emerged is striking. However, over the past decade there has also been a lack of government coordination of the devolved inspectorates. Given the Welsh administration's powers to influence the remits and inspection frameworks of these bodies, this is a missed opportunity.

In terms of the provision of advice on equalities, there is some evidence of progress. In the case of health and local government, pre-existing structures have adapted to the demands of devolution. In addition, new post-devolution bodies such as the Children and Family Court Advisory and Support Service (CAFCASS) Cymru have emerged. The Equality and Human Rights Commission (EHRC) also promises to offer more coordinated and comprehensive advice provision than seen previously, including human rights guidance from a Commission in Wales for the first time. Indeed, the provisions of the Equality Act (2006, s30, 2) effectively oblige the Commission to structure its operations in the context of quasi-federal Britain. Thus, the EHRC Wales Committee exercises devolved functions including information, research, education, training, advice and guidance. Moreover, the Commission in Wales has a legal right to advise devolved government on the equalities implications of its lawmaking (Equality Act, 2006, s20). It is too early to assess the wider impact of the EHRC, yet there is potential for it to exert a strong and positive influence. Overall, the trend that emerges in the wake of devolution is one of growing state capacity in relation to support and advice on equalities, but it is also one of uneven provision. It suggests the need for further development to address concerns that 'significant gaps remain in the geography and geometry of advice provision' (Borland et al., 2009: 6).

From a comparative perspective, there are similarities and contrasts in infrastructure developments in Wales, Scotland and Northern Ireland. In all three polities, pre-existing equalities-related organisations have, to varying extents, adapted to devolution. In terms of new bodies, the separate legal jurisdictions in Scotland and Northern Ireland have seen the creation of standalone human rights commissions. In all territories, constitutional reform has witnessed the comparatively rapid development of devolved state inspectorates, commissioners and allied bodies. In addition, Northern Ireland has its own equalities commission (with powers over some cross-border agencies). In each case, there is evidence of considerable variability in the extent to which public inspectorates oversee adherence to equalities law. Overall, the evolving nature of the 'equalities infrastructure' reflects the developing nature of devolution in the UK.

As the analysis in chapter 6 revealed, the framework of equalities-related law in Wales reflects the rise of multi-level governance. It is effectively composed of UN treaty obligations and EC directives (that apply to the UK as a whole), Westminster statutes and devolved enactments. Thus, over the past four decades, British legislation has outlawed discrimination on the grounds of race, sex, disability, religion or (non-) belief, sexual orientation and age. It applies to the provision of goods, facilities and services, and the exercise of public functions, including public policy-making. However, it does not afford consistent protection across all strands and all areas of activity, something that will partly be addressed when the provisions of the Equality Act (2010) come into effect. In common with 'regional', sub-state legislatures across Europe and elsewhere, quasi-federalism in the UK has also led to a series of equalities clauses in the devolution statutes; effectively, these 'constitutionalise' the promotion of equality by government. Thus, the Welsh administration's general equality duty goes beyond the British anti-discrimination framework and requires the Welsh ministers to have due regard to the principle that there should be equality of opportunity for *all* people. This imperative extends not only to the devolved executive's policy-making, but also its legislative functions. Analysis in chapter 6 revealed how the use of secondary legislation to promote equalities has been an established feature of devolution since 1999. Hundreds of statutory instruments have been passed and a growing number contain equalities provisions. For example, the Local Authorities (Model Code of Conduct) (Wales) Order (2008) requires members of local authorities to carry out their 'duties and responsibilities with due regard to the principle that there should be equality of opportunity for all people'.

Of major significance is the introduction of new legislative powers in the Government of Wales Act (2006). These allow the National Assembly to pass primary laws for Wales (known as Measures, and enforceable by the courts in the same way as parliamentary Acts). Analysis of the first Legislative Competence Orders transferring measure-making powers to the Assembly reveals that a significant number cover equality-related topics, such as the Welsh language, additional learning needs and mental health. Moreover, Regulatory Impact Assessment procedures (see GOWA, 2006, s76) require primary (and secondary) laws passed by the Assembly to be compatible with the government's general equality duty (GOWA, 2006, s77).

Taken together, these developments point to the increasing use of legal instruments to back equalities policies in the devolved context, and a growing divergence in equalities-related law applying in the jurisdictions of a quasi-federal UK. Cautious reading of the evidence from the first three terms of the National Assembly also suggests that these aspects mark a positive advancement. As devolution has matured, there has been an increasing emphasis on legislation as a 'hard' policy enforcement instrument, one that has the potential to decrease the likelihood of a policy implementation gap. This marks a key progression from the early years of the Assembly when public policy often contained declaratory statements around the promotion of equality, but lacked appropriate legal mechanisms to ensure that they were fully implemented. However, with little time elapsed since the provisions of the Government of Wales Act (2006) came into effect, it is too early to fully assess the impact that the Assembly's primary law making powers will have on the future promotion of equalities.

Policy discourse analysis and reference to evaluative studies in chapter 7 revealed that the creation of the National Assembly has led to the systematic political reprioritisation of equalities in public policy. Strikingly, all of the major policies and strategies issued by successive governments refer to the promotion of equalities as a crosscutting theme. At a symbolic level, at least, this strategic commitment to equalities is a major transition – it points to the realisation of one of the arguments of pro-devolution campaigners, that constitutional reform would deliver inclusive public policy to further the promotion of equalities (Chaney and Fevre, 2001).

Inclusive approaches to policy also resonate with the literature on mainstreaming equality – specifically, the need to engage with the groups targeted by policy (Beveridge and Nott, 2002; Donaghy 2004). Over the past decade, the majority of key strategies have been founded on consultation with those outside government. The systematic and diverse ways in which equalities considerations are now embedded in the language of policy-making is also noteworthy; it underlines the significant shift in the way in which public administration operates in the wake of devolution. On matters such as asylum seekers, refugees, forced marriage, honour based violence and domestic abuse, for the first time national Welsh strategies are now in existence. In areas of shared policy responsibility with Westminster (on issues such as child welfare, youth justice, domestic abuse and older people's services) there is some evidence of the Welsh government pursuing a more advanced approach than central government (such as incorporating compliance with the UN Charter on the Rights of the Child in devolved legislation establishing the Children's Commissioner). The general result is policy specifically tailored to the socio-economic and cultural specificities of Wales, rather than the pre-existing 'one-size fits all' approach evident in earlier Whitehall policies.

A further notable aspect of devolution is the rapid growth in government policy-making capacity. This is evident in the increasing volume of policies, consultations and evaluations, as well as the breadth of topics covered. The promotion of equalities has also been based on a diversity of approaches and policy instruments. These include the redistribution of resources and support for specific groups; promotion of equalities in accredited professional training; improving the nature of public service delivery for targeted groups; conveying rights to citizens by placing legal duties on devolved public bodies to promote equalities; and measures aimed at changing social attitudes around equality and discrimination. In instrumental terms, the evidence of a growing number of policy evaluations reveals that such policies are beginning to achieve equalities outcomes (for example, increase in numbers of disabled people participating in sports; increasing diversity of those holding public appointments; greater attention to equality and diversity in the post-2008 schools curriculum, GPs obliged to write an Annual Health Report for individuals with learning disabilities, etc.).

However, despite these positive developments, significant problems and challenges remain. In the Welsh case, the announcement from the outset by the Assembly that a generic mainstreaming approach would inform all policy-making was a bold and symbolic step. Yet, the systematic analysis of subsequent policy outputs shows the past decade to have been a period of 'institutional decoupling' (Chaney, 2006, 2009), or the means by which an organisation manages a disjuncture between formal rules and actual activities, such that it espouses one thing but generally practices another (Meyer and Rowan, 1991; Dahlström, 2004). Whilst successive administrations have advocated the need to mainstream equalities, as noted, until recently this has not generally been translated into policy outcomes (Rees and Chaney, 2010). Thus, whilst the majority of policies are integrated into the government's strategic vision and espouse the aim of promoting equalities, a number do little more that offer a declaration of intent (for example, Environment Strategy Action Plan 2008–11). In addition, not all policy documents cite the government's statutory duty to promote equality of opportunity. Analysis of the policies of the past ten years also reveals that there is a high level of variability in the way that different government departments address equalities issues. Generally, absent in a number of policy areas (for example, economic development, sustainable development, tourism, health) is a systematic approach, one that is based upon the use of equalities indicators; defined responsibility for implementation; measurable targets in a set timeframe; and feedback mechanisms to improve future effectiveness. It is an issue that continues to resonate, not only in Wales, but across the UK as noted in a recent UN report: 'many public bodies, including government ministries, have faced difficulties in developing results-based and action-oriented equality schemes and in mainstreaming equality into all policies and processes' (UN Committee on the Elimination of Discrimination against Women, 2008: 4).

In assessing progress, it should also be noted that Welsh ministers currently work within the constraints of the present devolution settlement whereby significant forces of policy convergence operate (Jeffery and Adams, 2006: 3). These include intergovernmental linkages (for example, Secretary of State for Wales/Wales Office as mediator between devolved government and UK institutions); intra-party negotiations (for example, between Welsh Labour and British Labour Party); and the reservation to Westminster of key powers that impact on equalities (for example, taxation, criminal justice and social security). Context-specific factors have also arrested the progress of the equalities agenda. These include major restructuring of the Welsh legislature on parliamentary lines (this followed the provisions of GOWA, 2006 and, although essential, diverted the energies of politicians and officials alike); fiscal constraints (the oft-criticised Barnett formula limits the resources available to the government and, in turn, the breadth and scale of its equalities policies); the National Assembly's chronic under-capacity (just 45 AMs if members of the Cabinet are excluded); and (notwithstanding a forthcoming referendum on further powers for the Assembly) the present arcane and cumbersome lawmaking process stemming from the opaque division of powers between devolved and central government.

However, against this backdrop, there are a number of grounds for cautious optimism. The government's revised Mainstreaming Strategy (WAG, 2006) has led to a series of measures to address the earlier failings. These include the introduction of an Inclusive Policymaking Tool (WAG, 2008(37)) that should result in a more systematic approach to mainstreaming equalities in policy, as well as the publication of Single Equality Plans (and related progress reports) by government departments. As detailed in chapter 7, there is emerging evidence that these measures are starting to have an impact, for example, through the increasing use of policy evaluations and the setting of equalities targets. However, it must be emphasised that there is much remaining work to be done before mainstreaming is fully embedded in policy-making through the systematic use of equalities indicators, impact assessments and budgeting techniques. Notwithstanding these issues, analysis also reveals the distinctive nature of some post-devolution equalities policies. Examples include the Older People's Strategy and Commissioner; reform of the public appointments process; the Children's Commissioner for Wales; extensive measures to increase the participation of young people in formal decision-making; and anticipated primary legislation for increasing the rights of Welsh speakers and creation of the post of language commissioner.

From a comparative perspective, contrasts and commonalities exist between the devolved countries of the UK. Both Scotland and Northern Ireland have stronger historical traditions of indigenous policy-making as well as separate legal systems. Arguably, this has meant that equalities groups have not had such a 'steep learning curve' in engaging in policy work as that experienced in Wales. A further key difference is the singular, post-conflict status of Northern Ireland.

This exerts a particular influence on the developing equalities agenda in that territory. Despite such contrasts, there are also striking similarities. These include the political subscription to mainstreaming; the need for more emphasis on securing equalities outcomes; scope for increased use of equality indicators, impact assessments and targets; and the need for greater accountability in policy implementation, and improvements in monitoring and evaluating policy.

As noted, one of the core arguments of pro-devolution campaigners in the 1980s and 1990s was that the creation of the National Assembly for Wales would advance political equality through a participatory mode of governance. This viewpoint was shared by many of those elected to the new legislature, including the former First Minister Rhodri Morgan AM, who spoke of the goal of achieving a 'new pluralism' in policy-making (Morgan, 2002). 'Lobbying' is a key element in attempts to secure participatory democracy, and refers quite simply to 'the practice of attempting to influence the decisions of government' (Rosenthal, 2001: 11). Analysis in chapter 8 reveals how devolution has created a nascent 'equalities lobby' with a potential membership and political influence that is significant in scale, on some measures involving almost half of all voluntary sector organisations in the country. This is a powerful corrective to those that choose to style equalities as a 'minority' or 'politically correct' undertaking. Nevertheless, major challenges relate to the lobby. A fundamental issue is how some equalities-related organisations interpret their own role and whether they see it having a policy dimension, or whether their *raison d'être* is solely concerned with service delivery and other non-lobbying activities. A further related question is the extent to which there is coordinated action around a collective notion of equality. Notwithstanding such matters, it is significant that over the past decade the lobby has benefited from continuing and extensive government funding. This has been a necessary strategy to increase policy-making capacity. The views of NGO managers underline the importance of this support. In the present economic downturn it remains to be seen whether any future scaling back in support will have a significant impact on the effectiveness of the lobby. It is also notable that the Assembly's present lack of full parliamentary powers present distinct challenges for equalities organisations owing to the complex division of policy responsibilities between Cardiff and Westminster. As a result, NGOs and others need to maintain a dual lobbying focus (an issue that is not as significant for their counterparts in Scotland and Northern Ireland). Unevenness is a further feature of the lobby, for whilst comparatively strong networks exist around disability, gender and children, other social groups lack these mobilising structures and, as a result, are weaker and more fragmented. This in turn raises questions about their ability to make their voices heard against the background of increasing competition between equalities strands and organisations as they compete for access to those in power. Nevertheless, it is clear that equalities organisations are using the structures of devolved governance to place their policy demands before government. For example, discourse analysis of the proceedings of the Assembly's Equality Committee reveals it to be acting as nexus between equalities NGOs and elected representatives. Similarly, analysis of the Third Sector Partnership Council meetings with government ministers, and the work of the new Petitions Committee, shows that these are also being used by exogenous interests to press equality claims on government. Weighed against this progress, further key challenges remain, not least in boosting the representativeness of equality policy networks and organisations, and the need to increase the numbers and types of NGOs that are aware of and able to use the new structures of devolved governance.

From a comparative perspective, Scotland and Northern Ireland again exhibit a number of commonalities with Wales. Following constitutional reform in 1998–9, all devolved UK polities were subject to similar concerns about the limited capacity of indigenous policy communities. As a result, a decade on, the devolved administrations continue to intervene to boost lobby capacity through measures such as the sponsorship of policy networks. In each country there has been variability in the level of engagement between government and organisations representing different equality strands. Whilst gender and disability organisations note aspects of progress, ethnic minority and faith organisations have generally been less engrossed in policy work. Frustrations are also evident in that, for many NGOs, the increased access to government has been somewhat process-oriented and has not always translated into clear policy outcomes. In all three territories there remain concerns about the need to broaden the circles of those engaged in lobbying beyond the well-networked, more established, better resourced organisations.

A further notable development, explored in chapter 8, is the way in which devolution has introduced electoral competition around equalities in the context of Welsh, Scottish and Northern Irish general elections. Since the first National Assembly elections in 1999, the political parties in Wales have given increasing attention to equalities matters as they seek to maximise support at the ballot box from a range of social groups in an increasingly heterogeneous electorate. This has been driven in part by civil and civic organisations seizing the political opportunity structures associated with devolved elections to issue their own equalities manifestos. Analysis reveals that, in turn, parties and candidates are adopting some of their policy proposals. Overall, this indicates that 'sub-state' electoral politics is an arena in which the interaction between parties and NGOs shapes the policy that is ultimately mandated in devolved elections.

To return to this book's core aim, it set out to chart the impact of constitutional reform on the promotion of gender and other modes of equality. It has identified the way in which the UK's devolution programme was partly shaped by equality campaigners' call for a more inclusive mode of governance, and that provisions in the devolution statutes have gone some way to address this demand. The evidence relating to the new governance structures reveals that they are generally leading to greater system openness and are allowing external interests to place equalities demands upon government. Moreover, policy analysis, evaluative studies and a growing body of law attest to the way that devolution has transformed the degree to which the public policy process addresses equalities issues in Wales, Scotland and Northern Ireland. This is a significant and positive discontinuity.

However, given the historical failure of central government to fully address entrenched patterns and processes of inequality, it is unrealistic to expect that new regional legislatures with limited powers will succeed in just one decade. Thus, in the devolved context, challenges remain. These include the need to increase devolved governments' engagement with equalities constituencies, and for a greater emphasis to be placed on securing equalities outcomes. There is emerging evidence that such issues are beginning to be addressed. Overall, the experience of the past decade indicates that 'regional' legislatures operating in the context of multi-level governance do have the potential to make a significant contribution to the promotion of equalities through policy-making based on local needs. Yet, further progress and ongoing political commitment is necessary if, over future years, mainstreaming practices are to be fully embedded in the policy work of devolved government.

Notes

1: Introduction: Equalities and Public Policy

[1] E.g. DLGC (2007) *Equalities Review*, and the UK Government's Equalities Office.

[2] *http://www.equalities.gov.uk/about/index.htm.*

[3] Women and Work Commission, 2006.

[4] DLGC, 2006.

[5] Feinstein, 2002.

[6] Parliamentary Written Answer – Hansard Column 583W, 1 February 2006, figures for 2004–5.

[7] Benabou, 1997.

[8] Wilkinson, 2005.

[9] Home Office, 2001. *http://www.image.guardian.co.uk/sys-files/Guardian/documents/2001/12/11/communitycohesionreport.pdf.*

[10] Office of the Deputy Prime Minister, 2006.

[11] Office of National Statistics, 2008.

[12] *http://webarchive.nationalarchives.gov.uk/+/http://www.dwp.gov.uk/mediacentre/pressreleases/2006/feb/drc-015-090206.asp/.*

[13] UK Government data cited by Stonewall: *http://www.stonewall.org.uk/information_bank/sexuality_key_questions/79.asp.*

[14] Office of National Statistics, 2008.

[15] Office of National Statistics, 2001.

[16] DLGC, 2008, pp. 6–7; DLGC, 2007a; EHRC, 2008b.

2: Theoretical Perspectives on Promoting Equality

[1] It should be noted that equality between social classes was not being advocated.

[2] 2000/78/EC of 27 November 2000, OJ L303/16.

[3] Tawney's principal focus was social welfare.

[4] Burchardt, 2008.

[5] Ibid.

3: Exploring Inequality and Discrimination in Wales, Scotland and Northern Ireland

1. Draws upon analysis by Dunkerley, 2007. Data: 2001 Census, unless otherwise stated.
2. ONS, 2008.
3. Niner, 2006.
4. Statistics for Wales, 2009.
5. Circa 2007; see Shipley, 2008.
6. Shipley, 2008.
7. 8.1% (234,100 people) did not answer the question regarding religion
8. 60 years of age for women, 65 for men.
9. WAG, 2008(5).
10. WAG, 2006j.
11. ONS, 2009b.
12. EOC, 2006.
13. Welsh Language Board, 2004, p. 6.
14. Welsh Language Board, 2007.
15. NAfW, 2003a.
16. Excluding full-time students.
17. Lee, 2006a.
18. WAG, 2008(5), WAG, 2008(32).
19. ONS, 2007b.
20. Lee, 2006b.
21. Yeandle et al., 2007.
22. Statistics for Wales, 2009, Table 2.1.
23. Circa 2004/5.
24. Statistics for Wales, 2007, p. 20.
25. National Assembly for Wales Statistical Directorate, 2005, p. 57.
26. NAfW, 2006b.
27. NAfW, 2006d.
28. Statistics for Wales, 2009, p. 18.
29. Pilgrim and Scourfield, 2007, p. 156.
30. Williams and Robinson, 2006.
31. Welsh Language Board, 2007.
32. WAG/Statistics for Wales, 2007, p. 63.
33. National Assembly for Wales Statistical Directorate, 2005, p. 56.
34. NAfW, 2006c, p. 17.
35. NAfW, 2006b.
36. NAfW, 2006b, p. 17.
37. Including subject areas not listed separately above.
38. NAfW (2006) and EOC Wales (2006), figures for 2004/5.
39. 2003/4, with the exception of Work Based Learning (WBL).

40 Including subject areas not listed separately above.
41 DCELLS, 2006/EOC Wales, 2006, circa 2003/4.
42 NAfW, 2006b.
43 Statistics for Wales, 2008, p. 2.
44 WAG, 2008(5).
45 Principal data source: Welsh Language Board, 2007, unless stated otherwise.
46 WAG, 2007c, p. 29.
47 WAG, 2007c, p. 29.
48 Statistics for Wales, 2007.
49 People with a current disability, including DDA disabled and work-limiting disability.
50 ONS, 2005 and EOC, 2006.
51 NAfW, 2006c.
52 Statistics for Wales, 2007.
53 Statistics for Wales, 2007, p. 27.
54 Statistics for Wales, 2007, p. 27. Data from the 2001 Census.
55 WAG, 2008(5).
56 NAfW, 2003b.
57 Welsh Language Board, 2007.
58 ONS, 2009a.
59 ONS, 2005, p. 12.
60 EOC Wales, 2006 and EHRC, 2009.
61 Including those not shown separately.
62 ONS, 2005, p. 15.
63 Cited in Rees, 1999, p. 33.
64 Williams and Robinson, 2006.
65 NAfW, 2005b, p. 64.
66 Last quarter of 2007.
67 National Offender Management Service, 2007.
68 NAfW, 2005b, p. 66.
69 Statistics for Wales, 2007, p. 18.
70 NAfW, 2005b, p. 67.
71 WAG, 2008(5).
72 Welsh Language Board, 2007, p. 4
73 Stonewall Cymru, 2006.
74 Stonewall Cymru, 2006, p. 6.
75 WAG, 2007c.
76 WAG, 2006k.
77 WAG, 2007c.
78 Statistics for Wales, 2007, p. 19.
79 WAG, 2008(5).
80 WAG, 2006k.

81 Williams and Robinson, 2006.
82 NAfW, 2005b, p. 73.
83 WAG, 2007c.
84 Welsh Consumer Council and EOC, 2005.
85 Welsh Consumer Council and EOC, 2005.
86 NAfW, 2006b.
87 NAfW, 2003b.
88 NAfW, 2006b.
89 Circa 2008.
90 ONS, 2005, p. 9.
91 EOC Wales, 2006.
92 'Welsh' denotes those normally domiciled in Wales regardless of national/ethnic origin.
93 2007.
94 Statistics for Wales, 2008.
95 Williams and Robinson, 2006.
96 Purposive sample of 403 individuals.
97 Stonewall Cymru, 2008 and anon, 'Gay hate crime convictions rise', 18 April 2009, *http://news.bbc.co.uk/1/hi/wales/8004548.stm.*
98 Welsh Women's Aid, 2005.
99 2008. Sample size 1,589.
100 EHRC, 2008a.
101 EHRC, 2008b, p. 15.
102 EHRC, 2008c, p. 20.
103 Excludes 'Neither' and 'Don't know/refused to answer' responses.
104 Scottish Executive National Statistics, 2006.
105 *http://www.gro-scotland.gov.uk/census/index.html.*
106 Bromley and Curtice, 2003.
107 Scottish Executive National Statistics, 2006, p.60.
108 *http://www.equalityhumanrights.com/en/scotland/news/Pages/PaygapScotlandnov08.aspx*, 27 November 2008.
109 EOC Scotland, 2006, p. 6.
110 EOC Scotland, 2006, p. 5.
111 EOC Scotland, 2006, p. 7.
112 EOC Scotland, 2006, p. 7.
113 Scottish Executive National Statistics, 2006, p. 220.
114 Scottish Social Attitudes Survey, 2006.
115 Scottish Executive National Statistics, 2006, p. 56
116 Scottish Executive National Statistics, 2006.
117 *http://www.copfs.gov.uk/About/Departmental-Overview/diversity/racist-crime/Statistics0506*, 27 November 2008.
118 Bromley and Curtice, 2003.
119 Scottish Social Attitudes Survey, 2006.

[120] Office for National Statistics, 2008.

[121] Bromley and Curtice, 2003.

[122] Scottish Executive National Statistics, 2006, p. 59.

[123] Scottish Executive National Statistics, 2006, p. 65.

[124] Scottish Executive National Statistics, 2006, p. 82.

[125] Scottish Executive National Statistics, 2006, p. 104.

[126] Scottish Executive National Statistics, 2006, p. 108.

[127] Scottish Executive National Statistics, 2006, p. 57; based on 2001 Census Data.

[128] Scottish Executive National Statistics, 2006, p. 119.

[129] *http://www.copfs.gov.uk/About/Departmental-Overview/diversity/racist-crime/Analysus*, 27 November 2008.

[130] Scottish Executive National Statistics, 2006, p. 59; circa 2006.

[131] Scottish Executive National Statistics, p. 106.

[132] 2006–7.

[133] *http://www.equality.nisra.gov.uk/default.asp623.htm.*

[134] Defined as 'any incident of threatening behaviour, violence, or abuse (psychological, physical, sexual, financial or emotional) by one family member against another or adults who are or have been intimate partners, regardless of gender, and whether a crime has occurred or not, will be recorded as domestic'.

[135] PSNI, 2008a.

[136] Northern Ireland Department of Education, 2008, Figure 4.

[137] PSNI, 2008b.

[138] Livesey et al., 2007, p. 54.

[139] Northern Ireland Department of Education, 2008, Table 7.

[140] Connolly, 2002.

[141] PSNI, 2008a.

[142] Northern Ireland Department of Health, Social Services and Public Health, 2004.

[143] PSNI, 2008b.

[144] Livesey, et al., 2007, p. 57.

[145] Equality Commission for Northern Ireland, 2008.

[146] PSNI, 2008a.

[147] ONS, 2008b.

[148] Livesey et al., 2007.

[149] Office of the Oversight Commissioner, 2007, p. 13.

[150] NI Department of Health, Social Services and Public Safety, 2004, p. 32.

[151] NIO, 2004.

[152] Age of household reference person by type of accommodation 2002–3; source, Continuous Household Survey.

4: Promoting Equality: A Governance Perspective

[1] Dafydd Wigley MP, Plaid Cymru, Hansard House of Commons Debates, 28 February 1996, Column 919.

[2] Standing Order 28.9.

[3] Third edition (first revision, September 2007).

[4] The First Minister and the Deputy First Minister are also each responsible for three personal nominations.

[5] Paragraph 34, Strand 1.

[6] *http://www.ofmdfmni.gov.uk/index/making-government-work/civic-forum-review/civic-forum-faqs.htm.* Accessed 2 September 2008.

[7] Third edition (first revision, September 2007).

[8] Reproduced from: *http://education.niassembly.gov.uk/information/ Elections_NIA.pdf.*

5: The Equalities 'Infrastructure' in the Devolved State

[1] *http://www.wales.nhs.uk/sites3/page.cfm?orgid=256&pid=3704.*

[2] *http://www.wales.nhs.uk/sites3/page.cfm?orgid=256&pid=3704.*

[3] Some RECs have broadened their remit beyond race to encompass other 'strands' of equality.

[4] Limited disaggregated Wales-only statistics provided in the 2007–8 ACAS Annual Report.

[5] Age equality regulations effective from October 2006

[6] Wales Audit Office, 2008, p. 10.

[7] Public Services Ombudsman for Wales, 2008, p. 19.

[8] CSSIW, 2008, p. 2.

[9] In addition to inspecting the work of NHS Wales, since April 2006 Healthcare Inspectorate Wales is responsible for regulating independent healthcare in Wales.

[10] Healthcare Inspectorate Wales, 2006.

[11] *http://www.hiw.org.uk/page.cfm?orgid=477&pid=13329.*

[12] Estyn, 2004.

[13] General Teaching Council for Wales, 2006a.

[14] Social Services Inspectorate for Wales, 2003.

[15] Social Services Inspectorate for Wales, 2004.

[16] Children's Commissioner for Wales, 2007a.

[17] This term has been superseded by The Civil Procedure (Modification of Supreme Court Act 1981) Order 2004. The current term is a 'mandatory order'. This compels a public body to act in respect of statutory provision.

[18] *http://www.sentw.gov.uk/.*

[19] That is to say they were not the subject of an order to strike out.

[20] For example, seven such claims were received in 2006–7

[21] *http://www.olderpeoplewales.com/*.

[22] Adapted from: *http://www.olderpeoplewales.com/index.php?id=16&L=0*.

[23] *http://new.wales.gov.uk/about/recruitment/publicapps/cpal?lang=en*.

[24] *http://www.publicappointmentscommissioner.org/What_we_do/ Promoting_Equal_Opportunities/*.

[25] *www.acas.org.uk*.

[26] The Secretary of State of EHRC's sponsoring department, on behalf of the Commission.

[27] Section 30, 2(a).

[28] Schedule 1, Section 32.

[29] *http://www.bord-na-gaidhlig.org.uk/about-us/the-gaelic-act.html*.

[30] *http://www.publicappointments.org/our_role/*.

[31] *http://www.audit-scotland.gov.uk/docs/local/2008/nr_081113_equalities. pdf*.

[32] *http://www.scotland.gov.uk/Topics/Justice/Civil/17838/10235*.

[33] *http://www.swia.gov.uk/swia/files/Argyll%20and%20Bute%20 Inspection%20Report.pdf*.

[34] *http://www.nihrc.org/index.php?option=com_content&task=view&id= 7&Itemid=12*.

[35] *http://www.ocpani.gov.uk/index/our-role.htm*.

[36] *http://www.niscc.info/home-1.aspx*.

[37] Under the terms of the Health and Personal Social Services (Quality, Improvement and Regulation) (Northern Ireland) Order (2003).

6: *Legislating for Equality in a Quasi-Federal UK*

[1] Quoted from *http://www.un.org/womenwatch/daw/cedaw/cedaw.htm*.

[2] *http://www.un.org/ageing/un_principles.html*.

[3] *http://www.un.org/ageing/un_principles.html*.

[4] *http://ec.europa.eu/employment_social/fundamental_rights/pdf/ey07/ com07_en.pdf*.

[5] See *http://www.justice.gov.uk/docs/act-studyguide.pdf*.

[6] Adapted from Equality Bill (2009) House of Commons 03.12.2009; *http://www.publications.parliament.uk/pa/ld200910/ldbills/020/en/ 2010020en.pdf*.

[7] Welsh Language Board, 2007b, p. 10.

[8] Cymdeithas yr Iaith Gymraeg, *http://cymdeithas.org* and the Welsh Language Board, 2006.

[9] Race Relations Order (Amendment) Regulations (Northern Ireland) (2003).

[10] 2000–1, 5 bills; 2001–2, 8 bills; 2002–3, 6 bills; 2003–4, 6 bills; 2004–5, 3 bills; 2005–6, 1 bill; 2006–7, 3 bills.

[11] *http://www.gov.ns.ca/legislature/HOUSE_OF_ASSEMBLY/NS_ Legislative_Procedures.pdf.*

[12] *Ley 4/2005, de 18 de febrero, para la Igualdad de Mujeres y Hombres*; adapted from Bustelo and Peterson, 2005.

[13] As reformed by Law 6/2006 of 19 July 2006.

[14] *http://www.opsi.gov.uk/legislation/wales/wsi2002/wsi_20020156_mi.pdf.*

[15] *http://new.wales.gov.uk/?view=Search+results&d-1337099- p=2&lang=en&paging=true#internal.*

[16] See *www.assemblywales.org/bus-home/buslegislation/bus-legislation-leg- process.htm.*

[17] Circular NC/C/05/10LDF. Securing Specialist Provision for Learners with Learning Difficulties and/or Disabilities (2005).

[18] Circular NC/C/05/05LDF – Student Support Arrangements 2005/6 (2005).

[19] Circular NAFWC 13/2006 – National Service Framework (NSF) for Older People in Wales (2006).

7: Analysing the Devolved Governments' Public Policy Approaches to the Promotion of Equality

[1] WAG, 2008(21); WAG, 2008(22); WAG, 2008(25); WAG, 2008(26); WAG, 2008(9); WAG, 2008(27); WAG, 2008(28); WAG, 2008(29); WAG, 2008(31).

[2] *http://new.wales.gov.uk/topics/educationandskills/policy_strategy_and_ planning/learning_pathways/?lang=en.* Accessed 24 September 2008.

[3] *http://www.hefcw.ac.uk/about_he_in_wales/wag_priorities_and_policies/ reaching_higher_targets.aspx.* Accessed 4 February 2010.

[4] Section 312, Education Act (1996).

[5] WAG Statement, Additional Learning Needs – Legislative Competence Order, 11 June 2007.

[6] OECD, 2006 cited in WAG, 2008(10), p. 5.

[7] *http://www.funkydragon.org.*

[8] *http://www.funkydragon.org/en/fe/page.asp?n1=2.*

[9] WAG/Save the Children Wales, 2007.

[10] *http://www.wyfsd.org/cms/index.php?&lan=en.*

[11] WAG, 2008(4).

[12] *http://www.funkydragon.org.uk/en/fe/page.asp?n1=2.*

13 *http://new.wales.gov.uk/topics/educationandskills/policy_strategy_and_ planning/schools/children_and_young_people/school-council- project/?lang=en.*

14 *http://www.opsi.gov.uk/legislation/wales/wsi2005/20053200e.htm.*

15 *http://new.wales.gov.uk/topics/educationandskills/policy_strategy_and_ planning/schools/children_and_young_people/cyppconsultations/?lang=en.*

16 WAG, 2007d, p. 5.

17 WAG, 2007a; WAG, 2007e; WAG, 2007f; WAG, 2007g

18 *http://new.wales.gov.uk/topics/childrenyoungpeople/childrenfirst/?lang=en.*

19 WAG, 2005.

20 WAG, 2006g.

21 See National Assembly for Wales (Transfer of Functions) Order 1999 (SI. 1999/672).

22 *http://careerswales.com/aboutus/.* Accessed 25 September 2008.

23 *http://careerswales.com/aboutus/.* Accessed 25 September 2008.

24 *http://www.englishtest.chwaraeteg.com/.* Accessed 18 September 2008.

25 *http://www.gowales.co.uk/en/student/workingInWales/keyIndustryProfiles/ publicSector/index.html.* Accessed 1 November 2008.

26 *http://www.wiseinwales.org.uk/faqs/index.html.*

27 *http://www.wiseinwales.org.uk/faqs/index.html.*

28 *http://www.wiseinwales.org.uk/faqs/index.html.*

29 These included the Royal National Institute for the Blind Cymru and the Black Ethnic Support Team.

30 Number of incidences (–) of the following key terms in the Environment Strategy Action Plan 2008–11: equal/equality (0); disabled/disability (0); age/older (0); faith (0); women/gender (0).

31 WAG, 2008(3), p. 57.

32 Adapted from Arad Consulting and Evans, 2007.

33 See http:*//www.scotland.gov.uk/Publications/2004/09/19976/43560.*

34 *http://www.payingforcareinwales.net.*

35 Care and Social Services Inspectorate Wales, 2007. Incidences of the following terms in the document: 'equality' (0), 'disabled/disability' (0), 'ethnic' (0). Care and Social Services Inspectorate Wales (2007) *Care Services in Wales Annual Report 2006–2007*, Cardiff, CSSIW. Incidences of the following terms in the document: 'equality' (1), 'disabled/disability' (3), 'ethnic' (0).

36 See *http://www.scotland.gov.uk/library3/social/wtem-00.asp.*

37 Scottish Government, 2008a, p. 48.

38 Scottish Government, 2007a, p. 88.

39 Scottish Government, 2007, p. 64.

40 Scottish Government, 2007, p. 119.

41 Scottish Government, 2008b, p. 6.

42 Scottish Government , 2007, p. 121.

43 Scottish Government, 2007.
44 Scottish Government, 2007, p. 160.
45 Scottish Government, 2008c, p. 11.
46 Scottish Government, 2008, p. 13, for the Pilot Evaluation Report, see: *http://www.scotland.gov.uk/Publications/2007/03/28153424/0.*
47 Scottish Government, 2008a.
48 Scottish Government, 2007, p. 212.
49 Scottish Government, 2007, p. 44.
50 No legislative timetable announced; see, for e.g., Northern Ireland Assembly debates, 10 September 2007, Oral Answers to Questions, Single Equality Bill.
51 It should be noted, however, that the UK government retained responsibility for primary legislation on the Welsh Language throughout the period of administrative devolution.
52 Under the Federation of Disability Sport Wales policy.

8: Lobbying and Electoral Competition on Equality Matters in the Devolved Polity

1   The summary database does not list language organisations under a separate heading
2   £993,000, *http://new.wales.gov.uk/publications/accessinfo/drnewhomepage/lifedrs2/lifedrs2007/1938456/?lang=en.*
3   *http://www.awema.org.uk/public/main.cfm?m1=c_5&m2=e_0&m3=e_0&m4=e_0.* Accessed 13 August 2008.
4   *http://www.womensvoice.org.uk/membership.php.* Accessed 14 August 2008.
5   *http://www.stonewallcymru.org.uk/cymru/english/default.asp.*
6   *http://www.stonewallcymru.org.uk/cymru/english/about_us/227.asp.* Accessed 13 August 2008.
7   *http://www.womensworkshop.org.uk/index.html.* Accessed 13 August 2008.
8   *http://www.disabilitywales.org/aboutus/index.html.* Accessed 14 August 2008.
9   *http://new.wales.gov.uk/publications/accessinfo/drnewhomepage/peopledrs2/peopledrs2008/1930149/?lang=en.*
10 *http://www.childreninwales.org.uk/aboutus/index.html.* Accessed 4 October 2008.
11 This is being piloted at the time of writing.
12 Ranging from £100 to a maximum of £2,000.
13 Children in Wales, 2007, p. 17.

14 *http://new.wales.gov.uk/publications/accessinfo/drnewhomepage/ peopledrs2/peopledrs2007/1928996/?lang=en.*

15 WAG, (2004).

16 *http://www.refugeevoicewales.org/documents/Annual%20Report%20 RVW-2006-2007.pdf.*

17 *http://wales.gov.uk/publications/accessinfo/drnewhomepage/ Internationaldrs/Internationaldrs2008/creatonofmigrantsforum/?lang=en.*

18 *http://new.wales.gov.uk/topics/equality/rightsequality/faith/ faithforum/?lang=en.*

19 Mission Statement: National Partnership Forum published 1 May 2005 at the first meeting of the National Partnership Forum for Older People in Wales.

20 National Partnership Forum for Older People in Wales, 2007 (unless otherwise stated).

21 *http://new.wales.gov.uk/topics/equality/rightsequality/faith/ engagement/?lang=en.* Accessed 29 September 2008.

22 *http://www.helptheaged.org.uk/en-cy/WhatWeDo/AboutUs/AcrossTheUK/.* In 2009–10 this organisation became Age UK after merging with Age Concern.

23 *http://www.refugeevoicewales.org/documents/Annual%20Report%20 RVW-2006-2007.pdf.*

24 *http://debbiewilkie.org/debbiewilkie/id7.html.* Accessed 2 September 2008.

25 *http://www.scottishwomensconvention.org/.*

26 *http://www.engender.org.uk.*

27 *http://www.communityni.org/index.cfm/section/article/page/womens_ policy_forum.*

28 See, for example, Minutes of the Women's Policy Forum, 22 April 2006, NICVA.

29 *http://www.coso.org.uk/publications.html.*

30 *http://www.dsdni.gov.uk/vcu_taskforce.*

31 $P = 0.001$.

32 Chi Squared $= 30.398$, df $= 8$, $P = 0.001$.

33 Welsh. Trans. 'Fair Play'. A state funded organisation to promote gender equality in the labour market.

34 $P = <0.001$, Chi Squared $= 23.6$, df $= 1$, $P = 0.00115$.

35 Minutes Of The Voluntary Sector Meeting With Sue Essex AM, 19 May 2005.

36 Meeting between Business Minister Jane Hutt AM and the Voluntary Sector, 10 June 2005.

37 Minutes of the Voluntary Sector meeting with Sue Essex AM (Minister for Finance, Local Government and Public Services) 19 October 2006.

[38] Meeting between the Business Minister and the Voluntary Sector, Thursday, 8 December 2005.
[39] 17 May 2004.
[40] 17 May 2004.
[41] 22 November 2004.
[42] 10 June 2005.
[43] 25 June 2003.
[44] 25 May 2006.
[45] 18 May 2004.
[46] 6 February 2006.
[47] 19 May 2005.
[48] 15 November 2004.
[49] 14 November 2004.
[50] 18 July 2007.
[51] 7 June 2006.
[52] 24 November 2005.
[53] 8 December 2005.
[54] 17 May 2004.
[55] 19 May 2005.
[56] 8 February 2006.
[57] 6 December 2005.
[58] 7 June 2006.
[59] 14 November 2005.
[60] 24 November 2005
[61] 18 July 2007.
[62] 7 June 2006.
[63] 10 June 2005.
[64] 25 May 2006.
[65] That is to say all meetings at the time of writing.
[66] 4 October 2007.
[67] 6 December 2007.
[68] 21 February 2008.
[69] In response, 30.8 per cent said that they were unsure/did not know.
[70] *http://www.wcb-ccd.org.uk/English/Reports/ar2001/annualreview2001. htm.*
[71] A WAG initiative initially put out for consultation in 2006 and subsequently renamed the 'Grassroots Fund', it provides small grants up to £5,000 for capacity building amongst local voluntary groups and is administered via County Voluntary Services.
[72] RNIB Cymru, 2008.
[73] Cardiff and the Vale Coalition of Disabled People, 2006, p. 3.
[74] Disability Wales, 2007, p. 28.
[75] Disability Wales, 2006, p. 10.

76 Independent Commission to Review the Voluntary Sector Scheme, 2006, p. 48.
77 Independent Commission to Review the Voluntary Sector Scheme, 2006, p. 48.
78 MEWN Cymru 2007, p. 36.
79 Independent Commission to Review the Voluntary Sector Scheme, 2006, p. 36.
80 Independent Commission to Review the Voluntary Sector Scheme, 2006, p. 48.
81 MEWN Cymru, 2007, p. 51.
82 All Wales Saheli Association/ WAG, 2006.
83 All Wales Saheli Association/ WAG, 2006.
84 All Wales Saheli Association/ WAG, 2006.
85 Stonewall Cymru, 2004, p. 3.
86 Stonewall Cymru, 2004, p. 4.
87 NAfW, 2008c, p. 31.
88 Independent Commission to Review the Voluntary Sector Scheme, 2006, p. 48.
89 Age Concern Cymru, 2007, p. 6
90 Help the Aged Wales, 2007, p. 3.
91 Help the Aged Wales, 2007, p. 3.
92 National Partnership Forum for Older People in Wales, 2007, p. 8.
93 Independent Commission to Review the Voluntary Sector Scheme, 2006, p. 48.
94 Save the Children, 2008, p. 6.
95 Children in Wales, 2007, p. 11.
96 Welsh Refugee Council, 2007, p. 9.
97 Save the Children, 2008, p. 6.
98 As identified by the search terms 'women' and 'gender' (excludes incidence of 'women' in reference to the party name Northern Ireland Women's Coalition).
99 Party wound up on 11 May 2006.
100 Age Concern Cymru et al., 2007, p. 8.
101 Age Concern Cymru et al., 2007, p. 8.
102 Age Concern Cymru et al., 2007, p. 8.
103 Age Concern Cymru et al., 2007, p. 8.
104 Age Concern Cymru et al., 2007, p. 4.
105 Housing Forum Cymru, 2006, p. 7.
106 Age Concern Cymru et al., 2007, p. 4.
107 Scope Cymru, 2007, p. 7.
108 Coalition on Charging Cymru, 2007, p. 8.
109 Age Concern Cymru et al., 2007, p. 8.
110 Age Concern Cymru et al., 2007, p. 8.

[111] Age Concern Cymru et al., 2007, p. 7.
[112] Christian Peoples Alliance in Wales, 2007, p. 22.
[113] Age Concern Cymru et al., 2007, p. 8.
[114] Age Concern Cymru et al., 2007, p. 4.
[115] Age Concern Cymru et al., 2007, p. 8.
[116] Age Concern Cymru et al., 2007, p. 7.
[117] Age Concern Cymru et al., 2007, p. 6.
[118] Age Concern Cymru, 2007b, p. 4.
[119] Age Concern Cymru et al., 2007, p. 6.
[120] Age Concern Cymru et al., 2007, p. 4.
[121] Age Concern Cymru et al., 2007, p. 4.
[122] Age Concern Cymru et al., 2007, p. 4.
[123] Wales Council for the Blind, 2003, p. 15.
[124] Wales Council for the Blind, 2003, p. 17.
[125] Scope Cymru, 2007, p. 3.
[126] Age Concern Cymru, 2007b, p. 3.
[127] Mind Cymru, 2007, p. 3.
[128] Coalition on Charging Cymru, 2007, p. 14.
[129] Tros Gynnal Hawliau Plant, et al., 2007, p. 6.
[130] Amnesty International et al., 2007, p. 16.
[131] Age Concern Cymru et al., 2007, p. 6.
[132] Welsh Refugee Council, 2007, p. 5.
[133] Age Concern Cymru, 2007, p. 6.
[134] Help the Aged Wales, 2007, p. 3.
[135] See also *http://www.assemblywales.org/abthome/abt-commission/about_us-public_attitudes_2008/about_us-public_attitudes_2008_attitudes_towards_the_assembly.htm*. Accessed 13 August 2008.

Bibliography

Abbas, T. (2005) 'Recent Developments to British Multicultural Theory, Policy and Practice: The Case of British Muslims', *Citizenship Studies*, 9, 2, 153–166.

Acheson, N. and Williamson, A. P. (2007) 'Civil society in multi-level public policy: the case of Ireland's two jurisdictions', *Policy and Politics*, 35, 1, 25–44.

Adams, J. and Robinson, P. (eds) (2002) *Devolution in practice: public policy differences within the UK*, London: IPPR.

Adamson, D. (2008) 'Still Living on the Edge?', in Chaney, P., Royles, E. and Thompson, A. (eds) *Contemporary Wales: An Review of Economic, Political and Social Research*, Cardiff: University of Wales Press.

Adamson, D. and Bromiley, R. (2008) *Community empowerment in practice – Lessons from Communities First*, York: Joseph Rowntree Foundation.

Adnett, N. (2005) *The European Social Model: Modernisation or Evolution?* Cheltenham: Edward Elgar.

Adriana, P. and Manolescu, I. (2006) Gender discrimination in Romania, *Journal of Organizational Change Management*, vol. 19, no. 6, 766–71.

Advisory Group On The Strategy For Older People In Wales (2007) *Report Of An Advisory Group On The Strategy For Older People In Wales*, Cardiff: AGSTOPW.

Age Concern Cymru (2007a) *Annual Report 2007*, Cardiff: Age Concern Cymru.

Age Concern Cymru (2007b) *A New Age Time to Deliver for Older People in Wales – Age Concern in Wales' Manifesto for the National Assembly*, Cardiff: Age Concern Cymru.

Age Concern Cymru, Citizens Advice Cymru, Children in Wales, Chwarae Teg, Commission for Racial Equality, Disability Rights Commission, Disability Wales, Equal Opportunities Commission, Faith Communities, Help the Aged, Minority

Ethnic Women's Network Wales (MEWN Cymru), North Wales Race Equality Network (NWREN), Race Equality First, South East Wales Racial Equality Council (SEWREC), Stonewall Cymru, Swansea Bay Racial Equality Council, The Valleys Race Equality Council, Wales Women's National Coalition (WWNC), Welsh Language Board, Welsh Women's Aid (2007) *Who are you talking to? Equality Manifesto for Wales – Welsh Assembly Elections 2007*, Cardiff: Age Concern Cymru et al.

Ahonen, S. (2002) 'From an Industrial to a Post-industrial Society: changing conceptions of equality in education', *Educational Review*, 54, 2, 1, 173–81.

Alcock, C., Daly, G., and Griggs, E. (2008) *Introducing Social Policy*, London: Longman.

Aldred, R. and Woodcock, J. (2008) 'Transport: challenging disabling environments', *Local Environment*, 13, 6, 485–96.

All-Wales Alliance for Research and Development in Health and Social Care (AWARD) (2007) *Strategy for Older People in Wales: An Interim Review*, Swansea: AWARD.

All Wales Convention (2009) *Report of the All Wales Convention*, Cardiff: All Wales Convention.

All Wales Saheli Association/Welsh Assembly Government (2006) *Muslim Women Talk Wales Project Report*, Cardiff: All Wales Saheli Association/Welsh Assembly Government.

Amnesty International; Asylum Justice; Cardiff Asylum Seeker Support Group; Children in Wales; Church Action on Poverty; Commission for Race Equality; Cytûn – Churches Together in Wales; Displaced People in Action; Newport and District Refugee Support Group; Oxfam; Refugee Voice Wales; Save the Children, Wales; Swansea Bay Asylum Seeker Support Group; Welsh Refugee Council (2007) *Child Poverty: National Assembly Elections 2007*, Cardiff: Amnesty International et al.

Annandale, E., Harvey, J., Cavers, D. and Dixon-Woods, M. (2007) Gender and access to healthcare in the UK: a critical interpretive synthesis of the literature, *Evidence and Policy: A Journal of Research, Debate and Practice*, 3, 4, 463–86.

Anon, (2008) 'Ysbytai: Wardiau un rhyw', 25.06.2008, *http://news.bbc.co.uk/welsh/hi/newsid_7470000/newsid_7473500/7473500.stm*

Anon, (2009) 'Gay hate crime convictions rise', 18.04.2009, *http://news.bbc.co.uk/1/hi/wales/8004548.stm*

Arad Consulting and Evans, H. (2007) *First Stage Evaluation of Iaith Pawb/Gwerthusiad Cam 1 o Iaith Pawb*, Cardiff: WAG.

Arbitration and Conciliation Service (2007) *ACAS Annual Report and Accounts 2006/07*, London: ACAS.

Arksey, H. (2007) 'Combining work and care: the reality of policy tensions for carers', *Benefits*, 15, 2, 139–49.

Arksey, H. and Glendinning, C. (2008) 'Combining Work and Care: Carers' Decision-making in the Context of Competing Policy Pressures', *Social Policy and Administration*, 42, 1, 1–18.

Arnot, M. (2003) 'Citizenship Education and Gender', in Lockyer, A., Crick, B. and Annette, J. (eds) *Education for Democratic Citizenship: Issues of Theory and Practice*, Aldershot: Ashgate.

Arts Wales (2008) *Moving Beyond Action Plan 2003/06, Summary Report on progress March 08*, Cardiff: Arts Wales.

Atkeson, L. (2003) 'Not All Cues are Created Equal: The Conditional Impact of Female Candidates on Political Engagement', *Journal of Politics*, 65:1, 1040–61.

Audit Office in Wales (2004) *Some Progress But Many Challenges In Providing Mental Health Services For Older People In Wales*, Press Release 5 November 2004, Cardiff: AOiW.

Ayim, M. (1998) 'Just How Correct is Political Correctness? A Critique of the Opposition's Arguments', *Argumentation*, 12, 4, 445–80.

Bache, I. and Flinders, M. (eds) (2004) *Multi-Level Governance in Theory and Practice,* Oxford: Oxford University Press.

Bagilhole, B. (2009) *Understanding Equal Opportunities and Diversity: The social differentiations and intersections of inequality*, Bristol: Policy Press.

Ballestrero, M. V. (1992) New Legislation in Italian Equality Law Act 125 of 10 April 1991 (the Positive Action Act), *Industrial Law Journal*, 21, 152–6.

Bancroft, A. (2000) 'No Interest in Land': Legal and Spatial Enclosure of Gypsy-Travellers in Britain', *Space and Polity*, 4, 1, 41–56.

Bardach, E. (2008) *A Practical Guide for Policy Analysis: The Eightfold Path to More Effective Problem Solving*, Washington: Congressional Quarterly Press.

Barnett Donaghy, T. (2002) 'Mainstreaming: Northern Ireland's Participative-Democratic Approach', Paper presented to the Jubilee conference of the Australasian Political Studies

Association, Australian National University, Canberra, October 2002.

Barnett Donaghy, T. (2004) 'Mainstreaming: Northern Ireland's participative democratic approach', *Policy and Politics*, 32, 1, 49–62.

Barnes, C., Mercer, G. (2004), 'Theorising and researching disability from a social model perspective', in Barnes, C., Mercer, G. (eds), *Implementing the Social Model of Disability: Theory and Research*, The Disability Press: Leeds.

Barquet, M. and Osses, S. (2005) 'Governability and Women's Citizenship', *Journal of Women, Politics and Policy*, vol. 27, nos 1–2, 9–30.

Bauer, M., McAuliffe, L. and Nay, R. (2007) 'Sexuality, health care and the older person: an overview of the literature', *International Journal of Older People Nursing*, 2, 1, 63–8.

Baumgardt, A. (2005) *A Critical Evaluation of the Application of Gender Budgeting on a Government Agency*, unpublished MSc dissertation, Cardiff University.

Bell, M. (2008) 'The Implementation of European Anti-Discrimination Directives: Converging towards a Common Model?', *The Political Quarterly*, vol. 79, no. 1, January-March 2008, 36–44.

Benabou, R. (1997) *Inequality and Growth*, London: NBER Working Paper 5658.

Benson, J. K. (1993) 'A Framework for Policy Analysis' in Miyakawa, T. (ed.) *The Science of Public Policy*, London: Routledge.

Bernard, M. and Phillips, J. (2000) 'The challenge of ageing in tomorrow's Britain', *Ageing and Society*, 20, 33–54.

Berthoud, R. and Blekesaune, M. (2007), *Persistent Employment Disadvantage. Report for the Equalities Review*, London: Equalities Review.

Bevan Foundation (2005) *A Childcare Revolution*, Tredegar: Bevan Foundation.

Bevan Foundation (2008) *Wales TUC Equal At Work Project: Equality and Trade Unions in Wales*, Tredegar: Bevan Foundation.

Beveridge, F. and Nott, S. (2002) 'Mainstreaming: A Case For Optimism And Cynicism', *Feminist Legal Studies*, 10, 299–311.

Bevir, M. (2008) 'The Westminster Model, Governance and Judicial Reform', *Parliamentary Affairs*, 21, 4, 1–18.

Bew, P., Gibben, P. and Patterson, H. (2002) *Northern Ireland 1921–2001: Political forces and social classes*, London: Serif.

Bhattacharyya, G., Ison, L. and Blair, M. (2004) *Minority Ethnic Attainment and Participation in Education and Training: The Evidence*, London: DfES.

Bischoff, I. (2005) 'Party competition in a heterogeneous electorate: The role of dominant-issue voters', *Public Choice*, 122: 1–2, 221–43.

Blair, T. (1996) *Speech by the Rt. Hon. Tony Blair MP, leader of the Labour Party to the Wales Labour Party Conference*, Brangwyn Hall, Swansea, Friday 10 May 1996.

Blair, T. (1998) *The Third Way – New Politics for the New Century*. Fabian Pamphlet 588, London: The Fabian Society.

Blair, T. (1999) *New Britain: My Vision Of A Young Country*, London: Basic Books.

Blanc, R., Le, G. and Jackson, S. (2006) 'Sexuality as cultural diversity within sport organisations', *International Journal of Sport Management and Marketing*, 2, 1–2, 30 119–33.

Blickenstaff, J. (2005) 'Women and science careers: leaky pipeline or gender filter?', *Gender and Education*, 17, 4, 369–86.

Blunkett, D. (2001) *Politics and Progress: Renewing Democracy and Civil Society*, London: Politicos.

Bohman, J. and Rehg, W. (eds) (1997) *Deliberative Democracy: Essays on Reason and Politics*, Cambridge: MIT Press.

Borland, J., Griffiths, A., Rees, O. with Collins, S., Dahiya, G., James, S. Kadanchirayil, A., Miller, S. and Pritchard-Jones, J. (2009) *Responding to Discrimination: The Geography and Geometry of Advice Provision in England, Scotland and Wales*, London: EHRC.

Boland, P. (2004) An Assessment of the Objective One Programme in Wales 1999–2003, in Chaney, P., Thompson, A. and Scourfield, J. (eds) *Contemporary Wales: An Annual Review of Economic and Social Research*, Cardiff: University of Wales Press, 17, 66–79.

Bowes, A. (2006) 'Mainstreaming Equality: Implications of the Provision of Support at Home for Majority and Minority Ethnic Older People', *Social Policy and Administration*, 40, 7, 739–57.

Boyles, C., McMillan, I., Bailey, P. and Mossey, S. (2008) 'Representations of disability in nursing and healthcare literature: an integrative review', *Journal of Advanced Nursing*, 62, 4, 428–37.

Bradbury, J. (1998) 'The Devolution Debate in Wales during the Major Governments: The Politics of a Developing Union State?', *Regional and Federal Studies*, 8, 1, 120–39.

Bradbury, J. and Stafford, I. (2008) 'Devolution and Public Policy in Wales: The case of Transport', in Chaney, P., Thompson, A. and Royles, E. (eds) *Contemporary Wales*, Cardiff: University of Wales Press.

British Broadcasting Corporation Trust (2008) *The BBC Trust Impartiality Report: BBC Network News And Current Affairs Coverage Of The Four UK Nations*, London: BBC Trust.

Breen, M.S. (2001) Strange Bedfellows: Queer Negotiations with Homophobia in the Arts, Politics, and Religion, *International Journal of Sexuality and Gender Studies*, 6, 4, 231–4.

Breitenbach, E. (2005) Gender Equality Policies in Scotland Since Devolution, *Scottish Affairs*, 56, summer, 10–21.

Breitenbach, E. (2005a) *The Scottish Executive and Equality, Paper Presented to Public Policy, Equality and Diversity in the Context of Devolution*, ESRC Seminar Series, Edinburgh University, November 2005.

Breitenbach, E. and Galligan, Y. (2006) 'Measuring gender equality: reflecting on experiences and challenges in the UK and Ireland', *Policy and Politics*, 34, 4, 597–614.

Broadnax, W. D. (2000) *Diversity and Affirmative Action in Public Services*, Boulder: Westview Press.

Bromley, J. and Curtice, J. (2003) *Attitudes to Discrimination in Scotland*, Edinburgh, Scottish Executive Social Research.

Brown, H. (1988) *Egalitarianism and the generation of inequality*, Oxford: Oxford University Press.

Budge, I., Robertson, D. and Hearl, D. (1987) *Ideology, Strategy and Party Change: Spatial Analyses of Post-War Election Programmes in 19 Democracies*, Cambridge: Cambridge University Press.

Budge, I. and Klingemann, H. D., Volkens, A., Bara, J. and Tanenbaum, E. (eds) (2001) *Mapping Policy Preferences: Estimates for Parties, Electors, and Governments 1945–1998*, Oxford: Oxford University Press.

Budlender, D., Elson, D., Hewitt, G., Mukhopadhyay, T. (2002) *Gender Budgets Make Cents: Understanding gender responsive budgets* London: Gender Affairs Department, Commonwealth Secretariat.

Budlender, D. and Sharp, R., with Allen, K. (1998) *How to do a gender-sensitive budget analysis: Contemporary research and practice*, Canberra: Australian Agency for International Development and London: Commonwealth Secretariat.

Bustelo, M. and Peterson, E. (2005) *The Evolution of Policy Discourses and Policy Instruments within the Spanish State Feminism. A Unified or Fragmented Landscape?* Paper presented at the Workshop 'State Feminism and Women's Movements: Assessing change of the last decade in Europe', ECPR Workshops, Granada, Spain, April 2005.

Burchardt, T. (2006) *Foundations for measuring equality: A discussion paper for the Equalities Review*, London: ESRC Research Centre for Analysis of Social Exclusion, London School of Economics.

Burchardt, T. (2008) *Background Note: Equality Measurement Framework 'selection of indicators' specialist consultation*, London: EHRC.

Business in the Community (1993) *Corporate Culture and Caring*, London: BIC.

Bytheway, B. and Johnson, J. (1990) 'On defining ageism', *Critical Social Policy*, 10, 27–39.

Byrne, D. (2005) *Social Exclusion*, 2nd edition, Maidenhead: Open University Press.

Bywaters, P. and McLeod, E. (1996) *Working for Equality in Health*, London: Routledge.

Cabinet Office (1999) *Modernising Government*, London: Cabinet Office.

Capability Scotland (2007) *Capability Scotland: Annual Review 2006/2007*, Edinburgh: Capability Scotland.

Carabine, J. (2004) 'Lesbian and Gay Politics and Participation in New Labour's Britain', *Social Politics*, 11, 2, 312–27.

Care and Social Services Inspectorate Wales (2007) *Chief Inspector's Overview – Care and Social Services in Wales 2006–2007*, Cardiff: CSS.

Care and Social Services Inspectorate Wales (2007) *Care Services in Wales Annual Report 2006–2007*, Cardiff: CSSIW.

Carley, M. (2006) 'Partnership and statutory local governance in a devolved Scotland', *International Journal of Public Sector Management*, 19, 3, 250–60.

Camarero, L. and Oliva, J. (2008) 'Exploring the Social Face of Urban Mobility: Daily Mobility as Part of the Social Structure in Spain', *International Journal of Urban and Regional Research*, 32, 2, 344–62.

Cameron Report (1969) *Disturbances in Northern Ireland: Report of the Commission appointed by the Governor of Northern Ireland*, Cmnd. 532, Belfast, HMSO.

Cann, J. (2004) 'Higher Education's Contribution to the Maintenance and Revitalization of Minority Official Languages: The Cases of Wales and New Brunswick', *Welsh Journal of Education*, 13, 1, 95–117.

Cardiff and the Vale Coalition of Disabled People (2006) *Coalition News*, Cardiff: Cardiff and the Vale Coalition of Disabled People.

Care and Social Services Inspectorate Wales (2008) *Performance Evaluation Of Local Authority Social Services 2007/08 – Handbook For Analysing Performance Information*, Cardiff: CSSIW.

Careers Wales (2006) *Executive Director's Report, Annual Review 04/05*, Cardiff: Careers Wales.

Carr, F. and Massey, A. (eds) (1999) *Public policy in the new Europe: Eurogovernance in theory and practice*, Cheltenham: Edward Elgar.

Carr, S. (2008) 'Sexuality and religion: a challenge for diversity strategies in UK social care service development and delivery', *Diversity in Health and Social Care*, 5, 2, 113–22.

Caudwell, J. (2007) 'Queering the Field? The complexities of sexuality within a lesbian-identified football team in England', *Gender, Place and Culture – A Journal of Feminist Geography*, 14, 2, 183–96.

Cavanagh, M. (2002) *Against Equality of Opportunity*, Oxford: Oxford University Press.

Chaney, P. and Fevre, R. (2001) 'Inclusive Governance and "Minority" Groups: The Role of the Third Sector in Wales', *Voluntas – International Journal of Third Sector Research*, 12, 2, 131–56.

Chaney, P. and Fevre, R. (2001) 'Ron Davies and the Cult of "Inclusiveness": Devolution and Participation in Wales', *Contemporary Wales*, 21–49.

Chaney, P. and Fevre, R. (2002) *An Absolute duty: The Equality Policies of the Government of the National Assembly for Wales and their Implementation: July 1999 to January 2002*, Report for the Equal Opportunities Commission, Disability Rights

Commission, and Commission for Racial Equality, Cardiff: Institute of Welsh Affairs.

Chaney, P. (2004) *A Preliminary Evaluation of the Close The Pay Gap Campaign in Wales*, Report commissioned by the Welsh Assembly Government, the Equal Opportunities Commission Wales and the Wales TUC, Cardiff: Welsh Assembly Government, the Equal Opportunities Commission Wales and the Wales TUC.

Chaney, P., Fevre, R. and Stephens, N. (2004) 'Setting the agenda? Women and policy-making in post-devolution Wales', in Breitenbach, E. (ed.) *Engendering Democracy: Women's Organisations and their Influence on Policy Making Within the Devolved Administrations in Northern Ireland, Scotland, and Wales, A Report of a Seminar Held on 5 December, 2003*, Belfast: Working Papers Series, University of Edinburgh/Queen's University Belfast.

Chaney, P. (2003) 'Social Capital and the Participation of Marginalized Groups in Government: A Study of the Statutory Partnership between the Third Sector and Devolved Government in Wales', *Public Policy and Administration*, vol. 17, 4, 22–39.

Chaney P. and Rees T. (2004) 'The Northern Ireland Section 75 Equality Duty: An International Perspective', in vol. 2, *Northern Ireland Office – The Section 75 Equality Duty Operational Review*, vol. 2, 1–51.

Chaney P, (2006) 'A Case of Institutional Decoupling: Equality and Public Policy in Post Devolution Wales', *Scottish Affairs*, 56, 22–34.

Chaney, P. (2007) 'Gender, Electoral Competition and Political Behaviour: Preliminary Analysis from the UK's Devolution Programme', *Contemporary Politics*, 13, 2, 93–118.

Chaney, P. (2008) 'Devolved Governance and the Substantive Representation of Women: The Second Term of the National Assembly for Wales, 2003–07', *Parliamentary Affairs*, 61, 2, 34–53.

Chaney, P. (2009) *Equal Opportunities and Human Rights: The First Decade of Devolution*, London: Equality and Human Rights Commission.

Charles, N. and Mackay, F. (2008) *Developing Domestic Abuse Strategies in Devolved Legislature: Scotland and Wales Compared*, Paper presented to the Engendering Devolution Conference, University of Warwick, 21 November 2008.

Children's Commissioner for Wales (2007a) *Annual review 2006–07*, Cardiff: Children's Commissioner for Wales.

Children in Wales (2007b) *Annual Report and Financial Summary 2006/07*, Cardiff: Children in Wales.

Childs, S. and Krook, M. L. (2006) 'Gender and Politics: The State of the Art', *Politics*, 26, 1, 18–28.

Chou, Y., Tzou, P., Pu, C. Kroger, T. and Lee, W. (2008) 'Respite care as a community care service: Factors associated with the effects on family carers of adults with intellectual disability in Taiwan', *Journal of Intellectual and Developmental Disability*, 33, 1, 12–21.

Christian Peoples Alliance in Wales (2007) *The Manifesto of The Christian Peoples Alliance in Wales Assembly Elections 2007*, Cardiff: Christian Peoples Alliance in Wales.

Chwarae Teg (2007) *Thousands able to adopt smarter working*, Press Release, 23 May 2007, Cardiff: Chwarae Teg.

Cichowski, R. A. (2004) 'Women's Rights, the European Court, and Supranational Constitutionalism', *Law and Society Review*, 38, 3, 489–512.

Clark, S. and Paechter, C. (2007) '"Why can't girls play football?" Gender dynamics and the playground', *Sport, Education and Society*, 12, 3, 261–76

Clarke, P. (2002) 'The Children's Commissioner for Wales', *Children and Society*, 16, 4, 287–90.

Clements, L. and Thomas, P. (1999) 'Human rights and the Welsh Assembly', *Planet: The Welsh Internationalist*, vol. 136, 7–11.

Coalition on Charging Cymru (2007) *Coalition on Charging Cymru renews its call for the abolition of domiciliary care charges – National Assembly For Wales elections May 2007*, Cardiff, Coalition on Charging Cymru.

Cohen, G. A. (1989) 'On the Currency of Egalitarian Justice', *Ethics*, 99, 4, 906–32.

Cohen, G. (1993) 'Equality of What? On Welfare, Goods, and Capabilities', in Nussbaum, M. and Sen, A. (eds), *The Quality of Life*, Oxford: Oxford University Press, pp. 9–29.

Cohen, J. (1997) 'Deliberation and democratic legitimacy', in Bohman, J. and Rehg, W. (eds) (1997) *Deliberative Democracy: Essays on Reason and Politics*, Cambridge: MIT Press.

Cole, M. (ed.) (2000) *Education, Equality and Human Rights*, London: Falmer-Routledge.

Cole, M. and Virdee, S. (2006) 'Racism and resistance: from Empire to new Labour', in Cole, M. (ed.), *Education, Equality and Human Rights: issues of gender, 'race', sexuality, disability and social class*, Second edition, London and New York: Routledge.

Cole, S. (2007) 'Transport Governance in Wales: A Study in Devolved Government', in Chaney, P., Royles, E. and Thompson, A. (eds) *Contemporary Wales: A Review of Economic, Political and Social Research*, Cardiff: University of Wales Press, 179–95.

Colebatch, H. K. (2002) *Policy* (2nd edition), Buckingham: OUP.

Coleman, J.S. (1988) 'Social capital and the creation of human capital', *American Journal of Sociology*, 94 supplement, s95–s120.

Collins, P. H. (1999) *Black Feminist Thought: Knowledge, Consciousness and the Politics of Empowerment*, New York: Routledge.

Commission of the European Communities (1998) *Gender Mainstreaming: Conceptual Framework, Methodology and Presentation of Good Practice* (EG-S-MS (98) 2).

Committee For The Office Of The First Minister And Deputy First Minister (2008) *Final Report on the Committee's Inquiry into Child Poverty in Northern Ireland*, Belfast: Northern Ireland Assembly Committee For The Office Of The First Minister And Deputy First Minister.

Commission of the European Communities (2000) *Implementation by the European Community of the platform for action adopted at the Fourth World Conference on Women in Beijing 1995*, Luxembourg: Office for Official Publications of the European Communities.

Committee on the Elimination of Discrimination against Women (2008) *Concluding observations of the Committee on the Elimination of Discrimination against Women: United Kingdom of Great Britain and Northern Ireland*, 41st session, 18 July 2008, New York, United Nations.

Committee on the Administration of Justice (2006) 'Equality in Northern Ireland: the rhetoric and the reality', Belfast: Committee on the Administration of Justice.

Committee For The Office Of The First Minister And Deputy First Minister (2008) *Final Report on the Committee's Inquiry into Child Poverty in Northern Ireland*, Belfast: Committee For The Office Of The First Minister And Deputy First Minister.

Committee on Standards in Public Life (1995) *Standards in Public Life*, London: HMSO.

Committee on the Administration of Justice (2006) *Equality in Northern Ireland: The Rhetoric and the Reality*, Belfast: Committee on the Administration of Justice.

Communities Scotland (2003), *Integrating Social Inclusion Partnerships and Community Planning Partnerships*, Edinburgh: Scottish Executive.

Compston, H. (ed.) (2004) *Handbook of public policy in Europe: Britain, France and Germany*, Basingstoke: Palgrave Macmillan.

Confederation of British Industry (1996) *A Winning Strategy – The Business Case for Equal Opportunities*, London: CBI.

Connell, R. (2007) 'News from the Coalface', *International Feminist Journal of Politics*, 9, 2, 137–53.

Consultative Steering Group on the Scottish Parliament (1998) *Shaping Scotland's Parliament*, Edinburgh: The Scottish Office.

Cornford, J. (2002) Foreword, in Adams, J. and Robinson, P. (eds) *Devolution in Practice: Public Policy Differences within the UK*, London: IPPR.

Council of Europe (2004) *Gender Mainstreaming*, Strasbourg: COE *http://www.coe.int/T/E/Human_Rights/Equality/02._Gender_ mainstreaming*

Crenshaw, K., Gotanda, N., Peller, G. and Thomas, K. (eds) (1995) *Critical race Theory: the Key Writings that Formed the Movement*, New York: New Press.

Crenshaw, K., (2000) *Gender-related aspects of race discrimination, United Nations Expert Meeting on Gender and Racial Discrimination*, Zagreb, Croatia, pp. 2–20. New York: United Nations.

Crozier, G (2005) '"There's a war against our children": Black educational underachievement revisited', *British Journal of Sociology of Education*, 26, 5, 585–98.

Daly, M. (1977) *Gyn/Ecology: Metaethics of Radical Feminism*, New York: Women's Press Ltd.

Daniels, K. and Macdonald, L. (2005) *Equality, Diversity and Discrimination*, London: Chartered Institute of Personnel and Development.

Davies, J. S. (2007) 'The Limits of Partnership: An Exit-Action Strategy', *Democratic Inclusion*, 55, 779–800.

Davies, M., Addis, S., MacBride-Stewart, S., and Shepherd, M. (undated) *The Health, Social Care and Housing Needs of Lesbian, Gay, Bisexual and Transgender Older people: literature review*, Cardiff: Cardiff University Institute of Society, Health and Ethics.

Dearlove, J. and Saunders, P. (1991) *Introduction to British Politics*, Cambridge: Polity.

DeLeon, P. (1998) 'Models of Policy Discourse: Insights versus Prediction', *Policy Studies Journal*, 26, 1, 147–61.

De Lima, P. (2005) 'An Inclusive Scotland? The Scottish Executive and Racial Equality', in G. Mooney and G. Scott (eds) *Exploring Social Policy in the 'New' Scotland*, Bristol: Policy Press.

Delamont, S. (1980) Sex roles and the school, in Moon, B and Shelton Mayes, A. (eds) *Teaching and Learning in the Secondary School*, Buckingham: OUP.

Department for education, lifelong learning and skills (2006) *Work-based learning provision 2004/05 at FE Institutions and other training providers*, Cardiff: DCELLS.

Department of Education Northern Ireland Executive (2008) *Review of Irish-Medium Education Report*, Belfast: Department of Education Northern Ireland Executive.

Department of Health, Social Services and Public Safety Northern Ireland (2006) *The Quality Standards for Health and Social Care*, Belfast: Department of Health, Social Services and Public Safety.

Department for Local Government and Communities (2006) *The Equalities Review: Interim Report for Consultation*, London: DLGC.

Department for Local Government and Communities (2007a) *Equalities Review*, London: UK Government, Department for Local Government and Communities.

Department for Communities and Local Government (2007b) *Discrimination Law Review A Framework for Fairness: Proposals for a Single Equality Bill for Great Britain*, London: Department for Communities and Local Government.

Department for Communities and Local Government (2008) *Framework for a Fairer Future – The Equality Bill*, London: Equalities Office.

Department of Trade and Industry/Women and Equality Unit (2004) *Changing World, Changing Lives: Women in the UK since 1999*, London: Department of Trade and Industry/Women and Equality Unit.

Diamond, P. (2004) *New Labour's Old Roots: Revisionist Thinkers in Labour's History 1931–97*, London: Imprint Academic.

Dickens, L. (1994) 'The Business Case for Women's Equality: Is the Carrot Better than the Stick?' *Employee Relations*, 16, 8, 5–18.

Disability Rights Commission (2006) *Equal Treatment: Closing the Gap. A formal investigation into physical health inequalities experienced by people with learning disabilities and/or mental health problems*, Manchester: DRC.

Disability Rights Commission (2007) *Equal Treatment: Closing the Gap – One Year On, Report of the Reconvened Formal Inquiry Panel of the DRC's Formal Investigation into the inequalities in physical health experienced by people with mental health problems and learning disabilities*, Cardiff: DRC.

Disability Wales (1998) *Disability Wales News* (Winter), no. 12, Caerphilly: Disability Wales.

Disability Wales (2006a) *Disability Equality in Action Project*, Caerphilly: Disability Wales.

Disability Wales (2006b) *Disability Wales Review 2005/06*, Caerphilly: Disability Wales.

Disability Wales (2007) 'Wales Disability Reference Group', *Disability Wales News*, Issue 72, Caerphilly: Disability Wales.

Dorey, P. (2005) *Policy Making in Britain: An Introduction*, London: Sage.

Dowling, F. (2006) 'Physical education teacher educators' professional identities, continuing professional development and the issue of gender equality', *Physical Education and Sport Pedagogy*, 11, 3, 247–63.

Downs, A. (1957) *An Economic Theory of Democracy*, New York: HarperCollins.

Dryzek, J. S. (2000) *Deliberative Democracy and Beyond: Liberals, Critics, Contestations*, Oxford: Oxford University Press.

Dubé, J. (1988) 'The Legible Woman: Annual Conference of the Welsh Union of Writers', *Radical Wales*, 20, 10–11.

Dubnova I. and Joss D. M. (1997) 'Women and domestic violence: global dimensions, health consequences and intervention strategies', *Work*, 9, 1, 79–88.

Dunkerley, D. (2007) 'Wales's Changing Population: A Demographic Overview', *Contemporary Wales*, 19, 116–26.

Dunkwu, K. (2001) 'Policy, equality and educational research', in Hill, D. and Cole, M. (eds) *Schooling and Equality: Fact, Concept and Policy*, London: Routledge Kogan Page.

Dunn, W. M. (2007) *Public Policy Analysis: An Introduction*, London: Prentice Hall.

Dworkin, R. (1977) *Taking rights seriously*, Cambridge: Harvard University Press.

Dworkin, A. (2006) *Heartbreak: The Political Manifesto of a Feminist Militant*, New York: Continuum International Publishing.

ECOTEC (2006) *Cross Cutting Themes Research Project (Objectives 1 and 3) Final Report*, C3008/April 2006, Cardiff: ECOTEC.

Edelmann, M. (1977) 'Political Language and Political Reality', *Political Studies*, 18, 1, 10–19.

Edelman, M. (1988) *Constructing the Political Spectacle*, Chicago: Chicago University Press.

Egan, D. (2007) *Combating child poverty in Wales: Are effective education strategies in place?* York: Joseph Rowntree Foundation.

Ekos Ltd (2009) *Ex Post Evaluation of the Rural Development Plan 2000–2006: Final Report*, Ekos: Glasgow.

Elman, R. (2008) *Sexual Equality in an Integrated Europe: Virtual Equality*, Basingstoke: Palgrave.

Elson, D. (1998) 'Integrating Gender issues into National Budgetary Policies and Procedures: Some policy options', *Journal of International Development*, 10, 929–41.

Elster, J. (ed.) (1998) *Deliberative Democracy*, Cambridge: Cambridge University Press.

Epstein, D. and O'Halloran, S. (1999) *Delegating Powers: A Transaction Cost Politics Approach to Policy Making Under Separate Powers*, Cambridge: Cambridge University Press.

Equality Commission for Northern Ireland (2005) *Final Report of Commission Investigation Under Paragraph 11 of Schedule 9 of the Northern Ireland Act 1998, Potential Failure To Comply With Approved Equality Scheme Subject To Investigation*, Belfast: Equality Commission for Northern Ireland.

Equality Commission for Northern Ireland (2007) *Section 75 – Keeping it effective: Reviewing the Effectiveness of Section 75 of the Northern Ireland Act 1998*, Belfast: Equality Commission for Northern Ireland.

Equality Commission for Northern Ireland (2008) *CEDAW Report, United Nations Convention on the Elimination of all forms of Discrimination Against Women*, Belfast: Equality Commission for Northern Ireland.

Equal Opportunities Commission (2003) *Mainstreaming: Everything you wanted to know about mainstreaming but were afraid to ask*, Manchester: Equal Opportunities Commission.

Equal Opportunities Commission (2006) *Facts about Women and Men in Wales*, Cardiff: Equal Opportunities Commission.

EOC Scotland (2006) *Facts About Women and Men in Scotland*, Edinburgh: Equal Opportunities Commission.

Equality and Human Rights Commission (2008a) *Insight: Work fit for all – disability, health and the experience of negative treatment in the British workplace*, London: Equality and Human Rights Commission.

Equality and Human Rights Commission (2008b) *Sex and Power 2008*, London: Equality and Human Rights Commission.

Equality and Human Rights Commission (2008c) *Who Do You See? Living Together in Wales Survey – The Workplace*, Cardiff: Equality and Human Rights Commission.

Equality and Human Rights Commission (2008d) *Who Do You See? Living Together in Wales Survey Research findings summary*, Cardiff: Equality and Human Rights Commission Wales.

Equality and Human Rights Commission (2009) *Who Runs Wales? The Road to Equality for Women*, Cardiff: Equality and Human Rights Commission.

Equality Commission for Northern Ireland (2007) *Keeping it Effective, Reviewing the Effectiveness of Section 75 of the Northern Ireland Act*, Belfast: Equality Commission for Northern Ireland.

Equality Commission for Northern Ireland (2008) *CEDAW Report, United Nations Convention on the Elimination of all forms of Discrimination Against Women*, Belfast: Equality Commission for Northern Ireland.

Equality Committee of the Scottish Parliament (2008) *Equal Opportunities Committee Report – Removing Barriers and Creating Opportunities: Review of Progress*, SP Paper 130 EO/S3/08/R2, Edinburgh: Equality Committee of the Scottish Parliament.

Equalities Office (2008) *Framework for a Fairer Future – The Equality Bill*, London: Equalities Office.

Equal Opportunities Commission Wales/NAfW (1999) *Different but Equal: Guidance on Achieving Sex Equality in Schools*, Cardiff: Equal Opportunities Commission Wales/NAfW.

Equal Opportunities Commission Scotland (2006) *Facts About Women and Men in Scotland*, Edinburgh: Equal Opportunities Commission Scotland.

Esping-Andersen, G., Gallie, D., Hemerijk, A and Myers, J. (2002) *Why We Need a New Welfare State*, New York: Oxford University Press.

Estyn (2004) *Guidance on the Inspection of Secondary Schools*, Cardiff: Estyn.

Estyn (2005a) *Equal opportunities and diversity in schools in Wales – Survey on the implementation of ACCAC guidance on the promotion of equal opportunities and diversity (2001) and the effectiveness of schools and LEAs in meeting statutory duties under race relations legislation*, Cardiff: Estyn.

Estyn (2005b) *The Education of Gypsy Traveller Learners: A survey of provision made by schools and local authorities to meet the needs of Gypsy Traveller learners*, Cardiff: Estyn.

Estyn (2007a) *A Report on the Careers Services in Wales: Good Practice in how Careers Wales Companies Challenge Gender Stereotyping*, Cardiff: Estyn.

Estyn (2007b) *The Annual Report of Her Majesty's Chief Inspector of Education and Training in Wales 2006–2007*, Cardiff: Estyn.

Estyn (2007c) *Disability Discrimination Act (1995) – The Practice of Schools and Local Education Authorities in Implementing their Duties*, Cardiff: Estyn.

Estyn (2005) *The Education of Gypsy Traveller Learners: A survey of provision made by schools and local authorities to meet the needs of Gypsy Traveller learners*, Cardiff: Estyn.

European Commission (1994) *White Paper on Social Policy*, Brussels: EC, COM (94) 333.

European Commission (2005) *Non-Discrimination And Equal Opportunities For All – A Framework Strategy, Communication From The Commission To The Council, The European Parliament, The European Economic and Social Committee and The Committee of the Regions*, Brussels: EC.

Falkmer T. (2001) 'Transport Mobility for Children and Adolescents with Cerebral Palsy', *Scandinavian Journal of Occupational Therapy*, 8, 3, 158.

Faulks, K. (2000) *Citizenship*, London: Routledge.

Fearon, K. (1996) 'Introduction', *Power, Politics, Positionings*, Belfast: Democratic Dialogue.

Felli, L. and Merlo, A. (2004) *Endogenous Lobbying*, CARESS Working Papers 00–03, University of Pennsylvania Center for Analytic Research and Economics in the Social Sciences.

Field, A. (2007) 'Counter-Hegemonic Citizenship: LGBT Communities and the Politics of Hate Crimes in Canada', *Citizenship Studies*, vol. 11, no. 3, July 2007, 247–62.

Feinstein, L. (2002) *Quantitative estimates of the social benefits of learning 2: Health (depression and obesity)*, London: Centre for Research on the Wider Benefits of Learning.

Fiorio, C. and Percoco, M. (2007) 'Would You Stick To Using Your Car Even If Charged? Evidence from Trento, Italy', *Transport Reviews*, 27, 5, 605–20.

Fischer, F. (2003a) *Reframing Public Policy: Discursive Politics and Deliberative Practices*, Oxford: Oxford University Press.

Fischer, F. (2003b) 'Beyond empiricism: Policy Analysis as Deliberative Practice', chapter 7 in M. A. Hajer and H. Wagenaar (eds) *Deliberative Policy Analysis: Understanding Governance in the Network Society*, Cambridge: Cambridge University Press.

Fischer, F. and Forester, J. (1993) *The Argumentative Turn in Policy Analysis*, London: UCL Press.

Fitzgerald, R. (2007) *Final Report and Evaluation of Phase 3 of the Equal Pay Campaign In Wales – Summary Report*, Glasgow: Fitzgerald Associates.

Fitzgerald, R. (2009) *Equal opportunities and the Scottish Parliament: A Progress Review*, Glasgow: Equality and Human Rights Commission.

Flynn, A., Marsden, T., Netherwood, A. and Pitts, R. (2008) *The Sustainable Development Effectiveness Report For The Welsh Assembly Government*, Cardiff: WAG.

Frankfurt H. G., (1987) 'Equality as a moral ideal', *Ethics*, 98, 21–43.

Franklin, M., Van der Eijk, C., Evans, D., Fotos, M., Hirczy de Mino, W., Marsh, M. and Wessels, B. (2004) *Voter Turnout and the Dynamics of Electoral Competition in Established Democracies Since 1945*, Cambridge: Cambridge University Press.

Flacke-Neudorfer, C. (2007) Tourism, Gender and Development in the Third World: A Case Study from Northern Laos, *Tourism and Hospitality Planning and Development*, 4, 2, 135–47.

Flores, William V. and Rina Benmayor (1997) *Latino Cultural Citizenship: Claiming Identity, Space, and Rights*. Boston: Beacon Press.

Floya, A. and Yuval-Davis, N. (1993), *Racialised boundaries*, London: Routledge.

Fortin, J. (1998) *Children's Rights and the Developing Law*, London: Butterworths.

Francis, B. (2000) 'The gendered subject: students' subject preferences and discussions of gender and subject ability', *Oxford Review of Education*, 26, 1, 35–48.

Fredman, S. (2000) 'Equality: A New Generation?', *Industrial Law Journal*, 30, 145–68.

Fredman, S. and Spencer, S. (2003) *Age as an Equality Issue*, Oxford: Hart Publishing.

Freeden, M. (1994) 'Political Concepts and Ideological Morphology', *Journal of Political Philosophy*, 2, 2, 140 –64.

French D. and Hainsworth J. (2001) '"There aren't any buses and the swimming pool is always cold!": obstacles and opportunities in the provision of sport for disabled people', *Managing Leisure*, 6, 1, 35–49.

Friedan, B. (2001) *The Feminine Mystique*, London: W. W. Norton and Company.

Fudge, S. (2007) 'Objective One and Community Development: Democratizing the Economic and Political Landscape in south Wales', in Chaney, P., Thompson, A. and Scourfield, J. (eds) *Contemporary Wales: An Annual Review of Economic and Social Research*, Cardiff: University of Wales Press, 19, 1–12.

Fukuyama, F. (1999) *The Great Disruption: Human Nature And The Reconstitution Of Social Order*, New York: Free Press.

Fukuyama, F. (2004) *State Building Governance and World Order in the Twenty-First Century*, London: Profile Books.

Furedy J. J. (2002) 'Reflections on the Dühring and Brand cases: Political correctness and the current abandonment of academic autonomy to the culture of comfort', *Journal of Economic Studies*, 29, 4–5, 332–44.

Gabel, S. and Peters, S. (2004) 'Presage of a paradigm shift? Beyond the social model of disability toward resistance theories of disability', *Disability and Society*, 19, 6, 585–600.

Gal, S. and Kligman, G. (2000) *The Politics of Gender after Socialism: A Comparative-Historical Essay*, Princeton: Princeton University Press.

Gant, R. and Walford, N. (1998) 'Telecommunications and disabled people: A rural perspective', *Health and Place*, 4, 3, 245–63.

Garrett, P., Dickson, H. and Whelan, A. (2008) 'What do non-English-speaking patients value in acute care? Cultural competency from the patient's perspective: a qualitative study', *Ethnicity and Health*, 13, 5, 479–96.

Gargarella, R. (1998) 'Full representation, deliberation and impartiality', in Elster, J. (ed.) (1998) *Deliberative Democracy*, Cambridge: Cambridge University Press.

Gaskell, C. (2008) 'But They Just Don't Respect Us': young people's experiences of (dis)respected citizenship and the New Labour Respect Agenda', *Children's Geographies*, 6, 3,223–38.

Gay, O. (1996) *The Quango Debate*, Research Paper 96/72, London: House of Commons Library.

Geddes, M. and Le Gales, P. (2001) 'Local Partnerships, Welfare Regimes and local governance', in M. Geddes and J. Benington (eds) *Local Partnerships and social exclusion in the European Union: New forms of local Social Governance?* London: Routledge, pp. 220–41.

General Teaching Council for Wales (2006a) *Statement of Professional Values and Practice*, Cardiff: General Teaching Council for Wales.

General Teaching Council for Wales (2006b) *A Professional Development Framework for Teachers in Wales*, Cardiff: General Teaching Council for Wales.

General Teaching Council for Wales (2007) *The Chartered Teacher Standards*, Cardiff: General Teaching Council for Wales.

Gershuny, J. (2000) *Changing Times: Work and Leisure in Post-industrial Society*, Oxford: Oxford University Press.

Gill, K. and Hough, S. (2007) 'Sexuality Training, Education and Therapy in the Healthcare Environment: Taboo, Avoidance, Discomfort or Ignorance?', *Sexuality and Disability*, 25, 2, 73–6.

Gillborn, D. (2005) 'Education policy as an act of white supremacy: whiteness, critical race theory and education reform, *Journal of Educational Policy,* 20, 4, 485–505.

Gillis, S., Howie, G. and Munford, R. (2007) *Third Wave Feminism: A Critical Exploration*, Basingstoke: Palgrave Macmillan.

Goodall, B. (2006) 'Disabled Access and Heritage Attractions', *Tourism Culture and Communication*, 7, 1, 57–78.

Government Equalities Office (2008a) *Framework for a Fairer Future – The Equality Bill*, London: Government Equalities Office.

Government Equalities Office (2008b) *Government Equalities Office, Business Plan 2008–9*, London: Government Equalities Office.

Gramsci, A. (2007) *Prison Notebooks*, New York: Columbia University Press.

Granovetter, M. (1985), 'Economic Action and Social Structure: the problem of embeddedness', *American Journal of Sociology*, vol. 78, pp. 481–510.

Gray, B., Robinson, C. and Seddon, D. (2008) 'Invisible Children: Young Carers of Parents with Mental Health Problems – The Perspectives of Professionals', *Child and Adolescent Mental Health*, 13, 4, 169–72.

Greed, C. (2006) 'Making The Divided City Whole: Mainstreaming Gender Into Planning in the United Kingdom', *Tijdschrift voor Economische en Sociale Geografie*, 97, 3, 267–80.

Green, I. A. (2004) 'Gay but not queer: Toward a post-queer study of sexuality', *Theory and Society*, 31, 521–45.

Greer, S. (2005) 'The Territorial Bases of Health Policymaking in the UK after Devolution', *Regional and Federal Studies*, vol. 15, no. 4, 501–18.

Griffiths, D. (1996) *Thatcherism and Territorial Politics*, Aldershot: Avebury.

Griffiths, D., Sigona, N., and Zetter, R. (2006) 'Integrative Paradigms, Marginal Reality: Refugee Community Organisations and Dispersal in Britain', *Journal of Ethnic and Migration Studies*, 32, 5, 881–98.

Grossman, G. and E. Helpman (1996) 'Electoral Competition and Special Interest Politics', *Review of Economic Studies*, 63, 265–86.

Gutmann, A. and Thompson, D. (1996) *Democracy and Disagreement*, Cambridge: MIT Press.

Habermas, J. (1981) *The Theory of Communicative Action*, London: Beacon Press.

Habermas, J. (1984) *The Philosophical Discourse of Modernity*, Cambridge: Polity.

Habermas, J. (1984) *The Theory of Communicative Action*, vol. 2: 'Lifeworld and System: A Critique of Functionalist Reason', London: Beacon Press.

Habermas, J. (1987) *The Philosophical Discourse of Modernity: Twelve Lectures*, trans. Frederick G. Lawrence, Cambridge: MIT Press.

Habermas, J. (1996) *Between facts and norms: Contributions to a discourse theory of law and democracy*, Cambridge: Polity Press.

Hadden, T., Mallinder, L., O'Connell, R. and Rainey, B. (2007) 'Equality, Good Relations and a Shared Future', in F. McCandless, R. Rowedge, T. Hadden (eds) 'Equality, Good Relations and a Shared Future', Working Paper, Belfast: QUB Human Rights Centre.

Housing Forum Cymru (2006) *A Vision for Housing in Wales*, Cardiff: Housing Forum Cymru.

Mallinder, L., O'Connell, R., Russell, D., Jarman, N. and Rainey, B. (eds) 'What to Do About Equality and Good Relations and a Shared Future?', *Fortnight*, May, no. 453.

Hafner-Burton, E. and Pollack, M. A. (2002) 'Gender Mainstreaming and Global Governance', *Feminist Legal Studies* 10, 285–98.

Hain, P. (1999) *A Welsh Third Way?*, Tribune Pamphlet, London: Tribune Publications.

Håkan, S. (2008) 'From a "University Agenda" to a "Collaborative Agenda" – An Inquiry into a Tendency in Swedish Higher Education', *Journal of Adult and Continuing Education*, 14, 1, 74–84.

Hall, A. and Mogyorody, V. (2007) 'Organic Farming, Gender, and the Labor Process', *Rural Sociology*, 72, 2, 289–316.

Hall, P. A. (1986) *Governing the Economy: The Politics of State Intervention in Britain and France*, Cambridge: Polity Press.

Hall, J. A. (1994) *The State: Critical Concepts*, London: Routledge.

Hankivsky, O. and Christoffersen, A. (2008) 'Intersectionality and the determinants of health: a Canadian perspective', *Critical Public Health*, 18, 3, 271–83.

Hansen, S. (1997) 'Talking About Politics: Gender and Contextual Effects on Political Proselytizing', *Journal of Politics*, 59, 2, 73–103.

Hanson, D. (1995) *Unelected, Unaccountable and Untenable: A Study of Appointments to Public Bodies in Wales*, Cardiff: WLP.

Hargreaves J. (1997) 'Women's Sport, Development, and Cultural Diversity: the South African Experience', *Women's Studies International Forum*, 20, 2, 191–209.

Harris J. (1999) 'Justice and Equal Opportunities in Health Care', *Bioethics*, 13, 5, 392–404.

Harvey, C. (2000) 'Governing after the Rights Revolution', *Journal Of Law And Society*, vol. 27, no. 1, 61–97.

Haylett, C. (2003) 'Culture, Class and Urban Policy: Reconsidering Equality', *Antipode*, 35, 1, 55–73.

Hayley F. (2005) 'Still feeling like a spare piece of luggage? Embodied experiences of (dis)ability in physical education and school sport', *Physical Education and Sport Pedagogy*, 0, 1, 41–59.

Hazell, R. (2007) 'The Continuing Dynamism of Constitutional Reform', *Parliamentary Affairs*, 60, 1, 1, 3–25.

Healey, P. (1997) *Collaborative Planning – Shaping places in fragmented societies*. Houndmills and London: Macmillan Press.

Healthcare Inspectorate Wales (2006) *Healthcare Inspectorate Wales Race Equality Action Plan*, Cardiff: Healthcare Inspectorate Wales.

Held, D. (1989) *Political theory and the modern state: essays on state, power and democracy*, Cambridge: Polity Press.

Hellier-Tinoco, R. (2005) 'Becoming-in-the-world-with-others: Inter-Act Theatre Workshop', *Research in Drama Education*, 10, 2, 159–73

Help the Aged Wales (2007) *Impact Report 2007*, Cardiff: Help the Aged Wales.

Her Majesty's Inspectorate of Constabulary for Scotland (2008a) *Thematic Inspection – The Police Response to Domestic Abuse*, Edinburgh: HMICS.

Her Majesty's Inspectorate of Constabulary for Scotland (2008b) *Thematic Inspection – Care of Detained and Arrested Children*, Edinburgh: HMICS.

Her Majesty's Inspector of Education (2007) *How good is our school? The Journey to Excellence*, Livingstone: HMIE.

H. M. Treasury (2006) *Prosperity for All in the Global Economy – World Class Skills*, London: H. M. Treasury.

Higher Education Funding Council for Wales (2008) *Disability of Applicants, Students and Staff of Welsh HEIs Compared to Population Distributions of Disability*, Cardiff: HEFCW.

Hilmar, R. (2005) 'Resources count, but votes decide? from neo-corporatist representation to neo-pluralist parliamentarism', *West European Politics*, 28, 4 740–63.

Hill, M. (2004) *The Public Policy Process*, London: Pearson Longman.

Hill, M. and Hupe, P. (2008) *Implementing Public Policy: An Introduction to the Study of Operational Governance*, London: Sage.

Hill, H. and Kenyon, R. (2007) *Promoting Equality and Diversity: A Practitioner's Guide*, Oxford: Oxford University Press.

Hill, M. (1997) *The Policy Process in the Modern State* (3rd edition), Harlow: Prentice Hall.

Hirst, P. and Barnett, A. (1993) 'Introduction', in Barnett, A., Ellis, C. and Hirst, P. (1993) *Debating the Constitution: New Perspectives on Constitutional Reform*, London: Polity Press, pp. 1–8.

Hodgson, L. (2004) 'Manufactured civil society: counting the cost', *Critical Social Policy*, 24, 2, 139–64.

Hollingsworth, K. and Douglas, G. (2002) 'Creating a children's champion for Wales? The Care Standards Act 2000 (Part V) and the Children's Commissioner for Wales Act 2001', *The Modern Law Review Limited*, 65, 1, 58–78.

Home Office (2001) *Community Cohesion: A Report of the Independent Review Team chaired by Ted Cantle*, London: Home Office.

Hood, C. (1991) 'A public management for all seasons?', *Public Administration*, 69, 1, 3–19.

Hood, C. (1995) 'Contemporary Public Management: A New Global Paradigm?', *Public Policy and Administration*, 10, 2, 104–17.

Hooghe, L. and Marks, G. (2001) *Multi-Level Governance and European Integration*, London: Rowman and Littlefield Pub Inc.

Hooks, B. (1981) *Ain't I a Woman? Black Women and Feminism*, Cambridge, MA: South End Press.

Hooks, B., (1990) *Yearning: Race, Gender, and Cultural Politics*, Boston, MA: South End Press.

Howell, J. (2006) 'Women's Political Participation in China: In Whose Interests Elections?', *Journal of Contemporary China*, vol. 15, no. 49, 603–19.

Howlett, M. (1991) 'Policy Instruments, Policy Styles and Policy Implementation: National Approaches to theories of Instrument Choice', *Policy Studies Journal*, 19, 2, 1–21.

Howard, E. (2008) 'The European Year of Equal Opportunities for All – 2007: Is the EU moving away from a formal idea of equality?', *European Law Journal*, 14, 2, 168–85.

Hughes, C. and Madoc-Jones, I. (2005) 'Meeting the Needs of Welsh Speaking Young People in Custody', *Howard Journal of Criminal Justice*, 44, 4, 374–86.

Hughes, O. (2004) *Public management and administration*, Basingstoke: Palgrave Macmillan.

Humphries, J. and Rubery, J. (eds) (1995) *The Economics of Equal Opportunities*, London: HMSO.

Independent Commission to Review the Voluntary Sector Scheme (2004) *Final Report*, Cardiff: Independent Commission to Review the Voluntary Sector Scheme.

Ineland, J. (2005) 'Logics and discourses in disability arts in Sweden: a neo- institutional perspective', *Disability and Society*, 20, 7, 749–62

Inglehart, R. and Norris, P. (2003) *Rising Tide: Gender Equality and Cultural Change Around the World*, Cambridge: Cambridge University Press.

Irvine, F., Roberts, G., Jones, P. Spencer, L. Baker, C. and Williams, C. (2006) 'Communicative sensitivity in the bilingual healthcare setting: A qualitative study of language awareness', *Journal of Advanced Nursing*, 53, 4, 422–34.

Freidrichs, J. (1998) 'Social Inequality, Segregation and Urban Conflict: The Case of Hamburg', in S. Musterd and W. J. M. Ostendorf (eds) *Urban Segregation and the Welfare State: Inequality and Exclusion in Western Cities*, London: Routledge.

Jessop, B. (2007) *State Power*, Cambridge: Polity.

John, P. (1998) *Analysing Public Policy*, London: Continuum.

Johnston, L. (2007) 'Mobilizing pride/shame: lesbians, tourism and parades', *Social and Cultural Geography*, 8, 1, 29–45.

Johnstone, M. and Kanitsaki, O. (2008) 'The politics of resistance to workplace cultural diversity education for health service providers: an Australian study', *Race, Ethnicity and Education*, 11, 2, 133–54.

Johnstone, M. and Kanitsaki, O. (2008) 'Cultural racism, language prejudice and discrimination in hospital contexts: an Australian study', *Diversity in Health and Social Care*, 5, 1, 19–30.

Jones, G. E. (2000) 'Policy-making in Welsh education: a historical perspective, 1889–1988', in R. Daugherty, R. Phillips and G. Rees (eds) *Education Policy-making in Wales: Explorations in Devolved Governance*, Cardiff: University of Wales Press.

Jones, G. E. (2007) 'The Welsh Universities and Devolution', *Welsh Journal of Education*, 14, 1, 21–42.

Jones, G. E. and Roderick, G. W. (2003) *A History of Education in Wales*, Cardiff: University of Wales Press.

Jordan, A. and Richardson, J. (1987) *British Politics and the Policy Process*, London: Unwin Hyman.

Kant, I. (1785) *Grundlegung zur Metaphysik der Sitten*, in Preußischen Akademie der Wissenschaften (ed.) *Kants Gesammelte Schriften*, Berlin: Gesammelte Schriften, 1902.

Kaplan, G. (1992) *Contemporary Western European Feminism*, London: Routledge.

Kay, R. (2007) *Gender, Equality and Difference During And After State Socialism*, Basingstoke: Palgrave.

Keaney, E. and Oskala, A. (2007) 'The Golden Age of the Arts? Taking Part Survey Findings on Older People and the Arts', *Cultural Trends*, 16, 4, 323–55.

Kearney, J. R. (2003) *Working Group on Government Policy for Support and Funding of the Voluntary and Community Sector – Report to the Task Force on Resourcing the Voluntary and Community Sector*, Belfast: Department for Social Government.

Keating, M. (2002) 'The Invention of Regions: Political Restructuring and Territorial Government in Western Europe', in Brenner, N., Jessop, B., Jones, M. and Macleod, L. (2002) (eds) *State/Space: A Reader*, London: Wiley Blackwell.

Keating, M. (2002) 'Devolution and public policy in the United Kingdom: divergence or convergence?', chapter 1 in Adams, J. and Robinson, P. (eds) *Devolution in Practice: Public Policy Differences within the UK*, London: IPPR.

Keating, M. and McEwen, N. (2005) 'Devolution and public policy in comparative perspective', *Regional and Federal Studies*, vol. 15, no. 4, 413–21.

Kenny, M. (2007) 'Gender, Institutions and Power: A Critical Review', *The British Journal of Politics and International Relations*, 7, 2, 91–100.

Kenway, P., Parsons, N., Carr, J. and Palmer, G. (2005) *Monitoring poverty and social exclusion in Wales 2005*, York: Joseph Rowntree Foundation.

Kitschelt, H. and Rehm, P. (2005) *Work, Family, and Politics Foundations of Electoral Partisan Alignments in Post-industrial Democracies*, paper presented to the Annual Meeting of the American Political Science Association, Washington, D.C. (1–4 September 2005).

Klijn, E. H. and Koppenjan, J. (1999) 'Network Management and Decision Making in Networks: A Multi-actor Approach to Governance', Working Paper 99, University of Twente, NIG.

Kolodinsky, J. (2001) 'Satisfaction of disabled rural elders and adults with the quality of community-based long-term care services', *International Journal of Consumer Studies*, 25, 2, 168–79.

Knox, C. (1999) 'Northern Ireland: At the Crossroads of Political and Administrative Reform', *Governance: An International Journal of Policy and Administration*, vol. 12, no. 3, 311–28.

Kofman, E. (1995) 'Citizenship for some, but not for others: spaces of citizenship in contemporary Europe', *Political Geography*, 14, 121–37.

Kooiman, J. and Van Vliet, M. (1993), 'Governance and public management', in Eliassen, K. A. and Kooiman, J. (eds), *Managing Public Organizations*, London: Sage.

Kosofsky Sedgwick, E. (1991) *Epistemology of the Closet*, Berkeley: University of California Press.

Laffin, M. (2000) 'Constitutional design: a framework for analysis', *Parliamentary Affairs*, 53, 3, 532–41.

Lambert, D. (1999) 'The Government of Wales Act – An Act for Laws to Be Ministered in Wales in Like Form As It Is in This Realm?', *Cambrian Law Review*, 30, 60–71.

Lambert, D. G. and Navarro, M. (2007) 'Some Effects Of The Government of Wales Act 2006: The Welsh Journey from Administrative Decentralization Passing Through Executive Devolution to Quasi-Legislative Devolution in Less Than Eight Years', *Contemporary Wales*, 20, 13–30.

Larner, W. (2000) 'Neo-liberalism: Policy, Ideology, Governmentality', *Studies in Political Economy*, 63, 5–26.

Larserud, S. and Taphorn, R. (2007) 'Designing for Equality: Women's quotas and women's political participation', *Development*, vol. 50, no. 1, 36–42.

Lee, R. (2006) *A Brief Analysis of the Labour Market by Main Equality Strands*, Cardiff: WAG.

Lee, R. (2006) *A Brief Analysis of Demographic Background by Main Equality Strands*, Cardiff: WAG.

Lewis, J. (1992) 'Gender and the development of welfare regimes', *Journal of European Social Policy*, 3, 159–73.

Lewis, J. (2006) 'Employment and Care: The Policy Problem, Gender Equality and the Issue of Choice', *Journal of Comparative Policy Analysis*, 8, 2, 103–14.

Lewis, G. (2008) *Hawl i'r Gymraeg*, Tal-y-bont: Y Lolfa.

Liff, S. and Dickens, L. (1999) 'Ethics and equality: reconciling false dilemmas', in J. Marshall and D. Winstanley (eds) *Ethical Issues in Contemporary Human Resource Management*, London: Macmillan.

Lindsay, I. (1998) 'The civic forum: the key to inclusiveness', *Welsh Democracy Review*, 3, 7–9.

Lindsay, I. (2006) *Discrimination: Successes And Failures Since Devolution*, Report of Forum on Discrimination, 30 September 2006, Edinburgh: Scottish Civic Forum.

Listhaug, O. and Grønflaten, L. (2007) 'Civic Decline? Trends in Political Involvement and Participation in Norway', 1965–2001, *Scandinavian Political Studies*, vol. 30, no. 2, 272–99.

Lister, R. (2003) *Citizenship: Feminist Perspectives* (2nd edition), Basingstoke: Palgrave Macmillan.

Lister, R. (1997) *Citizenship: Feminist Perspectives*, Basingstoke: Macmillan.

Livesey, G., McAleavy, G., Donegan, T., Duffy, J., O'Hagan, C., Adamson, G. and White, R. (2007) *The Nature and Extent of Bullying in Schools in the North of Ireland*, Belfast: N.I. Department of Education.

Livingstone, S. (2001) *Unequal opportunities? The impact of devolution on the equality agenda*, Third Seminar Paper of 'Devolution in Practice, Public policy differences within the UK – A joint Institute for Public Policy Research/Economic and Social Research Council Devolution Programme project', Queens University Belfast, 3 December.

Locke, J. (1690/1979) *An Essay Concerning Human Understanding*, Clarendon Edition of the Works of John Locke, Oxford: Oxford University Press.

Lockyer, A. (2003) 'Introduction and Review', in Lockyer, A.. Crick, B. and Annette, J. (eds) *Education for Democratic Citizenship: Issues of Theory and Practice*, Aldershot: Ashgate.

Lovecy, J. (2002) 'Gender Mainstreaming and the Framing of Women's Rights in Europe: The Contribution of the Council of Europe', *Feminist Legal Studies*, 10, 271–83.

Lovenduski, J. (2005) *Feminizing politics*, Cambridge: Polity.

Lowery, D and Gray, V. (2004) 'A Neopluralist Perspective on Research on Organized Interests', *Political Research Quarterly*, 57, 1, 164–75.

Lowery, D. (2007) 'Why Do Organized Interests Lobby? A Multi-Goal, Multi-Context Theory of Lobbying', *Polity*, 39, 1, 29–54.

Lowery, D. and Gray, F. (2004) 'A Neopluralist Perspective on Research on Organized Interests', in A. S. McFarland (ed.) *Neopluralism*, Lawrence: University of Kansas Press.

Lowndes, V. and Wilson, D. (2001) 'Social Capital and Local Governance: Exploring the Institutional Design Variable', *Political Studies*, 49, 629–47.

Lynch, P. (2001) *Scottish Government and Politics: An Introduction*, Edinburgh: Edinburgh University Press.

Lynch, K. and Lodge, A. (2002) *Equality and Power in Schools: Redistribution, Recognition and Representation*, London: Routledge Falmer.

Mabbett, D. (2008) 'Aspirational Legalism and the Role of the Equality and Human Rights Commission in Equality Policy', *The Political Quarterly*, 79, 1, 45–52.

Mac an Ghaill, M. (1999) *Contemporary Racisms and Ethnicities: Social and Cultural Transformations*, Buckingham: Open University Press.

McKay, A. and Gillespie, M. (2005) 'Women, Inequalities and Social Policy', in G. Mooney and G. Scott (eds) *Exploring Social Policy in the 'New' Scotland*, Bristol: Policy Press.

Mackay, F. and Bilton, K. (2001) *Equality Proofing Procedures In Drafting Legislation: International Comparisons*, Governance of Scotland Forum, University of Edinburgh, Scottish Executive Central Research Unit.

Mackay, F. and Bilton, K. (2003) *Learning From Experience: Lessons in Mainstreaming Equal Opportunities*, Edinburgh: Scottish Executive Social Research.

Mackay, F. (2009) 'Travelling the Distance? Equal Opportunities and the Scottish Parliament', in Jeffery, C. and Mitchell, J. (eds) *The Scottish Parliament 1999–2009: The First Decade*, Edinburgh: Luath Press Ltd/Hansard Society.

MacKinnon, K. (2004) 'Reversing Language Shift: Celtic Languages Today – Any Evidence? *Journal of Celtic Linguistics*, 8, 1, 109–32.

Macpherson, S. and Bond, S. (2009) *Equality Issues in Scotland: A Review of Research 2000–08*, Glasgow: Equality and Human Rights Commission.

Macpherson, W. (1999) *The Stephen Lawrence Inquiry: Report Of An Inquiry By Sir William Macpherson of Cluny*, London: The Stationery Office.

Madoc-Jones, I. (2004) 'Linguistic sensitivity, indigenous peoples and the mental health system in Wales', *International Journal of Mental Health Nursing*, 13, 4, 216–24.

Mansbridge, J. (1992) 'A deliberative perspective on neo-corporatism', *Politics and Society*, 20, 4, 493–505.

March, J. and Olsen, J. P. (1984) 'The new institutionalism: organisational factors in political life', *American Political Science Review*, 78, 732–49.

Marin-Lamellet C., Bruyas M.-P., Guyot L. (2000) The usability of the internet as a source of information for disabled travellers, *Recherche Transports Securite*, 68, 3–14.

Marks, D. (2001) 'Disability and cultural citizenship', in N. Stevenson (ed.) *Culture and Citizenship*, London: Sage.

Marsh, D. and Rhodes, R. A. W. (1992) *Policy Networks in British Government*, Oxford: Oxford University Press.

Marsh, D. (2008) Understanding British Government: Analysing Competing Models, *British Journal of Politics and International Relations*, 10, 2, 251–68.

Marshall, T. H. (1950) *Citizenship and Social Class and Other Essays*, Cambridge: Cambridge University Press.

Mason, A. (2006) *Levelling the Playing Field: The Idea of Equal Opportunity and Its Place in Egalitarian Thought*, Oxford: Oxford University Press.

McAllister, L. (1999) 'The Road to Cardiff Bay: The Process of Establishing the National Assembly for Wales', *Parliamentary Affairs*, 52, 634–48.

McBride, D. (1995) *Comparative State Feminism*, New York: Sage.

McCall, L. (2005) 'The Complexity of Intersectionality', *Signs: A Journal of Women in Culture and Society*, 30, 3, 1771–800.

McCrudden, C. (2004) *Mainstreaming Equality in Northern Ireland 1998–2004: A Review of the Issues Concerning the Operation of the Equality Duty in Section 75 of the Northern Ireland Act 1998*, Belfast: Northern Ireland Office.

McDonough, R. (1996) 'Integration or independence? in *Power, Politics, Positionings*, Belfast: Democratic Dialogue.

McKenzie, R. (2001) *Lifting Every Voice*, Cardiff: NAW/PCSU.

Meehan, E. (2003) *From Government to Governance, Civic Participation and 'New Politics'; the Context of Potential Opportunities for the Better Representation of Women*, Occasional Paper no. 5, Centre for Advancement of Women in Politics, School of Politics and International Studies, Queen's University Belfast.

Merrett, C. and Gruid, J. (2000) 'Small Business Ownership in Illinois: The Effect of Gender and Location on Entrepreneurial Success', *The Professional Geographer*, 52, 3, 425–36.

Miles, R. and Brown, M. (2003) *Racism*, 2nd edition, London: Routledge.

Miller, D. (1997) 'Equality and Justice', *Ratio*, 110, 3, 222–37.

Miller, D. (2000) *Citizenship and National identity*, Cambridge: Polity Press.

Miller, D. (2001) *Principles of Social Justice*, San Francisco: Harvard University Press.

Mind Cymru (2007) *Mind Cymru Manifesto*, Cardiff: Mind Cymru.

Minority Ethnic Women's Network Cymru (2007) *Voices from Within Report*, Cardiff: MEWN.

Mitchell, J. (2000) 'New Parliament, New Politics in Scotland', *Parliamentary Affairs*, vol. 53, no. 3, 605–21.

Modood, T. (2000) *Multiculturalism (Themes for the 21st Century Series)*, Basingstoke: Palgrave Macmillan.

Modood T. (2007) *Multiculturalism: A Civic Idea*, Cambridge: Polity.

Moghadam, V. and Senftova, L. (2005) 'Measuring women's empowerment: participation and rights in civil, political, social, economic, and cultural domains', *International Social Science Journal*, vol. 57, no. 2, 389–412

Mooney, G., Scott, G. and Williams, C. (2007) 'Rethinking social policy through devolution', *Critical Social Policy*, 26, 3, 483–97.

Moore M. E.; Parkhouse B. L.; Konrad A. M (2001) 'Women in sport management: advancing the representation through HRM structures', *Women in Management Review*, 16, 2, 51–61.

Moraga, C. and Anzaldúa, G. (1981) *This Bridge Called My Back*, Pittsburgh: Persephone Press.

Moran, M., Rein, M. and Goodin, R. (2008) *The Oxford Handbook of Public Policy*, Oxford: Oxford University Press.

Morgan, K. and Mungham, G. (2000) *Redesigning Democracy: The Making of the Welsh Assembly*, Bridgend: Seren.

Morgan, K. and Roberts, E. (1993) *The Democratic Deficit: A guide to Quangoland, Papers in Planning and Research No.144*, Cardiff: Cardiff University Dept. of City and Regional Planning.

Morgan, Rh. (2007) 'Who are you talking to? Disabled people in Wales', *Disability Wales*, 72, 34–6.

Morison, J. (2001) 'Democracy, Governance and Governmentality: Civic Public Space and Constitutional Renewal in Northern Ireland', *Oxford Journal of Legal Studies*, 21, 2, 287–310.

Morrison, A., Raju, D. and Sinha, N. (2007) *Gender Equality, Poverty and Economic Growth*, Policy Research Working Paper 4349, New York, The World Bank, Gender and Development Group, Poverty Reduction and Economic Management Network.

Morsink, J. (1999) *The Universal Declaration of Human Rights: origins, drafting, and intent*, Philadelphia: University of Pennsylvania Press.

Mumford, K. and Smith, P. (2007) *The Gender Earnings Gap In Britain: Including The Workplace*, The Manchester School, 75, 6, 653–72.

Murphy, M. C. (2007) 'Europeanization and the Sub-National Level: Changing Patterns of Governance in Northern Ireland', *Regional and Federal Studies*, 17, 3, 293– 315.

National Assembly for Wales (2000a) *Voluntary Sector Scheme*, Cardiff: NAfW.

National Assembly for Wales (2000b) *The National Assembly For Wales: Arrangements To Promote Equality Of Opportunity 1999– 2000*, Papers of the Committee on Equality of Opportunity, Cardiff: NAfW.

National Assembly for Wales (2000c), *Local Government Finance (Wales) Special Grant Report (No.2) Wales 2000 Special Grant for Asylum Seekers (Adults, Families of Asylum Seekers and Unaccompanied Asylum Seeking Children)*, Cardiff: NAfW.

National Assembly for Wales (2001a) *Special Educational Needs Code of Practice for Wales*, Cardiff: NAfW.

National Assembly for Wales (2001b) *Equal Pay Audit 2001*, papers of the Committee on Equality of Opportunity, 13 June 2001, Cardiff: NAfW.

National Assembly for Wales (2001c) *Environment, Planning & Transport Committee Consultation Report: Policy Review of Public Transport*, Cardiff: NAfW.

National Assembly for Wales (2001d) *The Transport Framework for Wales*, Cardiff: NAfW.

National Assembly for Wales (2001e) *Better Homes for People in Wales: A National Housing Strategy for Wales*, Cardiff: NAfW.

National Assembly for Wales (2002a) *Final Report on The Review Of Remuneration and Expenses of Chairs and Members of Assembly Sponsored Public Bodies and National Health Service Wales Bodies*, Papers of the Assembly Equality Committee, 30 January 2002, Cardiff: NAfW.

National Assembly for Wales (2002b) *Final Report on the Review Of Remuneration and Expenses of Chairs and Members of Assembly Sponsored Public Bodies and National Health Service Wales Bodies*, Papers of the Assembly Equality Committee, 30 January 2002, Cardiff: NAfW.

National Assembly for Wales (2003a) *Focus on Disability*, Cardiff: NAfW.

National Assembly for Wales (2003b) *Progress and Achievements on Public Appointments, Papers of the Assembly Equality Committee*, 30 March 2003, Cardiff: NAfW.

National Assembly for Wales (2003c) *Equality Committee's Review of Service Provision for Gypsies and Travellers*, Cardiff: NAfW.

National Assembly for Wales (2004a) *National Assembly for Wales Code of Practice for Ministerial Appointments to Public Bodies*, Cardiff: WAG.

National Assembly for Wales (2004b) *Learning Pathways 14–19 Guidance, National Assembly for Wales, Circular Number: 37/2004*, Cardiff: NAfW.

National Assembly for Wales (2005a) *Close the Pay Gap': Evaluation of Phase 2 and plans for Phase 3 of the Equal Pay Campaign*, Papers of the Committee on Equality Of Opportunity, 24 November 2005, Cardiff: NAfW.

National Assembly for Wales (2005b) *A Statistical Focus on Diversity in Wales*, Cardiff: NAfW.

National Assembly for Wales (2006a) *Stronger Partnerships for Better Outcomes Guidance, Circular – Children Act 2004, National Assembly for Wales Circular No: 35/2006 Date of Issue: August 2006*, Cardiff: NAfW.

National Assembly for Wales (2006b) *A Brief Analysis of Education by Main Equality Strands*, Cardiff: NAfW.

National Assembly for Wales (2006c) *HE enrolments at Welsh HEIs by subject, level and mode of study (gender)*, Cardiff: NAfW.

National Assembly for Wales (2006d) *A Brief Analysis of Transport by Main Equality Strands*, Cardiff: NAfW.

National Assembly for Wales (2007a) *Education, Lifelong Learning and Skills Committee Review of Additional Learning Requirements*, Cardiff: NAfW.

National Assembly for Wales (2007b) *Policy Review Project Report*, Papers of the Equality of Opportunity Committee, EOC (2)-02-07, Annex 2, Cardiff: NAfW

National Assembly for Wales (2007c) *Accessibility of Polling Stations in Wales Inquiry Cross Party Equality Committee*, Cardiff: NAfW.

National Assembly for Wales (2007d) *Standing Orders of the National Assembly*, Cardiff: NAfW.

National Assembly for Wales (2007e) *National Assembly Equality of Opportunity Committee, Equality and Human Rights Commission Briefing Paper*, 6 December 2007, Cardiff: NAfW.

National Assembly for Wales (2007f) *Progress with the Implementation of the Welsh Assembly Government's Childcare Strategy*, Proceedings of the National Assembly for Wales, The Committee on Equality of Opportunity, 28 February 2007, Cardiff: NAfW.

National Assembly for Wales (2008a) *Issues affecting Migrant Workers in Wales Cross Party Equality Committee*, Cardiff: NAfW.

National Assembly for Wales (2008b) *Accessibility of Information Report*, Cross Party Equality Committee: NAfW.

National Assembly for Wales (2008c) *The Funding of Voluntary Sector Organisations in Wales, Report of the Communities and Culture Committee*, Cardiff: NAfW.

NHS Wales (2001) *Improving health in Wales: A Plan for the NHS with its Partners*, Cardiff: NHS Wales.

National Offender Management Service (2007) *From Homeless to Home: The Accommodation Pathfinder for Female Offenders to Reduce Re- Offending in Wales: A Scoping Exercise*, Cardiff: National Offender Management Service.

National Partnership Forum for Older People in Wales (2007) *Second Report 2006–2007 – The National Partnership Forum for Older People in Wales*, Cardiff: The National Partnership Forum for Older People in Wales.

Netto, G. (2006) 'Vulnerability to Homelessness, Use of Services and Homelessness Prevention in Black and Minority Ethnic Communities', *Housing Studies*, 21, 4, 581–601.

Newman, J. (2001) *Modernising Governance*, London: Routledge.

Newman, J. (2002) 'Changing Governance, Changing Equality? New Labour, Modernization and Public Services', *Public Money and Management*, 22, 1, 7–14

Niner, P. (2006) *Accommodation Needs of Gypsy-Travellers in Wales: Report to the Welsh Assembly Government*, Cardiff: Welsh Assembly Government.

Niven, B. (2008) 'The EHRC: Transformational, Progressively Incremental or a Disappointment?', *The Political Quarterly*, 79, 1, 17–26.

Northern Ireland Office, (1998) *Proposals for a Civic Forum*, Belfast: NIO.

Northern Ireland Assembly (1999) *The Official Record of the Northern Ireland Assembly*, 8 March 1999, Belfast: NIA.

Northern Ireland Council for Ethnic Minorities (2008) *Annual Report 2007–8*, Belfast: NICEM.

Northern Ireland Council for Voluntary Action (2005) *State of the Third Sector*, Belfast: NICVA.

Northern Ireland Council for Voluntary Action (2006) *Minutes of the Women's Policy Forum*, 22 April, Belfast: NICVA.

Northern Ireland Council for Voluntary Action (2007) *Annual Report, 'Opportunities'*, December 2007, Belfast: NICVA.

Northern Ireland Council for Voluntary Action (2008) *Response to Consultation on Review of the Civic Forum*, Belfast: NICVA.

Northern Ireland Department of Health, Social Services and Public Health (2004a) *Equality and Inequalities in Health and Social Care in Northern Ireland*, Belfast: Northern Ireland Department of Health, Social Services and Public Health.

Northern Ireland Department of Health, Social Services and Public Safety (2004b) *Health And Social Care Inequalities, Monitoring System: First Update Bulletin 2004*, Belfast: Northern Ireland Department of Health, Social Services and Public Health.

Northern Ireland Department of Education (2008) *Statistical Press Release: Qualifications and Destinations of Northern Ireland School Leavers 2006/07 (Revised)*, Belfast, NIO.

Northern Ireland Office (2004) *NIO, Northern Ireland Crime Survey, 2003/4*, Belfast: NIO.

Northern Ireland Social Care Council (2008) *Corporate Plan 2008–2011*, Belfast: NISCC.

Northern Ireland Women's Coalition (NIWC) (1998) *Northern Ireland Women's Coalition: A New Voice For New Times*, Manifesto Assembly Elections 1998.

Nussbaum, M. (2000) *Women and Human Development: The Capabilities Approach*, Cambridge: Cambridge University Press.

Obinger, H., Leibfried, S. and Castles, F. G. (2005) *Federalism and the Welfare State: New World and European Experiences*, Cambridge: Cambridge University Press.

O'Brien, N. (2008) 'Equality and Human Rights: Foundations of a Common Culture?', *The Political Quarterly*, vol. 79, no. 1, 27–35.

O'Cinneide, C. (2002) *A Single Equality Body: Lessons from Abroad*, Manchester: EOC.

O'Cinneide, C. (2009) *The Place of Equal Opportunities in the Devolution Settlement: A Legal Analysis*, Glasgow: Equality and Human Rights Commission.

O'Neill, D. (1996) 'Health care for older people', in Bywaters, P. and McLeod, E. (eds) *Working for Equality in Health*, London: Routledge.

Office of the Commissioner for Public Appointments in Scotland (2006) *Code of Practice for Ministerial Appointments to Public Bodies in Scotland*, Edinburgh: Office of the Commissioner for Public Appointments in Scotland.

Office of the Commissioner for Public Appointments for Northern Ireland (1995) *Principles for Ministerial Appointments to Public Bodies in Northern Ireland*, Belfast: OCPANI.

Office of the Commissioner for Public Appointments for Northern Ireland (2008) *Annual Report 2007-8*, Belfast: OCPANI.

Office of the Deputy Prime Minister (2006) *State of the English Cities*, London: ODPM.

Office of the First Minister and Deputy First Minister of Northern Ireland (2005) *Partnerships in Northern Ireland*, Belfast: OFMDFMNI.

Office Of The First Minister And Deputy First Minister (2005a) *A Shared Future Policy and Strategic Framework for Good Relations in Northern Ireland*, Belfast: Office Of The First Minister And Deputy First Minister.

Office of the First Minister and Deputy First Minister (2006a) *Lifetime Opportunities' – Government's Anti-poverty and Social Inclusion Strategy for Northern Ireland*, Belfast: OFMDFM.

Office Of The First Minister And Deputy First Minister (2006b) *A Shared Future. First Triennial Action Plan 2006–2009*, Belfast: Office Of The First Minister And Deputy First Minister.

Office of the Oversight Commissioner (2007) *Report 19, May 2007*, Belfast: Office of the Oversight Commissioner.

Office for National Statistics (2001) *Census 2001*, London: ONS.

Office for National Statistics (2005) *Labour Force Survey Spring 2005*, London: ONS.

Office for National Statistics (2007a) *Statistics for Wales, Pupils with Statements of Special Educational Needs*, January 2007, SDR 79/2007, London: ONS.

Office for National Statistics (2007b) *Measuring Equality – A Review of Equality Data*, London: ONS.

Office for National Statistics (2008) *2008 Annual Survey of Hours and Earnings*, London: ONS.

Office for National Statistics (2009a) *News Release: Civil partnerships down 18 per cent in 2008*, London: ONS.

Office for National Statistics (2009b) *Statistical Bulletin: 2009 Annual Survey of Hours and Earnings*, London: ONS.

Older People's Commissioner for Wales (2008) *Annual Report*, Cardiff: Older People's Commissioner for Wales.

Oldfield, A. (1994) 'Citizenship: An Unnatural Practice?', in Turner, B. and Hamilton, P. (eds) *Citizenship: Critical Concepts*, London: Routledge.

Oliver, M. (1996) *Understanding Disability: From Theory to Practice*, Basingstoke: Macmillan Press.

Organisation for Economic Cooperation and Development (2006) *PISA 2006 Science Competencies for Tomorrow's World: Volume 1: Analysis*, Paris: OECD.

Osborne, M. and Slivinski, A. (1996) 'A Model of Political Competition with Citizen Candidates', *Quarterly Journal of Economics*, 111, 65–96.

Osler, A. and Morrison, M. (2002) 'Can Race Equality be Inspected? Challenges for Policy and Practice Raised by the OFSTED School Inspection Framework', *British Educational Research Journal*, vol. 28, no. 3, 327–38.

Osler A. (2000) 'The Crick Report: Difference, Equality and Racial Justice', *The Curriculum Journal*, 11, 1, 1 25–37.

Osmond, J. (1999a) *Adrift but Afloat: The civil service and the National Assembly*, Cardiff: IWA.

Paine, T. (1792/ 1999) *The Rights of Man*, New York: Dover Publications.

Palley, C. (1972) 'The Evolution, Disintegration and Possible Reconstruction of the Northern Ireland Constitution', *Anglo-American Law Review*, 1, 3 400–34.

Parekh, B. (2000) *The report of the Commission on the Future of Multi-Ethnic Britain*, London: Profile Books.

Paris, C., Gray, P. and Muir, J. (2002) 'Devolving Housing Policy and Practice in Northern Ireland 1998–2002', *Housing Studies*, 18, 2, 159–75.

Parsons, W. (1996) *Public Policy: An Introduction to the Theory and Practice of Policy Analysis*, Cheltenham: Edward Elgar.

Pascall, G. and Lewis, J. (2004) 'Emerging Gender Regimes and Policies for Gender Equality in a Wider Europe', *Journal of Social Policy*, 33, 373–94.

Patterson, I, (2007) 'Information sources used by older adults for decision making about tourist and travel destinations', *International Journal of Consumer Studies*, 31, 5, 528–33.

Pattie, C., Seyd, P. and Whiteley, P. (2004) *Citizenship in Britain: Values, Participation and Democracy*, Cambridge: Cambridge University Press.

Pelizzo, R. (2003) 'Party positions or party direction? An analysis of party manifesto data', *West European Politics*, 26, 2, 67–89.

Phillips, A. (1999) *Which Equalities Matter?* Cambridge: Polity.

Phillips, A. and Dustin, M. (2004) 'UK Initiatives on Forced Marriage: Regulation, Dialogue and Exit', *Political Studies*, 52, 531–51.

Phillips, T. (2007a) *Foreword, in Fairness and Freedom: The Final Report of the Equalities Review*, Norwich: Office of Public Sector Information.

Phillips, T. (2007b) 'Equality and human rights: siblings or just rivals?', *Benefits*, 15, 2, 127–38.

Phillipson, C. (1998) *Reconstructing Old Age: New Agendas in Social Theory and Social Practice*, London: Sage.

Phillipson, C. and Walker, A. (eds) (1986) *Ageing and Social Policy: A critical Assessment*, London: Gower.

Pierson, P. (1995) 'Fragmented Welfare States: Federal Institutions and the Development of Social Policy', *Governance*, 8, 4, 449–78.

Pilgrim, A. N. and Scourfield, J. (2007) 'Racist Bullying as it affects Children in Wales: A scoping study', *Contemporary Wales*, 20, 78–86.

Plaid Cymru (1999) *The Manifesto of Plaid Cymru – The Party of Wales*, Cardiff: Plaid Cymru.

Plaid Cymru (2007) *National Assembly Election Manifesto 2007*, Cardiff: Plaid Cymru.

Police Service of Northern Ireland (2008a) *The PSNI's statistical Report 1st April 2007–31st March 2008*, Belfast: PSNI.

Police Service of Northern Ireland (2008b) *Statistical Report No. 2, Domestic Incidents and Crimes 1st April 2007–31st March 2008*, Central Statistics Branch, Operational Support Department, Belfast: PSNI.

Portes, A. (1998), 'Social Capital: its origins and applications in modern sociology', *Annual Review of Sociology*, 24, 1–14.

Prokhovnik, R. (2005) *Making Policy, Shaping Lives*, Edinburgh: Edinburgh University Press/Open University Press.

Poulantzas, N. (1978) *State, Power, Socialism*, New York: Verso.

Pradhan Malla, S. (2000) 'Property Rights of Nepalese Women', in *A Baseline Study on Inheritance Right of Women*, Forum for Women, Law and development, Kathmandu: FWLD.

Patchett, K. (2005) 'Principle or Pragmatism? Legislating for Wales by West and Whitehall', in R. Hazell and R. Rawlings (eds), *Devolution, Law Making and the Constitution*, Exeter: Imprint Academic.

Public Service Management Wales (2008) *The Bigger Picture – Public Service Management Wales – Annual Report – 07/08*, Cardiff: Public Service Management Wales.

Public Services Ombudsman for Wales (2008) *The Annual Report 2007/08 of The Public Services Ombudsman for Wales*, Cardiff: Public Services Ombudsman for Wales.

Putnam, R. with Leonardi, R. and Nanettti, R.Y. (1993), *Making Democracy Work*, Princeton: Princeton University Press.

Rankin, P. L., and Vickers, J. (2001) *Women's movements and state feminism: Integrating Diversity into Public Policy*, Ottawa: Status of Women Canada.

Rawlings, R. (1998) 'The New Model Wales', *Journal of Law and Society*, 25, 4, 461–509.

Rawlings, R. (2003) *Delineating Wales: Constitutional, Legal and Administrative Aspects of National Devolution*, Cardiff: University of Wales Press.

Rawls, J. (1971) *A Theory of Justice*, Oxford: Oxford University Press/ Harvard University Press.

Rees, T. (1998) *Mainstreaming Equality in the European Union: Education, Training and Labour Market Policies*, London: Routledge.

Rees, G. (2004) 'Democratic Devolution and Education Policy in Wales: the Emergence of a National system?', *Contemporary Wales*, 17, 28–44.

Rees, T. and Chaney, P. (2010) 'Multilevel Governance, Equality and Human Rights', *Society and Social Policy*.

Rees, T. (1999) *Women and Work: Twenty-Five Years of Gender Equality in Wales*, Cardiff: University of Wales Press.

Rees, T. (2000) 'The Learning Region? Integrating Gender Equality into Regional Economic Development', *Policy and Politics*, 28, 2, 179–91.

Rees, O. (2010) 'Devolution and the Children's Commissioner For Wales: Challenges and Opportunities', in Chaney, P., Thompson, A. and Royles, E. (eds) *Contemporary Wales: An Annual Review of Economic, Political and Social Research*, Cardiff: University of Wales Press.

Reynolds, D. (2001) 'Ploughing Our Own Educational Furrow', *Agenda*, IWA, Autumn 2001, 19–24.

Rhodes, R. (1997) *Understanding Governance: Policy Networks, Governance, Reflexivity and Accountability*, Buckingham: Open University Press.

Rich, A. (1977) *Of Woman Born: Motherhood as Experience and Institution*, London: Virago Press.

Richard Commission (2004) *Report of the Richard Commission: Commission on the Powers and Electoral Arrangements of the National Assembly for Wales*, Cardiff: National Assembly for Wales.

Richard, I. (2006) *Speech to Institute of Welsh Politics Conference on 'The Future of Welsh Politics*, Cardiff, 20 September.

Richards, D., and Smith M., (2002) *Governance and Public Policy in the UK*, Oxford: Oxford University Press.

Riddell, S. (1992) *Gender and the Politics of the Curriculum*, London and New York: Routledge.

Ridley, F. F. and Wilson, D. (1995) *The Quango Debate*, Oxford: Oxford University/Hansard Society for Parliamentary Government.

Rolph, A. (2003) 'A Movement of its Own: The Women's Liberation Movement in South Wales', in G. H., Koloski, A. Neilson, A. and Robertson, E. (eds) *The Feminist Seventies*, University of York: Raw Nerve Books, pp. 127–38.

Rosenthal (2001) *The Third House: Lobbyists and Lobbying in the States*, New York: CQ Press.

Rousseau, J.-J. (1762/1987) *The Social Contract*, English translation by M. Cranston, Harmondsworth: Penguin.

Rowbotham, S. (1992) *Hidden from History: 300 Years of Women's Oppression and the Fight Against It*, London: Pluto Press.

Royal National Institute of Blind People Cymru (2008) *Victory for people with Wet AMD in Wales*, RNIB Cymru News, Cardiff: RNIB Cymru, June 25, 2008.

Sabatier, P. A. (ed.) (2006) *Theories of the Policy Process*, Boulder, CO: Westview Press.

Sabatier, P. A. and Jenkins Smith, H. (1999) *Policy Change and Learning: An Advocacy Coalition Approach*, Boulder, CO: Westview Press.

Sabatier, P. A. and Jenkins Smith, H. (1999) 'The Advocacy Coalition Framework: An Assessment' in Sabatier, P. A. (ed.) *Theories of the Policy Process*, Boulder CO: Westview Press, pp.117–66.

Santos, L. and Varejão, J. (2007) 'Employment, pay and discrimination in the tourism industry', *Tourism Economics*, 13, 2, 225–40.

Sapiro, V. and Conover, P. (1997) 'The Variable Gender Basis of Electoral Politics: Gender and Context in the 1992 US Election', *British Journal of Political Science*, 27:4, 497–523.

Save the Children (2008) *Save the Children Wales – What we do in Wales*, Cardiff: Save the Children.

Save the Children, The Bevan Foundation, the New Policy Institute and, Focus Consultancy (2008) *Children in Severe Poverty in Wales: An Agenda for Action*, Cardiff: Save the Children, The Bevan Foundation, the New Policy Institute and Focus Consultancy.

Schiek, D. and Chege, V. (2008) *European Union Non-discrimination Law: Comparative Perspectives on Multidimensional Equality Law*, London: Routledge-Cavendish.

Scheffler, S. (2003) 'What is Egalitarianism?', *Philosophy and Public Affairs*, 31, 5–39.

Scope Cymru (2007) *Time to Get Equal – Manifesto for Wales – Scope Cymru*, Cardiff, Scope Cymru.

Scott, J. (2001) *Power*, Oxford: Polity Press.

Scottish Executive (2005) *A Vision For The Voluntary Sector: The Next Phase Of Our Relationship*, Edinburgh: Scottish Executive.

Scottish Executive and National Statistics (2006) *High Level Summary of Equality Statistics: Key Trends for Scotland*, Edinburgh: Scottish Executive National Statistics.

Scottish Government (2007) *Better Health, Better Care: Action Plan*, Edinburgh: Scottish Government.

Scottish Government (2008a) *Disability Equality Scheme Annual Report 2008*, Edinburgh: Scottish Government.

Scottish Government (2008b) *Gender Equality Scheme Annual Report 2008*, Edinburgh: Scottish Government.

Scottish Government (2008c) *Race Equality Scheme Annual Report 2008*, Edinburgh: Scottish Government.

Scottish Government (2008d) *Enterprising Third Sector: Action Plan 2008–2011*, Edinburgh: Scottish Government.

Scottish Government (2009) *Draft Budget 2010/11: Equality Statement*, Edinburgh: Scottish Government.

Scottish Parliament (2007) *Standing Orders of the Scottish Parliament*, Edinburgh: Scottish Parliament.

Sharpe, L. J. (1993) 'The United Kingdom: The Disjointed Meso', in L. J. Sharpe (ed.) *The Rise of Meso Government in Europe*, London: Sage.

Shaw, G., Veitch, C. and Coles, T. (2005) 'Access, Disability, And Tourism: Changing Responses in the United Kingdom', *Tourism Review International*, 8, 3, 167–76

Sherlock, A. (2000) 'Born Free, but Everywhere in Chains? A legal analysis of the first year of the National Assembly for Wales', *Cambrian Law Review*, 31, 61–72

Selznick, P. (1996) 'Institutionalism "old" and "new"', *Administrative Science Quarterly*, 41, 270–7.

Sen, A. (1997) 'Equality of What?', in R. Goodin, and P. Pettit (eds) *Contemporary Political Philosophy*, Oxford: Blackwell.

Sen, A. K. (1984) *Resources, Values and Development*, Oxford: Blackwell.

Sen, A. K. (1992) *Inequality Re-examined*, Oxford: Clarendon Press.

Sen, A. K. (1993) 'Capability and Well-Being', in M. Nussbaum and A. K. Sen (eds), *The Quality of Life*, Oxford: Oxford University Press.

Sen, A. K., (2005) 'Human Rights and Capabilities', *Journal of Human Development*, 6, 2, 151–66.

Shakespeare, T. and Watson, N. (1997) 'Defending the social model', *Disability and Society*, 12, 2, 293–300.

Shakespeare, T. and Watson, N. (2001) 'The social model of disability: an outdated ideology?', in: S. Barnartt and B. Altman (eds) *Exploring theories and expanding methodologies: where we are and where we need to go* (London: JAI), 9–28.

Shipley, I. (2008) *Statistics on migrant workers in Wales*, Cardiff: Welsh Assembly Government.

Siraj- Blatchford, I., Milton, E., Laugharne, J. and Charles, F. (2007) 'Developing the Foundation Phase for 3–7-year-olds in Wales', *The Welsh Journal of Education*, 14, 43–68.

Skelcher, C. (2005) 'Jurisdictional Integrity, Polycentrism, and the Design of Democratic Governance', *Governance*, 18 (1), 89–110.

Skelcher, C., Mathur, N. and Smith, M. (2005) 'The Public Governance of Collaborative Spaces: Discourse, Design and Democracy', *Public Administration*, 83 3, 573–96.

Skocpol, T. (1997) 'Bringing the State Back in', in Hill, M. (ed.) *The Policy Process: A Reader*, 2nd edition, London: Pearson Prentice Hall.

Smith, M. J. (1993) *Pressure, Power and Policy*, Hemel Hempstead: Harvester Wheatsheaf.

Social Services Inspectorate for Wales (2003) *National Minimum Standards For Fostering Services*, Cardiff: Social Services Inspectorate for Wales.

Social Services Inspectorate for Wales (2004) *National Minimum Standards For Boarding Schools*, Cardiff: Social Services Inspectorate for Wales.

Soper, K. (1994) 'Feminism, humanism and postmodernism', in M. Evans (ed.) *The Woman Question*, London: Sage.

Soutphommasane, T. (2005) 'Grounding multicultural citizenship: From minority rights to civic pluralism', *Journal of Intercultural Studies*, 26, 4, 401–16.

Spargo, T. (1999) *Foucault and Queer Theory*, Cambridge: Icon Books.

331

Special Education Needs Tribunal for Wales (2007) *Special Educational Needs Tribunal for Wales – Annual Report 2006–2007*, Llandrindod Wells: SENTW.

Spicker, P. (2006) *Policy analysis for practice: applying social policy*, Bristol: Policy Press.

Sports Council For Wales (2007) *Equality Scheme*, Cardiff: Sports Council For Wales.

Squire, V. (2008) 'Accounting for the Dominance of Control: Inter-party Dynamics and Restrictive Asylum Policy in Contemporary Britain', *British Politics*, 3, 2, 241–61.

Squires, J. (2005) 'Is Mainstreaming Transformative? Theorizing Mainstreaming in the Context of Diversity and Deliberation', *Social Politics*, 12, 3, 366–88.

Squires, J. (2008) 'Intersecting Inequalities: Reflecting on the Subjects and Objects of Equality', *The Political Quarterly*, vol. 79, no. 1, 28–54.

Statistics for Wales (2009) *Gypsy and Traveller Caravan Count July 2009, SDR 197/2009*, Cardiff: Statistics for Wales.

Statistics for Wales (2007) *A Social Audit of the Muslim Community in Wales*, Cardiff: Statistics for Wales.

Statistics for Wales (2008) *International Comparisons of Education Indicators*, Cardiff: Statistics for Wales.

Statistics for Wales (2009) *Schools in Wales: Examination Performance 2008*, Cardiff: Statistics for Wales.

Steinem, G. (1995) *Outrageous Acts and Everyday Rebellions*, New York: Holt Paperbacks.

Sterling, R. (2005) 'Promoting Democratic Government through Partnerships?', chapter 7 in Newman, J. (ed.) *Remaking Governance: Peoples, Politics and the Public Sphere*, Bristol: Polity Press.

Stetson, D. and Mazur, A. (1995) *Comparative State Feminism*, London: Sage.

Stonewall Cymru (2004a) *Stonewall Cymru Annual Review 2003–4*, Cardiff: Stonewall Cymru.

Stonewall Cymru, (2004b) *Count us in! Addressing the needs of Wales' forgotten 'community of interest' A Stonewall Cymru Assessment Report*, Cardiff: Stonewall Cymru.

Stonewall Cymru (2006) *The Housing Needs of Lesbian, Gay and Bisexual (LGB) People in Wales*, Cardiff: Stonewall Cymru.

Stonewall Cymru (2008a) *Have you experienced homophobic hate crime? A guide on how the Criminal Justice agencies respond to homophobic hate crime, and the steps you can take towards stopping it*, Cardiff: Stonewall Cymru.

Stonewall (2008b) *Homophobic hate crime The Gay British Crime Survey 2008*, London: Stonewall.

Student Finance Wales/Welsh Assembly Government (2007) *Guide To Funding – Making Learning Work For You*, Cardiff: Student Finance Wales/WAG.

Sullivan, M. (2004) 'Wales Devolution and Health Policy: Policy Experimentation and Differentiation to Improve Health', *Contemporary Wales*, 17, 44–65.

Sullivan, N. (2003) *A Critical Introduction to Queer Theory*, Edinburgh: Edinburgh University Press.

Sykes, P. (2000) *Presidents and prime ministers: conviction politics in the Anglo-American tradition*, Lawrence: University Press of Kansas.

Syson, F. and Wood, E. (2005) 'Local authority arts events and the South Asian community: unmet needs – a UK case study', *Managing Leisure*, 11, 4, 245–58

Takeda, H. (2006) 'Gendering the Japanese political system: The gender-specific pattern of political activity and women's political participation', *Japanese Studies*, vol. 26, no. 2, 185–98.

Tamale, S. (1999) *When Hens Begin to Crow: Gender and Parliamentary Politics in Uganda*, Boulder CO: Westview Press.

Tawney, R. H. (1931) *Equality*, London, Routledge.

Taylor-Gooby, P. (1985) *Public Opinion, Ideology, and State Welfare*, London: Routledge Kegan and Paul.

Temkin, L. (1986) 'Inequality', *Philosophy and Public Affairs 15*, reprinted in L. Pojman and R. Westmoreland (eds) *Equality. Selected Readings*, Oxford: Oxford University Press, 1997, pp. 75–88.

Tomlinson, S. (2008) *Race and education: policy and politics in Britain*, Maidenhead: Open University Press.

Thompson, N. (2003) *Promoting Equality: Challenging Discrimination and Oppression*, 2nd edition, Basingstoke: Palgrave.

Tonkiss, F. (2000), 'Trust, Social Capital and Economy', pp. 72–89 in F. Tonkiss and A. Passey (eds) *Trust and Civil Society*, London: Macmillan.

Torres, C. A. (2006) 'Democracy, Education, and Multiculturalism: Dilemmas of Citizenship in a Global World', in Lauder, H., Brown, P., Dillabough, J. and Halsey, A. H. (eds) *Education, Globalization and Social Change*, Oxford: Oxford University Press.

Tros Gynnal Hawliau Plant, NSPC Cymru, Barnados Cymru, Save the Children Wales (2007) *Manifesto – Child Poverty, National Assembly Elections 2007*, Cardiff: Tros Gynnal Hawliau Plant, NSPC Cymru, Barnados Cymru, Save the Children Wales.

Tully, J. (1995) *Strange multiplicity: constitutionalism in an age of diversity*, Cambridge and New York: Cambridge University Press.

Turner, B. (1993) 'Outline of a Theory of Citizenship', in Turner, B. and Hamilton, P. (eds) *Citizenship: Critical Concepts*, London: Routledge.

United Nations (1995) *UN Fourth World Conference on Women (Beijing, 1995) global platform for action*, New York: United Nations.

United Nations Committee on the Elimination of Discrimination against Women (2008) *Reports submitted by States parties under article 18 of the Convention on the Elimination of All Forms of Discrimination against Women – Sixth periodic report of States parties: United Kingdom of Great Britain and Northern Ireland*, New York: UN.

Ussher, J. and Sandoval, M. (2008) 'Gender differences in the construction and experience of cancer care: The consequences of the gendered positioning of carers', *Psychology and Health*, 23, 8, 945–63.

Van der Vleuten, J. M. (2007) *The Price of Gender Equality: Members States and Governance in the European Union*, London: Ashgate Publishing.

Vasak, K and Alston, P. (1982) *The International Dimensions of Human Rights*, Westport, CN: Greenwood Press.

Veijola, S. and Jokinen, E. (2008) 'Towards a Hostessing Society? Mobile Arrangements of Gender and Labour', *Nordic Journal of Women's Studies*, 16, 3, 166–81.

Verba, S., Nie, N. H. and Kim, J. (1987) *Participation and Political Equality: A Seven-nation Comparison*, Chicago: University of Chicago Press.

Verloo, M. and Roggeband, C. (1996) 'Gender impact assessment: the development of a new instrument in the Netherlands', *Impact Assessment*, vol. 14, 3–20.

Verloo, M. (2007) *Multiple Meanings of Gender Equality: A Critical Frame Analysis of Gender Policies in Europe*, Budapest: Central European University Press.

Vile, M. J. C. (1969) *Constitutionalism and the Separation of Powers*, Oxford: Oxford University Press.

Vizard, P. and Burchardt, T. (2007) *Developing a capability list: Final Recommendations of the Equalities Review Steering Group on Measurement*, CASE paper 121, London: LSE.

Vlastos, G. (1962) 'Justice and Equality', in Richard Brandt (ed.) *Social Justice*, Englewood Cliffs NJ: Prentice Hall.

Waaldijk, Bonini-Baraldi, M. (2006) *Sexual Orientation Discrimination in the European Union: National Laws and the Employment Equality Directive*, Cambridge: Cambridge University Press.

Walby, S. (1989) 'Theorising Patriarchy', *Sociology*, 23, 2, 213–34.

Walby, S. (2004) 'The European Union and Gender Equality: Emergent Varieties of Gender Regime', *Social Politics*, 11, 1, 4–29.

Walby, S., Armstrong, J. and Humphreys, L. (2008) *Review of Equality Statistics*, London: EHRC.

Wales Audit Office (2005) *Press Release: 'A Long Way to Go', Adult mental health services in Wales must improve to meet Assembly Government targets*, Cardiff: WAO, 10 October 2005.

Wales Audit Office (2007) *Tackling Homelessness in Wales: A Review of the Effectiveness of the National Homelessness Strategy*, Cardiff: WAO.

Wales Audit Office (2008) *Auditor General for Wales Annual Report and Accounts April 2007 to March 2008*, Cardiff: WAO.

Wales Council for Voluntary Action (2008a) *All Wales Database of Voluntary organisations*, Cardiff: WCVA.

Wales Council for Voluntary Action (2008b) *Welsh Assembly Government: Consultation on a Single Equality Scheme – Comments from Equality and Human Rights Coalition*, Cardiff: WCVA.

Wales Council for the Blind (2003) *A Manifesto from Visually Impaired People in Wales*, Cardiff: Wales Council for the Blind.

Wales Economic Funding Office (1999) *Single Programme Document: Objective One Economic Development Aid for West Wales and the Valleys*, Cardiff: WEFO.

Wales Office (2005) *Better Governance for Wales*, Cm 6582, London: The Stationery Office.

Walker, D.M. (1980) *The Oxford Companion to Law*, Oxford: Clarendon Press.

Ward, N. and McNicholas, K. (1998) 'Reconfiguring rural development in the UK: Object 5b and the new rural governance', *Journal of Rural Studies*, vol. 14, no. 1, 27–39.

Warren, J. (2007) 'Young Carers: Conventional or Exaggerated Levels of Involvement in Domestic and Caring Tasks?', *Children and Society*, 21, 2, 136–46.

Webb Review (2007) *Independent Review of the Mission and Purpose of Further Education in Wales*, St Asaph: WAG.

Weimer, D. and Vining, A. (2004) *Policy Analysis: Concepts and Practice*, London: Prentice Hall.

Welsh Assembly Government (2001a) *Cabinet Written Statement: Inclusion of the UN Convention on the Rights of the Child in the Children's Commissioner for Wales Regulations*, 26 June 2001.

Welsh Assembly Government (2001b) *Wales – The Learning Country*, Cardiff: WAG.

Welsh Assembly Government (2002a) *Reaching Higher: Higher Education and the Learning Country: A Strategy for the Higher Education Sector in Wales*, Cardiff: WAG.

Welsh Assembly Government (2002b) *When I'm 64 . . . and more*, Cardiff: WAG.

Welsh Assembly Government (2002c) *Black, Minority Ethnic Housing Action Plan for Wales*, Cardiff: WAG.

Welsh Assembly Government (2002d) *A Winning Wales The National Economic Development Strategy of the Welsh Assembly Government*, Cardiff: WAG.

Welsh Assembly Government (2002e) *Wales for Innovation – The Welsh Assembly Government's Action Plan for Innovation*, Cardiff: WAG.

Welsh Assembly Government (2002f) *Creative Future: Cymru Greadigol – A Culture Strategy for Wales*, Cardiff: WAG.

Welsh Assembly Government (2002g) *Childcare Action Plan*, Cardiff: WAG.

Welsh Assembly Government (2003a) *The Strategy for Older People in Wales*, Cardiff: WAG.

Welsh Assembly Government (2003b) *Wales a Better Country*, Cardiff: WAG.

Welsh Assembly Government (2003c) *Survey Report: Ethnic Minority Achievement Grant (EMAG) Effective Use Of Resources*, Cardiff: WAG/Estyn.

Welsh Assembly Government (2003d) *Homelessness Strategy*, Cardiff: WAG.

Welsh Assembly Government (2003e) *Iaith Pawb*, Cardiff: WAG.

Welsh Assembly Government (2003f) *Survey Report: Ethnic Minority Achievement Grant (EMAG) Effective Use Of Resources*, Cardiff: Estyn.

Welsh Assembly Government (2004a) *Children and Young People: Rights To Action*, Cardiff: WAG.

Welsh Assembly Government (2004b) Cabinet Statement, Services for Asylum Seekers and Refugees in Wales, 3 February 2004, by Edwina Hart, Minister for Social Justice and Regeneration, Cardiff: WAG.

Welsh Assembly Government (2004c) *Making the Connections: Delivering Better Services for Wales – The Welsh Assembly Government vision for public services*, Cardiff: WAG.

Welsh Assembly Government (2004d) *All Wales Youth Offending Strategy*, Cardiff: WAG.

Welsh Assembly Government (2004e) *Sustainable Development Scheme, 'Starting to Live Differently*, Cardiff: WAG.

Welsh Assembly Government (2004f) *The Sustainable Development Action Plan 2004–07*, Cardiff: WAG.

Welsh Assembly Government (2005a) *A Fair Future for our Children*, Cardiff: WAG.

Welsh Assembly Government (2005b) *Flying Start*, Cardiff: WAG.

Welsh Assembly Government (2005c) *National Homelessness Strategy For Wales 2006–2008*, Cardiff: WAG.

Welsh Assembly Government (2005d) *Wales: A Vibrant Economy – The Welsh Assembly Government's Strategic Framework for Economic Development*, Cardiff: WAG.

Welsh Assembly Government (2005e) *Designed for Life, Creating World Class Health Care for the Twenty-First Century*, Cardiff: WAG.

Welsh Assembly Government (2005f) *Accommodation Needs of Gypsy Travellers in Wales*, Cardiff: WAG.

Welsh Assembly Government (2005g) *Review of Social Landlords' Implementation of the Black, Minority Ethnic (BME) Housing Action Plan for Wales*, Cardiff: WAG.

Welsh Assembly Government (2005h) *Climbing Higher: The Welsh Assembly Government Strategy for Sport and Physical Activity*, Cardiff: WAG.

Welsh Assembly Government (2005i) *Adult Mental Health Services – Raising the Standard, The Revised Adult Mental Health National Service Framework and an Action Plan for Wales*, Cardiff: WAG.

Welsh Assembly Government (2005j) *Refugee Housing Action Plan*, Cardiff: WAG.

Welsh Assembly Government (2005k) *Tackling Domestic Abuse: The All Wales National Strategy*, Cardiff: WAG.

Welsh Assembly Government (2005l) *National Service Framework for Older People*, Cardiff: WAG.

Welsh Assembly Government (2005m) *Healthy Ageing Action Plan*, Cardiff: WAG.

Welsh Assembly Government/Arts Council for Wales (2006) *Moving On: An Arts and Disability Strategy for Wales*, Cardiff: WAG/ Arts Council for Wales.

Welsh Assembly Government (2006a) *Refugee Housing Action Plan*, Cardiff: WAG.

Welsh Assembly Government (2006b) *Designed to Work: A workforce strategy to deliver Designed for Life*, Cardiff: WAG.

Welsh Assembly Government (2006c) *Summary of Consultation Responses to Wales: A Vibrant Economy*, Cardiff: WAG.

Welsh Assembly Government (2006d) *Review of Local Service Delivery: Report to the Welsh Assembly Government*, Cardiff: WAG.

Welsh Assembly Government (2006e), *Interim evaluation of Communities First: Final Report*, Cardiff: WAG.

Welsh Assembly Government (2006f) *Making the Connections: Delivering Beyond Boundaries*, Cardiff: WAG.

Welsh Assembly Government (2006g) *Child Poverty Implementation Plan – Phase 1 Proposals*, Cardiff: WAG.

Welsh Assembly Government (2006h) *The Learning Country: Vision into Action* Cardiff: WAG.

Welsh Assembly Government (2006i) *Climbing Higher – The Next Steps*, Cardiff: WAG.

Welsh Assembly Government (2006j) *Statistical Article: A brief analysis of Demographic Background by Main Equality Strands*, Cardiff: WAG.

Welsh Assembly Government (2006k) *A brief analysis of Health by main equality strands*, Cardiff: WAG.

Welsh Assembly Government (2006l) *Sixth Annual Equality Report*, Cardiff: WAG.

Welsh Assembly Government (2006m) *Better Homes for People in Wales A National Housing Strategy for Wales Action Plan*, Cardiff: WAG.

Welsh Assembly Government (2006n) *Environment Strategy for Wales*, Cardiff: WAG.

Welsh Assembly Government (2006o) *National Tourism Strategy – Achieving Our Potential 2006–13*, Cardiff: WAG.

Welsh Assembly Government/Save the Children Wales (2007) *The Children and Young People's Participation Consortium For Wales and the Participation Unit*, Cardiff: WAG/Save the Children Wales.

Welsh Assembly Government (2007a) *Partnership and Managing Change*, Cardiff: WAG.

Welsh Assembly Government (2007b) *Counsel General urges debate over changing legal landscape*, WAG Press Release, 21 September 2007, Cardiff: WAG.

Welsh Assembly Government (2007c) *Statistical Focus on Men and Women in Wales*, Cardiff: WAG.

Welsh Assembly Government (2007d) *Review Of Promoting Equality Fund*, Cardiff: WAG.

Welsh Assembly Government (2007e) *The Eighth Annual Equality Report: 2006–2007*, Cardiff: WAG.

Welsh Assembly Government (2007f) *Local participation strategies 0–25 Guidance Welsh – Guidance Welsh Assembly Government Circular No: 025/2007*, August 2007, Cardiff: WAG.

Welsh Assembly Government (2007g) *Welsh Assembly Government Guidance on Local Participation Strategies 0–25, Statement of information, April 2, 2007*, Cardiff: WAG.

Welsh Assembly Government (2007h) *Voluntary Sector Scheme Annual Report 2006–07*, Cardiff: WAG.

Welsh Assembly Government (2007i) *Carers' Strategy for Wales Action Plan 2007*, Cardiff: WAG,

Welsh Assembly Government (2007j) *Communities First Guidance*, Cardiff: WAG.

Welsh Assembly Government (2007k) *One Wales*, Cardiff: WAG.

Welsh Assembly Government (2007l) *Draft Minority Ethnic Housing Action Plan 2008–2011*, Cardiff: WAG.

Welsh Assembly Government (2007m) *Communities First Guidance*, Cardiff: WAG.

Welsh Assembly Government (2007n) *Welsh Assembly Government Statement, Youth Justice System in Wales, 20 November 2007, by Edwina Hart, Minister for Health and Social Services*, Cardiff: WAG.

Welsh Assembly Government (2007o) *The Rural Development Plan 2007–2013*, Cardiff: WAG.

Welsh Assembly Government (2007p) *A Strategy For Social Services in Wales over the next Decade: Fulfilled Lives, Supportive Communities*, Cardiff: WAG.

Welsh Assembly Government (2007q) *A Science Policy for Wales*, Cardiff: WAG.

Welsh Assembly Government (2007r) *Statement on Policy and Practice for Adults with a Learning Disability*, Cardiff: WAG.

Welsh Assembly Government (2007s) *Grass Roots Fund: Guidelines & Notes for Applicants*, Cardiff: WAG.

Welsh Assembly Government (2008(1)) *Sports Council for Wales Remit Letter 2008–09*, Cardiff: WAG.

Welsh Assembly Government (2008(2)) *Delivering Emergency Care Services: An Integrated Approach for Delivering Unscheduled Care in Wales*, Cardiff: WAG.

Welsh Assembly Government (2008(3)) *Wales Assembly Government One Wales Delivery Plan 2007–2011*, Cardiff: WAG.

Welsh Assembly Government (2008(4)) *Welsh Assembly Government Gypsy Traveller Site Management Guidance*, Cardiff: WAG.

Welsh Assembly Government (2008(5)) *Statistical Focus on Older People*, Cardiff: WAG.

Welsh Assembly Government (2008(6)) *The Strategy for Older People in Wales 2008–2013*, Cardiff: WAG.

Welsh Assembly Government (2008(7)) *Iaith Pawb and Welsh Language Scheme – Annual Report 2007–08*, Cardiff: WAG.

Welsh Assembly Government (2008(8)) *Building a Society for All Ages: Draft Intergenerational Practice Strategy For Wales*, Cardiff: WAG.

Welsh Assembly Government (2008(9)) *Covering Letter: 'Local Vision – Statutory Guidance on developing and delivering Community Strategies'*, Cardiff: WAG.

Welsh Assembly Government (2008(10)) *Minority Ethnic Youth Forum*, Cardiff: WAG.

Welsh Assembly Government (2008(11)) *Voluntary Sector strategy 'The Third dimension'*, Cardiff: WAG.

Welsh Assembly Government (2008(12)) *Voluntary Sector Scheme*, Cardiff: WAG.

Welsh Assembly Government (2008(13)) *Partnership Council Scheme*, Cardiff: WAG.

Welsh Assembly Government (2008(14)) *School Effectiveness Framework: Building effective learning communities together*, Cardiff: WAG.

Welsh Assembly Government (2008(15)) *Improving the Health of Health of Homeless and Specific Vulnerable Groups' Standards 2008–9*, Cardiff: WAG.

Welsh Assembly Government (2008(16)) *Forced Marriage And Honour Based Violence Three Year Action Plan April 2008–March 2011*, Cardiff: WAG.

Welsh Assembly Government (2008(17)) *Welsh Ministers' Regulatory Impact Assessment Code for Subordinate Legislation*, Cardiff: WAG.

Welsh Assembly Government (2008(18)) *One Wales: Connecting the Nation – The Wales Transport Strategy*, Cardiff: WAG.

Welsh Assembly Government (2008(19)) *Local Vision: Statutory Guidance from the Welsh Assembly Government on Developing and Delivering Community Strategies*, Cardiff: WAG.

Welsh Assembly Government (2008(20)) *Minority Ethnic Housing Action Plan 2008–2011*, Cardiff: WAG.

Welsh Assembly Government (2008(21)) *Art and design in the National Curriculum for Wales*, Cardiff: WAG.

Welsh Assembly Government (2008(22)) *Welsh in the National Curriculum for Wales*, Cardiff: WAG.

Welsh Assembly Government (2008(23)) *Voices and Choices: A proposed right for children to appeal to the Special Educational Needs Tribunal for Wales*, Cardiff: WAG.

Welsh Assembly Government (2008(24)) *School Effectiveness Framework – Guidance*, Cardiff: WAG.

Welsh Assembly Government (2008(25)) *Geography in the National Curriculum for Wales*, Cardiff: WAG.

Welsh Assembly Government (2008(26)) *English in the National Curriculum for Wales*, Cardiff: WAG.

Welsh Assembly Government (2008(27)) *Music in the National Curriculum for Wales*, Cardiff: WAG.

Welsh Assembly Government (2008(28)) *History in the National Curriculum for Wales*, Cardiff: WAG.

Welsh Assembly Government (2008(29)) *Personal and Social Education in the National Curriculum for Wales*, Cardiff: WAG.

Welsh Assembly Government (2008(30)) *2008–09 Final Budget New Plans*, Cardiff: WAG.

Welsh Assembly Government (2008(31)) *Making the most of learning Implementing the revised curriculum*, Cardiff: WAG.

Welsh Assembly Government (2008(32)) *Statistical Focus on Older People*, Cardiff: WAG.

Welsh Assembly Government (2008(33)) *Skills That Work for Wales: A Skills and Employment Strategy and Action Plan*, Cardiff: WAG.

Welsh Assembly Government (2008(34)) *Refugee Inclusion Strategy*, Cardiff: WAG.

Welsh Assembly Government (2008(35)) *Environment Strategy Action Plan 2008–11*, Cardiff: WAG.

Welsh Assembly Government (2008(36)) *Foundation Phase: Framework for Children's Learning for 3 to 7-year-olds in Wales*, Cardiff: WAG.

Welsh Assembly Government (2008(37)) *Initial Impact Assessment Toolkit*, Cardiff: WAG.

Welsh Assembly Government (2009a) *21st Century Higher Education Strategy and Plan for Wales – For Our Future*, Cardiff: WAG.

Welsh Assembly Government (2009b) *Ten Year Homelessness Plan for Wales 2009–19*, Cardiff: WAG.

Welsh Assembly Government (2009c) *Single Equality Scheme 2009–13*, Cardiff: WAG.

Welsh Conservatives (1999) *Election Manifesto for the National Assembly Elections*, Cardiff: Welsh Conservatives.

Welsh Conservatives (2007) *Vote Welsh Conservative for a change*, Cardiff: Welsh Conservatives.

Welsh Consumer Council and the Equal Opportunities Commission in Wales (2005) *Gender and Bus Travel in Wales*, Cardiff: Welsh Consumer Council and the Equal Opportunities Commission in Wales.

Welsh Development Agency (2000) *Entrepreneurship Action Plan For Wales: Strategy Document*, Cardiff: WDA.

Welsh European Funding Office (2007) *West Wales and the Valleys, Convergence Operational Programme European Social Fund 2007–2013*, Cardiff: WEFO.

Welsh Labour Party (1999) *Working Hard for Wales: Labour's Manifesto for the National Assembly*, Cardiff: WLP.

Welsh Labour (2007) *Building a Better Wales – 2007 Welsh Labour Election Manifesto*, Cardiff: Welsh Labour.

Welsh Language Board (2004) *2004 Welsh Language Use Survey*, Cardiff: ByIG/WLB.

Welsh Language Board (2006) *Position Statement on the Legislative Position of the Welsh Language*, Cardiff: WLB.

Welsh Language Board (2007a) *Estimation of the number of Welsh speakers in England*, Cardiff: ByIG/WLB.

Welsh Language Board (2007b) *The Vitality Of Welsh: A Statistical Balance Sheet*, Cardiff: Bwrdd yr Iaith Gymraeg/Welsh Language Board.

Welsh Liberal Democrats (1999) *Guarantee Delivery: Liberal Democrat Manifesto for the National Assembly for Wales 1999*, Cardiff: WLDP.

Welsh Liberal Democrats (2007) *A Fair, Green Future – The Welsh Liberal Democrat manifesto for the Welsh General Election 2007*, Cardiff: Welsh Liberal Democrats.

Welsh Local Government Association (2007) *Report – Local Government and Contemporary Equality Issues*, Papers of the Local Government and Public Services Committee, National Assembly for Wales, 7 March 2007.

Welsh Local Government Association (2008a) *The Equality Improvement Framework For Wales*, Cardiff: WLGA.

Welsh Local Government Association (2008b) *Welsh Local Government Association Annual Report from the Equalities Team*, Cardiff: WLGA.

Welsh Office (1977) *Welsh Economic Trends, No.4*, Cardiff: Welsh Office.

Welsh Office (1997) *White Paper, A Voice For Wales/Papur Gwyn, Llais Dros Gymru*, Cm 3718, London: Stationery Office.

Welsh Office (1985) *Digest of Welsh historical statistics 1700–1974*, Cardiff: Welsh Office.

Welsh Office (1999) *The Government's Expenditure Plans 1999–2000 to 2001–2002: A Departmental Report by the Welsh Office and the Office of Her Majesty's Chief Inspector of Schools in Wales*, Cardiff: National Assembly for Wales.

Welsh Refugee Council (2007) *Impact Report 2004–2005*, Cardiff: Welsh Refugee Council.

Welsh Women's Aid (2005) *Annual Report*, Cardiff: Welsh Women's Aid.

West P., Reeder A., Milne B. J. and Poulton, R. (2002) 'Worlds apart: a comparison between physical activities among youth in Glasgow, Scotland and Dunedin, New Zealand', *Social Science and Medicine*, 54, 4, 607–19.

Whipple, M. (2005) 'The Dewey-Lippmann Debate Today: Communication Distortions, Reflective Agency, and Participatory Democracy', *Sociological Theory*, 23, 2, 156–78.

White, A., Jones, E., and James, D. (2005) 'There's a Nasty Smell in the Kitchen! Gender and Power in the Tourism Workplace in Wales', *Tourism Culture and Communication*, 6, 1, 37–49.

White, S. (2006) *Equality*, Oxford: Blackwell.

Whitehead, J. (1996) 'Sex stereotypes, gender identity and subject choice at 'A' level', *Educational Research*, 38, 147–60.

Whyte, J. (1983) 'How much discrimination was there under the unionist regime, 1921–1968?', in T. Gallagher and J. O'Connell (eds) *Contemporary Irish Studies*, Manchester: Manchester University Press.

Wildavsky, A. (1987) *Speaking Truth to Power: The Art and Craft of Policy Analysis*, 2nd edition, London: Macmillan.

Wilkinson, R. G. (2005) *The Impact of Inequality*, London: Routledge.

Williams, C. (2003) 'The Impact of Labour on Policies for Children and Young People in Wales', *Children and Society*, 17, 247–53.

Williams, C. (2003) 'Children and Young People in Wales', *Children and Society*, 17, 3, 247–53.

Williams, C. (2006) 'Black and ethnic minority associations in Wales', in Day, G., Dunkerley, D. and Thompson, A. (eds) *Civil Society in Wales*, Cardiff: University of Wales Press.

Williams, C., Borland, J., Griffiths, A., Roberts, G. and Morris, E. (2003) *Snakes and Ladders Advice and Support for Discrimination Cases in Wales*, Cardiff: EOC Wales.

Williams, C. H. (2004) 'Iaith Pawb: The Doctrine of Plenary Inclusion', in Chaney, P., Thompson, A. and Scourfield, J. (eds) *Contemporary Wales: Review of the Assembly's First Term*, Cardiff: University of Wales Press, 17, 1–27.

Williams, C. H. (2007) *Language and Governance*, Cardiff: UWP.

Williams, C. H. (2008) *Linguistic Minorities in Democratic Context*, Basingstoke: Palgrave Macmillan.

Williams, M. and Robinson, A. (2006) *Counted In: A report for Stonewall Cymru and the Welsh Assembly Government SME Equality Project*, Cardiff: Stonewall Cymru.

Williams, R. (2009) *Y Coleg Ffederal: Report to the Minister for Children, Education, Lifelong Learning and Skills*, Cardiff: WAG.

Wilson, F. L. (1990) 'Neo-corporatism and the rise of new social movements', in Dalton, R. J. and Kuechler, M. (eds) *Challenging the Political Order: New Social and Political Movements in Western Democracies*, Cambridge: Polity Press.

Wilson, R. (2007) 'Rhetoric meets reality: Northern Ireland's equality agenda', *Benefits*, 15, 2, 151–62.

Wolf, N. (1994) *Fire with Fire: New Female Power and How It Will Change the 21st Century*, London and New York: Vintage Books.

Wolff, J. (2007) 'Social Justice and Public Policy: A view from Political Philosophy', in G. Craig, D. Gordon, and T. Burchardt (eds) *Social Justice and Public Policy: Seeking Fairness in Diverse Societies*, Bristol: Policy Press.

Women and Work Commission (2006) *Shaping a Fairer Future*, Whitehall: UK Government Women and Equality Unit.

Wollstonecraft, M. (1792/ 2004) *Vindication of the Rights of Women*, Harmondsworth: Penguin Classics.

Wright, A. (1996) *Citizens and subjects: An Essay on British Politics*, London and New York: Routledge.

Wright, C., Weekes, D. and McGlaughlin, A. (2004) *'Race', class, and gender in exclusion from school*, London: Falmer Press.

Wyn Jones, R. (1998) *Memorandum submitted to the Welsh Affairs Select Committee, 'Broadcasting and Political Culture in Wales'*, London: HMSO.

Yanow, D. (1993) *How Does a Policy Mean? Interpreting Policy and Organizational Actions*, Washington DC: Georgetown University Press.

Yanow, D. (1999) *Conducting Interpretive Policy Analysis*, London: Sage.

Yates, K. (2005) 'Understanding the experiences of mobility-disabled tourists', *International Journal of Tourism Policy*, 1, 2, 153–66.

Yeandle, S., Bennett, C. and Buckner, L. (2007) *Carers, Employment and Services in their Local Context*, Leeds: Carers UK and University of Leeds.

Young, I. M. (1983) 'Rights to Intimacy in a Complex Society', *Journal of Social Philosophy*, 14, 2, 47–52.

Young, I. M (1990) *Justice and the Politics of Difference*, Princeton, NJ: Princeton University Press.

Younger, M. and Warrington, M. (2007) 'Closing the Gender Gap? Issues of gender equity in English secondary schools', *Discourse: Studies in the Cultural Politics of Education*, 28, 2, 219–42.

Index